As They Said It

Volume II

Reconstruction to the Present, 3e

by Nunn McGinty Publishing

Printed in the United States of America

Cover design: Mira Digital Publishing

ISBN-10:1-60803-005-9

ISBN-13: 978-1-60803-005-7

Nunn McGinty Publishing
Spring, Texas

Table of Contents

Introduction

As They Said It: Documents, Speeches, and Statements in U.S. History from the Civil War to the Present

Many millions of words have been written about history by journalists, professors, and others, and we have a rich variety of stories and interpretations because of that, and they are vital to our understanding of the past.

But even more important are the words of the people who made those histories themselves, and the purpose of this collection is to reveal these primary sources to the reader, to get beyond the stories we've been told and look at the fundamental ideas and words and actions of those who we usually write about, to let the presidents, judges, radicals, protestors, and others tell history in their own words.

This collection will present a representative set of documents, court cases, famous speeches and other records that were created by the primary actors in U.S. history from the Civil War era t o the present. There are statements by politicians justifying foreign conquest and others condemning it. Some records are defenses of American racism and others are attacks on U.S. segregation and racial hatred. Included are some of the more important supreme court cases in the era, covering issues such as Civil Rights, abortion, gay rights, torture and other issues.

Put simply, we can learn a great deal about our past by reading the words of those who have analyzed and interpreted it, but we can only get a more thorough understanding of history by looking at original documents, cases, speeches and statements by the people who were involved in these crucial issues while they were taking place and in their own words.

I

The Triumph of Industrial Capitalism and Its Challenges

Several deep problems confronted American leaders in the aftermath of a bloody and costly Civil War. The U.S. had to reunify the states, rebuild vast parts of the country that had been devastated, recreate a national political system and, most importantly, try to create a new social system to bring in African-Americans who had been enslaved for over two centuries. All of this, too, had to be done in the larger context of a national transformation to an industrial capitalist economic system.

The documents in this chapter speak to that larger economic transformation and some of challenges it faced, from workers and from farmers. In the years from the end of the Civil War to the beginning of the 20th century the country was deeply divided with national strikes, agrarian uprisings, and perhaps the greatest political challenge, the Populists, to capitalist hegemony in the nation's history. At the end of this struggle, those challenges had been beaten back and the country was irrevocably on a path toward becoming a global capitalist power.

Keeping the Rabble in Line

Rutherford B. Hayes Diary entry, August 5, 1877

Amid "The Great Uprising" of 1877, a series of industrial strikes throughout the entire United States, President Rutherford B. Hayes spoke out against labor.

August 5, 1877

The strikes have been put down by force; but now for the real remedy. Can't something [be] done by education of the strikers, by judicious control of the capitalists, by wise general policy to end or diminish the evil? The railroad strikers, as a rule, are good men, sober, intelligent, and industrious. The mischiefs are: —

1. Strikers prevent men willing to work from doing so.

2. They seize and hold the property of their employers.

3. The consequent excitement furnishes an opportunity for the dangerous criminal classes to destroy life and property.

Now, "every man has a right, if he sees fit to, to quarrel with his own bread and butter, but he has no right to quarrel with the bread and butter of other people." Every man has a right to determine for himself the value of his own labor, but he has no right to determine for other men the value of their labor. (Not good.)

Every man has a right to refuse to work if the wages don't suit him, but he has no right to prevent others from working if they are suited with the wages.

Haymarket Martyr Louis Lingg Says Good-bye

Louis Lingg, an anarchist convicted of sedition in the Haymarket bombings and sentenced to death, met his end defiantly.

Court of Justice! With the same irony with which you have regarded my efforts to win in this "free land of America," a livelihood such as humankind is worthy to enjoy, do you now, after condemning me to death, concede me the liberty of making a final speech.

I accept your concession; but it is only for the purpose of exposing the injustice, the calumnies and the outrages which have been heaped upon me.

You have accused me of murder, and convicted me: What proof have you brought that I am guilty?

In the first place, you have brought this fellow Seliger to testify against me. Him I have helped to make bombs, and you have further proven that with the assistance of another, I took those bombs to No. 58 Clybourn avenue, but what you have not proven—even with the assistance of your bought "squealer," Seliger, who would appear to have acted such a prominent part in the affair—is that any of those bombs were taken to the haymarket.

A couple of chemists also, have been brought here as specialists, yet they could only state that the metal of which the haymarket bomb was made bore a certain resemblance to those bombs of mine, and your Mr. Ingham has vainly endeavored to deny that the bombs were quite different. He had to admit that there was a difference of a full half inch in their diameters, although he suppressed the fact that there was also a difference of a quarter of an inch in the thickness of the shell. This is the kind of evidence upon which you have convicted me.

It is not murder, however, of which you have convicted me. The judge has stated that much only this morning in his resume of the case, and Grinnell has repeatedly asserted that we were being tried not for murder, but for anarchy, so the condemnation is— that I am an anarchist!

What is anarchy? This is a subject which my comrades have explained with sufficient clearness, and it is unnecessary for me to go over it again. They have told you plainly enough what our aims are. The state's attorney, however, has not given you that information. He has merely criticized and condemned, not the doctrines of anarchy, but our methods of giving them practical effect, and even here he has maintained a discreet silence as to the fact that those methods were forced upon us by the brutality of the police. Grinnell's own proffered remedy for our grievances is the ballot and combination of trades unions, and Ingham has even avowed the desirability of a six-hour movement! But the fact is, that at every attempt to wield the ballot, at every endeavor to combine the efforts of workingmen, you have displayed the brutal violence of the police club, and this is why I have recommended rude force, to combat the ruder force of the police.

You have charged me with despising "law and order."What does your "law and order" amount to? Its representatives are the police, and they have thieves in their ranks. Here sits Captain Schaack. He has himself admitted to me that my hat and books have been stolen from him in his office—stolen by policemen. These are your defenders of property rights! The detectives again, who arrested me, forced their way into my room like housebreakers, under false pretenses, giving the name of a carpenter, Lorenz, of Burlington street. They have sworn that I was alone in my room, therein perjuring themselves. You have not subpoenaed this lady, Mrs. Klein, who was present, and could have sworn that the aforesaid detectives broke into my room under false pretenses, and that their testimonies are perjured

But let us go further. In Schaack we have a captain of the police, and he also has perjured himself. He has sworn that I admitted to him being present at the Monday night meeting, whereas I distinctly informed him that I was at a carpenters' meeting at Zepf's Hall. He has sworn again that I told him that I also learned to make bombs from Herr Most's book. That also is a perjury.

Let us go still a step higher among these representatives of law and order. Grinnell and his associates have permitted perjury, and I say that they have done it knowingly. The proof has been adduced by my counsel, and with my own eyes I have seen Grinnell point out to Gilmer, eight days before he came upon the stand, the persons of the men whom he was to swear against.

While I, as I have stated above, believe in force for the sake of winning for myself and fellow-workmen a livelihood such as men ought to have, Grinnell, on the other hand, through his police and other rogues, has suborned perjury in order to murder seven men, of whom I am one. Grinnell had the pitiful courage here in the courtroom, where I could not defend myself, to call me a coward! The scoundrel! A fellow who has leagued himself with a parcel of base, hireling knaves, to bring me to the gallows. Why? For no earthly reason save a contemptible selfishness—a desire to 'rise in the world"—to "make money," forsooth.

This wretch—who, by means of the perjuries of other wretches is going to murder seven men—is the fellow who calls me "coward"! And yet you blame me for despising such "defenders of the law" such unspeakable hypocrites!

Anarchy means no domination or authority of one man over another, yet you call that "disorder." A system which advocates no such "order" as shall require the services of rogues and thieves to defend it you call "disorder."

The Judge himself was forced to admit that the state's attorney had not been able to connect me with the bombthrowing. The latter knows how to get around it, however. He charges me with being a "conspirator." How does he prove it? Simply by declaring the International Working People's Association to be a "conspiracy." I was a member of that body, so he has the charge securely fastened on me. Excellent! Nothing is too difficult for the genius of a state's attorney!

It is hardly incumbent upon me to review the relations which I occupy to my companions in misfortune. I can say truly and openly that I am not as intimate with my fellow prisoners as I am with Captain Schaack.

The universal misery, the ravages of the capitalistic hyena have brought us together in our agitation, not as persons, but as workers in the same cause. Such is the "conspiracy" of which you have convicted me.

I protest against the conviction, against the decision of the court. I do not recognize your law, jumbled together as it is by the nobodies of bygone centuries, and I do not recognize the decision of the court. My own counsel have conclusively proven from the decisions of equally high courts that a new trial must be

granted us. The state's attorney quotes three times as many decisions from perhaps still higher courts to prove the opposite, and I
am convinced that if, in another trial, these decisions should be
supported by twenty-one volumes, they will adduce one hundred
in support of the contrary, if it is anarchists who are to be tried.
And not even under such a law—a law that a schoolboy must
despise—not even by such methods have they been able to
"legally" convict us.

They have suborned perjury to boot.

I tell you frankly and openly, I am for force. I have already told
Captain Schaack, "if they use cannons against us, we shall use
dynamite against them." I repeat that I am the enemy of the
"order"of today, and I repeat that, with all my powers, so long as
breath remains in me, I shall combat it. I declare again, frankly
and openly, that I am in favor of using force. I have told Captain
Schaack, and I stand by it,"if you cannonade us, we shall dynamite you."You laugh! Perhaps you think,"you'll throw no more
bombs"; but let me assure you I die happy on the gallows, so
confident am I that the hundreds and thousands to whom I have
spoken will remember my words; and when you shall have
hanged us, then—mark my words—they will do the bombthrowing! In this hope do I say to you: I despise you. I despise your
order, your laws, your force-propped authority. Hang me for it!

Dawes Act: An Act to Provide for the Allotment of Lands in Severalty to Indians on the Various Reservations, and to Extend the Protection of the Laws of the United States and the Territories over the Indians, and for Other Purposes.

Be it enacted by the Senate and House of Representatives of the United States of
America in Congress assembled, That in all cases where any tribe or band of Indians
has been, or shall hereafter be, located upon any reservation created for their use,
either by treaty stipulation or by virtue of an act of Congress or executive order setting apart the same for their use, the President of the United States be, and he

hereby is, authorized, whenever in his opinion any reservation or any part thereof of such Indians is advantageous for agricultural and grazing purposes, to cause said reservation, or any part thereof, to be surveyed, or resurveyed if necessary, and to allot the lands in said reservation in severalty to any Indian located thereon in quantities as follows:

> To each head of a family, one-quarter of a section;

> To each single person over eighteen years of age, one-eighth of a section;

> To each orphan child under eighteen years of age, one-eighth of a section; and

> To each other single person under eighteen years now living, or who may be born prior to the date of the order of the President directing an allotment of the lands embraced in any reservation, one-sixteenth of a section:

> **Provided,** That in case there is not sufficient land in any of said reservations to allot lands to each individual of the classes above named in quantities as above provided, the lands embraced in such reservation or reservations shall be allotted to each individual of each of said classes pro rata in accordance with the provisions of this act: And provided further, That where the treaty or act of Congress setting apart such reservation provides the allotment of lands in severalty in quantities in excess of those herein provided, the President, in making allotments upon such reservation, shall allot the lands to each individual Indian belonging thereon in quantity as specified in such treaty or act: And provided further, That when the lands allotted are only valuable for grazing purposes, an additional allotment of such grazng lands, in quantities as above provided, shall be made to each individual.

> **SEC. 2.** That all allotments set apart under the provisions of this act shall be selected by the Indians, heads of families selecting for their minor children, and the agents shall select for each orphan child, and in such manner as to embrace the improvements of the Indians making the selection. where the improvements of two or more Indians have been made on the same legal subdivision of land, unless they shall otherwise agree, a provisional line may be run dividing said lands between them, and the amount to which each is entitled shall be equalized in the assignment of the remain-

der of the land to which they are entitled under his act: Provided, That if any one entitled to an allotment shall fail to make a selection vithin four years after the President shall lirect that allotments may be made on a particular reservation, the Secretary of the Interior may direct the agent of such tribe or band, if such there be, and if there be no agent, then a special agent appointed for that purpose, to make a selection for such Indian, which selection shall be allotted as in cases where selections are made by the Indians, and patents shall issue in like manner.

SEC. 3. That the allotments provided for in this act shall be made by special agents appointed by the President for such purpose, and the agents in charge of the respective reservations on which the allotments are directed to be made, under such rules and regulations as the Secretary of the Interior may from time to time prescribe, and shall be certified by such agents to the Commissioner of Indian Affairs, in duplicate, one copy to be retained in the Indian Office and the other to be transmitted to the Secretary of the Interior for his action, and to be deposited in the General Land Office.

SEC. 4. That where any Indian not residing upon a reservation, or for whose tribe no reservation has been provided by treaty, act of Congress, or executive order, shall make settlement upon any surveyed or unsurveyed lands of the United States not otherwise appropriated, he or she shall be entitled, upon application to the local land-office for the district in which the lands arc located, to have the same allotted to him or her, and to his or her children, in quantities and manner as provided in this act for Indians residing upon reservations; and when such settlement is made upon unsurveyed lands, the grant to such Indians shall be adjusted upon the survey of the lands so as to conform thereto; and patents shall be issued to them for such lands in the manner and with the restrictions as herein provided. And the fees to which the officers of such local land-office would have been entitled had such lands been entered under the general laws for the disposition of the public lands shall be paid to them, from any moneys in the Treasury of the United States not otherwise appropriated, upon a statement of an account in their behalf for such fees by the Commissioner of the General Land Office, and a certification of such account to the Secretary of the Treasury by the Secretary of the Interior.

SEC. 7. That in cases where the use of water for irrigation is necessary to render the lands within any Indian reservation available for agricultural purposes, the Secretary of the Interior be, and he is hereby, authorized to prescribe such rules and regulations as he may deem necessary to secure a just and equal distribution thereof among the Indians residing upon any such reservation; and no oother appropriation or grant of water by any riparian proprietor shall permitted to the damage of any other riparian proprietor.

SEC. 8. That the provisions of this act shall not extend to the territory occupied by the Cherokees, Creeks, Choctaws, Chickasaws, Seminoles, and Osage, Miamies and Peorias, and Sacs and Foxes, in the Indian Territory, nor to any of the reservations of the Seneca Nation of New York Indians in the State of New York, nor to that strip of territory in the State of Nebraska adjoining the Sioux Nation on the south added by executive order.

SEC. 9. That for the purpose of making the surveys and resurveys mentioned in section two of this act, there be, and hereby is, appropriated, out of any moneys in the Treasury not otherwise appropriated, the sum of one hundred thousand dollars, to be repaid proportionately out of the proceeds of the sales of such land as may be acquired from the Indians under the provisions of this act.

SEC. 10. That nothing in this act contained shall be so canstrued to affect the right and power of Congress to grant the right of way through any lands granted to an Indian, or a tribe of Indians, for railroads or other highways, or telegraph lines, for the public use, or condemn such lands to public uses, upon making just compensation.

SEC. 11. That nothing in this act shall be so construed as to prevent the removal of the Southern Ute Indians from their present reservation in Southwestern Colorado to a new reservation by and with consent of a majority of the adult male members of said tribe.

Approved, February, 8, 1887.

Documents on the Pullman Strike

Thomas W. Heathcoate, inside finisher, Pullman Car Works, testimony before U. S. Strike Commission, August 1894.

> ....a man has to do about four times as much work at piecework as he has to do at day work, because the pieces are cut down so low it is almost impossible for a man, unless he is an expert , to make $1.90 a day at the work. For instance, take the desk behind which you sit. I take the making of that desk today for $20; I go to work on it, and, being an expert, make $4 a day at it; then the foreman says to me "the next time I will not give you but $18 for making it. " Well, I take another desk at that and by hard work still make $4 per day at it. The next time he cuts the price down to $16. I still by using more effort, working hard, make $4 per day at it. He then cuts the price down to $12 and I can only make $3 per day at it. ...He then gives the desk to some other man who is not as expert in doing the work, and that man cannot make $1.25 per day at it.

★   ★   ★

Thomas H. Wickes, second vice-president, Pullman Company, responses to questions posed by the commissioners of the U.S. Strike Commission, August 1894.

> Commissioner Kernan: after having taken a contract at an estimated basis of wages, [was] a cut made in the wages during the construction of such cars.

> Answer: I know of no such instance. The only cut that was made that I know anything about was last November the day scale was agreed upon at that time. I know of no cut since that. There might have been an adjustment of piecework prices since that

> Commissioner Kernan: It has been claimed here that you not only cut the wages in the way you have suggested, but that subsequently during the course of construction of cars, by a readjustment of the prices paid for piecework, a further substantial reduction was made in the cost.

> Answer: I know of no such instance, but there are always two parties to a contract in piecework; one party is the workmen themselves, and the other is the foreman, or whoever is in charge. It is a contract made between our company and the workmen.

Commissioner Kernan: Do you mean that the foreman was in a position where he might have himself, by a readjustment of piece prices, reduced the cost of these cars?'

Answer: Possibly.

Commissioner Kernan: Well, is his action in that respect taken of his own motion and without consultation directly with the officers?

Answer: The foreman of a shop is supposed to be competent to fix the piecework prices; to make all piecework prices.

Commissioner Kernan: Well, now, is it not possible under a system permitting him to do that, that his arbitrary action might result in some injustices being done?

Answer: There is a possibility of that; yes sir; that is one of the matters that would have been investigated.

Commissioner Kernan: That was one of the matters complained of, was it not?

Answer: Yes sir.

Commissioner Kernan: You did not carry your investigation to the point of ascertaining what proof there was in that because the strike came?

Answer: We were not allowed to.... There was no work going on at all in our shops since this strike. We have been very busily engaged in other matters. These men went out on the llth of May and severed their connection with the company; therefore there was no further investigation as far as they were concerned....

★   ★   ★

Excerpt, U.S. Strike Commission Report, November 14, 1894.

If we exclude the aesthetic and sanitary features at Pullman, the rents there are from 20 to 25 per cent higher than rents in Chicago or surrounding towns for similar accommodations. . The aesthetic features are admired by visitors, but have little money value to employees, especially when they lack bread....

The company's claim that the workmen need not hire its tenements and can live elsewhere if they choose is not entirely tenable. The fear of losing work keeps them in Pullman as long as there are tenements unoccupied, because the company is supposed, as a matter of business, to give a preference to its tenants when work is slack. The employees, believing that a tenant at Pullman has this advantage, naturally feel some compulsion to rent at Pullman, and thus to stand well with the management. Exceptional and necessary expert workmen do not share this feeling to the same extent and are more free to hire or own homes elsewhere. While reducing wages the company made no reduction in rents. Its position is that the two matters are distinct....

★   ★   ★

Thomas H. Wickes, second vice-president, Pullman Company, questioning before the Strike Commission, August 1894.

Question: Has the company had any policy with reference to labor unions among its help?

Wickes: No, we never objected to unions except in one instance. I presume that there are quite a number of unions in our shops now.

Question: What are they?

Wickes: I couldn't tell you, but I have heard of some of them. I suppose the cabinetmakers have a union, and I suppose the car builders have a union....

Question: The only objection you ever made was to the American Railway Union, wasn't it?

Wickes: Yes, sir.

Question: What was the basis of your objection to that union?

Wickes: Our objection to that was that we would not treat with our men as members of 'the American Railway Union, and we would not treat with them as members of any union. We treat with them as individuals and as men....

Question: Don't you think, Mr. Wickes, that would give the corporation a very great advantage over those men if it could take them up one at a time and discuss the question with them. With the ability that you have got, for instance, where do you think the man would stand in each discussion?

Wickes: The man has got probably more ability than I have.

Question: You think that it would be fair to your men for each one of them to come before you and take up the question of his grievances and attempt to maintain his end of the discussion, do you?

Wickes: I think so, yes. If he is not able to do that, that is his misfortune.

Question: Don't you think that the fact that you represent a vast concentration of capital, and are selected for that because of your ability to represent it, entitles him if he pleases to unite with all of the men of his craft and select the ablest one they have got to represent the cause?

Wickes: As a union?

Question: As a union.

Wickes: They have the right, yes sir. We have the right to say whether we will receive them or not.

Question: Do you think you have any right to refuse to recognize that right in treating with the men?

Wickes: Yes, sir; if we choose to.

Question: Then you think you have the right to refuse to recognize a union of men designed for the purpose of presenting... to your company the grievances which all complain of or which any complain of?

Wickes: That is the policy of the company; yes, sir. If we were to receive these men as representatives of the unions they could probably force us to pay any wage which they saw fit, and get the Pullman Company in the same shape that some of the railroads are by making concessions which ought not to be made.

Question: Don't you think that the opposite policy, to wit, that all your dealings with the men, as individuals, in case you sought to abuse your power, might enable you to pay to the men ... just what you saw fit?

Wickes: Well, of course a man in an official position, if he is arbitrary and unfair, could work a great deal of injustice to the men; no doubt about that. But then it is a man's privilege to go to work somewhere else.

Question: Don't you recognize as to many men, after they had become settled in a place at work of that kind, that really that privilege does not amount to much?

Wickes: We find that the best men usually come to the front; the best of our men don't give us any trouble with unions or anything else. It is only the inferior men—that is, the least competent—that give us the trouble....

★   ★   ★

Thomas H. Wickes, second vice-president, Pullman Company, statement to the U. S. Strike Commission, August 1894.

On June 1 [1893], two members of the Civic Federation called upon me to consider some methods of conciliation and arbitration. I explained the situation to them and informed them that we did not consider there was any proper subject for arbitration. On the next day two other members of the Civic Federation called and we had a similar discussion.

On the 15th of June, 12 persons, calling themselves a committee from the American Railway Union, called upon me to request that there should be an arbitration. I informed them, in reply, that the company declined to consider any communication from the American Railway Union as representing the former employees of the company.

On the next day a committee of six of our former employees called upon me and requested that there should be an arbitration. I informed them that we did not consider that there was any proper subject for arbitration.

On the 22nd of June Messrs. F. E. Pollans, B. W. Lovejoy, and C. A. Timlin, claiming to be a committee of three of the American Railway Union, called upon me and stated that they were instructed to notify the Pullman Company that, unless it agreed to arbitration, a boycott would be declared to stop the running of Pullman cars, taking effect at 12 o'clock noon, Tuesday, the 26th day of June. I replied to this statement that the company declined to consider any communication from the American Railway Union on the subject. ...

★   ★   ★

George M. Pullman, responses to questions posed by the commissioners of the U.S. Strike Commission, August 27, 1894.

> Question: What are those matters that are proper subjects for arbitration?
>
> Pullman: A matter of opinion would be a proper subject for arbitration, as, for instance, a question of title, or a disagreement on a matter of opinion but as to whether a fact that I know to be true is true or not, I could not agree to submit to arbitration. Take the case in hand, the question as to whether the shops at Pullman shall be continuously operated at a loss or not, is one which it was impossible for the company, as a matter of principle, to submit to the opinion of any third party....
>
> Question: You use the expression, "impossible to be submitted." Why is it impossible?
>
> Pullman: Because it would violate a principle.
>
> Question: What principle?
>
> Pullman: The principle that a man should have the right to manage his own property....

★   ★   ★

George M. Pullman, responses to questions posed by commissioners of the U.S. Strike Commission, August 27, 1894.

> Commissioner Worthington: Now, let me ask you, does the company now make it a condition, in taking back any of those who were on the strike, that they shall surrender their card of membership in the American Railway Union?

Pullman: We do. That is the only union, however. We have never discriminated against any labor union whatever, except the American Railway Union.

Commissioner Worthington: Have you had any other labor organization in Pullman?

Pullman: I do not know as to that. We have never made any question whatever on that in the hiring of the men.

Commissioner Worthington: Has there ever been one that you know of?

Pullman: I presume they have, although I am not able to say definitely about it.

Commissioner Worthington: Is not this American Railway Union the first labor organization that your employees as employees have belonged to that has come to your knowledge?

Pullman: I have no recollection of any contact with a labor organization other than the railway union.

Commissioner Worthington: And the policy now, as I understand it, of the Pullman Palace Car Company is that it will retain no one in its employ that belongs to this branch of organized labor?

Pullman: The policy is that it will retain no one that belongs to the American Railway Union. It has not discriminated against any other labor organizations.

Commissioner Worthington: And you do not know that there is any other one out there to discriminate against?

Answer: I don't know as a fact, but I presume there is.

Commissioner Worthington: But if there was one, you would not have discriminated against it?

Pullman: I say we have never discriminated against other labor organizations. If I should desire to make any further statement hereafter, I may make it, I suppose.

Farmers in Revolt

Bryan's "Cross of Gold" Speech: Mesmerizing the Masses

At the 1896 Democratic Party Convention, the young mayor of Omaha, Nebraska, William Jennings Bryan, advocated relief for farmers and "free silver" in one of the most famous political speeches in U.S. history—the "Cross of God" speech.

> I would be presumptuous, indeed, to present myself against the distinguished gentlemen to whom you have listened if this were but a measuring of ability; but this is not a contest among persons. The humblest citizen in all the land when clad in the armor of a righteous cause is stronger than all the whole hosts of error that they can bring. I come to speak to you in defense of a cause as holy as the cause of liberty—the cause of humanity. When this debate is concluded, a motion will be made to lay upon the table the resolution offered in commendation of the administration and also the resolution in condemnation of the administration. I shall object to bringing this question down to a level of persons. The individual is but an atom; he is born, he acts, he dies; but principles are eternal; and this has been a contest of principle.
>
> Never before in the history of this country has there been witnessed such a contest as that through which we have passed. Never before in the history of American politics has a great issue been fought out as this issue has been by the voters themselves.
>
> On the 4th of March, 1895, a few Democrats, most of them members of Congress, issued an address to the Democrats of the nation asserting that the money question was the paramount issue of the hour; asserting also the right of a majority of the Democratic Party to control the position of the party on this paramount issue; concluding with the request that all believers in free coinage of silver in the Democratic Party should organize and take charge of and control the policy of the Democratic

Party. Three months later, at Memphis, an organization was perfected, and the silver Democrats went forth openly and boldly and courageously proclaiming their belief and declaring that if successful they would crystallize in a platform the declaration which they had made; and then began the conflict with a zeal approaching the zeal which inspired the crusaders who followed Peter the Hermit. Our silver Democrats went forth from victory unto victory, until they are assembled now, not to discuss, not to debate, but to enter up the judgment rendered by the plain people of this country.

But in this contest, brother has been arrayed against brother, and father against son. The warmest ties of love and acquaintance and association have been disregarded. Old leaders have been cast aside when they refused to give expression to the sentiments of those whom they would lead, and new leaders have sprung up to give direction to this cause of freedom. Thus has the contest been waged, and we have assembled here under as binding and solemn instructions as were ever fastened upon the representatives of a people.

We do not come as individuals. Why, as individuals we might have been glad to compliment the gentleman from New York [Senator Hill], but we knew that the people for whom we speak would never be willing to put him in a position where he could thwart the will of the Democratic Party. I say it was not a question of persons; it was a question of principle; and it is not with gladness, my friends, that we find ourselves brought into conflict with those who are now arrayed on the other side. The gentleman who just preceded me [Governor Russell] spoke of the old state of Massachusetts. Let me assure him that not one person in all this convention entertains the least hostility to the people of the state of Massachusetts.

But we stand here representing people who are the equals before the law of the largest cities in the state of Massachusetts. When you come before us and tell us that we shall disturb your business interests, we reply that you have disturbed our business interests by your action. We say to you that you have made too limited in its application the definition of a businessman. The man who is employed for wages is as much a businessman as his employer. The attorney in a country town is as much a businessman as the corporation counsel in a great metropolis. The merchant at the

crossroads store is as much a businessman as the merchant of
New York. The farmer who goes forth in the morning and toils
all day, begins in the spring and toils all summer, and by the
application of brain and muscle to the natural resources of this
country creates wealth, is as much a businessman as the man who
goes upon the Board of Trade and bets upon the price of grain.
The miners who go 1,000 feet into the earth or climb 2,000 feet
upon the cliffs and bring forth from their hiding places the precious metals to be poured in the channels of trade are as much
businessmen as the few financial magnates who in a backroom
corner the money of the world.

We come to speak for this broader class of businessmen. Ah. my
friends, we say not one word against those who live upon the
Atlantic Coast; but those hardy pioneers who braved all the dangers of the wilderness, who have made the desert to blossom as
the rose—those pioneers away out there, rearing their children
near to nature's heart, where they can mingle their voices with
the voices of the birds—out there where they have erected
schoolhouses for the education of their children and churches
where they praise their Creator, and the cemeteries where sleep
the ashes of their dead—are as deserving of the consideration of
this party as any people in this country.

It is for these that we speak. We do not come as aggressors. Our
war is not a war of conquest. We are fighting in the defense of
our homes, our families, and posterity. We have petitioned, and
our petitions have been scorned. We have entreated, and our
entreaties have been disregarded. We have begged, and they have
mocked when our calamity came.

We beg no longer; we entreat no more; we petition no more. We
defy them!

The gentleman from Wisconsin has said he fears a Robespierre.
My friend, in this land of the free you need fear no tyrant who
will spring up from among the people. What we need is an
Andrew Jackson to stand as Jackson stood, against the encroach-
ments of aggregated wealth.

They tell us that this platform was made to catch votes. We reply
to them that changing conditions make new issues; that the principles upon which rest Democracy are as everlasting as the hills;

but that they must be applied to new conditions as they arise. Conditions have arisen and we are attempting to meet those conditions. They tell us that the income tax ought not to be brought in here; that is not a new idea. They criticize us for our criticism of the Supreme Court of the United States. My friends, we have made no criticism. We have simply called attention to what you know. If you want criticisms, read the dissenting opinions of the Court. That will give you criticisms.

They say we passed an unconstitutional law. I deny it. The income tax was not unconstitutional when it was passed. It was not unconstitutional when it went before the Supreme Court for the first time. It did not become unconstitutional until one judge changed his mind; and we cannot be expected to know when a judge will change his mind.

The income tax is a just law. It simply intends to put the burdens of government justly upon the backs of the people. I am in favor of an income tax. When I find a man who is not willing to pay his share of the burden of the government which protects him, I find a man who is unworthy to enjoy the blessings of a government like ours.

He says that we are opposing the national bank currency. It is true. If you will read what Thomas Benton said, you will find that he said that in searching history he could find but one parallel to Andrew Jackson. That was Cicero, who destroyed the conspiracies of Cataline and saved Rome. He did for Rome what Jackson did when he destroyed the bank conspiracy and saved America.

We say in our platform that we believe that the right to coin money and issue money is a function of government. We believe it. We believe it is a part of sovereignty and can no more with safety be delegated to private individuals than can the power to make penal statutes or levy laws for taxation.

Mr. Jefferson, who was once regarded as good Democratic authority, seems to have a different opinion from the gentleman who has addressed us on the part of the minority. Those who are opposed to this proposition tell us that the issue of paper money is a function of the bank and that the government ought to go out of the banking business. I stand with Jefferson rather than with them, and tell them, as he did, that the issue of money is a function of the government and that the banks should go out of the governing business.

They complain about the plank which declares against the life tenure in office. They have tried to strain it to mean that which it does not mean. What we oppose in that plank is the life tenure that is being built up in Washington which establishes an office-holding class and excludes from participation in the benefits the humbler members of our society. . . .

Let me call attention to two or three great things. The gentleman from New York says that he will propose an amendment providing that this change in our law shall not affect contracts which, according to the present laws, are made payable in gold. But if he means to say that we cannot change our monetary system without protecting those who have loaned money before the change was made, I want to ask him where, in law or in morals, he can find authority for not protecting the debtors when the act of 1873 was passed when he now insists that we must protect the creditor. He says he also wants to amend this platform so as to provide that if we fail to maintain the parity within a year that we will then suspend the coinage of silver. We reply that when we advocate a thing which we believe will be successful we are not compelled to raise a doubt as to our own sincerity by trying to show what we will do if we are wrong.

I ask him, if he will apply his logic to us, why he does not apply it to himself. He says that he wants this country to try to secure an international agreement. Why doesn't he tell us what he is going to do if they fail to secure an international agreement. There is more reason for him to do that than for us to expect to fail to maintain the parity. They have tried for thirty years— thirty years—to secure an international agreement, and those are waiting for it most patiently who don't want it at all.

Now, my friends, let me come to the great paramount issue. If they ask us here why it is we say more on the money question than we say upon the tariff question, I reply that if protection has slain its thousands the gold standard has slain its tens of thousands. If they ask us why we did not embody all these things in our platform which we believe, we reply to them that when we have restored the money of the Constitution, all other necessary reforms will be possible, and that until that is done there is no reform that can be accomplished.

Why is it that within three months such a change has come over the sentiments of the country? Three months ago, when it was confidently asserted that those who believed in the gold standard would frame our platforms and nominate our candidates, even the advocates of the gold standard did not think that we could elect a President; but they had good reasons for the suspicion, because there is scarcely a state here today asking for the gold standard that is not within the absolute control of the Republican Party.

But note the change. Mr. McKinley was nominated at St. Louis upon a platform that declared for the maintenance of the gold standard until it should be changed into bimetallism by an international agreement. Mr. McKinley was the most popular man among the Republicans ; and everybody three months ago in the Republican Party prophesied his election. How is it today? Why, that man who used to boast that he looked like Napoleon, that man shudders today when he thinks that he was nominated on the anniversary of the Battle of Waterloo. Not only that, but as he listens he can hear with ever increasing distinctness the sound of the waves as they beat upon the lonely shores of St. Helena.

Why this change? Ah, my friends. is not the change evident to anyone who will look at the matter? It is because no private character, however pure, no personal popularity, however great, can protect from the avenging wrath of an indignant people the man who will either declare that he is in favor of fastening the gold standard upon this people, or who is willing to surrender the right of self-government and place legislative control in the hands of foreign potentates and powers. . . .

We go forth confident that we shall win. Why? Because upon the paramount issue in this campaign there is not a spot of ground upon which the enemy will dare to challenge battle. Why, if they tell us that the gold standard is a good thing, we point to their platform and tell them that their platform pledges the party to get rid of a gold standard and substitute bimetallism. If the gold standard is a good thing, why try to get rid of it? If the gold standard, and I might call your attention to the fact that some of the very people who are in this convention today and who tell you that we ought to declare in favor of international bimetallism and thereby declare that the gold standard is wrong and that the principles of bimetallism are better—these very people four months ago were open and avowed advocates of the gold standard and telling us that we could not legislate two metals together even with all the world.

I want to suggest this truth, that if the gold standard is a good thing we ought to declare in favor of its retention and not in favor of abandoning it; and if the gold standard is a bad thing, why should we wait until some other nations are willing to help us to let it go?

Here is the line of battle. We care not upon which issue they force the fight. We are prepared to meet them on either issue or on both. If they tell us that the gold standard is the standard of civilization, we reply to them that this, the most enlightened of all nations of the earth, has never declared for a gold standard, and both the parties this year are declaring against it. If the gold standard is the standard of civilization, why, my friends, should we not have it? So if they come to meet us on that, we can present the history of our nation. More than that, we can tell them this, that they will search the pages of history in vain to find a single instance in which the common people of any land ever declared themselves in favor of a gold standard. They can find where the holders of fixed investments have.

Mr. Carlisle said in 1878 that this was a struggle between the idle holders of idle capital and the struggling masses who produce the wealth and pay the taxes of the country; and my friends, it is simply a question that we shall decide upon which side shall the Democratic Party fight. Upon the side of the idle holders of idle capital, or upon the side of the struggling masses? That is the question that the party must answer first; and then it must be answered by each individual hereafter. The sympathies of the Democratic Party, as described by the platform, are on the side of the struggling masses, who have ever been the foundation of the Democratic Party.

There are two ideas of government. There are those who believe that if you just legislate to make the well-to-do prosperous, that their prosperity will leak through on those below. The Democratic idea has been that if you legislate to make the masses prosperous their prosperity will find its way up and through every class that rests upon it.

You come to us and tell us that the great cities are in favor of the gold standard. I tell you that the great cities rest upon these broad and fertile prairies. Burn down your cities and leave our farms, and your cities will spring up again as if by magic. But destroy our farms and the grass will grow in the streets of every city in the country.

My friends, we shall declare that this nation is able to legislate for its own people on every question without waiting for the aid or consent of any other nation on earth, and upon that issue we expect to carry every single state in the Union.

I shall not slander the fair state of Massachusetts nor the state of New York by saying that when citizens are confronted with the proposition, "Is this nation able to attend to its own business?"— I will not slander either one by saying that the people of those states will declare our helpless impotency as a nation to attend to our own business. It is the issue of 1776 over again. Our ancestors, when but 3 million, had the courage to declare their political independence of every other nation upon earth. Shall we, their descendants, when we have grown to 70 million, declare that we are less independent than our forefathers? No, my friends, it will never be the judgment of this people. Therefore, we care not upon what lines the battle is fought. If they say bimetallism is good but we cannot have it till some nation helps us, we reply that, instead of having a gold standard because England has, we shall restore bimetallism, and then let England have bimetallism because the United States have.

If they dare to come out in the open field and defend the gold standard as a good thing, we shall fight them to the uttermost, having behind us the producing masses of the nation and the world. Having behind us the commercial interests and the laboring interests and all the toiling masses, we shall answer their demands for a gold standard by saying to them, you shall not press down upon the brow of labor this crown of thorns. You shall not crucify mankind upon a cross of gold.

People's Party Platform:
Adopted at St. Louis, July 24, 1896

The People's party, assembled in National Convention, reaffirms its allegiance to the principles declared by the founders of the Republic, and also to the fundamental principles of just government as enunciated in the platform of the party in 1892. We recognize that, through the connivance of the present and preceding Administrations, the country has reached a crisis in its national life as predicted in our declaration four years ago, and that prompt and patriotic action is the supreme duty of the hour. We realize that, while we have political independence, our financial and industrial independence is yet to be attained by restoring to our country the constitutional control and exercise of the functions necessary to a people's government, which functions have been basely surrendered by our public servant to corporate monopolies. The influence of European money changers has been more potent in shaping legislation than the voice of the American people. Executive power and patronage have been used to corrupt our Legislatures and defeat the will of the people, and plutocracy has thereby been enthroned upon the ruins of Democracy. To restore the Government intended by the fathers and for the welfare and prosperity of this and future generations, we demand the establishment of an economic and financial system which shall make us masters of our own affairs and independent of European control by the adoption of the following:

Declaration of Principles

FIRST. We demand a national money, safe and sound, issued by the General Government only, without the intervention of banks of issue, to be a full legal tender for all debts, public and private; a just, equitable, and efficient means of distribution direct to the people and through the lawful disbursements of the Government.

SECOND. We demand the free and unrestricted coinage of silver and gold at the present ratio of 16 to 1, without waiting for the consent of foreign nations.

THIRD. We demand the volume of circulating medium be speedily increased to an amount sufficient to meet the demands of the business and population and to restore the just level of prices of labor and production.

FOURTH. We denounce the sale of bonds and the increase of the public interest-bearing debt made by the present Administration as unnecessary and without authority of law, and demand that no more bonds be issued except by specific act of Congress.

FIFTH. We demand such legislation as will prevent the demonetization of the lawful money of the United States by private contract.

SIXTH. We demand that the Government, in payment of its obligations, shall use its option as to the kind of lawful money in which they are to be paid, and we denounce the present and preceding Administrations for surrendering this option to the holders of Government obligations.

SEVENTH. We demand a graduated income tax to the end that aggregated wealth shall bear its just proportion of taxation, and we regard the recent decision of the Supreme Court relative to the Income Tax law as a misinterpretation of the Constitution and an invasion of the rightful powers of Congress over the subject of taxation.

EIGHTH. We demand that postal savings banks be established by the Government for the safe deposit of the savings of the people and to facilitate exchange.

Transportation

FIRST. Transportation being a means of exchange and a public necessity, the Government should own and operate the railroads in the interest of the people and on a non-partisan basis, to the end that all may be accorded the same treatment in transportation and that the tyranny and political power now exercised by the great railroad corporations, which result in the impairment if not the destruction of the political rights and personal liberties of the citizen, may be destroyed. Such ownership is to be accomplished gradually, in a manner consistent with sound public policy.

SECOND. The interest of the United States in the public highways built with public moneys and the proceeds of extensive grants of land to the Pacific Railroads should never be alienated, mortgaged, or sold, but guarded and protected for the general welfare as provided by the laws organizing such railroads. The foreclosure of existing liens of the United States on these roads should at once follow default in the payment thereof by the debtor companies; and at the foreclosure sales of said roads the

Government shall purchase the same if it becomes necessary to protect its interests therein, or if they can be purchased at a reasonable price; and the Government shall operate said railroads as public highways for the benefit of the whole people and not in the interest of the few under suitable provisions for protection of life and property, giving to all transportation interests equal privileges and equal rates for fares and freights.

THIRD. We denounce the present infamous schemes for refuding these debts, and demand that the laws now applicable thereto be executed and administered according to their interest and spirit.

Telegraph

The telegraphic, like the Post-office system, being a necessity for the transmission of news, should be owned and operated by the Government in the interest of the people.

Land

FIRST. True policy demands that the National and State legislation shall be such as will ultimately enable every prudent and industrious citizen to secure a home, and, therefore, the land should not be monopolized for speculative purposes. All lands now held by railroads and other corporations in excess of their actual needs, should by lawful means be reclaimed by the Government and held for natural settlers only, and private land monopoly as well as alien ownership should be prohibited.

SECOND. We condemn the frauds by which the land grant Pacific Railroad Companies have, through the connivance of the Interior Department, robbed multitudes of actual bona fide settlers of their homes and miners of their claims, and we demand legislation by Congress which will enforce the exception of mineral land from such grants after as well as before the patent.

THIRD. We demand that bona fide settlers on all public lands be granted free homes, as provided in the National Homestead law, and that no exception be made in the case of Indian reservations when opened for settlement, and that all lands not now patented come under this demand.

Direct Legislation

We favor a system of direct legislation, through the initiative and referendum, under proper constitutional safeguards.

General Propositions

FIRST. We demand the election of President, Vice-President, and United States Senators by a direct vote of the people.

SECOND. We tender to the patriotic people of the country our deepest sympathies in their heroic struggle for political freedom and independence, and we believe the time has come when the United States, the great Republic of the world, should recognize that Cuba is and of right ought to be a free and independent State.

THIRD. We favor home rule in the Territories and the District of Columbia, and the early admission of the Territories as States.

FOURTH. All public salaries should be made to correspond to the price of labor and its products.

FIFTH. In times of great industrial depression idle labor should be employed on public works as far as practicable.

SIXTH. The arbitrary course of the courts in assuming to imprison citizens for indirect contempt, and ruling them by injunction, should be prevented by proper legislation.

SEVENTH. We favor just pensions for our disabled Union soldiers.

EIGHTH. Believing that the elective franchise and an untrammelled ballot are essential to government of, for, and by the people, the People's party condemn the wholesale system of disfrachisement adopted in some of the States as unrepublican and undemocratic, and we declare it to be the duty of the several State Legislatures to take such action as will secure a full, free and fair ballot and honest count.

NINTH. While the foregoing propositions constitute the platform upon which our party stands, and for the vindication of which its organization will be maintained, we recognize that the great and pressing issue of the pending campaign, upon which the present election will turn, is the financial question, and upon this great and specific issue between the parties we cordially invite the aid and co-operation of all organizations and citizens agreeing with us upon this vital question.

Shying Away: Labor Leaders Steer Clear of the Farmers' Alliance

Samuel Gompers, the head of the biggest union in the United States, the American Federation of Labor [AFL], rejected calls for worker-farmer solidarity and dealth a huge blow to working peoples' causes and their ability to take political action.

> We will soon be in the throes of a political campaign. The passions of men will be sought to be aroused, their prejudices and supposed ignorance played upon and brought into action. The partisan zealot, the political mounteback, the statesman for revenue only, as well as the effervescent, bucolic political party, cure-all sophist and fakir, will be rampant. The dear workingman and his interests will be the theme of all alike, who really seek party advantage and success, though civilization fall, labor be crushed and relapse into barbarism be the result.

> We are on the eve of events which will place our members, our unions and our entire movement to a most critical test, a test which may mean either a partial dissolution of our organizations, or their growth, extension and development. It is because of the great trust committed to my care that a timely word of advice and warning is given lest our members be taken unawares, fail to profit by the experience of labor organizations which have weathered the storms, and those others whose only evidence of former greatness or existence are their epitaphs folly, blunders, calamities. "Learn to see in another's calamity the ills which you should avoid" is a maxim which Syrus declared more than nineteen hundred years ago; and it is as applicable to our times as it was when first penned.

> Whatever labor secures now or secured in the past is due to the efforts of the workers themselves in their own organizations—the trades unions on trade union lines, on trade union action. When

in previous years the workers were either unorganized or poorly organized, the political trickster scarcely ever have a second thought to the dear workingman and his interests. During the periods of fair or blossoming organization the political soothsayers attempted by cajolery and baiting to work their influence into the labor organizations; to commit them to either party or the other.

There are many organizations which may declare that their unions are safe from such influences, and, lulled into a fancied security, permit the virus of political partisanship to be injected into their very being; laying their unions liable to the most malignant diseases of division, antagonism and disruption. Bear in mind that the modern political party freebooter finds his prototype in the one who "For ways that are dark and tricks that are in vain the heathen (political) Chinese is peculiar?"

The industrial field is littered with more corpses of organizations destroyed by the damning influence of partisan political action than from all other causes combined. Nor must it be at all lost sight of that this does not only apply to local or national trade unions but also to previous efforts of labor at national federation. The National Labor Union, in its time a great federation, after it committed itself to political partisan action, went to the limbo of movements which no longer moved. After that act it acted no more. No convention of that organization was ever after held.

In the light of that experience the American Federation of Labor has always declared and maintained that the unions of labor are above, and should be beyond, the power and influence of political parties. It was with these great object lessons still dangling before our vision, . . . like the sword of Damocles hanging over our heads by a single thread, which, severed by a failure to profit by past experience, may leave us headless, and the whole body of organized labor bleeding to death, a hapless victim of our own folly, serfs or slaves to the cupidity of corporate monopolistic greed, that the A. F. of L. at its last convention resolved that,

"Party politics, whether they be Democratic, Republican, Socialistic, Populistic, Prohibition, or any other shall have no place in the conventions of the American Federation of Labor."

This action, while it directly decrees the course for the conventions of the A. F. of L. is also a declamation of policy and principle and hence applies equally to all affiliated organizations.

The power of the trade unions is extending to all classes and influencing public sympathy and public judgment. Let us build up our organizations upon a solid basis . . . , that they may endure for all time, that they may be our protectors, our defenders in our struggle for justice and right; that we may turn the in the hour of our trials with the confidence of our manhood maintained, and in the hour of our triumphs to pay them the meed of praise and glory of victories won, men, women and children saved, our civilization and emancipation assured.

Let the watchword be: No political party domination over the trade unions; no political party influence over trade union action.

Long live the trade union! Long live the American Federation of Labor!

II

Imperialism and Democracy

Even though the economic system of industrial capitalism had triumphed and become firmly entrenched, problems remained. The economy was producing more goods than could be consumed at home and great amounts of capital, money to be invested and recirculated for profit, was piling up with no place to invest it ["surplus capital"].

The solution to this crisis became foreign conquest, with the U.S. invading and taking control of Hawai'i, Cuba and the Philippines, among other places. Some national leaders saw great advantage in this conquest, which would involve both armies and bankers [so-called dollar diplomacy]. But others, such as William Jennings Bryan, attacked this new empire as a violation of national principles of republicanism and self-government.

By the early part of the 20th Century, the United States was clearly embarked on a mission to open up lands all over the globe so that American businesses could trade and invest, to create a global "open door" for commerce and finance. By the outset of a major war in Europe in 1914, the Americans were poised for global power and used the war to become a global financial power.

But this power came with a cost, as the American concept of "democracy" was exposed to the harsh light of hypocrisy, with the government taking action against those who would protest, who would exercise their right to free speech, against the war or in favor of an expanded idea of democracy.

1898 and Its Aftermath

Albert Beveridge: The March of the Flag

The March of the Flag

It is a noble land that God has given us; a land that can feed and clothe the world; a land whose coastlines would inclose half the countries of Europe; a land set like a sentinel between the two imperial oceans of the globe, a greater England with a nobler destiny.

It is a mighty people that He has planted on this soil; a people sprung from the most masterful blood of history; a people perpetually revitalized by the virile, man-producing working-folk of all the earth; a people imperial by virtue of their power, by right of their institutions, by authority of their Heaven-directed purposes-the propagandists and not the misers of liberty.

It is a glorious history our God has bestowed upon His chosen people; a history heroic with faith in our mission and our future; a history of statesmen who flung the boundaries of the Republic out into unexplored lands and savage wilderness; a history of soldiers who carried the flag across blazing deserts and through the ranks of hostile mountains, even to the gates of sunset; a history of a multiplying people who overran a continent in half a century; a history of prophets who saw the consequences of evils inherited from the past and of martyrs who died to save us from them; a history divinely logical, in the process of whose tremendous reasoning we find ourselves today.

Therefore, in this campaign, the question is larger than a party question. It is an American question. It is a world question. Shall the American people continue their march toward the commercial supremacy of the world? Shall free institutions broaden their blessed reign as the children of liberty wax in strength, until the empire of our principles is established over the hearts of all mankind?

Have we no mission to perform no duty to discharge to our fellow man? Has God endowed us with gifts beyond our deserts and marked us as the people of His peculiar favor, merely to rot in our own selfishness, as men and nations must, who take cowardice for their companion and self for their deity-as China has, as India has, as Egypt has?

Shall we be as the man who had one talent and hid it, or as he who had ten talents and used them until they grew to riches? And shall we reap the reward that waits on our discharge of our high duty; shall we occupy new markets for what our farmers raise, our factories make, our merchants sell-aye, and please God, new markets for what our ships shall carry?

Hawaii is ours; Porto Rico is to be ours; at the prayer of her people Cuba finally will be ours; in the islands of the East, even to the gates of Asia, coaling stations are to be ours at the very least; the flag of a liberal government is to float over the Philippines, and may it be the banner that Taylor unfurled in Texas and Fremont carried to the coast.

The Opposition tells us that we ought not to govern a people without their consent. I answer, The rule of liberty that all just government derives its authority from the consent of the governed, applies only to those who are capable of self-government We govern the Indians without their consent, we govern our territories without their consent, we govern our children without their consent. How do they know what our government would be without their consent? Would not the people of the Philippines prefer the just, humane, civilizing government of this Republic to the savage, bloody rule of pillage and extortion from which we have rescued them?

And, regardless of this formula of words made only for enlightened, self-governing people, do we owe no duty to the world? Shall we turn these peoples back to the reeking hands from which we have taken them? Shall we abandon them, with Germany, England, Japan, hungering for them? Shall we save them from those nations, to give them a self-rule of tragedy?

They ask us how we shall govern these new possessions. I answer: Out of local conditions and the necessities of the case methods of government will grow. If England can govern foreign lands, so can America. If Germany can govern foreign lands, so can America. If they can supervise protectorates, so can America. Why is it more difficult to administer Hawaii than Nevs Mexico or California? Both had a savage and an alien population: both were more remote from the seat of government when they came under our dominion than the Philippines are today.

Will you say by your vote that American ability to govern has decayed, that a century s experience in self-rule has failed of a result? Will you affirm by your vote that you are an infidel to American power and practical sense? Or will you say that ours is the blood of government; ours the heart of dominion; ours the brain and genius of administration? Will you remember that we do but what our fathers did-we but pitch the tents of liberty farther westward, farther southward-we only continue the march of the flag?

The march of the flag! In 1789 the flag of the Republic waved over 4,000,000 souls in thirteen states, and their savage territory which stretched to the Mississippi, to Canada, to the Floridas. The timid minds of that day said that no new territory was needed, and, for the hour, they were right. But Jefferson, through whose intellect the centuries marched; Jefferson, who dreamed of Cuba as an American state, Jefferson, the first Imperialist of the Republic-Jefferson acquired that imperial territory which swept from the Mississippi to the mountains, from Texas to the British possessions, and the march of the flag began!

The infidels to the gospel of liberty raved, but the flag swept on! The title to that noble land out of which Oregon, Washington, Idaho and Montana have been carved was uncertain: Jefferson, strict constructionist of constitutional power though he was, obeyed the Anglo-Saxon impulse within him, whose watchword is, "Forwardl": another empire was added to the Republic, and the march of the flag went on!

Those who deny the power of free institutions to expand urged every argument, and more, that we hear, today; but the people's judgment approved the command of their blood, and the march of the flag went on!...

WILLIAM JENNINGS BRYAN:
The Paralyzing Influence of Imperialism

IF IT IS RIGHT for the United States to hold the Philippine Islands permanently and imitate European empires in the government of colonies, the Republican Party ought to state its position and defend it, but it must expect the subject races to protest against such a policy and to resist to the extent of their ability.

The Filipinos do not need any encouragement from Americans now living. Our whole history has been an encouragement, not only to the Filipinos but to all who are denied a voice in their own government. If the Republicans are prepared to censure all who have used language calculated to make the Filipinos hate foreign domination, let them condemn the speech of Patrick Henry. When he uttered that passionate appeal, "Give me liberty or give me death," he expressed a sentiment which still echoes in the hearts of men.

Let them censure Jefferson; of all the statesmen of history none have used words so offensive to those who would hold their fellows in political bondage. Let them censure Washington, who declared that the colonists must choose between liberty and slavery. Or, if the statute of limitations has run against the sins of Henry and Jefferson and Washington, let them censure Lincoln, whose Gettysburg speech will be quoted in defense of popular government when the present advocates of force and conquest are forgotten.

Someone has said that a truth once spoken can never be recalled. It goes on and on, and no one can set a limit to its ever widening influence. But if it were possible to obliterate every word written or spoken in defense of the principles set forth in the Declaration of Independence, a war of conquest would still leave its legacy of perpetual hatred, for it was God Himself who placed in every human heart the love of liberty. He never made a race of people so low in the scale of civilization or intelligence that it would welcome a foreign master.

Those who would have this nation enter upon a career of empire must consider not only the effect of imperialism on the Filipinos but they must also calculate its effects upon our own nation. We cannot repudiate the principle of self-government in the Philippines without weakening that principle here.

Lincoln said that the safety of this nation was not in its fleets, its armies, its forts, but in the spirit which prizes liberty as the heritage of all men, in all lands, everywhere, and he warned his countrymen that they could not destroy this spirit without planting the seeds of despotism at their own doors.

Even now we are beginning to see the paralyzing influence of imperialism. Heretofore this nation has been prompt to express its sympathy with those who were fighting for civil liberty. While our sphere of activity has been limited to the Western Hemisphere, our sympathies have not been bounded by the seas. We have felt it due to ourselves and to the world, as well as to those who were struggling for the right to govern themselves, to proclaim the interest which our people have, from the date of their own independence, felt in every contest between human rights and arbitrary power. . . .

A colonial policy means that we shall send to the Philippine Islands a few traders, a few taskmasters, and a few officeholders, and an army large enough to support the authority of a small fraction of the people while they rule the natives.

If we have an imperial policy we must have a great standing army as its natural and necessary complement. The spirit which will justify the forcible annexation of the Philippine Islands will justify the seizure of other islands and the domination of other people, and with wars of conquest we can expect a certain, if not rapid, growth of our military establishment.

That a large permanent increase in our regular army is intended by Republican leaders is not a matter of conjecture but a matter of fact. In his message of Dec. 5, 1898, the President asked for authority to increase the standing army to 100,000. In 1896 the army contained about 25,000. Within two years the President asked for four times that many, and a Republican House of Representatives complied with the request after the Spanish treaty had been signed, and when no country was at war with the United States.

If such an army is demanded when an imperial policy is contemplated but not openly avowed, what may be expected if the people encourage the Republican Party by endorsing its policy at the polls?

A large standing army is not only a pecuniary burden to the people and, if accompanied by compulsory service, a constant source of irritation but it is even a menace to a republican form of government. The army is the personification of force, and militarism will inevitably change the ideals of the people and turn the thoughts of our young men from the arts of peace to the science of war. The government which relies for its defense upon its citizens is more likely to be just than one which has at call a large body of professional soldiers.

A small standing army and a well-equipped and well-disciplined state militia are sufficient at ordinary times, and in an emergency the nation should in the future as in the past place its dependence upon the volunteers who come from all occupations at their country's call and return to productive labor when their services are no longer required – men who fight when the country needs fighters and work when the country needs workers. . . .

Some argue that American rule in the Philippine Islands will result in the better education of the Filipinos. Be not deceived. If we expect to maintain a colonial policy, we shall not find it to our advantage to educate the people. The educated Filipinos are now in revolt against us, and the most ignorant ones have made the least resistance to our domination. If we are to govern them without their consent and give them no voice in determining the taxes which they must pay, we dare not educate them lest they learn to read the Declaration of Independence and the Constitution of the United States and mock us for our in consistency.

The principal arguments, however, advanced by those who enter upon a defense of imperialism are:

First, that we must improve the present opportunity to become a world power and enter into international politics.

Second, that our commercial interests in the Philippine Islands and in the Orient make it necessary for us to hold the islands permanently.

Third, that the spread of the Christian religion will be facilitated by a colonial policy.

Fourth, that there is no honorable retreat from the position which the nation has taken.

The first argument is addressed to the nation's pride and the second to the nation's pocketbook. The third is intended for the church member and the fourth for the partisan.

It is sufficient answer to the first argument to say that for more than a century this nation has been a world power. For ten decades it has been the most potent influence in the world. Not only has it been a world power but it has done more to affect the policies of the human race than all the other nations of the world combined. Because our Declaration of Independence was promulgated, others have been promulgated. Because the patriots of 1776 fought for liberty, others have fought for it. Because our Constitution was adopted, other constitutions have been adopted.

The growth of the principle of self-government, planted on American soil, has been the overshadowing political fact of the 19th century. It has made this nation conspicuous among the nations and given it a place in history, such as no other nation has ever enjoyed. Nothing has been able to check the onward march of this idea. I am not willing that this nation shall cast aside the omnipotent weapon of truth to seize again the weapons of physical warfare. I would not exchange the glory of this republic for the glory of all the empires that have risen and fallen since time began.

The permanent chairman of the last Republican National Convention presented the pecuniary argument in all its baldness when he said:

We make no hypocritical pretense of being interested in the Philippines solely on account of others. While we regard the welfare of those people as a sacred trust, we regard the welfare of the American people first. We see our duty to ourselves as well as to others. We believe in trade expansion. By every legitimate means within the province of government and constitution we mean to stimulate the expansion of our trade and open new markets.

This is the commercial argument. It is based upon the theory that war can be rightly waged for pecuniary advantage and that it is profitable to purchase trade by force and violence. Franklin denied both of these propositions. When Lord Howe asserted that the acts of Parliament which brought on the Revolution were necessary to prevent American trade from passing into foreign channels, Franklin replied:

To me it seems that neither the obtaining nor retaining of any trade, howsoever valuable, is an object for which men may justly spill each other's blood; that the true and sure means of extending and securing commerce are the goodness and cheapness of commodities, and that the profits of no trade can ever be equal to the expense of compelling it and holding it by fleets and armies. I consider this war against us, therefore, as both unjust and unwise.

I place the philosophy of Franklin against the sordid doctrine of those who would put a price upon the head of an American soldier and justify a war of conquest upon the ground that it will pay. The Democratic Party is in favor of the expansion of trade. It would extend our trade by every legitimate and peaceful means; but it is not willing to make merchandise of human blood.

But a war of conquest is as unwise as it is unrighteous. A harbor and coaling station in the Philippines would answer every trade and military necessity and such a concession could have been secured at any time without difficulty. It is not necessary to own people in order to trade with them. We carry on trade today with every part of the world, and our commerce has expanded more rapidly than the commerce of any European empire. We do not own Japan or China, but we trade with their people. We have not absorbed the republics of Central and South America, but we trade with them. Trade cannot be permanently profitable unless it is voluntary.

When trade is secured by force, the cost of securing it and retaining it must be taken out of the profits, and the profits are never large enough to cover the expense. Such a system would never be defended but for the fact that the expense is borne by all the people while the profits are enjoyed by a few.,

Imperialism would be profitable to the Army contractors; it would be profitable to the shipowners, who would carry live soldiers to the Philippines and bring dead soldiers back; it would be profitable to those who would seize upon the franchises, and it would be profitable to the officials whose salaries would be fixed here and paid over there; but to the farmer, to the laboring man, and to the vast majority of those engaged in other occupations, it would bring expenditure without return and risk without reward...

The Open Door Note: U.S. Secretary of State, John Hay, September 6, 1899

At the time when the Government of the United States was informed by that of Germany that it had leased from His Majesty the Emperor of China the port of Kiao-chao and the adjacent territory in the province of Shantung, assurances were given to the ambassador of the United States at Berlin by the Imperial German minister for foreign affairs that the rights and privileges insured by treaties with China to citizens of the United States would not thereby suffer or be in anywise impaired within the area over which Germany had thus obtained control.

More recently, however, the British Government recognized by a formal agreement with Germany the exclusive right of the latter country to enjoy in said leased area and the contiguous "sphere of influence or interest" certain privileges, more especially those relating to railroads and mining enterprises; but as the exact nature and extent of the rights thus recognized have not been clearly defined, it is possible that serious conflicts of interest may at any time arise not only between British and German subjects within said area, but that the interests of our citizens may also be jeopardized thereby.

Earnestly desirous to remove any cause of irritation and to insure at the same time to the commerce of all nations in China the undoubted benefits which should accrue from a formal recognition by the various powers claiming "spheres of interest" that they shall enjoy perfect equality of treatment for their commerce and navigation within such "spheres," the Government of the

United States would be pleased to see His German Majesty's Government give formal assurances, and lend its cooperation in securing like assurances from the other interested powers, that each, within its respective sphere of whatever influence—

First. Will in no way interfere with any treaty port or any vested interest within any so-called "sphere of interest" or leased territory it may have in China.

Second. That the Chinese treaty tariff of the time being shall apply to all merchandise landed or shipped to all such ports as are within said "sphere of interest" (unless they be "free ports"), no matter to what nationality it may belong, and that duties so leviable shall be collected by the Chinese Government.

Third. That it will levy no higher harbor dues on vessels of another nationality frequenting any port in such "sphere" than shall be levied on vessels of its own nationality, and no higher railroad charges over lines built, controlled, or operated within its "sphere" on merchandise belonging to citizens or subjects of other nationalities transported through such "sphere" than shall be levied on similar merchandise belonging to its own nationals transported over equal distances.

The liberal policy pursued by His Imperial German Majesty in declaring Kiao-chao a free port and in aiding the Chinese Government in the establishment there of a custom-house are so clearly in line with the proposition which this Government is anxious to see recognized that it entertains the strongest hope that Germany will give its acceptance and hearty support.

The recent ukase of His Majesty the Emperor of Russia declaring the port of Ta-lien-wan open during the whole of the lease under which it is held from China to the merchant ships of all nations, coupled with the categorical assurances made to this Government by His Imperial Majesty's representative at this capital at the time and since repeated to me by the present Russian ambassador, seem to insure the support of the Emperor to the proposed measure. Our ambassador at the Court of St. Petersburg has in consequence been instructed to submit it to the Russian Government and to request their early consideration of it. A copy of my instruction on the subject to Mr. Tower is herewith inclosed for your confidential information.

The commercial interests of Great Britain and Japan will be so clearly served by the desired declaration of intentions, and the views of the Governments of these countries as to the desirability of the adoption of measures insuring the benefits of equality of treatment of all foreign trade throughout China are so similar to those entertained by the United States, that their acceptance of the propositions herein outlined and their cooperation in advocating their adoption by the other powers can be confidently expected. I inclose herewith copy of the instruction which I have sent to Mr. Choate on the subject.

In view of the present favorable conditions, you are instructed to submit the above considerations to His Imperial German Majesty's Minister for Foreign Affairs, and to request his early consideration of the subject.

Copy of this instruction is sent to our ambassadors at London and at St. Petersburg for their information.

The Roosevelt Corollary to the Monroe Doctrine

President Theodore Roosevelt's Annual Message to Congress, December 6, 1904

Foreign Policy

In treating of our foreign policy and of the attitude that this great Nation should assume in the world at large, it is absolutely necessary to consider the Army and the Navy, and the Congress, through which the thought of the Nation finds its expression, should keep ever vividly in mind the fundamental fact that it is impossible to treat our foreign policy, whether this policy takes shape in the effort to secure justice for others or justice for ourselves, save as conditioned upon the attitude we are willing to take toward our Army, and especially toward our Navy. It is not merely unwise, it is contemptible, for a nation, as for an individual, to use high-sounding language to proclaim its purposes, or to take positions which are ridiculous if unsupported by potential force, and then to refuse to provide this force. If there is no intention of providing and keeping the force necessary to back up a strong attitude, then it is far better not to assume such an attitude.

The steady aim of this Nation, as of all enlightened nations, should be to strive to bring ever nearer the day when there shall prevail throughout the world the peace of justice. There are kinds of peace which are highly undesirable, which are in the long run as destructive as any war. Tyrants and oppressors have many times made a wilderness and called it peace. Many times peoples who were slothful or timid or shortsighted, who had been enervated by ease or by luxury, or misled by false teachings, have shrunk in unmanly fashion from doing duty that was stern and that needed self-sacrifice, and have sought to hide from their own minds their shortcomings, their ignoble motives, by calling them love of peace. The peace of tyrannous terror, the peace of craven weakness, the peace of injustice, all these should be shunned as we shun unrighteous war. The goal to set before us as a nation, the goal which should be set before all mankind, is the attainment of the peace of justice, of the peace which comes when each nation is not merely safe-guarded in its own rights, but scrupulously recognizes and performs its duty toward others. Generally peace tells for righteousness; but if there is conflict between the two, then our fealty is due first to the cause of righteousness. Unrighteous wars are common, and unrighteous peace is rare; but both should be shunned. The right of freedom and the responsibility for the exercise of that right can not be divorced. One of our great poets has well and finely said that freedom is not a gift that tarries long in the hands of cowards. Neither does it tarry long in the hands of those too slothful, too dishonest, or too unintelligent to exercise it. The eternal vigilance which is the price of liberty must be exercised, sometimes to guard against outside foes; although of course far more often to guard against our own selfish or thoughtless shortcomings.

If these self-evident truths are kept before us, and only if they are so kept before us, we shall have a clear idea of what our foreign policy in its larger aspects should be. It is our duty to remember that a nation has no more right to do injustice to another nation, strong or weak, than an individual has to do injustice to another individual; that the same moral law applies in one case as in the other. But we must also remember that it is as much the duty of the Nation to guard its own rights and its own interests as it is the duty of the individual so to do. Within the

Nation the individual has now delegated this right to the State, that is, to the representative of all the individuals, and it is a maxim of the law that for every wrong there is a remedy. But in international law we have not advanced by any means as far as we have advanced in municipal law. There is as yet no judicial way of enforcing a right in international law. When one nation wrongs another or wrongs many others, there is no tribunal before which the wrongdoer can be brought. Either it is necessary supinely to acquiesce in the wrong, and thus put a premium upon brutality and aggression, or else it is necessary for the aggrieved nation valiantly to stand up for its rights. Until some method is devised by which there shall be a degree of international control over offending nations, it would be a wicked thing for the most civilized powers, for those with most sense of international obligations and with keenest and most generous appreciation of the difference between right and wrong, to disarm. If the great civilized nations of the present day should completely disarm, the result would mean an immediate recrudescence of barbarism in one form or another. Under any circumstances a sufficient armament would have to be kept up to serve the purposes of international police; and until international cohesion and the sense of international duties and rights are far more advanced than at present, a nation desirous both of securing respect for itself and of doing good to others must have a force adequate for the work which it feels is allotted to it as its part of the general world duty. Therefore it follows that a self-respecting, just, and far-seeing nation should on the one hand endeavor by every means to aid in the development of the various movements which tend to provide substitutes for war, which tend to render nations in their actions toward one another, and indeed toward their own peoples, more responsive to the general sentiment of humane and civilized mankind; and on the other hand that it should keep prepared, while scrupulously avoiding wrongdoing itself, to repel any wrong, and in exceptional cases to take action which in a more advanced stage of international relations would come under the head of the exercise of the international police. A great free people owes it to itself and to all mankind not to sink into helplessness before the powers of evil.

Policy Toward Other Nations of the Western Hemisphere

It is not true that the United States feels any land hunger or entertains any projects as regards the other nations of the Western Hemisphere save such as are for their welfare. All that this country desires is to see the neighboring countries stable, orderly, and prosperous. Any country whose people conduct themselves well can count upon our hearty friendship. If a nation shows that it knows how to act with reasonable efficiency and decency in social and political matters, if it keeps order and pays its obligations, it need fear no interference from the United States. *Chronic wrongdoing, or an impotence which results in a general loosening of the ties of civilized society, may in America, as elsewhere, ultimately require intervention by some civilized nation, and in the Western Hemisphere the adherence of the United States to the Monroe Doctrine may force the United States, however reluctantly, in flagrant cases of such wrongdoing or impotence, to the exercise of an international police power.* If every country washed by the Caribbean Sea would show the progress in stable and just civilization which with the aid of the Platt Amendment Cuba has shown since our troops left the island, and which so many of the republics in both Americas are constantly and brilliantly showing, all question of interference by this Nation with their affairs would be at an end. Our interests and those of our southern neighbors are in reality identical. They have great natural riches, and if within their borders the reign of law and justice obtains, prosperity is sure to come to them. While they thus obey the primary laws of civilized society they may rest assured that they will be treated by us in a spirit of cordial and helpful sympathy. *We would interfere with them only in the last resort, and then only if it became evident that their inability or unwillingness to do justice at home and abroad had violated the rights of the United States or had invited foreign aggression to the detriment of the entire body of American nations.* It is a mere truism to say that every nation, whether in America or anywhere else, which desires to maintain its freedom, its independence, must ultimately realize that the right of such independence can not be separated from the responsibility of making good use of it.

In asserting the Monroe Doctrine, in taking such steps as we have taken in regard to Cuba, Venezuela, and Panama, and in endeavoring to circumscribe the theater of war in the Far East, and to secure the open door in China, we have acted in our own interest as well as in the interest of humanity at large. There are, however, cases in which, while our own interests are not greatly involved, strong appeal is made to our sympathies. Ordinarily it is very much wiser and more useful for us to concern ourselves with striving for our own moral and material betterment here at home than to concern ourselves with trying to better the condition of things in other nations. We have plenty of sins of our own to war against, and under ordinary circumstances we can do more for the general uplifting of humanity by striving with heart and soul to put a stop to civic corruption, to brutal lawlessness and violent race prejudices here at home than by passing resolutions and wrongdoing elsewhere. Nevertheless there are occasional crimes committed on so vast a scale and of such peculiar horror as to make us doubt whether it is not our manifest duty to endeavor at least to show our disapproval of the deed and our sympathy with those who have suffered by it. The cases must be extreme in which such a course is justifiable. There must be no effort made to remove the mote from our brother's eye if we refuse to remove the beam from our own. But in extreme cases action may be justifiable and proper. What form the action shall take must depend upon the circumstances of the case; that is, upon the degree of the atrocity and upon our power to remedy it. The cases in which we could interfere by force of arms as we interfered to put a stop to intolerable conditions in Cuba are necessarily very few. Yet it is not to be expected that a people like ours, which in spite of certain very obvious shortcomings, nevertheless as a whole shows by its consistent practice its belief in the principles of civil and religious liberty and of orderly freedom, a people among whom even the worst crime, like the crime of lynching, is never more than sporadic, so that individuals and not classes are molested in their fundamental rights—it is inevitable that such a nation should desire eagerly to give expression to its horror on an occasion like that of the massacre of the Jews in Kishenef, or when it witnesses such systematic and long-extended cruelty and oppression as the cruelty and oppression of which the Armenians have been the victims, and which have won for them the indignant pity of the civilized world.

The Platt Amendment, 1903

Article I. The Government of Cuba shall never enter into any treaty or other compact with any foreign power or powers which will impair or tend to impair the independence of Cuba, nor in any manner authorize or permit any foreign power or powers to obtain by colonization or for military or naval purposes, or otherwise, lodgment in or control over any portion of said island.

Article II. The Government of Cuba shall not assume or contract any public debt to pay the interest upon which, and to make reasonable sinking-fund provision for the ultimate discharge of which, the ordinary revenues of the Island of Cuba, after defraying the current expenses of the Government, shall be inadequate.

Article III. The Government of Cuba consents that the United States may exercise the right to intervene for the preservation of Cuban independence, the maintenance of a government adequate for the protection of life, property, and individual liberty, and for discharging the obligations with respect to Cuba imposed by the Treaty of Paris on the United States, now to be assumed and undertaken by the Government of Cuba. . . .

Article V. The Government of Cuba will execute, and, as far as necessary, extend the plans already devised, or other plans to be mutually agreed upon, for the sanitation of the cities of the island, to the end that a recurrence of epidemic and infectious diseases may be prevented, thereby assuring protection to the people and commerce of Cuba, as well as to the commerce of the Southern ports of the United States and the people residing therein....

Article VII. To enable the United States to maintain the independence of Cuba, and to protect the people thereof, as well as for its own defense, the Government of Cuba will sell or lease to the United States lands necessary for coaling or naval stations, at certain specified points, to be agreed upon with the]?resident of the United States.

WILLIAM HOWARD TAFT: Dollar Diplomacy

The foreign relations of the United States actually and potentially affect the state of the Union to a degree not widely realized and hardly surpassed by any other factor in the welfare of
the whole nation. The position of the United States in the moral,
intellectual, and material relations of the family of nations should
be a matter of vital interest to every patriotic citizen. The
national prosperity and power impose upon us duties which we
cannot shirk if we are to be true to our ideals. The tremendous
growth of the export trade of the United States has already made
that trade a very real factor in the industrial and commercial
prosperity of the country. With the development of our industries, the foreign commerce of the United States must rapidly
become a still more essential factor in its economic welfare.

Whether we have a farseeing and wise diplomacy and are not
recklessly plunged into unnecessary wars, and whether our foreign
policies are based upon an intelligent grasp of present-day world
conditions and a clear view of the potentialities of the future, or
are governed by a temporary and timid expediency or by narrow
views befitting an infant nation, are questions in the alternative
consideration of which must convince any thoughtful citizen that
no department of national polity offers greater opportunity for
promoting the interests of the whole people on the one hand, or
greater chance on the other of permanent national injury, than
that which deals with the foreign relations of the United States.

The fundamental foreign policies of the United States should be
raised high above the conflict of partisanship and wholly dissoci-
ated from differences as to domestic policy. In its foreign affairs
the United States should present to the world a united front. The
intellectual, financial, and industrial interests of the country and
the publicist, the wage earner, the farmer, and citizen of whatever
occupation must cooperate in a spirit of high patriotism to promote that national solidarity which is indispensable to national
efficiency and to the attainment of national ideals. . . .

The diplomacy of the present administration has sought to
respond to modern ideas of commercial intercourse. This policy
has been characterized as substituting dollars for bullets. It is one
that appeals alike to idealistic humanitarian sentiments, to the

dictates of sound policy and strategy, and to legitimate commercial aims. It is an effort frankly directed to the increase of American trade upon the axiomatic principle that the government of the United States shall extend all proper support to every legitimate and beneficial American enterprise abroad.

How great have been the results of this diplomacy, coupled with the maximum and minimum provision of the Tariff Law, will be seen by some consideration of the wonderful increase in the export trade of the United States. Because modern diplomacy is commercial, there has been a disposition in some quarters to attribute to it none but materialistic aims. How strikingly erroneous is such an impression may be seen from a study of the results by which the diplomacy of the United States can be judged.

In the field of work toward the ideals of peace, this government negotiated, but to my regret was unable to consummate, two arbitration treaties which set the highest mark of the aspiration of nations toward the substitution of arbitration and reason for war in the settlement of international disputes. Through the efforts of American diplomacy, several wars have been prevented or ended. I refer to the successful tripartite mediation of the Argentine Republic, Brazil, and the United States between Peru and Ecuador; the bringing of the boundary dispute between Panama and Costa Rica to peaceful arbitration; the staying of warlike preparations when Haiti and the Dominican Republic were on the verge of hostilities; the stopping of a war in Nicaragua; the halting of internecine strife in Honduras.

The government of the United States was thanked for its influence toward the restoration of amicable relations between the Argentine Republic and Bolivia. The diplomacy of the United States is active in seeking to assuage the remaining ill feeling between this country and the Republic of Colombia. In the recent civil war in China, the United States successfully joined the other interested powers in urging an early cessation of hostilities. An agreement has been reached between the governments of Chile and Peru whereby the celebrated Tacna-Arica dispute, which has so long embittered international relations on the west coast of South America, has at last been adjusted. Simultaneously came the news that the boundary dispute between Peru and Ecuador had entered upon a stage of amicable settlement.

The position of the United States in reference to the Tacna–Arica dispute between Chile and Peru has been one of nonintervention, but one of friendly influence and pacific counsel throughout the period during which the dispute in question has been the subject of interchange of views between this government and the two governments immediately concerned. In the general easing of international tension on the west coast of South America, the tripartite mediation, to which I have referred, has been a most potent and beneficent factor.

In China the policy of encouraging financial investment to enable that country to help itself has had the result of giving new life and practical application to the open door policy. The consistent purpose of the present administration has been to encourage the use of American capital in the development of China by the promotion of those essential reforms to which China is pledged by treaties with the United States and other powers. The hypothecation to foreign bankers in connection with certain industrial enterprises, such as the Hukuang railways, of the national revenues upon which these reforms depended, led the Department of State, early in the administration, to demand for American citizens participation in such enterprises, in order that the United States might have equal rights and an equal voice in all questions pertaining to the disposition of the public revenues concerned.

The same policy of promoting international accord among the powers having similar treaty rights as ourselves in the matters of reform, which could not be put into practical effect without the common consent of all, was likewise adopted in the case of the loan desired by China for the reform of its currency. The principle of international cooperation in matters of common interest upon which our policy had already been based in all of the above instances has admittedly been a great factor in that concert of the powers which has been so happily conspicuous during the perilous period of transition through which the great Chinese nation has been passing.

In Central America the aim has been to help such countries as Nicaragua and Honduras to help themselves. They are the immediate beneficiaries. The national benefit to the United States is twofold. First, it is obvious that the Monroe Doctrine is more vital in the neighborhood of the Panama Canal and the zone of the Caribbean than anywhere else. There, too, the maintenance of that doctrine falls most heavily upon the United States. It is therefore essential that the countries within that sphere shall be removed from the jeopardy involved by heavy foreign debt and chaotic national finances and from the ever present danger of international complications due to disorder at home. Hence, the United States has been glad to encourage and support American bankers who were willing to lend a helping hand to the financial rehabilitation of such countries because this financial rehabilitation and the protection of their customhouses from being the prey of would-be dictators would remove at one stroke the menace of foreign creditors and the menace of revolutionary disorder.

The second advantage to the United States is one affecting chiefly all the Southern and Gulf ports and the business and industry of the South. The republics of Central America and the Caribbean possess great natural wealth. They need only a measure of stability and the means of financial regeneration to enter upon an era of peace and prosperity, bringing profit and happiness to themselves and at the same time creating conditions sure to lead to a flourishing interchange of trade with this country.

I wish to call your especial attention to the recent occurrences in Nicaragua, for I believe the terrible events recorded there during the revolution of the past summer – the useless loss of life, the devastation of property, the bombardment of defenseless cities, the killing and wounding of women and children, the torturing of noncombatants, to exact contributions, and the suffering of thousands of human beings – might have been averted had the Department of State, through approval of the loan convention by the Senate, been permitted to carry out its now well-developed policy of encouraging the extending of financial aid to weak Central American states, with the primary objects of avoiding just such revolutions by assisting those republics to rehabilitate their finances, to establish their currency on a stable basis, to remove the customhouses from the danger of revolutions by arranging for their secure administration, and to establish reliable banks.

During this last revolution in Nicaragua, the government of that republic having admitted its inability to protect American life and property against acts of sheer lawlessness on the part of the malcontents, and having requested this government to assume that office, it became necessary to land over 2,000 Marines and Bluejackets in

Nicaragua. Owing to their presence the constituted government of Nicaragua was free to devote its attention wholly to its internal troubles, and was thus enabled to stamp out the rebellion in a short space of time. When the Red Cross supplies sent to Granada had been exhausted, 8,000 persons having been given food in one day upon the arrival of the American forces, our men supplied other unfortunate, needy Nicaraguans from their own haversacks.

I wish to congratulate the officers and men of the United States Navy and Marine Corps who took part in reestablishing order in Nicaragua upon their splendid conduct, and to record with sorrow the death of seven American Marines and Bluejackets. Since the reestablishment of peace and order, elections have been held amid conditions of quiet and tranquillity. Nearly all the American Marines have now been withdrawn. The country should soon be on the road to recovery. The only apparent danger now threatening Nicaragua arises from the shortage of funds. Although American bankers have already rendered assistance, they may naturally be loath to advance a loan adequate to set the country upon its feet without the support of some such convention as that of June 1911, upon which the Senate has not yet acted. . . .

It is not possible to make to the Congress a communication upon the present foreign relations of the United States so detailed as to convey an adequate impression of the enormous increase in the importance and activities of those relations. If this government is really to preserve to the American people that free opportunity in foreign markets which will soon be indispensable to our prosperity, even greater efforts must be made. Otherwise the American merchant, manufacturer, and exporter will find many a field in which American trade should logically predominate preempted through the more energetic efforts of other governments and other commercial nations.

There are many ways in which, through hearty cooperation, the legislative and executive branches of this government can do much. The absolute essential is the spirit of united effort and singleness of purpose. I will allude only to a very few specific examples of action which ought then to result.

America cannot take its proper place in the most important fields for its commercial activity and enterprise unless we have a Merchant

Marine. American commerce and enterprise cannot be effectively fostered in those fields unless we have good American banks in the countries referred to. We need American newspapers in those countries and proper means for public information about them.

We need to assume the permanency of a trained foreign service. We need legislation enabling the members of the foreign service to be systematically brought in direct contact with the industrial, manufacturing, and exporting interests of this country in order that American businessmen may enter the foreign field with a clear perception of the exact conditions to be dealt with and the officers themselves may prosecute their work with a clear idea of what American industrial and manufacturing interests require.

Congress should fully realize the conditions which obtain in the world as we find ourselves at the threshold of our middle age as a nation. We have emerged full grown as a peer in the great concourse of nations. We have passed through various formative periods. We have been self-centered in the struggle to develop our domestic resources and deal with our domestic questions. The nation is now too mature to continue in its foreign relations those temporary expedients natural to a people to whom domestic affairs are the sole concern.

In the past, our diplomacy has often consisted, in normal times, in a mere assertion of the right to international existence. We are now in a larger relation with broader rights of our own and obligations to others than ourselves. A number of great guiding principles were laid down early in the history of this government. The recent task of our diplomacy has been to adjust those principles to the conditions of today, to develop their corollaries, to find practical applications of the old principles expanded to meet new situations. Thus are being evolved bases upon which can rest the superstructure of policies which must grow with the destined progress of this nation.

The successful conduct of our foreign relations demands a broad and a modern view. We cannot meet new questions nor build for the future if we confine ourselves to outworn dogmas of the past and to the perspective appropriate at our emergence from colonial times and conditions. The opening of the Panama Canal will mark a new era in our international life and create new and worldwide conditions which, with their vast correlations and consequences, will obtain for hundreds of years to come. We must not wait for events to overtake us unawares. With continuity of purpose we must deal with the problems of our external relations by a diplomacy modern, resourceful, magnanimous, and fittingly expressive of the high ideals of a great nation.

The Great War

President Woodrow Wilson's Appeal for Neutrality: Message to the Senate, August 19, 1914

My fellow countrymen: I suppose that every thoughtful man in America has asked himself, during these last troubled weeks, what influence the European war may exert upon the United States, and I take the liberty of addressing a few words to you in order to point out that it is entirely within our own choice what its effects upon us will be and to urge very earnestly upon you the sort of speech and conduct which will best safeguard the Nation against distress and disaster.

The effect of the war upon the United States will depend upon what American citizens say and do. Every man who really loves America will act and speak in the true spirit of neutrality, which is the spirit of impartiality and fairness and friendliness to all concerned. The spirit of the Nation in this critical matter will be determined largely by what individuals and society and those gathered in public meetings do and say, upon what newspapers and magazines contain, upon what ministers utter in their pulpits, and men proclaim as their opinions on the street.

The people of the United States are drawn from many nations, and chiefly from the nations now at war. It is natural and inevitable that there should be the utmost variety of sympathy and desire among them with regard to the issues and circumstances of the conflict. Some will wish one nation, others another, to succeed in the momentous struggle. It will be easy to excite passion and difficult to allay it. Those responsible for exiting it will assume a heavy responsibility, responsibility for no less a thing than that the people of the United States, whose love of their country and whose loyalty to its Government should unite them as Americans all, bound in honor and affection to think first of her and her interests, may be divided in camps of hostile opinion, hot against each other, involved in the war itself in impulse and opinion if not in action.

Such divisions amongst us would be fatal to our peace of mind and might seriously stand in the way of the proper performance of our duty as the one great nation at peace, the one people holding itself ready to play a part of impartial mediation and speak the counsels of peace and accommodation, not as a partisan, but as a friend.

I venture, therefore, my fellow countrymen, to speak a solemn word of warning to you against that deepest, most subtle, most essential breach of neutrality which may spring out of partisanship, out of passionately taking sides. The United States must be neutral in fact as well as in name during these days that are to try men's souls. We must be impartial in thought as well as in action, must put a curb upon our sentiments as well as upon every transaction that might be construed as a preference of one party to the struggle before another.

My thought is of America. I am speaking, I feel sure, the earnest wish and purpose of every thoughtful American that this great country of ours, which is, of course, the first in our thoughts and in our hearts, should show herself in this time of peculiar trial a Nation fit beyond others to exhibit the fine poise of undisturbed judgment, the dignity of self-control, the efficiency of dispassionate action; a Nation that neither sits in judgment upon others nor is disturbed in her own counsels and which keeps herself fit and free to do what is honest and disinterested and truly serviceable for the peace of the world.

Shall we not resolve to put upon ourselves the restraints which will bring to our people the happiness and the great and lasting influence for peace we covet for them?

Secretary of State Bryan Opposes Loans to Belligerents: August 10, 1914

Secretary of State William Jennings Bryan to President Woodrow Wilson, August 10, 1914:

> I beg to communicate to you an important matter which has come before the Department. Morgan Company of New York have asked whether there would be any objection to their making a loan to the French Government and also the Rothschilds— I suppose that is intended for the French Government. I have conferred with Mr. Lansing and he knows of no legal objection to financing this loan, but I have suggested to him the advisability of presenting to you an aspect of the case which is not legal but I believe to be consistent with our attitude in international matters. It is whether it would be advisable for this Government to take the position that it will not approve of any loan to a belligerent nation. The reasons that I would give in support of this proposition are:
>
> **First:** Money is the worst of all contrabands because it commands everything else. The question of making loans contraband by international agreement has been discussed, but no action has been taken. I know of nothing that would do more to prevent war than an international agreement that neutral nations would not loan to belligerents. While such an agreement would be of great advantage, could we not by our example hasten the reaching of such an agreement? We are the one great nation which is not involved, and our refusal to loan to any belligerent would naturally tend to hasten a conclusion of the war. We are responsible for the use of our influence through example, and as we cannot tell what we can do until we try, the only way of testing our influence is to set the example and observe its effect. This is the fundamental reason in support of the suggestion submitted.
>
> **Second:** There is a special and local reason, it seems to me, why this course would be advisable. Mr. Lansing observed in the discussion of the subject that a loan would be taken by those in sympathy with the country in whose behalf the loan was negotiated. If we approved of a loan to France we could not, of course, object to a loan to Great Britain, Germany, Russia, or to any

other country, and if loans were made to these countries, our citizens would be divided into groups, each group loaning money to the country which it favors and this money could not be furnished without expressions of sympathy. These expressions of sympathy are disturbing enough when they do not rest upon pecuniary interests—they would be still more disturbing if each group was pecuniarily interested in the success of the nation to whom its members had loaned money.

Third: The powerful financial interests which would be connected with these loans would be tempted to use their influence through the newspapers to support the interests of the Government to which they had loaned because the value of the security would be directly affected by the result of the war. We would thus find our newspapers violently arrayed on one side or the other, each paper supporting a financial group and pecuniary interest, All of this influence would make it all the more difficult for us to maintain neutrality as our action on various questions that would arise would affect one side or the other and powerful financial interests would be thrown into the balance.... As we cannot prevent American citizens going abroad at their own risk, so we cannot prevent dollars going abroad at the risk of the owners, but the influence of the Government is used to prevent American citizens from doing this. Would the Government not be justified in using its influence against the enlistment of the nation's dollars in a foreign war?

Wilson's War Message to Congress: February 3, 1917

Gentlemen of the Congress:

I have called the Congress into extraordinary session because there are serious, very serious, choices of policy to be made, and made immediately, which it was neither right nor constitutionally permissible that I should assume the responsibility of making.

On the 3d of February last I officially laid before you the extraordinary announcement of the Imperial German Government that on and after the 1st day of February it was its purpose to put aside all restraints of law or of humanity and use its submarines to sink every vessel that sought to approach either the ports of Great Britain and Ireland or the western coasts of Europe or any of the ports controlled by the enemies of Germany within the Mediterranean. That had seemed to be the object of the German submarine warfare earlier in the war, but since April of last year the Imperial Government had somewhat restrained the commanders of its undersea craft in conformity with its promise then given to us that passenger boats should not be sunk and that due warning would be given to all other vessels which its submarines might seek to destroy, when no resistance was offered or escape attempted, and care taken that their crews were given at least a fair chance to save their lives in their open boats. The precautions taken were meagre and haphazard enough, as was proved in distressing instance after instance in the progress of the cruel and unmanly business, but a certain degree of restraint was observed The new policy has swept every restriction aside. Vessels of every kind, whatever their flag, their character, their cargo, their destination, their errand, have been ruthlessly sent to the bottom without warning and without thought of help or mercy for those on board, the vessels of friendly neutrals along with those of belligerents. Even hospital ships and ships carrying relief to the sorely bereaved and stricken people of Belgium, though the latter were provided with safe-conduct through the proscribed areas by the German Government itself and were distinguished by unmistakable marks of identity, have been sunk with the same reckless lack of compassion or of principle.

I was for a little while unable to believe that such things would in fact be done by any government that had hitherto subscribed to the humane practices of civilized nations. International law had its origin in the at tempt to set up some law which would be respected and observed upon the seas, where no nation had right of dominion and where lay the free highways of the world. By painful stage after stage has that law been built up, with meagre enough results, indeed, after all was accomplished that could be accomplished, but always with a clear view, at least, of what the heart and conscience of mankind demanded. This minimum of right the German Government has swept aside under the plea of retaliation and necessity and because it had no weapons which it could use at sea except these which it is impossible to employ as it is employing them without throwing to the winds all scruples of humanity or of respect for the understandings that were supposed to underlie the intercourse of the world. I am not now thinking of the loss of property involved, immense and serious as that is, but only of the wanton and wholesale destruction of the lives of noncombatants, men, women, and children, engaged in pursuits which have always, even in the darkest periods of modern history, been deemed innocent and legitimate. Property can be paid for; the lives of peaceful and innocent people can not be. The present German submarine warfare against commerce is a warfare against mankind.

It is a war against all nations. American ships have been sunk, American lives taken, in ways which it has stirred us very deeply to learn of, but the ships and people of other neutral and friendly nations have been sunk and overwhelmed in the waters in the same way. There has been no discrimination. The challenge is to all mankind. Each nation must decide for itself how it will meet it. The choice we make for ourselves must be made with a moderation of counsel and a temperateness of judgment befitting our character and our motives as a nation. We must put excited feeling away. Our motive will not be revenge or the victorious assertion of the physical might of the nation, but only the vindication of right, of human right, of which we are only a single champion.

"Safe for Democracy" for Whom?

Espionage Act—June 15, 1917

An Act To punish acts of interference with the foreign relations, the neutrality, and the foreign commerce of the United States, to punish espionage, and better to enforce the criminal laws of the United States, and for other purposes.

TITLE XII

SEC. 3. Whoever, when the United States is at war, shall willfully make or convey false reports or false statements with intent to interfere with the operation or success of the military or naval forces of the United States or to promote the success of its enemies and whoever, when the United States is at war, shall willfully cause or attempt to cause insubordination, disloyalty, mutiny, or refusal of duty, in the military or naval forces of the United States, or shall willfully obstruct the recruiting or enlistment service of the United States, to the injury of the service or of the United States, shall be punished by a fine of not more than $10,000 or imprisonment for not more than twenty years, or both.

TITLE XII

SECTION I, Every letter, writing, circular, postal card, picture, print, engraving, photograph, newspaper, pamphlet, book, or other publication, matter or thing, of any kind, in violation of any of the provisions of this Act is hereby declared to be non-mailable matter and shall not be conveyed in the mails or delivered from any post office or by any letter carrier....

SEC. 2. Every letter, writing, circular, postal card, picture, print, engraving, photograph, newspaper, pamphlet, book, or other publication, matter or thing, of any kind, containing any matter advocating or urging treason, insurrection, or forcible resistance to any law of the United States, is hereby declared to be non-mailable.

Eugene V. Debs: The Canton, Ohio Speech

Eugene Victor Debs, labor leader and Socialist candidate for President, was imprisoned because of this speech for alleged anti-American activities. From his prison cell, Debs received over one million votes for President in the election of 1920.

COMRADES, FRIENDS and fellow-workers, for this very cordial greeting, this very hearty reception, I thank you all with the fullest appreciation of your interest in and your devotion to the cause for which I am to speak to you this afternoon. [Applause.]

To speak for labor; to plead the cause of the men and women and children who toil; to serve the working class, has always been to me a high privilege; [Applause] a duty of love.

I have just returned from a visit over yonder [pointing to the workhouse], where three of our most loyal comrades are paying the penalty for their devotion to the cause of the working class. [Applause.] They have come to realize, as many of us have, that it is extremely dangerous to exercise the constitutional right of free speech in a country fighting to make democracy safe in the world. [Applause.]

I realize that, in speaking to you this afternoon, there are certain limitations placed upon the right of free speech. I must be exceedingly careful, prudent, as to what I say, and even more careful and prudent as to how I say it. [Laughter.] I may not be able to say all I think; [Laughter and applause] but I am not going to say anything that I do not think. [Applause.] I would rather a thousand times be a free soul in jail than to be a syco-phant and coward in the streets. [Applause and shouts.] They may put those boys in jail—and some of the rest of us in jail—but they can not put the Socialist movement in jail. [Applause and shouts.] Those prison bars separate their bodies from ours, but their souls are here this afternoon. [Applause and cheers.] They are simply paying the penalty that all men have paid in all the ages of history for standing erect, and for seeking to pave the way to better conditions for mankind. [Applause.]

If it had not been for the men and women who, in the past, have had the moral courage to go to jail, we would still be in the jun-gles. [Applause.]

This assemblage is exceedingly good to look upon. I wish it were possible for me to give you what you are giving me this after-noon. [Laughter.] What I say here amounts to but little; what I see here is exceedingly important. [Applause.] You workers in Ohio, enlisted in the greatest cause ever organized in the interest of your class, are making history today in the face of threatening opposition of all kinds—history that is going to be read with profound interest by coming generations. [Applause.]

There is but one thing you have to be concerned about, and that is that you keep foursquare with the principles of the international Socialist movement. [Applause.] It is only when you begin to compromise that trouble begins. [Applause.] So far as I am concerned, it does not matter what others may say, or think, or do, as long as I am sure that I am right with myself and the cause. [Applause.] There are so many who seek refuge in the popular side of a great question. As a Socialist, I have long since learned how to stand alone. [Applause.] For the last month I have been traveling over the Hoosier State; and, let me say to you, that, in all my connection with the Socialist movement, I have never seen such meetings, such enthusiasm, such unity of purpose; never have I seen such a promising outlook as there is today, notwithstanding the statement published repeatedly that our leaders have deserted us. [Laughter.] Well, for myself, I never had much faith in leaders. [Applause and laughter.] I am willing to be charged with almost anything, rather than to be charged with being a leader. I am suspicious of leaders, and especially of the intellectual variety. [Applause.] Give me the rank and file every day in the week. If you go to the city of Washington, and you examine the pages of the Congressional Directory, you will find that almost all of those corporation lawyers and cowardly politicians, members of Congress, and misrepresentatives of the masses—you will find that almost all of them claim, in glowing terms, that they have risen from the ranks to places of eminence and distinction. I am very glad I cannot make that claim for myself. [Laughter.] I would be ashamed to admit that I had risen from the ranks. When I rise it will be with the ranks, and not from the ranks. [Applause.]

When I came away from Indiana, the comrades said: "When you cross the line and get over into the Buckeye State, tell the comrades there that we are on duty and doing duty. Give them for us, a hearty greeting, and tell them that we are going to make a record this fall that will be read around the world." [Applause.]

The Socialists of Ohio, it appears, are very much alive this year. The party has been killed recently [laughter], which, no doubt, accounts for its extraordinary activity. [Laughter.] There is nothing that helps the Socialist Party so much as receiving an occasional deathblow. [Laughter and cheers.] The oftener it is killed the more active, the more energetic, the more powerful it becomes.

They who have been reading the capitalist newspapers realize what a capacity they have for lying. We have been reading them lately. They know all about the Socialist Party—the Socialist movement, except what is true. [Laughter.] Only the other day they took an article that I had written—and most of you have read it—most of you members of the party, at least—and they made it appear that I had undergone a marvelous transformation. [Laughter.] I had suddenly become changed—had in fact come to my senses; I had ceased to be a wicked Socialist, and had become a respectable Socialist [laughter], a patriotic Socialist—as if I had ever been anything else. [Laughter.]

What was the purpose of this deliberate misrepresentation? It is so self-evident that it suggests itself. The purpose was to sow the seeds of dissension in our ranks; to have it appear that we were divided among ourselves; that we were pitted against each other, to our mutual undoing. But Socialists were not born yesterday. [Applause.] They know how to read capitalist newspapers [laughter and applause]; and to believe exactly the opposite of what they read. [Applause and laughter.]

Why should a Socialist be discouraged on the eve of the greatest triumph in all the history of the Socialist movement? [Applause.] It is true that these are anxious, trying days for us all—testing days for the women and men who are upholding the banner of labor in the struggle of the working class of all the world against the exploiters of all the world [applause]; a time in which the weak and cowardly will falter and fail and desert. They lack the fiber to endure the revolutionary test; they fall away; they disappear as if they had never been. On the other hand, they who are animated by the unconquerable spirit of the social revolution; they who have the moral courage to stand erect and assert their convictions; stand by them; fight for them; go to jail or to hell for them, if need be [applause and shouts]—they are writing their names, in this crucial hour—they are writing their names in faceless letters in the history of mankind. [Applause.]

Those boys over yonder—those comrades of ours—and how I love them! Aye, they are my younger brothers [laughter and applause]; their very names throb in my heart, thrill in my veins, and surge in my soul. [Applause.] I am proud of them; they are there for us; [applause] and we are here for them. [Applause, shouts and cheers.] Their lips, though temporarily mute, are more eloquent than ever before; and their voice, though silent, is heard around the world. [Great applause.]

Are we opposed to Prussian militarism? [Laughter.] [Shouts from the crowd of "Yes. Yes."] Why, we have been fighting it since the day the Socialist movement was born; [applause] and we are going to continue to fight it, day and night, until it is wiped from the face of the earth. [Thunderous applause and cheers.] Between us there is no truce—no compromise.

These are the gentry who are today wrapped up in the American flag, who shout their claim from the housetops that they are the only patriots, and who have their magnifying glasses in hand, scanning the country for evidence of disloyalty, eager to apply the brand of treason to the men who dare to even whisper their opposition to Junker rule in the United States. No wonder Sam Johnson declared that "patriotism is the last refuge of the scoundrel." He must have had this Wall Street gentry in mind, or at least their prototypes, for in every age it has been the tyrant, the oppressor and the exploiter who has wrapped himself in the cloak of patriotism, or religion, or both to deceive and overawe the people. [Applause.]

They would have you believe that the Socialist Party consists in the main of disloyalists and traitors. It is true in a sense not at all to their discredit. We frankly admit that we are disloyalists and traitors to the real traitors of this nation; [applause] to the gang that on the Pacific coast are trying to hang Tom Mooney and Warren Billings in spite of their well-known innocence and the protest of practically the whole civilized world. [Applause, shouts and cheers.]

Every solitary one of these aristocratic conspirators and would-be murderers claims to be an arch-patriot; every one of them insists that the war is being waged to make the world safe for democracy. What humbug! What rot! What false pretense! These autocrats, these tyrants, these red-handed robbers and murderers, the "patriots," while the men who have the courage to stand face to face with them, speak the truth, and fight for their exploited victims—they are the disloyalists and traitors. If this be true, I want to take my place side by side with the traitors in this fight. [Great applause.]

The other day they sentenced Kate Richards O'Hare to the penitentiary for five years. Think of sentencing a woman to the penitentiary simply for talking. [Laughter.] The United States, under plutocratic rule, is the only country that would send a woman to prison for five years for exercising the right of free speech. [Applause.] If this be treason, let them make the most of it. [Applause.]

Let me review a bit of history in connection with this case. I have known Kate Richards O'Hare intimately for twenty years. I am familiar with her public record. Personally I know her as if she were my own sister. All who know Mrs. O'Hare know her to be a woman of unquestioned integrity. [Applause.] And they also know that she is a woman of unimpeachable loyalty to the Socialist movement. [Applause.] When she went out into North Dakota to make her speech, followed by plain-clothes men in the service of the government intent upon effecting her arrest and securing her prosecution and conviction—when she went out there, it was with the full knowledge on her part that sooner or later these detectives would accomplish their purpose. She made her speech, and that speech was deliberately misrepresented for the purpose of securing her conviction. The only testimony against her was that of a hired witness. And when the farmers, the men and women who were in the audience she addressed— when they went to Bismarck where the trial was held to testify in her favor, to swear that she had not used the language she was charged with having used, the judge refused to allow them to go upon the stand. This would seem incredible to me if I had not had some experience of my own with federal courts.

Who appoints our federal judges? The people? In all the history of the country, the working class have never named a federal judge. There are 121 of these judges and every solitary one holds his position, his tenure, through the influence and power of corporate capital. The corporations and trusts dictate their appointment. And when they go to the bench, they go, not to serve the people, but to serve the interests that place them and keep them where they are.

Why, the other day, by a vote of five to four—a kind of craps game—come seven, come 'leven [laughter]—they declared the

child labor law unconstitutional—a law secured after twenty
years of education and agitation on the part of all kinds of people. And yet, by a majority of one, the Supreme Court, a body of
corporation lawyers, with just one exception, wiped that law
from the statute books, and this in our so-called democracy, so
that we may continue to grind the flesh and blood and bones of
puny little children into profits for the Junkers of Wall Street.
[Applause.] And this in a country that boasts of fighting to make
the world safe for democracy! [Laughter.] The history of this
country is being written in the blood of the childhood the
industrial lords have murdered.

These are not palatable truths to them. They do not like to hear
them; and what is more they do not want you to hear them. And
that is why they brand us as undesirable citizens [laughter and
applause], and as disloyalists and traitors. If we were actual traitors—traitors to the people and to their welfare and progress, we
would be regarded as eminently respectable citizens of the republic; we would hold high office, have princely incomes, and ride
in limousines; and we would be pointed out as the elect who
have succeeded in life in honorable pursuit, and worthy of emu-
lation by the youth of the land. It is precisely because we are dis-
loyal to the traitors that we are loyal to the people of this nation.
[Applause.]

Scott Nearing! You have heard of Scott Nearing. [Applause.] He
is the greatest teacher in the United States. [Applause.] He was in
the University of Pennsylvania until the Board of Trustees, consisting of great capitalists, captains of industry, found that he was
teaching sound economics to the students in his classes. This
sealed his fate in that institution. They sneeringly charged—just
as the same usurers, money-changers, pharisees, hypocrites
charged the Judean Carpenter some twenty centuries ago—that
he was a false teacher and that he was stirring up the people.

The Man of Galilee, the Carpenter, the workingman who became
the revolutionary agitator of his day soon found himself to be an
undesirable citizen in the eyes of the ruling knaves and they had
him crucified. And now their lineal descendants say of Scott
Nearing, "He is preaching false economics. We cannot crucify him
as we did his elder brother but we can deprive him of employment and so cut off his income and starve him to death or into

submission. [Applause.] We will not only discharge him but place his name upon the blacklist and make it impossible for him to earn a living. He is a dangerous man for he is teaching the truth and opening the eyes of the people." And the truth, oh, the truth has always been unpalatable and intolerable to the class who live out of the sweat and misery of the working class. [Applause.]

Max Eastman [applause] has been indicted and his paper suppressed, just as the papers with which I have been connected have all been suppressed. What a wonderful compliment they pay us! [Laughter and applause.] They are afraid that we may mislead and contaminate you. You are their wards; they are your guardians and they know what is best for you to read and hear and know. [Laughter.] They are bound to see to it that our vicious doctrines do not reach your ears. And so in our great democracy, under our free institutions, they flatter our press by suppression; and they ignorantly imagine that they have silenced revolutionary propaganda in the United States. What an awful mistake they make for our benefit! As a matter of justice to them we should respond with resolutions of thanks and gratitude. Thousands of people who had never before heard of our papers are now inquiring for and insisting upon seeing them. They have succeeded only in arousing curiosity in our literature and propaganda. And woe to him who reads Socialist literature from curiosity! He is surely a goner. [Applause.] I have known of a thousand experiments but never one that failed.

How stupid and shortsighted the ruling class really is! Cupidity is stone blind. It has no vision. The greedy, profit-seeking exploiter cannot see beyond the end of his nose. He can see a chance for an "opening"; he is cunning enough to know what graft is and where it is, and how it can be secured, but vision he has none—not the slightest. He knows nothing of the great throbbing world that spreads out in all directions. He has no capacity for literature; no appreciation of art; no soul for beauty. That is the penalty the parasites pay for the violation of the laws of life. The Rockefellers are blind. Every move they make in their game of greed but hastens their own doom. Every blow they strike at the Socialist movement reacts upon themselves. Every time they strike at us they hit themselves. It never fails. [Applause.] Every time they strangle a Socialist paper they add a thousand voices proclaiming the truth of the principles of socialism and the ideals of the Socialist movement. They help us in spite of themselves.

Socialism is a growing idea; an expanding philosophy. It is spreading over the entire face of the earth: It is as vain to resist it as it would be to arrest the sunrise on the morrow. It is coming, coming, coming all along the line. Can you not see it? If not, I advise you to consult an oculist. There is certainly something the matter with your vision. It is the mightiest movement in the history of mankind. What a privilege to serve it! I have regretted a thousand times that I can do so little for the movement that has done so much for me. [Applause.] The little that I am, the little that I am hoping to be, I owe to the Socialist movement. [Applause.] It has given me my ideas and ideals; my principles and convictions, and I would not exchange one of them for all of Rockefeller's bloodstained dollars. [Cheers.] It has taught me how to serve—a lesson to me of priceless value. It has taught me the ecstasy in the handclasp of a comrade. It has enabled me to hold high communion with you, and made it possible for me to take my place side by side with you in the great struggle for the better day; to multiply myself over and over again, to thrill with a fresh-born manhood; to feel life truly worthwhile; to open new avenues of vision; to spread out glorious vistas; to know that I am kin to all that throbs; to be class-conscious, and to realize that, regardless of nationality, race, creed, color or sex, every man, every woman who toils, who renders useful service, every member of the working class without an exception, is my comrade, my brother and sister—and that to serve them and their cause is the highest duty of my life. [Great applause.]

And in their service I can feel myself expand; I can rise to the stature of a man and claim the right to a place on earth—a place where I can stand and strive to speed the day of industrial freedom and social justice.

Yes, my comrades, my heart is attuned to yours. Aye, all our hearts now throb as one great heart responsive to the battle cry of the social revolution. Here, in this alert and inspiring assemblage [applause] our hearts are with the Bolsheviki of Russia. [Deafening and prolonged applause.] Those heroic men and women, those unconquerable comrades have by their incomparable valor and sacrifice added fresh luster to the fame of the international movement. Those Russian comrades of ours have made greater sacrifices, have suffered more, and have shed more heroic blood than any like number of men and women anywhere on

earth; they have laid the foundation of the first real democracy
that ever drew the breath of life in this world. [Applause.] And
the very first act of the triumphant Russian revolution was to
proclaim a state of peace with all mankind, coupled with a fer-
vent moral appeal, not to kings, not to emperors, rulers or diplomats but to the people of all nations. [Applause.] Here we have
the very breath of democracy, the quintessence of the dawning
freedom. The Russian revolution proclaimed its glorious triumph
in its ringing and inspiring appeal to the peoples of all the earth.
In a humane and fraternal spirit new Russia, emancipated at last
from the curse of the centuries, called upon all nations engaged
in the frightful war, the Central Powers as well as the Allies, to
send representatives to a conference to lay down terms of peace
that should be just and lasting. Here was the supreme opportunity to strike the blow to make the world safe for democracy.
[Applause.] Was there any response to that noble appeal that in
some day to come will be written in letters of gold in the history of the world? [Applause.] Was there any response whatever
to that appeal for universal peace? [From the crowd. "No!"] No,
not the slightest attention was paid to it by the Christian nations
engaged in the terrible slaughter.

The capitalist system affects to have great regard and reward for
intellect, and the capitalists give themselves full credit for having
superior brains. When we have ventured to say that the time
would come when the working class would rule they have
bluntly answered "Never! it requires brains to rule." The workers
of course have none. And they certainly try hard to prove it by
proudly supporting the political parties of their masters under
whose administration they are kept in poverty and servitude.

They are continually talking about your patriotic duty. It is not
their but your patriotic duty that they are concerned about.
There is a decided difference. Their patriotic duty never takes
them to the firing line or chucks them into the trenches.

Now what you workers need is to organize, not along craft lines
but along revolutionary industrial lines. [Applause.] All of you
workers in a given industry, regardless of your trade or occupation, should belong to one and the same union.

Political action and industrial action must supplement and
sustain each other. You will never vote the Socialist republic into

existence. You will have to lay its foundations in industrial organization. The industrial union is the forerunner of industrial democracy. In the shop where the workers are associated is where industrial democracy has its beginning. Organize according to your industries! Get together in every department of industrial service! United and acting together for the common good your power is invincible.

When you have organized industrially you will soon learn that you can manage as well as operate industry. You will soon realize that you do not need the idle masters and exploiters. They are simply parasites. They do not employ you as you imagine but you employ them to take from you what you produce, and that is how they function in industry. You can certainly dispense with them in that capacity. You do not need them to depend upon for your jobs. You can never be free while you work and live by their sufferance. You must own your own tools and then you will control your own jobs, enjoy the products of your own labor and be free men instead of industrial slaves.

Organize industrially and make your organization complete. Then unite in the Socialist Party. Vote as you strike and strike as you vote.

Your union and your party embrace the working class. The Socialist Party expresses the interests, hopes and aspirations of the toilers of all the world.

Get your fellow workers into the industrial union and the political party to which they rightly belong, especially this year, this historic year in which the forces of labor will assert themselves as they never have before. This is the year that calls for men and women who have courage, the manhood and womanhood to do their duty.

Get into the Socialist Party and take your place in its ranks; help to inspire the weak and strengthen the faltering, and do your share to speed the coming of the brighter and better day for us all. [Applause.]

When we unite and act together on the industrial field and when we vote together on election day we shall develop the supreme power of the one class that can and will bring permanent peace to the world. We shall then have the intelligence, the courage and the power for our great task. In due time industry will be organized on a cooperative basis. We shall conquer the public power. We shall then transfer the title deeds of the railroads, the telegraph lines, the mines, mills and great industries to the people in their collective capacity; we shall take possession of all these social utilities in the name of the people. We shall then have industrial democracy. We shall be a free nation whose government is of and by and for the people.

And now for all of us to do our duty! The clarion call is ringing in our ears and we cannot falter without being convicted of treason to ourselves and to our great cause.

Do not worry over the charge of treason to your masters, but be concerned about the treason that involves yourselves. [Applause.] Be true to yourself and you cannot be a traitor to any good cause on earth.

Yes, in good time we are going to sweep into power in this nation and throughout the world. We are going to destroy all enslaving and degrading capitalist institutions and re-create them as free and humanizing institutions. The world is daily changing before our eyes. The sun of capitalism is setting; the sun of socialism is rising. It is our duty to build the new nation and the free republic. We need industrial and social builders. We Socialists are the builders of the beautiful world that is to be. We are all pledged to do our part. We are inviting—aye challenging you this afternoon in the name of your own manhood and womanhood to join us and do your part.

In due time the hour will strike and this great cause triumphant—the greatest in history—will proclaim the emancipation of the working class and the brotherhood of all mankind. [Thunderous and prolonged applause.]

Amendment XIX

The right of citizens of the United States to vote shall not be denied or abridged by the United States or by any state on account of sex.

Congress shall have power to enforce this article by appropriate legislation.

Margaret Sanger:
"The Morality of Birth Control"

The meeting tonight is a postponement of one which was to have taken place at the Town Hall last Sunday evening. It was to be a culmination of a three day conference, two of which were held at the Hotel Plaza, in discussing the Birth Control subject in its various and manifold aspects.

The one issue upon which there seems to be most uncertainty and disagreement exists in the moral side of the subject of Birth Control. It seemed only natural for us to call together scientists, educators, members of the medical profession and the theologians of all denominations to ask their opinion upon this uncertain and important phase of the controversy. Letters were sent to the most eminent men and women in the world. We asked in this letter, the following questions:

1. Is over-population a menace to the peace of the world?

2. Would the legal dissemination of scientific Birth Control information through the medium of clinics by the medical profession be the most logical method of checking the problem of over-population?

3. Would knowledge of Birth Control change the moral attitude of men and women toward the marriage bond or lower the moral standards of the youth of the country?

4. Do you believe that knowledge which enables parents to limit the families will make for human happiness, and raise the moral, social and intellectual standards of population?

We sent such a letter not only to those who, we thought, might agree with us, but we sent it also to our known opponents. Most of these people answered. Every one who answered did so with sincerity and courtesy, with the exception of one group whose reply to this important question as demonstrated at the Town Hall last Sunday evening was a disgrace to liberty-loving people, and to all traditions we hold dear in the United States. I believed that the discussion of the moral issue was one which did not solely belong to theologians and to scientists, but belonged to the people. And because I believed that the people of this country may and can discuss this subject with dignity and with intelligence I desired to bring them together, and to discuss it in the open.

When one speaks of moral, one refers to human conduct. This implies action of many kinds, which in turn depends upon the mind and the brain. So that in speaking of morals one must remember that there is a direct connection between morality and brain development. Conduct is said to be action in pursuit of ends, and if this is so, then we must hold the irresponsibility and recklessness in our action is immoral, while responsibility and forethought put into action for the benefit of the individual and the race becomes in the highest sense the finest kind of morality.

We know that every advance that woman has made in the last half century has been made with opposition, all of which has been based upon the grounds of immorality. When women fought for higher education, it was said that this would cause her to become immoral and she would lose her place in the sanctity of the home. When women asked for the franchise it was said that this would lower her standard of morals, that it was not fit that she should meet with and mix with the members of the opposite sex, but we notice that there was no objection to her meeting with the same members of the opposite sex when she went to church.

The church has ever opposed the progress of woman on the ground that her freedom would lead to immorality. We ask the church to have more confidence in women. We ask the opponents of this movement to reverse the methods of the church, which aims to keep women moral by keeping them in fear and in ignorance, and to inculcate into them a higher and truer morality based upon knowledge. And ours is the morality of knowledge. If we cannot trust woman with the knowledge of her own body, then I claim that two thousand years of Christian teaching has proved to be a failure.

We stand on the principle that Birth Control should be available to every adult man and woman. We believe that every adult man and woman should be taught the responsibility and the right use of knowledge. We claim that woman should have the right over her own body and to say if she shall or if she shall not be a mother, as she sees fit. We further claim that the first right of a child is to be desired. While the second right is that it should be conceived in love, and the third, that it should have a heritage of sound health.

Upon these principles the Birth Control movement in America stands. When it comes to discussing the methods of Birth Control, that is far more difficult. There are laws in this country which forbid the imparting of practical information to the mothers of the land. We claim that every mother in this country, either sick or well, has the right to the best, the safest, the most scientific information. This information should be disseminated directly to the mothers through clinics by members of the medical profession, registered nurses and registered midwives.

Our first step is to have the backing of the medical profession so that our laws may be changed, so that motherhood may be the function of dignity and choice, rather than one of ignorance and chance. Conscious control of offspring is now becoming the ideal and the custom in all civilized countries. Those who oppose it claim that however desirable it may be on economic or social grounds, it may be abused and the morals of the youth of the country may be lowered. Such people should be reminded that there are two points to be considered. First, that such control is the inevitable advance in civilization. Every civilization involves an increasing forethought for others, even for those yet unborn. The reckless abandonment of the impulse of the moment and the careless regard for the consequences, is not morality. The selfish gratification of temporary desire at the expense of suffering to lives that will come may seem very beautiful to some, but it is not our conception of civilization, or is it our concept of morality.

In the second place, it is not only inevitable, but it is right to control the size of the family for by this control and adjustment we can raise the level and the standards of the human race. While Nature's way of reducing her numbers is controlled by disease, famine and war, primitive man has achieved the same results by infanticide, exposure of infants, the abandonment of children, and by abortion. But such ways of controlling population is no longer possible for us. We have attained high standards of life, and along the lines of science must we conduct such control. We must begin farther back and control the beginnings of life. We must control conception. This is a better method, it is a more civilized method, for it involves not only greater forethought for others, but finally a higher sanction for the value of life itself.

Society is divided into three groups. Those intelligent and wealthy members of the upper classes who have obtained knowledge of Birth Control and exercise it in regulating the size of their families. They have already benefited by this knowledge, and are today considered the most respectable and moral members of the community. They have only children when they desire, and all society points to them as types that should perpetuate their kind.

The second group is equally intelligent and responsible. They desire to control the size of their families, but are unable to obtain knowledge or to put such available knowledge into practice.

The third are those irresponsible and reckless ones having little regard for the consequence of their acts, or whose religious scruples prevent their exercising control over their numbers. Many of this group are diseased, feeble-minded, and are of the pauper element dependent entirely upon the normal and fit members of society for their support. There is no doubt in the minds of all thinking people that the procreation of this group should be stopped. For if they are not able to support and care for themselves, they should certainly not be allowed to bring offspring into this world for others to look after. We do not believe that filling the earth with misery, poverty and disease is moral. And it is our desire and intention to carry on our crusade until the perpetuation of such conditions has ceased.

We desire to stop at its source the disease, poverty and feeble-mindedness and insanity which exist today, for these lower the standards of civilization and make for race deterioration. We know that the masses of people are growing wiser and are using their own minds to decide their individual conduct. The more people of this kind we have, the less immorality shall exist. For the more responsible people grow, the higher do they and shall they attain real morality.

III

After the War: Disillusion and Hope

Americans, in fact the people of the world, saw the Great War as a tragic and futile endeavor, with millions dead and the world still a dangerous place. In the period after the Great War, the U.S. had to face two great challenges—avoid another global conflict and confront a great economic depression. Neither effort really succeeded, as another global war erupted in Europe and turned even more catastrophic than the previous "Great War."

As we will see, there were attempts to avoid world conflicts, both by international agreement and by creating an "isolationist" mood at home by arguing that U.S. involvement in the earlier war was a mistake. At the same time, Americans were slammed with a huge economic disaster, caused by irresponsible behavior by the ruling class at home and the failure to create a new global economic order after the earlier war.

Within a decade, America was a very different place because of these problems. Franklin Roosevelt promised a "new deal" to the American people, but when his initial efforts did not stem the depression, critics came along to demand a more "people-oriented" approach to politics and economics, one that put working people first instead of the corporations.

At the same time, fascists in Europe and Asia provoked another world war, one that the Americans, once they decided to engage in it, used to rise to global power, through the strength of its economy and its weaponry, particularly the Atomic Bomb. At the end of it all, the U.S., as it had after the earlier war, tried to create a new world order, one based on international agreements and laws.

To End All Wars

The Versailles Treaty June 28, 1919: Part V Military, Naval and Air Clauses

In order to render possible the initiation of a general limitation of the armaments of all nations, Germany undertakes strictly to observe the military, naval and air clauses which follow.

SECTION I: MILITARY CLAUSES

CHAPTER I: EFFECTIVES AND CADRES OF THE GERMAN ARMY

ARTICLE 159

The German military forces shall be demobilised and reduced as prescribed hereinafter.

ARTICLE 160

1. By a date which must not be later than March 31, 1920, the German Army must not comprise more than seven divisions of infantry and three divisions of cavalry.

   After that date the total number of effectives in the Army of the States constituting Germany must not exceed one hundred thousand men, including officers and establishments of depots. The Army shall be devoted exclusively to the maintenance of order within the territory and to the control of the frontiers.

   The total effective strength of officers, including the personnel of staffs, whatever their composition, must not exceed four thousand.

2. Divisions and Army Corps headquarters staffs shall be organised in accordance with Table No. 1 annexed to this Section.

The number and strengths of the units of infantry, artillery, engineers, technical services and troops laid down in the aforesaid Table constitute maxima which must not be exceeded.

The following units may each have their own depot:

An Infantry regiment; A Cavalry regiment; A regiment of Field Artillery; A battalion of Pioneers.

3. The divisions must not be grouped under more than two army corps headquarters staffs.

    The maintenance or formation of forces differently grouped or of other organisations for the command of troops or for preparation for war is forbidden.

    The Great German General Staff and all similar organisations shall be dissolved and may not be reconstituted in any form.

    The officers, or persons in the position of officers, in the Ministries of War in the different States in Germany and in the Administrations attached to them, must not exceed three hundred in number and are included in the maximum strength of four thousand laid down in the third sub-paragraph of paragraph (1) of this Article.

ARTICLE 161

Army administrative services consisting of civilian personnel not included in the number of effectives prescribed by the present Treaty will have such personnel reduced in each class to one-tenth of that laid down in the Budget of 1913.

ARTICLE 162

The number of employees or officials of the German States such as customs officers, forest guards and coastguards, shall not exceed that of the employees or officials functioning in these capacities in 1913.

The number of gendarmes and employees or officials of the local or municipal police may only be increased to an extent corresponding to the increase of population since 1913 in the districts or municipalities in which they are employed.

These employees and officials may not be assembled for military training.

ARTICLE: 163

The reduction of the strength of the German military forces as provided for in Article 160 may be effected gradually in the following manner:

Within three months from the coming into force of the present Treaty the total number of effectives must be reduced to 200,000 and the number of units must not exceed twice the number of those laid down in Article 160.

At the expiration of this period, and at the end of each subsequent period of three months, a Conference of military experts of the Principal Allied and Associated Powers will fix the reductions to be made in the ensuing three months, so that by March 31, 1920, at the latest the total number of German effectives does not exceed the maximum number of 100,000 men laid down in Article 160. In these successive reductions the same ratio between the number of officers and of men, and between the various kinds of units, shall be maintained as is laid down in that Article.

CHAPTER II: ARMAMENT, MUNITIONS AND MATERIAL

ARTICLE 168

The manufacture of arms, munitions, or any war material, shall only be carried out in factories or works the location of which shall be communicated to and approved by the Governments of the Principal Allied and Associated Powers, and the number of which they retain the right to restrict.

Within three months from the coming into force of the present Treaty, all other establishments for the manufacture, preparation, storage or design of arms, munitions, or any war material whatever shall be closed down. The same applies to all arsenals except those used as depots for the authorised stocks of munitions. Within the same period the personnel of these arsenals will be dismissed.

ARTICLE 169

Within two months from the coming into force of the present Treaty German arms, munitions and war material, including anti-aircraft material, existing in Germany in excess of the quantities allowed, must be surrendered to the Governments of the Principal Allied and Associated Powers to be destroyed or rendered useless. This will also apply to any special plant intended for the manufacture of military material, except such as may be recognised as necessary for equipping the authorised strength of the German army.

The surrender in question will be effected at such points in German territory as may be selected by the said Governments.

Within the same period arms, munitions and war material, including anti-aircraft material, of origin other than German, in whatever state they may be, will be delivered to the said Governments, who will decide as to their disposal.

Arms and munitions which on account of the successive reductions in the strength of the German army become in excess of the amounts authorised by Tables II and III annexed to this Section must be handed over in the manner laid down above within such periods as may be decided by the Conferences referred to in Article 163.

ARTICLE 170

Importation into Germany of arms, munitions and war material of every kind shall be strictly prohibited.

The same applies to the manufacture for, and export to, foreign countries of arms, munitions and war material of every kind.

ARTICLE 171

The use of asphyxiating, poisonous or other gases and all analogous liquids, materials or devices being prohibited, their manufacture and importation are strictly forbidden in Germany.

The same applies to materials specially intended for the manufacture, storage and use of the said products or devices.

The manufacture and the importation into Germany of armoured cars, tanks and all similar constructions suitable for use in war are also prohibited.

ARTICLE 172

Within a period of three months from the coming into force of the present Treaty, the German Government will disclose to the Governments of the Principal Allied and Associated Powers the nature and mode of manufacture of all explosives, toxic substances or other like chemical preparations used by them in the war or prepared by them for the purpose of being so used.

SECTION III: AIR CLAUSES

ARTICLE 198

The armed forces of Germany must not include any military or naval air forces.

Germany may, during a period not extending beyond October 1, 1919, maintain a maximum number of one hundred seaplanes or flying boats, which shall be exclusively employed in searching for submarine mines, shall be furnished with the necessary equipment for this purpose, and shall in no case carry arms, munitions or bombs of any nature whatever.

In addition to the engines installed in the seaplanes or flying boats above mentioned, one spare engine may be provided for each engine of each of these craft.

No dirigible shall be kept.

ARTICLE 199

Within two months from the coming into force of the present Treaty the personnel of air forces on the rolls of the German land and sea forces shall be demobilised. Up to October 1, 1919, however, Germany may keep and maintain a total number of one thousand men, including officers, for the whole of the cadres and personnel, flying and non-flying, of all formations and establishments.

ARTICLE 200

Until the complete evacuation of German territory by the Allied and Associated troops, the aircraft of the Allied and Associated Powers shall enjoy in Germany freedom of passage through the air, freedom of transit and of landing.

ARTICLE 201

During the six months following the coming into force of the present Treaty, the manufacture and importation of aircraft, parts of aircraft, engines for aircraft, and parts of engines for aircraft, shall be forbidden in all German territory.

ARTICLE 202

On the coming into force of the present Treaty, all military and naval aeronautical material, except the machines mentioned in the second and third paragraphs of Article 198, must be delivered to the Governments of the Principal Allied and Associated Powers.

Delivery must be effected at such places as the said Governments may select, and must be completed within three months.

In particular, this material will include all items under the following heads which are or have been in use or were designed for warlike purposes:

Complete aeroplanes and seaplanes, as well as those being manufactured, repaired or assembled.

Dirigibles able to take the air, being manufactured, repaired or assembled.

Plant for the manufacture of hydrogen.

Dirigible sheds and shelters of every kind for aircraft.

Pending their delivery, dirigibles will, at the expense of Germany, be maintained inflated with hydrogen; the plant for the manufacture of hydrogen, as well as the sheds for dirigibles may at the discretion of the said Powers, be left to Germany until the time when the dirigibles are handed over.

Engines for aircraft.

Nacelles and fuselages.

Armament (guns, machine guns, light machine guns, bombdropping apparatus, torpedo-dropping apparatus, synchronisation apparatus, aiming apparatus).

Munitions (cartridges, shells, bombs loaded or unloaded, stocks of explosives or of material for their manufacture).

Instruments for use on aircraft.

Wireless apparatus and photographic or cinematograph apparatus for use on aircraft.

Component parts of any of the items under the preceding heads.

The material referred to above shall not be removed without special permission from the said Governments.

SECTION IV: INTER-ALLIED COMMISSIONS OF CONTROL.

ARTICLE 203

All the military, naval and air clauses contained in the present Treaty, for the execution of which a time-limit is prescribed, shall be executed by Germany under the control of Inter-Allied Commissions specially appointed for this purpose by the Principal Allied and Associated Powers.

ARTICLE 204

The Inter-Allied Commissions of Control will be specially charged with the duty of seeing to the complete execution of the delivery, destruction, demolition and rendering things useless to be carried out at the expense of the German Government in accordance with the present Treaty.

They will communicate to the German authorities the decisions which the Principal Allied and Associated Powers have reserved the right to take, or which the execution of the military, naval and air clauses may necessitate.

ARTICLE 205

The Inter-Allied Commissions of Control may establish their organisations at the seat of the central German Government.

They shall be entitled as often as they think desirable to proceed to any point whatever in German territory, or to send subcommissions, or to authorise one or more of their members to go, to any such point.

ARTICLE 207

The upkeep and cost of the Commissions of Control and the expenses involved by their work shall be borne by Germany.

SECTION V: GENERAL ARTICLES.

ARTICLE 213

So long as the present Treaty remains in force, Germany undertakes to give every facility for any investigation which the Council of the League of Nations, acting if need be by a majority vote, may consider necessary.

Kellogg-Briand Pact

BY THE PRESIDENT OF THE UNITED STATES OF AMERICA

A PROCLAMATION

WHEREAS a Treaty between the President of the United States Of America, the President of the German Reich, His Majesty the King of the Belgians, the President of the French Republic, His Majesty the King of Great Britain, Ireland and the British Dominions beyond the Seas, Emperor of India, His Majesty the King of Italy, His Majesty the Emperor of Japan, the President of the Republic of Poland, and the President of the Czechoslovak Republic, providing for the renunciation of war as an instrument of national policy, was concluded and signed by their respective Plenipotontiaries at Paris on the twenty-seventh day of August, one thousand nine hundred and twenty-eight, the original of which Treaty, being in the English and the French languages, is word for word as follows:

THE PRESIDENT OF THE GERMAN REICH, THE PRESIDENT OF THE UNITED STATES OF AMERICA, HIS MAJESTY THE KING OF THE BELGIANS, THE PRESIDENT OF THE FRENCH REPUBLIC, HIS MAJESTY THE KING OF GREAT BRITAIN IRELAND AND THE BRITISH DOMINIONS BEYOND THE SEAS, EMPEROR OF INDIA, HIS MAJESTY THE KING OF ITALY, HIS MAJESTY THE EMPEROR OF JAPAN, THE PRESIDENT OF THE REPUBLIC OF POLAND THE PRESIDENT OF THE CZECHOSLOVAK REPUBLIC,

Deeply sensible of their solemn duty to promote the welfare of mankind;

Persuaded that the time has, come when a frank renunciation of war as an instrument of na tional policy should be made to the end that the peaceful and friendly relations now existing between their peoples may be perpetuated;

Convinced that all changes in their relations with one another should be sought only by pacific means and be the result of a peaceful and orderly process, and that any signatory Power which shall hereafter seek to promote its ts national interests by resort to war a should be denied the benefits furnished by this Treaty;

Hopeful that, encouraged by their example, all the other nations of the world will join in this humane endeavor and by adhering to the present Treaty as soon as it comes into force bring their peoples within the scope of its beneficent provisions, thus uniting the civilized nations of the world in a common renunciation of war as an instrument of their national policy;

Have decided to conclude a Treaty and for that purpose have appointed as their respective who, having communicated to one another their full powers found in good and due form have agreed upon the following articles:

ARTICLE I

The High Contracting Parties solemnly declare in the names of their respective peoples that they condemn recourse to war for the solution of international controversies, and renounce it, as an instrument of national policy in their relations with one another.

ARTICLE II

The High Contracting Parties agree that the settlement or solution of all disputes or conflicts of whatever nature or of whatever origin they may be, which may arise among them, shall never be sought except by pacific means.

ARTICLE III

The present Treaty shall be ratified by the High Contracting Parties named in the Preamble in accordance with their respective constitutional requirements, and shall take effect as between them as soon as all their several instruments of ratification shall have been deposited at Washington.

This Treaty shall, when it has come into effect as prescribed in the preceding paragraph, remain open as long as may be necessary for adherence by all the other Powers of the world. Every instrument evidencing the adherence of a Power shall be deposited at Washington and the Treaty shall immediately upon such deposit become effective as; between the Power thus adhering and the other Powers parties hereto.

It shall be the duty of the Government of the United States to furnish each Government named in the Preamble and every Government subsequently adhering to this Treaty with a certified copy of the Treaty and of every instrument of ratification or adherence. It shall also be the duty of the Government of the United States telegraphically to notify such Governments immediately upon the deposit with it of each instrument of ratification or adherence.

IN FAITH WHEREOF the respective Plenipotentiaries have signed this Treaty in the French and English languages both texts having equal force, and hereunto affix their seals.

DONE at Paris, the twenty seventh day of August in the year one thousand nine hundred and twenty-eight.

AND WHEREAS it is stipulated in the said Treaty that it shall take effect as between the High Contracting Parties as soon as all the several instruments of ratification shall have been deposited at Washington;

AND WHEREAS the said Treaty has been duly ratified on the parts of all the High Contracting Parties and their several instruments of ratification have been deposited with the Government of the United States of America, the last on July 24, 1929;

NOW TIIEREFORE, be it known that I, Herbert Hoover, President of the United States of America, have caused the said Treaty to be made public, to the end that the same and every article and clause thereof may be observed and fulfilled with good faith by the United States and the citizens thereof.

IN TESTIMONY WHEREOF, I have hereunto set my hand and caused the seal of the United States to be affixed.

DONE at the city of Washington this twenty-fourth day of July in the year of our Lord one thousand nine hundred and twenty-nine, and of the Independence of the United States of America the one hundred and fifty-fourth

HERBERT HOOVER
By the President:

HENRY L STIMSON
Secretary of State

The Nye Report

FINDINGS

I. NATURE OF THE MUNITIONS COMPANIES

The committee finds, under the head of "the nature of the industrial and commercial organizations engaged in the manufacture of or traffic in arms, ammunitions, or other implements of war" that almost none of the munitions companies in this country confine themselves exclusively to the manufacture of military materials. Great numbers of the largest suppliers to the Army and Navy (Westinghouse, General Electric, du Pont, General Motors, Babcock & Wilcox, etc.) are predominantly manufacturers of materials for civilian life. Others, such as the aviation companies and Colt's Patent Firearms Co., supply the greatest portion of their output to the military services. In addition to the manufacturers there are several sales companies which act as agents for various manufacturers. There are also brokers dealing largely in old and second-hand supplies. In case of war, other companies, not at present producing any munitions, would be called upon to furnish them.

The Army manufactures its own rifles, cartridges, and field artillery. The Navy manufactures most of its own propellant powder, its own guns, and half of the battleships.

II. THE SALES METHODS OF THE MUNITIONS COMPANIES

The Committee finds, under the head of sales methods of the munitions companies, that almost without exception, the American munitions companies investigated have at times resorted to such unusual approaches, questionable favors and commissions, and methods of "doing the needful" as to constitute, in effect, a form of bribery of foreign governmental officials or of their close friends in order to secure business.

The committee realizes that these were field practices by the agents of the companies, and were apparently in many cases part of a level of competition set by foreign companies, and that the heads of the American companies were, in cases, apparently unaware of their continued existence and shared the committee's distaste and disapprobation of such practices.

The committee accepts the evidence that the same practices are resorted to by European munitions companies, and that the whole process of selling arms abroad thus, in the words of a Colt agent, has "brought into play the most despicable side of human nature; lies, deceit, hypocrisy, greed, and graft occupying a most prominent part in the transactions."

The committee finds such practices on the part of any munitions company, domestic or foreign, to be highly unethical, a discredit to American business, and an unavoidable reflection upon those

American governmental agencies which have unwittingly aided in the transactions so contaminated.

The committee finds, further, that not only are such transactions highly unethical, but that they carry within themselves the seeds of disturbance to the peace and stability of those nations in which they take place. In some nations, violent changes of administration might take place immediately upon the revelation of all details of such transactions. Mr. Lammot du Pont stated that the publication of certain du Pont telegrams (not entered in the record) might cause a political repercussion in a certain South American country. At its February 1936 hearings, the committee also suppressed a number of names of agents and the country in which they were operating, in order to avoid such repercussions.

The committee finds, further, that the intense competition among European and American munitions companies with the attendant bribery of governmental officials tends to create a corrupt officialdom, and thereby weaken the remaining democracies of the world at their head.

The committee finds, further, that the constant availability of munitions companies with competitive bribes ready in outstretched hands does not create a situation where the officials involved can, in the nature of things, be as much interested in peace and measures to secure peace as they are in increased armaments.

The committee finds also that there is a very considerable threat to the peace and civic progress of other nations in the success of the munitions makers and of their agents in corrupting the officials of any one nation and thereby selling to that one nation an armament out of proportion to its previous armaments. Whether such extraordinary sales are procured through bribery or through other forms of salesmanship, the effect of such sales is to produce fear, hostility, and greater munitions orders on the p art of neighboring countries, culminating in economic strain and collapse or war.

The committee elsewhere takes note of the contempt of some of the munitions companies for those governmental departments and officials interested in securing peace, and finds here that continual or even occasional corruption of other governments naturally leads to a belief that all governments, including our own, must be controlled by economic forces entirely.

III. THEIR ACTIVITIES CONCERNING PEACE EFFORTS

The committee finds, under this head, that there is no record of any munitions company aiding any proposals for limitation of armaments, but that, on the contrary, there is a record of their active opposition by some to almost all such proposals, of resentment toward them, of contempt for those responsible for them, and of violation of such controls whenever established, and of rich profiting whenever such proposals failed.

Following the peaceful settlement of the Tacna-Arica dispute between Peru and Chile, L. Y. Spear, vice president of Electric Boat Co. (which supplied submarines to Peru) wrote to Commander C. W. Craven, of Vickers-Armstrong (which supplied material to Chile):

> It is too bad that the pernicious activities of our State Department have put the brake on armament orders from Peru by forcing resumption of formal diplomatic relations with Chile

When the proposal to control the international traffic in arms was made in 1924 the Colt licensee in Belgium wrote:

> It is, of course, understood that our general interest is to prevent the hatching up of a new agreement plan "under such a form" (as Sir Eric Drummond says) "that it may be accepted by the governments of all the countries who manufacture arms and munitions of war."

It then proposed methods of "lengthening the controversies" and to "wear out the bodies occupied with this question."

The first great peace effort after the war was incorporated in the Treaty of Versailles and in the treaty of peace between the United States and Germany in the form of a prohibition on the manufacture, import, and export of arms by Germany. The manufacture and export of military powder by German companies, in violation of these treaty provisions first took place in 1924 and was known to the Nobel Co. (predecessors of Imperial Chemical Industries) of England and to the du Pont Co., but was not brought to the attention of the Department of State. The du Pont officials explained that the violation was allowed because of the close commercial relations between the British and German chemical companies. Later, United Aircraft licensed a German company for the manufacture of its airplane engines. Sperry Gyroscope also licensed a German company for the manufacture of its equipment. Both the engines and the equipment were of military availability. (See part V, B, secs. II and III.)

The second peace effort was made in 1922, when the Washington Disarmament Conference took place, not long after the American shipbuilding companies had received post-war awards of destroyers at a cost of $149,000,000, and while battleships whose construction was left pending in 1917 were being completed. The naval part of that conference succeeded in stopping a naval race. There was however, no effective action taken in regard to checking the use of poison gas, which was the other main subject for consideration. The committee's record is incomplete on the activities of the munitions companies in this connection, but does show their opposition to proposals for control of the chemical industry and their interest in the choice of chemical advisers to the American delegation. The conference had been preceded by the sale of all the German chemical patents to the American companies for a small sum, extensive propaganda and expenditures for high-tariff protection on grounds of national defense, and the instigation and writing of news stories from London and Paris designed to give the American public the impression that France and England were engaged in the construction of great poison-gas factories of their own to offset the German ones. Some of these were written by a du Pont agent under an assumed name. The Washington Conference operated in this atmosphere, and contented itself with repeating the declarations of The Hague conventions respecting the use of poisonous gases in warfare which had been violated during the war. Several delegations pointed out that this was no progress at all, but simply a reaffirmation of supposedly existing international law.

The embargo placed at the request of the Central (Nanking) Chinese Government on exports of arms to China was, according to the evidence, violated by American and European munitions companies. Shipments via Europe and Panama were frequently considered as a means of evading the embargo.

The Geneva Arms Control Conference of 1925 was watched carefully by the American and European munitions makers. They knew the American military delegates to the conference several weeks before the public was informed of their names, and one of them told the munitions makers that he believed a licensing system (the sine qua non of any control) to be undesirable. Du Pont representatives made known their objections to publicity. At a conference at the Department of Commerce (prior to the convening of the Geneva Conference) the objections of the munitions manufacturers were considered carefully and reservations to the draft convention to be discussed at Geneva were made. State Department documents not entered into the record ,give credit to the American delegation to the Geneva Conference for weakening the proposed draft convention in two important respects. The du Pont representatives (who attended the meeting at the Department of Commerce) later remarked of the final draft of the convention regarding the arms traffic signed at Geneva in 1925:

> There will be some few inconveniences to the manufacture of munitions in their export trade, but in the main they will not he hampered materially.

The draft convention was widely advertised as a large step forward in the direction of control of the traffic in arms. It has, in 1936, not yet been ratified by sufficient States to put it into effect.

The influence of American naval shipbuilding companies on the Geneva Disarmament Conference of 1927 has been described in the committee's report on Naval Shipbuilding (74th Cong., Rept. 944). Their agent at Geneva claimed credit for the failure of that conference, which came at a time when the Big Three shipyards had been given orders by the Navy for $53,744,000 in cruisers, which would have been cut materially in case the conference had been a success. He was paid by the shipbuilders into 1929. The Navy has not denied to the committee that this agent of the shipbuilders was in possession of confidential Navy Department documents during the time of his activity at Geneva.

Following the Geneva conference an arms embargo resolution was introduced in 1928 by the chairman of the American delegation to that conference, Representative Burton of Ohio. The munitions manufacturers, cocky with their success at Geneva, consulted with such allied interests as the Sporting Arms and

Ammunition Manufacturers Institute, and found it unnecessary to appear in the front ranks of opposition to this resolution. In 1932 Representative Fish introduced a resolution for a multilateral agreement renouncing the sale and export of arms. Du Pont representatives were active in lining up War and Navy opposition to it. In 1932-33 President Hoover supported an arms embargo which drew the comment from a du Pont representative:

> Regarding the attempts of Mr. Hoover and the "cooky pushers" in the State Department to effect embargoes on munitions sent out of the country, I do not believe there is the least occasion for alarm at present.

The munitions people were active in opposition to the arms embargo proposal which was adopted in the Senate without opposition. Senator Bingham of Connecticut succeeded in killing the bill on reconsideration and received the thanks of the munitions people and of their organization, the Army Ordnance Association. The War Department also opposed the embargo.

In 1932, another disarmament conference was held at Geneva. By this time the failure to prevent the rearmament of Germany, described above, had resulted in great profits to the French steel industry which had received large orders for the building of the continuous line of fortifications across the north of France, to the French munitions companies, and profits were beginning to flow into the American and English pockets from German orders for aviation matériel. This in turn resulted in a French and English aviation race, and with Germany openly rearming the much-heralded disarmament conference which convened in 1932 has failed completely. It was pointed out by a committee member that Du Pont representatives were aware that—

> the effect of the failure to check the [Versailles] treaty violation even goes to the extent of making a subsequent disarmament convention, if not improbable in its success, at least calculated to produce only an unworkable document.

In 1934, Congress adopted a joint resolution prohibiting, in effect, sales of munitions to Bolivia and Paraguay, then engaged in the Chaco War, for a period of almost 6 years. During these 6 years, the munitions companies had profited largely from the defeat of the Burton embargo proposal, offered in 1928.

The Chaco embargo, according to indictments issued by a Federal grand jury, was violated by the Curtiss-Wright Export Corporation and the Curtiss Aeroplane Motor Co. The lower court has held the embargo unconstitutional on the ground of delegation of power to the President.

Mayrink-Veiga, agents for many munitions companies in Brazil suggested that the embargo could be evaded by the shipment of planes to Europe first, stating that to be the Curtiss and Bellanca procedure.

In 1935, after a year of hearings by the special committee, a neutrality bill was passed including an embargo on arias, ammunition, and implements of war in the event of a state of war between two or more foreign states, and including a munitions-control board with power to issue export licenses. The Secretary of State has announced that not all the companies supposed to register under this law have done so. In 1936 an attempt was made to amend the neutrality law by holding the exports of necessary war materials (oil, copper, steel, etc.) to belligerents to normal quotas. This was defeated. Considerable quantities of those materials were already being exported to Italy, one of the belligerents in the Italo-Ethiopian War, and some of the exporting companies had connections and investments in Italy.

IV. THE EFFECT OF ARMAMENTS ON PEACE

The committee finds, under the head of the effect of armament, on peace, that some of the munitions companies have occasionally had opportunities to intensify the fears of people for their neighbors and have used them to their own profit.

The committee finds, further, that the very quality which in civilian life tends to lead toward progressive civilization, namely the improvements of machinery, has been used by the munitions makers to scare nations into a continued frantic expenditure for the latest improvements in devices of warfare. The constant message of the traveling salesman of the munitions companies to the rest of the world has been that they now had available for sale something new, more dangerous and more deadly than ever before and that the potential enemy was or would be buying it.

While the evidence before this committee does not show that wars have been started solely because of the activities of munitions makers and their agents, it is also true that wars rarely have one single cause, and the committee finds it to be against the peace of the world for selfishly interested organizations to be left free to goad and frighten nations into military activity.

The committee finds, further, that munitions companies engaged in bribery find themselves involved in the civil and military politics of other nations, and that this is an unwarranted form of intrusion into the affairs of other nations and undesirable representation of the character and methods of the people of the United States.

The export field of our munitions companies has been South America and China, with occasional excursions into Poland, Turkey, Siam, Italy, Japan, and other nations. There was less important dynamite loose in either South America or China than in western Europe. The activities of the munitions makers in Europe were of greater importance to the peace of the western world than their activities in either South America or China. It will remain for commissions with full powers in the large European nations to report on the provocative activities of their companies, particularly to investigate the statements made in the French Chamber of Deputies, that Skoda in Czechoslovakia, a subsidiary of Schneider-Creusot, financed the Hitler movement to power, which, more than any one other event, can be credited with causing the present huge rearmament race in Europe, so profitable to the European steel, airplane, and munitions companies.

In South America there have, in the post-war years, been moments of severe tension, occasionally breaking out into war. One of these moments apparently came directly after the World War, when Chile bought from Vickers a considerable battle fleet. This caused agitation in Brazil, Argentina, and Peru, with Vickers taking the lead in Chile and Argentina, and Electric Boat Co. in Peru and Brazil. The situation was apparently so delicate that an administration countermanded an offer from the United States Navy to sell destroyers to Peru inasmuch as the sale might encourage an outbreak of war between Chile and Peru (exhibits 54, 57).

Later tension developed between Peru and Chile over the Tacna-Arica matter and Aubry, the Electric Boat Co. agent, felt that if he brought the contracts for submarines for Peru—

> it would be a great blunder going to Argentina, for instance, via Chile (In this business we have to be tactful and a little diplomatist) and so in regard to Brazil as well as to the Argentine now that affairs are going to take place at the same time (exhibit 69).

Mr. Carse, president of Electric Boat, recognized the danger of armament when he pointed out in regard to financing Peruvian purchases "the armament which this money could purchase would not insure victory, as the other nation has much stronger armament and would tend more to bring conflict to a point than if they did not purchase the armament" (exhibit 61). It was sold, nevertheless.

The spreading effects of such fears were reported by Vice President Sutphen of Electric Boat:

> It appears that there has been quite an agitation in Bolivia, as you know, and a revolution has occurred there recently, and in the opinion of the bankers it has been instigated largely by Peru to have Bolivia join with her in opposition to Chile (ex. 60).

Chile was the country which bought the original increased armaments. It was in this connection that Spear wrote Craven of the "pernicious activities" of the United States Department of State in helping the resumption of diplomatic relations between Chile and Peru.

The naval armament had its military side. Evidence read into the record during the Colt Co. hearing in 1936 indicated an arms race with intense activity on the part of all machine-gun manu-facturers. The country which was credited with starting military armament "out of all proportion with that of other countries in South America" was identified as a country whose officials were the most susceptible to bribes.

The Department of Commerce obligingly furnished Colts the information that the arms race was bringing about a cabinet cri-sis in one of the countries reluctant to participate in it.

The statement of a Federal Laboratories salesman that "the unsettled condition in South America has been a great thing for me" is the key, and also, "We are certainly in one hell of a business where a fellow has to wish for trouble to make a living."

Colombia and Peru, at the time of the Leticia incident, were each kept well informed by the munitions companies of the proposed purchases of the other nation. The evidence of the Colt agent in Peru was that the Vickers agent, after unloading a huge armament order on Peru, had boasted to the Peruvians that he would sell "double the amount, and more modern, to the Chilean Government." When a limited amount of materiel, such as machine guns, was available, Bolivia could be forced into ordering them on the threat that unless she acted quickly, Paraguay would get them. Killing the back-country Indians of South America with airplanes, bombs, and machine guns boiled down to an order to get busy because "these opera bouffe revolutions are usually short-lived, and we must make the most of the opportunity"

In China the munitions companies report that there was a certain amount of feeling between the Central (Nanking) Government and the Canton Government. The Boeing agent was able to sell 10 planes to the Canton Government. Referring to the Nanking (recognized) Government he wrote:

> Their anger at us in selling airplanes to the Cantonese is more than offset by the fact that the Cantonese have gotten ahead of them and will have better equipment than they will have. In other words, the Canton sale is quite a stimulant to the sale up here.

The company, interested in making sales also to the recognized Nanking Government, replied:

> If the present deal with the Cantonese can be put through, without unreasonable demands being made upon us, it is to our advantage to successfully conclude the business if for no other reason but for the effect it would have on the Nanking Government.

All this may be little more to the munitions people than a highly profitable game of bridge with special attention on all sides to the technique of the "squeeze" play, but to a considerable part of the world's inhabitants there is still something frightful in death by machinery, and the knowledge that neighboring governments have acquired the latest and fastest engines of destruction leads to suspicion that those engines are meant to be used, and are not simply for play and show.

At the time a naval bill for $617,000,000 was before Congress, the president of the Bath Iron Works in Maine asked the publisher of a string of newspapers to reprint a Japanese war-scare story, although the Chinese source of that story had been thoroughly discredited editorially by the newspaper originally publishing it, the New York Herald Tribune. He thanked the publisher for playing up the scare story (Report on Naval Shipbuilding).

Attempts to sell munitions frequently involve bribery, which, to be effective, must go to those high in authority. This is apt to involve the companies in the politics of foreign nations. Federal Laboratories, by putting itself at the disposal of the administration of Cuba and two opposing factions, all at the same time, is a case in point. The Colt agent in Peru reported on his helping overthrow the general in charge of ordnance orders. American airplane companies reported on the political influence of French and English airplane companies, in a certain European country. Sperry Gyroscope's representative reported on Vickers' (English) political influence in Spain, as did also Electric Boat Co. officials.

The political power of the companies is best indicated, however, by a letter from Mr. John Ball, director of the Soley Armament Co Ltd., of England, in which he pointed out that "the stocks we control are of such magnitude that the sale of a big block of them could alter the political balance of power of the smaller States."

V. THEIR RELATIONS WITH THE UNITED STATES GOVERNMENT

The committee first, under this head, repeats its report on naval shipbuilding, in which "the committee finds, under the head of influence and lobbying of shipbuilders, that the Navy contractors, subcontractors, and suppliers constitute a very large and influential financial group", and "the committee finds that the matter of national defense should be above and separated from lobbying and the use of political influence by self-interested groups and that it has not been above or separated from either of them."

The committee finds, further, that the munitions companies have secured the active support of the War, Navy, Commerce, and even State Departments in their sales abroad, even when the material was to be produced in England or Italy.

The committee finds that by their aid and assistance to munitions companies the War, Navy, and Commerce Departments condone, in effect, in the eyes of those foreign officials cognizant of the details of the transactions the unethical practices of the companies which characterize their foreign sales efforts.

The committee finds that the munitions companies have constantly exerted pressure on the War Department to allow the exportation of the most recent American improvements in warfare, and have usually been successful in securing it, and have also furnished plans of important new machines of war to their foreign agents in advance of any release by the War Department.

The committee finds that the War Department encourages the sale of modern equipment abroad in order that the munitions companies may stay in business and be available in the event of another war, and that this consideration outranks the protection of secrets. (General Ruggles was quoted: "It was vastly more important to encourage the du Pont Co. to continue in the manufacture of propellants for military use, than to endeavor to protect secrets relating to the manufacture.")

The committee finds that as improvements are developed here, often with the cooperation of the military services, and these improvements presumably give the United States a military advantage, we are in the anomalous position of being forced to let the other nations have the advantages which we have obtained for ourselves, in order to keep the munitions manufacturers going, so that the United States can take advantage of the same improvements which its companies have sold abroad.

The committee finds, from official documents it has not entered into the record, that the United States naval missions to Brazil and Peru have been given considerable help to American munitions makers, and that their participation and leadership in war games directed at "a potential enemy" have not advanced the cause of peace in South America, and that their activity can be misinterpreted by neighboring countries as support of any military plans of the nations to which they are attached.

The committee finds, from official documents which it has not entered into the record, that the sales of munitions to certain South American nations in excess of their normal capacity to pay, was one of the causes for the defaults on certain South American bonds; and that the sales of the munitions was, in effect, financed by the American bond purchasers, and the loss on the bonds was borne by the same people.

The committee finds that the Army Ordnance Association, consisting of personnel from the munitions companies, constitutes a self-interested organization and has been active in War Department politics and promotions.

The committee finds that the Navy League of the United States has solicited and accepted contributions from steamship companies, the recipients of subsidy benefits, and that it has solicited contributions from companies with large foreign investments on the ground that these would profit from a large navy and that its contributors have at times been persons connected with Navy supplies. The committee also finds that the Navy League together with various Navy officials have engaged in political activity looking toward the defeat of Congressmen unfavorable to Navy League and Navy views.

The committee finds, further, that any close associations between munitions and supply companies on the one hand and the service departments on the other hand, of the kind which existed in Germany before the World War, constitutes an unhealthy alliance in that it brings into being a self-interested political power which operates in the name of patriotism and satisfies interests which are, in large part, purely selfish, and that such associations are an inevitable part of militarism, and are to be avoided in peacetime at all costs.

The committee finds, finally, that the neutrality bill of 1936, to which all its members gave their support and which provides for an embargo on the export of arms, ammunitions, and implements of war to belligerents, was a much needed forward step, and that the establishment of a Munitions Control Board, under the

Department of State, should satisfactorily prevent the shipment of arms to other than recognized governments.

VI. INTERNATIONAL AGREEMENTS OF MUNITIONS COMPANIES

The committee finds, under this head, that, among the companies investigated, the following have the most extensive foreign arrangements: F. I. du Pont do Nemours Co., Colt's Patent Firearms Co., Electric Boat Co., Sperry Gyroscope Co., Pratt & Whitney Aircraft Co.

The committee finds that the usual form of arrangement is a license to a foreign ally involving rights to manufacture and sell in certain parts of the world, together with more or less definite price-fixing agreements and occasionally profit-sharing arrangements, and that in effect the world is partitioned by parties at interest.

The committee finds that the granting of licenses to manufacture and sell to nations against which there were embargoes, such as Germany, was in practice a violation of the interest of such embargoes and nullified them.

The committee finds that the international commercial interests of such large organizations as du Pont and Imperial Chemical Industries may precede in the minds of those companies the importance of national policy as described publicly by the foreign office or State Department, and that such considerations of commercial interest were apparently foremost in the rearming of Germany beginning in 1924 and in the sale of a process which could he used to manufacture cheaper munitions in Japan in 1932, shortly after Secretary of State Stimson had taken steps to express the disapproval of this Nation for Japan's military activities in Manchuokuo. Several aviation companies also licensed Japan for the use of their material in Manchuokuo at a time when the United States Government refused recognition to it. Recognition by munitions companies may be far more important than diplomatic recognition.

The committee finds that the licensing of American inventions to allied companies in foreign nations is bound to involve in some form the recurrence of experiences similar to those in the last war in which Electric Boat Co. patents were used in German submarines and aided them in the destruction of American lives, and ships, and that in peacetime the licensing involves the manufacture abroad, at lower costs, of American material.

VII. THE CHEMICAL INDUSTRY AND MUNITIONS

The committee finds a general acknowledgment of the importance of the commercial chemical industry to the manufacture of such instruments of warfare as high explosives and gasses, that most of the large industrial nations have granted their chemical companies considerable measures of protection in the interests of national defense, and that no effective control has to date been established over these large military resources.

These findings were concurred in by all members of the committee.

Depression and New Deals

First Inaugural Address of Franklin D. Roosevelt

SATURDAY, MARCH 4, 1933

I am certain that my fellow Americans expect that on my induction into the Presidency I will address them with a candor and a decision which the present situation of our Nation impels. This is preeminently the time to speak the truth, the whole truth, frankly and boldly. Nor need we shrink from honestly facing conditions in our country today. This great Nation will endure as it has endured, will revive and will prosper. So, first of all, let me assert my firm belief that the only thing we have to fear is fear itself—nameless, unreasoning, unjustified terror which paralyzes needed efforts to convert retreat into advance. In every dark hour of our national life a leadership of frankness and vigor has met with that understanding and support of the people themselves which is essential to victory. I am convinced that you will again give that support to leadership in these critical days.

In such a spirit on my part and on yours we face our common difficulties. They concern, thank God, only material things. Values have shrunken to fantastic levels; taxes have risen; our ability to pay has fallen; government of all kinds is faced by serious curtailment of income; the means of exchange are frozen in the currents of trade; the withered leaves of industrial enterprise lie on every side; farmers find no markets for their produce; the savings of many years in thousands of families are gone.

More important, a host of unemployed citizens face the grim problem of existence, and an equally great number toil with little return. Only a foolish optimist can deny the dark realities of the moment.

Yet our distress comes from no failure of substance. We are stricken by no plague of locusts. Compared with the perils which our forefathers conquered because they believed and were not afraid, we have still much to be thankful for. Nature still offers her bounty and human efforts have multiplied it. Plenty is at our doorstep, but a generous use of it languishes in the very sight of the supply. Primarily this is because the rulers of the exchange of mankind's goods have failed, through their own stubbornness and their own incompetence, have admitted their failure, and abdicated. Practices of the unscrupulous money changers stand indicted in the court of public opinion, rejected by the hearts and minds of men.

True they have tried, but their efforts have been cast in the pattern of an outworn tradition. Faced by failure of credit they have proposed only the lending of more money. Stripped of the lure of profit by which to induce our people to follow their false leadership, they have resorted to exhortations, pleading tearfully for restored confidence. They know only the rules of a generation of self-seekers. They have no vision, and when there is no vision the people perish.

The money changers have fled from their high seats in the temple of our civilization. We may now restore that temple to the ancient truths. The measure of the restoration lies in the extent to which we apply social values more noble than mere monetary profit.

Happiness lies not in the mere possession of money; it lies in the joy of achievement, in the thrill of creative effort. The joy and moral stimulation of work no longer must be forgotten in the mad chase of evanescent profits. These dark days will be worth all they cost us if they teach us that our true destiny is not to be ministered unto but to minister to ourselves and to our fellow men.

Recognition of the falsity of material wealth as the standard of success goes hand in hand with the abandonment of the false belief that public office and high political position are to be valued only by the standards of pride of place and personal profit; and there must be an end to a conduct in banking and in business which too often has given to a sacred trust the likeness of callous and selfish wrongdoing. Small wonder that confidence languishes, for it thrives only on honesty, on honor, on the sacredness of obligations, on faithful protection, on unselfish performance; without them it cannot live.

Restoration calls, however, not for changes in ethics alone. This Nation asks for action, and action now.

Our greatest primary task is to put people to work. This is no unsolvable problem if we face it wisely and courageously. It can be accomplished in part by direct recruiting by the Government itself, treating the task as we would treat the emergency of a war, but at the same time, through this employment, accomplishing greatly needed projects to stimulate and reorganize the use of our natural resources.

Hand in hand with this we must frankly recognize the overbalance of population in our industrial centers and, by engaging on a national scale in a redistribution, endeavor to provide a better use of the land for those best fitted for the land. The task can be helped by definite efforts to raise the values of agricultural products and with this the power to purchase the output of our cities. It can be helped by preventing realistically the tragedy of the growing loss through foreclosure of our small homes and our farms. It can be helped by insistence that the Federal, State, and local governments act forthwith on the demand that their cost be drastically reduced. It can be helped by the unifying of relief activities which today are often scattered, uneconomical, and unequal. It can be helped by national planning for and supervision of all forms of transportation and of communications and other utilities which have a definitely public character. There are many ways in which it can be helped, but it can never be helped merely by talking about it. We must act and act quickly.

Finally, in our progress toward a resumption of work we require two safeguards against a return of the evils of the old order; there must be a strict supervision of all banking and credits and invest- ments; there must be an end to speculation with other people's money, and there must be provision for an adequate but sound currency.

There are the lines of attack. I shall presently urge upon a new Congress in special session detailed measures for their fulfillment, and I shall seek the immediate assistance of the several States.

Through this program of action we address ourselves to putting our own national house in order and making income balance outgo. Our international trade relations, though vastly important, are in point of time and necessity secondary to the establishment of a sound national economy. I favor as a practical policy the putting of first things first. I shall spare no effort to restore world trade by international economic readjustment, but the emergency at home cannot wait on that accomplishment.

The basic thought that guides these specific means of national recovery is not narrowly nationalistic. It is the insistence, as a first consideration, upon the interdependence of the various ele- ments in all parts of the United States—a recognition of the old and permanently important manifestation of the American spirit of the pioneer. It is the way to recovery. It is the immediate way. It is the strongest assurance that the recovery will endure.

In the field of world policy I would dedicate this Nation to the policy of the good neighbor—the neighbor who resolutely respects himself and, because he does so, respects the rights of others— the neighbor who respects his obligations and respects the sanctity of his agreements in and with a world of neighbors.

If I read the temper of our people correctly, we now realize as we have never realized before our interdependence on each other; that we can not merely take but we must give as well; that if we are to go forward, we must move as a trained and loyal army willing to sacrifice for the good of a common discipline, because without such discipline no progress is made, no leadership becomes effective. We are, I know, ready and willing to submit our lives and property to such discipline, because it makes possible a leadership which aims at a larger good. This I propose to offer, pledging that the larger purposes will bind upon us all as a sacred obligation with a unity of duty hitherto evoked only in time of armed strife.

With this pledge taken, I assume unhesitatingly the leadership of this great army of our people dedicated to a disciplined attack upon our common problems.

Action in this image and to this end is feasible under the form of government which we have inherited from our ancestors. Our Constitution is so simple and practical that it is possible always to meet extraordinary needs by changes in emphasis and arrangement without loss of essential form. That is why our constitutional system has proved itself the most superbly enduring political mechanism the modern world has produced. It has met every stress of vast expansion of territory, of foreign wars, of bitter internal strife, of world relations.

It is to be hoped that the normal balance of executive and legislative authority may be wholly adequate to meet the unprecedented task before us. But it may be that an unprecedented demand and need for undelayed action may call for temporary departure from that normal balance of public procedure.

I am prepared under my constitutional duty to recommend the measures that a stricken nation in the midst of a stricken world may require. These measures, or such other measures as the Congress may build out of its experience and wisdom, I shall seek, within my constitutional authority, to bring to speedy adoption.

But in the event that the Congress shall fail to take one of these two courses, and in the event that the national emergency is still critical, I shall not evade the clear course of duty that will then confront me. I shall ask the Congress for the one remaining instrument to meet the crisis—broad Executive power to wage a war against the emergency, as great as the power that would be given to me if we were in fact invaded by a foreign foe.

For the trust reposed in me I will return the courage and the devotion that befit the time. I can do no less.

We face the arduous days that lie before us in the warm courage of the national unity; with the clear consciousness of seeking old and precious moral values; with the clean satisfaction that comes from the stem performance of duty by old and young alike. We aim at the assurance of a rounded and permanent national life.

We do not distrust the future of essential democracy. The people of the United States have not failed. In their need they have registered a mandate that they want direct, vigorous action. They have asked for discipline and direction under leadership. They have made me the present instrument of their wishes. In the spirit of the gift I take it.

In this dedication of a Nation we humbly ask the blessing of God. May He protect each and every one of us. May He guide me in the days to come.

Huey Long: "Share the Wealth"

Huey Long: Now in the third year of his administration, we find more of our people unemployed than at any other time. We find our houses empty and our people hungry, many of them half-clothed and many of them not clothed at all.

Mr. Hopkins announced twenty-two millions on the dole, a new high-water mark in that particular sum, a few weeks ago. We find not only the people going further into debt, but that the United States is going further into debt. The states are going further into debt, and the cities and towns are even going into bankruptcy. The condition has become deplorable. Instead of his promises, the only remedy that Mr. Roosevelt has prescribed is to borrow more money if he can and to go further into debt. The last move was to borrow $5 billion more on which we must pay interest for the balance of our lifetimes, and probably during the lifetime of our children. And with it all, there stalks a slimy specter of want, hunger, destitution, and pestilence, all because of the fact that in the land of too much and of too much to wear, our president has failed in his promise to have these necessities of life distributed into the hands of the people who have need of them.

Now, my friends, you have heard me read how a great New York newspaper, after investigations, declared that all I have said about the bad distribution of this nation's wealth is true. But we have been about our work to correct this situation. That is why the Share Our Wealth societies are forming in every nook and corner of America. They're meeting tonight. Soon there will be Share Our Wealth societies for everyone to meet. They have a great work to perform.

Here is what we stand for in a nutshell:

Number one, we propose that every family in America should at least own a homestead equal in value to not less than one third the average family wealth. The average family wealth of America, at normal values, is approximately $16,000. So our first proposition means that every family will have a home and the comforts of a home up to a value of not less than around $5,000 or a little more than that.

Number two, we propose that no family shall own more than three hundred times the average family wealth, which means that no family shall possess more than a wealth of approximately $5 million—none to own less than $5,000, none to own more than $5 million. We think that's too much to allow them to own, but at least it's extremely conservative.

Number three, we propose that every family shall have an income equal to at least one third of the average family income in America. If all were allowed to work, there'd be an income of from $5,000 to $10,000 per family. We propose that one third would be the minimum. We propose that no family will have an earning of less than around $2,000 to $2,500 and that none will have more than three hundred times the average less the ordinary income taxes, which means that a million dollars would be the limit on the highest income.

We also propose to give the old-age pensions to the old people, not by taxing them or their children, but by levying the taxes upon the excess fortunes to whittle them down, and on the excess incomes and excess inheritances, so that the people who reach the age of sixty can be retired from the active labor of life and given an opportunity to have surcease and ease for the balance of the life that they have on earth.

We also propose the care for the veterans, including the cash payment of the soldiers' bonus. We likewise propose that there should be an education for every youth in this land and that no youth would be dependent upon the financial means of his parents in order to have a college education.

Huey P. Long: "Every Man a King"

Is that a right of life, when the young children of this country are being reared into a sphere which is more owned by 12 men that is by 120,000,000 people?

Ladies and gentlemen, I have only 30 minutes in which to speak to you this evening, and I, therefore, will not be able to discuss in detail so much as I can write when I have all of the time and space that is allowed me for the subjects, but I will undertake to sketch them very briefly without manuscript or preparation, so that you can understand them so well as I can tell them to you tonight.

I contend, my friends, that we have no difficult problem to solve in America, and that is the view of nearly everyone with whom I have discussed the matter here in Washington and elsewhere throughout the United States—that we have no very difficult problem to solve.

It is not the difficulty of the problem which we have; it is the fact that the rich people of this country—and by rich people I mean the super-rich—will not allow us to solve the problems, or rather the one little problem that is afflicting this country, because in order to cure all of our woes it is necessary to scale down the big fortunes, that we may scatter the wealth to be shared by all of the people.

We have a marvelous love for this Government of ours; in fact, it is almost a religion, and it is well that it should be, because we have a splendid form of government and we have a splendid set of laws. We have everything here that we need, except that we have neglected the fundamentals upon which the American Government was principally predicated.

How may of you remember the first thing that the Declaration of Independence said? It said, "We hold these truths to be self-evident, that there are certain inalienable rights of the people, and among them are life, liberty, and the pursuit of happiness"; and it said, further, "We hold the view that all men are created equal."

Now, what did they mean by that? Did they mean, my friends, to say that all me were created equal and that that meant that any one man was born to inherit $10,000,000,000 and that another child was to be born to inherit nothing?

Did that mean, my friends, that someone would come into this world without having had an opportunity, of course, to have hit one lick of work, should be born with more than it and all of its children and children's children could ever dispose of, but that another one would have to be born into a life of starvation?

That was not the meaning of the Declaration of Independence when it said that all men are created equal of "That we hold that all men are created equal."

Now was it the meaning of the Declaration of Independence when it said that they held that there were certain rights that were inalienable—the right of life, liberty, and the pursuit of happiness. Is that right of life, my friends, when the young children of this country are being reared into a sphere which is more owned by 12 men than it is by 120,000,000 people?

Is that, my friends, giving them a fair shake of the dice or anything like the inalienable right of life, liberty, and the pursuit of happiness, or anything resembling the fact that all people are created equal; when we have today in America thousands and hundreds of thousands and millions of children on the verge of starvation in a land that is overflowing with too much to eat and too much to wear? I do not think you will contend that, and I do not think for a moment that they will contend it.

Now let us see if we cannot return this Government to the Declaration of Independence and see if we are going to do anything regarding it. Why should we hesitate or why should we quibble or why should we quarrel with one another to find out what the difficulty is, when we know what the Lord told us what the difficulty is, and Moses wrote it out so a blind man could see it, then Jesus told us all about it, and it was later written in the Book of James, where everyone could read it?

I refer to the Scriptures, now, my friends, and give you what it says not for the purpose of convincing you of the wisdom of myself, not for the purpose ladies and gentlemen, of convincing you of the fact that I am quoting the Scripture means that I am to be more believed than someone else; but I quote you the Scripture, rather refer you to the Scripture, because whatever you see there you may rely upon will never be disproved so long as you or your children or anyone may live; and you may further depend upon the fact that not one historical fact that the Bible has ever contained has ever yet been disproved by any scientific discovery or by reason of anything that has been disclosed to man through his own individual mind or through the wisdom of the Lord which the Lord has allowed him to have.

But the Scripture says, ladies and gentlemen, that no country can survive, or for a country to survive it is necessary that we keep the wealth scattered among the people, that nothing should be held permanently by any one person, and that 50 years seems to be the year of jubilee in which all property would be scattered about and returned to the sources from which it originally came, and every seventh year debt should be remitted.

Those two things the Almighty said to be necessary—I should say He knew to be necessary, or else He would not have so pre- scribed that the property would be kept among the general run of the people and that everyone would continue to share in it; so that no one man would get half of it and hand it down to a son, who takes half of what was left, and that son hand it down to another one, who would take half of what was left, until, like a snowball going downhill, all of the snow was off of the ground except what the snowball had.

I believe that was the judgment and the view and the law of the Lord, that we would have to distribute wealth every so often, in order that there could not be people starving to death in a land of plenty, as there is in America today. We have in American today more wealth, more goods, more food, more clothing, more houses than we have ever had. We have everything in abundance here. We have the farm problem, my friends, because we have too much cotton, because we have too much wheat, and have too much corn, and too much potatoes.

We have a home-loan problem because we have too many houses, and yet nobody can buy them and live in them.

We have trouble, my friends, in the country, because we have too much money owing, the greatest indebtedness that has ever been given to civilization, where it has been shown that we are incapable of distributing to the actual things that are here, because the people have not money enough to supply themselves with them, and because the greed of a few men is such that they think it is necessary that they own everything, and their pleasure consists in the starvation of the masses, and in their possessing things they cannot use, and their children cannot use, but who bask in the splendor of sunlight and wealth, casting darkness and despair and impressing it on everyone else.

"So, therefore," said the Lord, in effect, "if you see these things that now have occurred and exist in this and other countries, there must be a constant scattering of wealth in any country if this country is to survive."

"Then," said the Lord, in effect, "every seventh year there shall be a remission of debts; there will be no debts after 7 years." That was the law.

Now, let us take America today. We have in American today, ladies and gentlemen, $272,000,000,000 of debt. Two hundred and seventy-two thousand millions of dollars of debts are owed by the various people of this country today. Why, my friends, that cannot be paid. It is not possible for that kind of debt to be paid.

The entire currency of the United States is only $6,000,000,000. That is all of the money that we have got in America today. All the actual money you have got in all of your banks, all that you have got in the Government Treasury, is $6,000,000,000; and if you took all that money and paid it out today you would still owe $266,000,000,000; and if you took all that money and paid again you would still owe $260,000,000,000; and if you took it, my friends, 20 times and paid it you would still owe $150,000,000,000.

You would have to have 45 times the entire money supply of the United States today to pay the debts of the people of America, and then they would just have to start out from scratch, without a dime to go on with.

So, my friends, it is impossible to pay all of these debts, and you might as well find out that it cannot be done. The United States Supreme Court has definitely found out that it could not be done, because, in a Minnesota case, it held that when a State has postponed the evil day of collecting a debt it was a valid and constitutional exercise of legislative power.

Now, ladies and gentlemen, if I may proceed to give you some other words that I think you can understand—I am not going to belabor you by quoting tonight—I am going to tell you what the wise men of all ages and all times, down even to the present day, have all said: That you must keep the wealth of the country scattered, and you must limit the amount that any one man can own. You cannot let any man own $300,000,000,000 or $400,000,000,000. If you do, one man can own all of the wealth that they United States has in it.

Now, my friends, if you were off on an island where there were 100 lunches, you could not let one man eat up the hundred lunches, or take the hundred lunches and not let anybody else eat any of them. If you did, there would not be anything else for the balance of the people to consume.

So, we have in America today, my friends, a condition by which about 10 men dominate the means of activity in at least 85 percent of the activities that you own. They either own directly everything or they have got some kind of mortgage on it, with a very small percentage to be excepted. They own the banks, they own the steel mills, they own the railroads, they own the bonds, they own the mortgages, they own the stores, and they have chained the country from one end to the other, until there is not any kind of business that a small, independent man could go into today and make a living, and there is not any kind of business that an independent man can go into and make any money to buy an automobile with; and they have finally and gradually and steadily eliminated everybody from the fields in which there is a living to be made, and still they have got little enough sense to think they ought to be able to get more business out of it anyway.

If you reduce a man to the point where he is starving to death and bleeding and dying, how do you expect that man to get hold of any money to spend with you? It is not possible. Then, ladies and gentlemen, how do you expect people to live, when the wherewith cannot be had by the people?

In the beginning I quoted from the Scriptures. I hope you will understand that I am not quoting Scripture to convince you of my goodness personally, because that is a thing between me and my Maker, that is something as to how I stand with my Maker and as to how you stand with your Maker. That is not concerned with this issue, except and unless there are those of you who would be so good as to pray for the souls of some of us. But the Lord gave his law, and in the Book of James they said so, that the rich should weep and howl for the miseries that had come upon them; and, therefore, it was written that when the rich hold goods they could not use and could not consume, you will inflict punishment on them, and nothing but days of woe ahead of them.

Then we have heard of the great Greek philosopher, Socrates, and the greater Greek philosopher, Plato, and we have read the dialog between Plato and Socrates, in which one said that great riches brought on great poverty, and would be destructive of a country. Read what they said. Read what Plato said; that you must not let any one man be too poor, and you must not let any one man be too rich; that the same mill that grinds out the extra rich is the mill that will grind out the extra poor, because, in order that the extra rich can become so affluent, they must necessarily take more of what ordinarily would belong to the average man.

It is a very simple process of mathematics that you do not have to study, and that no one is going to discuss with you.

So that was the view of Socrates and Plato. That was the view of the English statesmen. That was the view of American statesmen. That was the view of American statesmen like Daniel Webster, Thomas Jefferson, Abraham Lincoln, William Jennings Bryan, and Theodore Roosevelt, and even as late as Herbert Hoover and Franklin D. Roosevelt.

Both of these men, Mr. Hoover and Mr. Roosevelt, came out and said there had to be a decentralization of wealth, but neither one of them did anything about it. But, nevertheless, they recognized the principle. The fact that neither one of them ever did anything about it is their own problem that I am not undertaking to criticize; but had Mr. Hoover carried out what he says ought to be done, he would be retiring from the President's office, very probably, 3 years from now, instead of 1 year ago; and had Mr. Roosevelt proceeded along the lines that he stated were necessary for the decentralization of wealth, he would have gone, my friends, a long way already, and within a few months he would have probably reached a solution of all of the problems that afflict this country.

But I wish to warn you now that nothing that has been done up to this date has taken one dime away from these big-fortune holders; they own just as much as they did, and probably a little bit more; they hold just as many of the debts of the common people as they ever held, and probably a little bit more; and unless we, my friends, are going to give the people of this country a fair shake of the dice, by which they will all get something out of the funds of this land, there is not a chance on the topside of this God's eternal earth by which we can rescue this country and rescue the people of this country.

It is necessary to save the Government of the country, but is much more necessary to save the people of America. We love this country. We love this Government. It is a religion, I say. It is a kind of religion people have read of when women, in the name of religion, would take their infant babes and throw them into the burning flame, where they would be instantly devoured by the all-consuming fire, in days gone by; and there probably are some people of the world even today, who, in the name of religion, throw their tear-dimmed eyes into the sad faces of their fathers and mothers, who cannot given them food and clothing they both needed, and which is necessary to sustain them, and that goes on day after day, and night after night, when day gets into darkness and blackness, knowing those children would arise in the morning without being fed, and probably to bed at night without being fed.

Yet in the name of our Government, and all alone, those people undertake and strive as hard as they can to keep a good government alive, and how long they can stand that no one knows. If I were in their place tonight, the place where millions are, I hope that I would have what I might say—I cannot give you the word to express the kind of fortitude they have; that is the word—I hope that I might have the fortitude to praise and honor my Government that had allowed me here in this land, where there is too much to eat and too much to wear, to starve in order that a handful of men can have so much more than they can ever eat or they can ever wear.

Now, we have organized a society, and we call it "Share Our Wealth Society," a society with the motto "every man a king."

Every man a king, so there would be no such thing as a man or woman who did not have the necessities of life, who would not be dependent upon the whims and caprices and ipsi dixit of the financial martyrs for a living. What do we propose by this society? We propose to limit the wealth of big men in the country. There is an average of $15,000 in wealth to every family in America. That is right here today.

We do not propose to divide it up equally. We do not propose a division of wealth, but we propose to limit poverty that we will allow to be inflicted upon any man's family. We will not say we are going to try to guarantee any equality, or $15,000 to families. No; but we do say that one third of the average is low enough for any one family to hold, that there should be a guaranty of a family wealth of around $5,000; enough for a home, and automobile, a radio, and the ordinary conveniences, and the opportunity to educate their children; a fair share of the income of this land thereafter to that family so there will be no such thing as merely the select to have those things, and so there will be no such thing as a family living in poverty and distress.

We have to limit fortunes. Our present plan is that we will allow no one man to own more than $50,000,000. We think that with that limit we will be able to carry out the balance of the program. It may be necessary that we limit it to less than $50,000,000. It may be necessary, in working out of the plans, that no man's fortune would be more than $10,000,000 or $15,000,000. But be that as it may, it will still be more than any one man, or any one man and his children and their children, will be able to spend in their lifetimes; and it is not necessary or reasonable to have wealth piled up beyond that point where we cannot prevent poverty among the masses.

Another thing we propose is old-age pension of $30 a month for everyone that is 60 years old. Now, we do not give this pension to a man making $1,000 a year, and we do not give it to him if he has $10,000 in property, but outside of that we do.

We will limit hours of work. There is not any necessity of having over-production. I think all you have got to do, ladies and gentlemen, is just limit the hours of work to such an extent as people will work only so long as is necessary to produce enough for all of the people to have what they need. Why, ladies and gentleman, let us say that all of these labor-saving devices reduce hours down to where you do not have to work but 4 hours a day; that is enough for these people, and then praise be the name of the Lord, if it gets that good. Let it be good and not a curse, and then we will have 5 hours a day and 5 days a week, or even less that that, and we might give a man a whole month off during a year, or give him 2 months; and we might do what other countries have seen fit to do, and what I did in Louisiana, by having schools by which adults could go back and learn the things that have been discovered since they went to school.

We will not have any trouble taking care of the agricultural situation. All you have to do is balance your production with your consumption. You simply have to abandon a particular crop that you have too much of, and all you have to do is store the surplus for the next year, and the Government will take it over. When you have good crops in the area in which the crops that have been planted are sufficient for another year, put in your public works in the particular year when you do not need to raise any more, and by that means you get everybody employed. When the Government has enough of any particular crop to take care of all of the people, that will be all that is necessary; and in order to do all of this, our taxation is going to be to take the billion-dollar fortunes and strip them down to frying size, not to exceed $50,000,000, and it is necessary to come to $10,000,000, we will come to $10,000,000. We have worked the proposition out to guarantee a limit upon property (and no man will own less than one third the average), and guarantee a reduction of fortunes and a reduction of hours to spread wealth throughout this country. We would care for the old people above 60 and take them away from this thriving industry and given them a chance to enjoy the necessities and live in ease, and thereby lift from the market the labor which would probably create a surplus of commodities.

Those are the things we propose to do. "Every man a king." Every man to eat when there is something to eat; all to wear something when there is something to wear. That makes us all sovereign.

You cannot solve these things through these various and sundry alphabetical codes. You can have the N.R.A. and P.W.A. and C.W.A. and the U.U.G. and G.I.N. and any other kind of "dadgummed" lettered code. You can wait until doomsday and see 25 more alphabets, but that is not going to solve this proposition. Why hide? Why quibble? You know what the trouble is. The man that says he does not know what the trouble is just hiding his face to keep from seeing the sunlight.

God told you what the trouble was. The philosophers told you what the trouble was; and when you have a country where one man owns more than 100,000 people, or a million people, and when you have a country where there are four men, as in America, that have got more control over things than all the 120,000,000 people together, you know what the trouble is.

We had these great incomes in this country; but the farmer, who plowed from sunup to sundown, who labored here from sunup to sundown for 6 days a week, wound up at the end of the with practically nothing.

And we ought to take care of the veterans of the wars in this program. That is a small matter. Suppose it does cost a billion dollars a year—that means that the money will be scattered throughout this country. We ought to pay them a bonus. We can do it. We ought to take care of every single one of the sick and disabled veterans. I do not care whether a man got sick on the battlefield or did not; every man that wore the uniform of this country is entitled to be taken care of, and there is money enough to do it; and we need to spread the wealth of the country, which you did not do in what you call the N.R.A.

If the N.R.A. has done any good, I can put it all in my eye without having it hurt. All I can see that N.R.A. has done is to put the little man out of business—the little merchant in his store, the little Dago that is running a fruit stand, or the Greek shoe-shining stand, who has to take hold of a code of 275 pages and study with a spirit level and compass and looking-glass; he has to hire a Philadelphia lawyer to tell him what is in the code; and by the time he learns what the code is, he is in jail or out of business; and they have got a chain code system that has already put him out of business. The N.R.A. is not worth anything, and I said so when they put it through.

Now, my friends, we have got to hit the root with the axe. Centralized power in the hands of a few, with centralized credit in the hands of a few, is the trouble.

Get together in your community tonight or tomorrow and organize one of our Share Our Wealth societies. If you do not understand it, write me and let me send you the platform; let me give you the proof of it.

This is Huey P. Long talking, United States Senator, Washington, D.C. Write me and let me send you the data on this proposition. Enroll with us. Let us make known to the people what we are going to do. I will send you a button, if I have got enough of them left. We have got a little button that some of our friends designed, with our message around the rim of the button, and in the center "Every man a king." Many thousands of them are meeting through the United States, and every day we are getting hundreds and hundreds of letters. Share Our Wealth societies are now being organized, and people have it within their power to relieve themselves from this terrible situation.

Look at what the Mayo brothers announced this week, these greatest scientists of all the world today, who are entitled to have more money than all the Morgans and the Rockefellers, or anyone else, and yet the Mayos turn back their big fortunes to be used for treating the sick, and said they did not want to lay up fortunes in this earth, but wanted to turn them back where they would do some good; but the other big capitalists are not willing to do that, are not willing to do what these men, 10 times more worthy, have already done, and it is going to take a law to require them to do it.

Organize your Share Our Wealth Society and get your people to meet with you, and make known your wishes to your Senators and Representatives in Congress.

Now, my friends, I am going to stop. I thank you for this opportunity to talk to you. I am having to talk under the auspices and by the grace and permission of the National Broadcasting System tonight, and they are letting me talk free. If I had the money, and I wish I had the money, I would like to talk to you more often on this line, but I have not got it, and I cannot expect these people to give it to me free except on some rare instance. But, my friends, I hope to have the opportunity to talk with you, and I am writing to you, and I hope that you will get up and help in the work, because the resolution and bills are before Congress, and we hope to have your help in getting together and organizing your Share Our Wealth society.

Now, that I have but a minute left, I want to say that I suppose my family is listening in on the radio in New Orleans, and I will say to my wife and three children that I am entirely well and hope to be home before many more days, and I hope they have listened to my speech tonight, and I wish them and all their neighbors and friends everything good that may be had.

I thank you, my friends, for your kind attention, and I hope you will enroll with us, take care of your own work in the work of this Government, and share or help in our Share Our Wealth society.

I thank you.

The Wagner Act of 1935

SEC. 7. Employees shall have the right of self-organization, to form, join, or assist labor organizations, to bargain collectively through representatives of their own choosing, and to engage in concerted activities, for the purpose of collective bargaining or other mutual aid or protection.

SEC. 8. It shall be an unfair labor practice for an employer-

1. To interfere with, restrain, or coerce employees in the exercise of the rights guaranteed in section 7.

2. To dominate or interfere with the formation or administration of any labor organization or contribute financial or other support to it: Provided, That... an employer shall not be prohibited from permitting employees to confer with him during working hours without loss of time or pay.

3. By discrimination in regard to hire or tenure of employment or any term or condition of employment to encourage or discourage membership in any labor organization: Provided, That nothing in this Act or in any other statute of the United States, shall preclude an employer from making an agreement with a labor organization (not established, maintained, or assisted by any action defined in this Act as an unfair labor practice) to require as a condition of employment membership therein, if such labor organization is the representative of the employees in the appropriate collec tive bargaining unit covered by such agreement when made.

4. To discharge or otherwise discriminate against an employee because he has filed charges or given testimony under this Act.

5. To refuse to bargain collectively with the representatives of his employees.

New Wars

Atlantic Charter

AUGUST 14, 1941

The President of the United States of America and the Prime Minister, Mr. Churchill, representing His Majesty's Government in the United Kingdom, being met together, deem it right to make known certain common principles in the national policies of their respective countries on which they base their hopes for a better future for the world.

First, their countries seek no aggrandizement, territorial or other;

Second, they desire to see no territorial changes that do not accord with the freely expressed wishes of the peoples concerned;

Third, they respect the right of all peoples to choose the form of government under which they will live; and they wish to see sovereign rights and self government restored to those who have been forcibly deprived of them;

Fourth, they will endeavor, with due respect for their existing obligations, to further the enjoyment by all States, great or small, victor or vanquished, of access, on equal terms, to the trade and to the raw materials of the world which are needed for their economic prosperity;

Fifth, they desire to bring about the fullest collaboration between all nations in the economic field with the object of securing, for all, improved labor standards, economic advancement and social security;

Sixth, after the final destruction of the Nazi tyranny, they hope to see established a peace which will afford to all nations the means of dwelling in safety within their own boundaries, and which will afford assurance that all the men in all lands may live out their lives in freedom from fear and want;

Seventh, such a peace should enable all men to traverse the high seas and oceans without hindrance;

Eighth, they believe that all of the nations of the world, for realistic as well as spiritual reasons must come to the abandonment of the use of force. Since no future peace can be maintained if land, sea or air armaments continue to be employed by nations which threaten, or may threaten, aggression outside of their frontiers, they believe, pending the establishment of a wider and permanent system of general security, that the disarmament of such nations is essential. They will likewise aid and encourage all other practicable measure which will lighten for peace-loving peoples the crushing burden of armaments.

Franklin D. Roosevelt

Winston S. Churchill

Bretton Woods Conference

This Conference at Bretton Woods, representing nearly all the peoples of the world, has considered matters of international money and finance which are important for peace and prosperity. The Conference has agreed on the problems needing attention, the measures which should be taken, and the forms of international cooperation or organization which are required. The agreements reached on these large and complex matters are without precedent in the history of international economic relations.

I. THE INTERNATIONAL MONETARY FUND

Since foreign trade affects the standard of life of every people, all countries have a vital interest in the system of exchange of national currencies and the regulations and conditions which govern its working. Because these monetary transactions are international exchanges, the nations must agree on the basic rules which govern the exchanges if the system is to work smoothly. When they do not agree, and when single nations and small groups of nations attempt by special and different regulations of the foreign exchanges to gain trade advantages, the result is instability, a reduced volume of foreign trade, and damage to national economies. This course of action is likely to lead to economic warfare and to endanger the worlds peace.

The Conference has therefore agreed that broad international action is necessary to maintain an international monetary system which will promote foreign trade. The nations should consult and agree on international monetary changes which affect each other. They should outlaw practices which are agreed to be harmful to world prosperity, and they should assist each other to overcome short-term exchange difficulties.

The Conference has agreed that the nations here represented should establish for these purposes a permanent international body, The International Monetary Fund, with powers and resources adequate to perform the tasks assigned to it. Agreement has been reached concerning these powers and resources and the additional obligations which the member countries should undertake. Draft Articles of Agreement on these points have been prepared.

II. THE INTERNATIONAL BANK FOR RECONSTRUCTION AND DEVELOPMENT

It is in the interest of all nations that post-war reconstruction should be rapid. Likewise, the development of the resources of particular regions is in the general economic interest. Programs of reconstruction and development will speed economic progress everywhere, will aid political stability and foster peace.

The Conference has agreed that expanded international investment is essential to provide a portion of the capital necessary for reconstruction and development.

The Conference has further agreed that the nations should cooperate to increase the volume of foreign investment for these purposes, made through normal business channels. It is especially important that the nations should cooperate to share the risks of such foreign investment, since the benefits are general.

The Conference has agreed that the nations should establish a permanent international body to perform these functions, to be called The International Bank for Reconstruction and Development. It has been agreed that the Bank should assist in providing capital through normal channels at reasonable rates of interest and for long periods for projects which will raise the productivity of the borrowing country. There is agreement that the Bank should guarantee loans made by others and that through their subscriptions of capital in all countries should share with the borrowing country in guaranteeing such loans. The Conference has agreed on the powers and resources which the Bank must have and on the obligations which the member countries must assume, and has prepared draft Articles of Agreement accordingly.

The Conference has recommended that in carrying out the policies of the institutions here proposed special consideration should be given to the needs of countries which have suffered from enemy occupation and hostilities.

The proposals formulated at the Conference for the establishment of the Fund and the Bank are now submitted, in accordance with the terms of the invitation, for consideration of the governments and people of the countries represented.

Atomic Scientists: Petition to the President of the United States

A Petition to the President of the United States

Discoveries of which the people of the United States are not aware may affect the welfare of this nation in the near future. The liberation of atomic power which has been achieved places atomic bombs in the hands of the Army. It places in your hands, as Commander-in-Chief, the fateful decision whether or not to sanction the use of such bombs in the present phase of the war against Japan.

We, the undersigned scientists, have been working in the field of atomic power. Until recently, we have had to fear that the United States might be attacked by atomic bombs during this war and that her only defense might lie in a counterattack by the same means. Today, with the defeat of Germany, this danger is averted and we feel impelled to say what follows:

The war has to be brought speedily to a successful conclusion and attacks by atomic bombs may very well be an effective method of warfare. We feel, however, that such attacks on Japan could not be justified, at least not unless the terms which will be imposed after the war on Japan were made public in detail and Japan were given an opportunity to surrender.

If such public announcement gave assurance to the Japanese that they could look forward to a life devoted to peaceful pursuits in their homeland and if Japan still refused to surrender our nation might then, in certain circumstances, find itself forced to resort to the use of atomic bombs. Such a step, however, ought not to be made at any time without seriously considering the moral responsibilities which are involved.

The development of atomic power will provide the nations with new means of destruction. The atomic bombs at our disposal represent only the first step in this direction, and there is almost no limit to the destructive power which will become available in the course of their future development. Thus a nation which sets the precedent of using these newly liberated forces of nature for purposes of destruction may have to bear the responsibility of opening the door to an era of devastation on an unimaginable scale.

If after this war a situation is allowed to develop in the world which permits rival powers to be in uncontrolled possession of these new means of destruction, the cities of the United States as well as the cities of other nations will be in continuous danger of sudden annihilation. All the resources of the United States, moral and material, may have to be mobilized to prevent the advent of such a world situation. Its prevention is at present the solemn responsibility of the United States—singled out by virtue of her lead in the field of atomic power.

The added material strength which this lead gives to the United States brings with it the obligation of restraint and if we were to violate this obligation our moral position would be weakened in the eyes of the world and in our own eyes. It would then be more difficult for us to live up to our responsibility of bringing the unloosened forces of destruction under control.

In view of the foregoing, we, the undersigned, respectfully petition: first, that you exercise your power as Commander-in-Chief, to rule that the United States shall not resort to the use of atomic bombs in this war unless the terms which will be imposed upon Japan have been made public in detail and Japan knowing these terms has refused to surrender; second, that in such an event the question whether or not to use atomic bombs be decided by you in light of the considerations presented in this petition as well as all the other moral responsibilities which are involved.

White House Press Release Anouncing the Bombing of Hiroshima, August 6, 1945

STATEMENT BY THE PRESIDENT OF THE UNITED STATES

Sixteen hours ago an American airplane dropped one bomb on Hiroshima and destroyed its usefulness to the enemy. That bomb had more power than 20,000 tons of TNT. It had more than two thousand times the blast power of the British "Grand Slam" which is the largest bomb ever yet used in the history of warfare.

The Japanese began the war from the air at Pearl Harbor. They have been repaid many fold. And the end is not yet. With this bomb we have now added a new and revolutionary increase in destruction to supplement the growing power of our armed forces. In their present form these bombs are now in production and even more powerful forms are in development.

It is an atomic bomb. It is a harnessing of the basic power of the universe. The force from which the sun draws its power has been loosed against those who brought war to the Far East.

Before 1939, it was the accepted belief of scientists that it was theoretically possible to release atomic energy. But no one knew any practical method of doing it. By 1942, however, we knew that the Germans were working feverishly to find a way to add atomic energy to the other engines of war with which they hoped to enslave the world. But they failed. We may be grateful to Providence that the Germans got the V-1's and V-2's late and in limited quantities and even more grateful that they did not get the atomic bomb at all.

The battle of the laboratories held fateful risks for us as well as the battles of the air, land, and sea, and we have now won the battle of the laboratories as we have won the other battles.

Beginning in 1940, before Pearl Harbor, scientific knowledge useful in was pooled between the United States and Great Britain, and many priceless helps to our victories have come from that arrangement. Under that general policy the research on the atomic bomb was begun. With American and British scientists working together we entered the race of discovery against the Germans.

The United States had available the large number of scientists of distinction in the many needed areas of knowledge. It had the tremendous industrial and financial resources necessary for the project and they could be devoted to it without undue impairment of other vital war work. In the United States the laboratory work and the production plants, on which a substantial start had already been made, would be out of reach of enemy bombing, while at that time Britain was exposed to constant air attack and was still threatened with the possibility of invasion. For these reasons Prime Minister Churchill and President Roosevelt agreed that it was wise to carry on the project here. We now have two great plants and many lesser works devoted to the production of atomic power. Employment during peak construction numbered 125,000 and over 65,000 individuals are even now engaged in operating the plants. Many have worked there for two and a half years. Few know what they have been producing. They see great quantities of material going in and they see nothing coming out of these plants, for the physical size of the explosive charge is exceedingly small. We have spent two billion dollars on the greatest scientific gamble in history—and won.

But the greatest marvel is not the size of the enterprise, its secrecy, nor its cost, but the achievement of scientific brains in putting together infinitely complex pieces of knowledge held by many men in different fields of science into a workable plan. And hardly less marvelous has been the capacity of industry to design and of labor to operate, the machines and methods to do things never done before so that the brainchild of many minds came forth in physical shape and performed as it was supposed to do. Both science and industry worked under the direction of the United States Army, which achieved a unique success in managing so diverse a problem in the advancement of knowledge in an amazingly short time. It is doubtful if such another combination could be got together in the world. What has been done is the greatest achievement of organized science in history. It was done under pressure and without failure.

We are now prepared to obliterate more rapidly and completely every productive enterprise the Japanese have above ground in any city. We shall destroy their docks, their factories, and their communications. Let there be no mistake; we shall completely destroy Japan's power to make war.

It was to spare the Japanese people from utter destruction that the ultimatum of July 26 was issued at Potsdam. Their leaders promptly rejected that ultimatum. If they do not now accept our terms they may expect a rain of ruin from the air, the like of which has never been seen on this earth. Behind this air attack will follow sea and land forces in such number that and power as they have not yet seen and with the fighting skill of which they are already well aware.

The Secretary of War, who has kept in personal touch with all phases of the project, will immediately make public a statement giving further details.

His statement will give facts concerning the sites at Oak Ridge near Knoxville, Tennessee, and at Richland, near Pasco, Washington, and an installation near Santa Fe, New Mexico. Although the workers at the sites have been making materials to be used producing the greatest destructive force in history they have not themselves been in danger beyond that of many other occupations, for the utmost care has been taken of their safety.

The fact that we can release atomic energy ushers in a new era in man's understanding of nature's forces. Atomic energy may in the future supplement the power that now comes from coal, oil, and falling water, but at present it cannot be produced on a bases to compete with them commercially. Before that comes there must be a long period of intensive research. It has never been the habit of the scientists of this country or the policy of this government to withhold from the world scientific knowledge. Normally, therefore, everything about the work with atomic energy would be made public.

But under the present circumstances it is not intended to divulge the technical processes of production or all the military applications. Pending further examination of possible methods of protecting us and the rest of the world from the danger of sudden destruction.

I shall recommend that the Congress of the United States con-sider promptly the establishment of an appropriate commission to control the production and use of atomic power within the United States. I shall give further consideration and make further recommendations to the Congress as to how atomic power can become a powerful and forceful influence towards the mainte-nance of world peace.

Geneva Convention (III) Relative to the Treatment of Prisoners of War; August 12, 1949

PART III: CAPTIVITY

SECTION I: BEGINNING OF CAPTIVITY

ARTICLE 17

Every prisoner of war, when questioned on the subject, is bound to give only his surname, first names and rank, date of birth, and army, regimental, personal or serial number, or failing this, equivalent information.

If he wilfully infringes this rule, he may render himself liable to a restriction of the privileges accorded to his rank or status.

Each Party to a conflict is required to furnish the persons under its jurisdiction who are liable to become prisoners of war, with an identity card showing the owner's surname, first names, rank, army, regimental, personal or serial number or equivalent information, and date of birth. The identity card may, furthermore, bear the signature or the fingerprints, or both, of the owner, and may bear, as well, any other information the Party to the conflict may wish to add concerning persons belonging to its armed forces. As far as possible the card shall measure 6.5 x 10 cm. and shall be issued in duplicate. The identity card shall be shown by the prisoner of war upon demand, but may in no case be taken away from him.

No physical or mental torture, nor any other form of coercion, may be inflicted on prisoners of war to secure from them information of any kind whatever. Prisoners of war who refuse to answer may not be threatened, insulted, or exposed to unpleasant or disadvantageous treatment of any kind. Prisoners of war who, owing to their physical or mental condition, are unable to state their identity, shall be handed over to the medical service. The identity of such prisoners shall be established by all possible means, subject to the provisions of the preceding paragraph.

The questioning of prisoners of war shall be carried out in a language which they understand.

ARTICLE 18

All effects and articles of personal use, except arms, horses, military equipment and military documents, shall remain in the possession of prisoners of war, likewise their metal helmets and gas masks and like articles issued for personal protection. Effects and articles used for their clothing or feeding shall likewise remain in their possession, even if such effects and articles belong to their regulation military equipment.

At no time should prisoners of war be without identity documents. The Detaining Power shall supply such documents to prisoners of war who possess none.

Badges of rank and nationality, decorations and articles having above all a personal or sentimental value may not be taken from prisoners of war.

Sums of money carried by prisoners of war may not be taken away from them except by order of an officer, and after the amount and particulars of the owner have been recorded in a special register and an itemized receipt has been given, legibly inscribed with the name, rank and unit of the person issuing the said receipt. Sums in the currency of the Detaining Power, or which are changed into such currency at the prisoner's request, shall be placed to the credit of the prisoner's account as provided in Article 64.

The Detaining Power may withdraw articles of value from prisoners of war only for reasons of security; when such articles are withdrawn, the procedure laid down for sums of money impounded shall apply.

Such objects, likewise sums taken away in any currency other than that of the Detaining Power and the conversion of which has not been asked for by the owners, shall be kept in the custody of the Detaining Power and shall be returned in their initial shape to prisoners of war at the end of their captivity.

ARTICLE 19

Prisoners of war shall be evacuated, as soon as possible after their capture, to camps situated in an area far enough from the combat zone for them to be out of danger.

Only those prisoners of war who, owing to wounds or sickness, would run greater risks by being evacuated than by remaining where they are, may be temporarily kept back in a danger zone.

Prisoners of war shall not be unnecessarily exposed to danger while awaiting evacuation from a fighting zone.

ARTICLE 20

The evacuation of prisoners of war shall always be effected humanely and in conditions similar to those for the forces of the Detaining Power in their changes of station.

The Detaining Power shall supply prisoners of war who are being evacuated with sufficient food and potable water, and with the necessary clothing and medical attention. The Detaining Power shall take all suitable precautions to ensure their safety during evacuation, and shall establish as soon as possible a list of the prisoners of war who are evacuated.

If prisoners of war must, during evacuation, pass through transit camps, their stay in such camps shall be as brief as possible.

SECTION II: INTERNMENT OF PRISONERS OF WAR

CHAPTER I: GENERAL OBSERVATIONS

ARTICLE 21

The Detaining Power may subject prisoners of war to internment. It may impose on them the obligation of not leaving, beyond certain limits, the camp where they are interned, or if the said camp is fenced in, of not going outside its perimeter. Subject to the provisions of the present Convention relative to penal and disciplinary sanctions, prisoners of war may not be held in close confinement except where necessary to safeguard their health and then only during the continuation of the circumstances which make such confinement necessary.

Prisoners of war may be partially or wholly released on parole or promise, in so far as is allowed by the laws of the Power on which they depend. Such measures shall be taken particularly in cases where this may contribute to the improvement of their state of health. No prisoner of war shall be compelled to accept liberty on parole or promise.

Upon the outbreak of hostilities, each Party to the conflict shall notify the adverse Party of the laws and regulations allowing or forbidding its own nationals to accept liberty on parole or promise. Prisoners of war who are paroled or who have given their promise in conformity with the laws and regulations so notified, are bound on their personal honour scrupulously to fulfil, both towards the Power on which they depend and towards the Power which has captured them, the engagements of their paroles or promises. In such cases, the Power on which they depend is bound neither to require nor to accept from them any service incompatible with the parole or promise given.

ARTICLE 22

Prisoners of war may be interned only in premises located on land and affording every guarantee of hygiene and healthfulness. Except in particular cases which are justified by the interest of the prisoners themselves, they shall not be interned in penitentiaries.

Prisoners of war interned in unhealthy areas, or where the climate is injurious for them, shall be removed as soon as possible to a more favourable climate.

The Detaining Power shall assemble prisoners of war in camps or camp compounds according to their nationality, language and customs, provided that such prisoners shall not be separated from prisoners of war belonging to the armed forces with which they were serving at the time of their capture, except with their consent.

ARTICLE 23

No prisoner of war may at any time be sent to, or detained in areas where he may be exposed to the fire of the combat zone, nor may his presence be used to render certain points or areas immune from military operations.

Prisoners of war shall have shelters against air bombardment and other hazards of war, to the same extent as the local civilian population. With the exception of those engaged in the protection of their quarters against the aforesaid hazards, they may enter such shelters as soon as possible after the giving of the alarm. Any other protective measure taken in favour of the population shall also apply to them.

Detaining Powers shall give the Powers concerned, through the intermediary of the Protecting Powers, all useful information regarding the geographical location of prisoner of war camps.

Whenever military considerations permit, prisoner of war camps shall be indicated in the day-time by the letters PW or PG, placed so as to be clearly visible from the air. The Powers concerned may, however, agree upon any other system of marking. Only prisoner of war camps shall be marked as such.

ARTICLE 24

Transit or screening camps of a permanent kind shall be fitted out under conditions similar to those described in the present Section, and the prisoners therein shall have the same treatment as in other camps.

IV

Containment Abroad and at Home

As soon as the Second World War ended, the U.S. and Soviet Union, allies in the fight against the Nazis, became rivals for world power. The Americans, with a huge advantage in economic and political power, embarked on a mission to expand its influence all over the globe and a "cold war" against the Russians ensued. In this great struggle, the U.S. was committed to stopping "communism," which was defined broadly to include neutral and nationalist states, everywhere, even though, as its own government agencies admitted, it had predominant power over the Soviet Union.

Just as importantly, this cold war extended into affairs at home, as the government, using the exaggerated threat of communism, suppressed groups and individuals like labor and African-Americans who were trying to expand the notion of democracy inside the U.S.

By the 1950s, the U.S. had effectively controlled "subversives" at home and extended its grab for power into new lands, all over the globe.

From National Interest to World Power

Truman Doctrine

PRESIDENT HARRY S. TRUMAN'S ADDRESS BEFORE A JOINT SESSION OF CONGRESS, MARCH 12, 1947

Mr. President, Mr. Speaker, Members of the Congress of the United States:

The gravity of the situation which confronts the world today necessitates my appearance before a joint session of the Congress. The foreign policy and the national security of this country are involved.

One aspect of the present situation, which I wish to present to you at this time for your consideration and decision, concerns Greece and Turkey.

The United States has received from the Greek Government an urgent appeal for financial and economic assistance. Preliminary reports from the American Economic Mission now in Greece and reports from the American Ambassador in Greece corroborate the statement of the Greek Government that assistance is imperative if Greece is to survive as a free nation.

I do not believe that the American people and the Congress wish to turn a deaf ear to the appeal of the Greek Government.

Greece is not a rich country. Lack of sufficient natural resources has always forced the Greek people to work hard to make both ends meet. Since 1940, this industrious and peace loving country has suffered invasion, four years of cruel enemy occupation, and bitter internal strife.

When forces of liberation entered Greece they found that the retreating Germans had destroyed virtually all the railways, roads, port facilities, communications, and merchant marine. More than a thousand villages had been burned. Eighty-five per cent of the children were tubercular. Livestock, poultry, and draft animals had almost disappeared. Inflation had wiped out practically all savings.

As a result of these tragic conditions, a militant minority, exploiting human want and misery, was able to create political chaos which, until now, has made economic recovery impossible.

Greece is today without funds to finance the importation of those goods which are essential to bare subsistence. Under these circumstances the people of Greece cannot make progress in solving their problems of reconstruction. Greece is in desperate need of financial and economic assistance to enable it to resume purchases of food, clothing, fuel and seeds. These are indispensable for the subsistence of its people and are obtainable only from abroad. Greece must have help to import the goods necessary to restore internal order and security, so essential for economic and political recovery.

The Greek Government has also asked for the assistance of experienced American administrators, economists and technicians to insure that the financial and other aid given to Greece shall be used effectively in creating a stable and self-sustaining economy and in improving its public administration.

The very existence of the Greek state is today threatened by the terrorist activities of several thousand armed men, led by Communists, who defy the government's authority at a number of points, particularly along the northern boundaries. A Commission appointed by the United Nations security Council is at present investigating disturbed conditions in northern Greece and alleged border violations along the frontier between Greece on the one hand and Albania, Bulgaria, and Yugoslavia on the other.

Meanwhile, the Greek Government is unable to cope with the situation. The Greek army is small and poorly equipped. It needs supplies and equipment if it is to restore the authority of the government throughout Greek territory. Greece must have assistance if it is to become a self-supporting and self-respecting democracy.

The United States must supply that assistance. We have already extended to Greece certain types of relief and economic aid but these are inadequate.

There is no other country to which democratic Greece can turn.

No other nation is willing and able to provide the necessary support for a democratic Greek government.

The British Government, which has been helping Greece, can give no further financial or economic aid after March 31. Great Britain finds itself under the necessity of reducing or liquidating its commitments in several parts of the world, including Greece.

We have considered how the United Nations might assist in this crisis. But the situation is an urgent one requiring immediate action and the United Nations and its related organizations are not in a position to extend help of the kind that is required.

It is important to note that the Greek Government has asked for our aid in utilizing effectively the financial and other assistance we may give to Greece, and in improving its public administration. It is of the utmost importance that we supervise the use of any funds made available to Greece; in such a manner that each dollar spent will count toward making Greece self-supporting, and will help to build an economy in which a healthy democracy can flourish.

No government is perfect. One of the chief virtues of a democracy, however, is that its defects are always visible and under democratic processes can be pointed out and corrected. The Government of Greece is not perfect. Nevertheless it represents eighty-five per cent of the members of the Greek Parliament who were chosen in an election last year. Foreign observers, including 692 Americans, considered this election to be a fair expression of the views of the Greek people.

The Greek Government has been operating in an atmosphere of chaos and extremism. It has made mistakes. The extension of aid by this country does not mean that the United States condones everything that the Greek Government has done or will do. We have condemned in the past, and we condemn now, extremist measures of the right or the left. We have in the past advised tolerance, and we advise tolerance now.

Greece's neighbor, Turkey, also deserves our attention.

The future of Turkey as an independent and economically sound state is clearly no less important to the freedom-loving peoples of the world than the future of Greece. The circumstances in which Turkey finds itself today are considerably different from those of Greece. Turkey has been spared the disasters that have beset Greece. And during the war, the United States and Great Britain furnished Turkey with material aid.

Nevertheless, Turkey now needs our support.

Since the war Turkey has sought financial assistance from Great Britain and the United States for the purpose of effecting that modernization necessary for the maintenance of its national integrity.

That integrity is essential to the preservation of order in the Middle East.

The British government has informed us that, owing to its own difficulties can no longer extend financial or economic aid to Turkey.

As in the case of Greece, if Turkey is to have the assistance it needs, the United States must supply it. We are the only country able to provide that help.

I am fully aware of the broad implications involved if the United States extends assistance to Greece and Turkey, and I shall discuss these implications with you at this time.

One of the primary objectives of the foreign policy of the United States is the creation of conditions in which we and other nations will be able to work out a way of life free from coercion. This was a fundamental issue in the war with Germany and Japan. Our victory was won over countries which sought to impose their will, and their way of life, upon other nations.

To ensure the peaceful development of nations, free from coercion, the United States has taken a leading part in establishing the United Nations, The United Nations is designed to make possible lasting freedom and independence for all its members. We shall not realize our objectives, however, unless we are willing to help free peoples to maintain their free institutions and their national integrity against aggressive movements that seek to impose upon them totalitarian regimes. This is no more than a frank recognition that totalitarian regimes imposed on free peoples, by direct or indirect aggression, undermine the foundations of international peace and hence the security of the United States.

The peoples of a number of countries of the world have recently had totalitarian regimes forced upon them against their will. The Government of the United States has made frequent protests against coercion and intimidation, in violation of the Yalta agreement, in Poland, Rumania, and Bulgaria. I must also state that in a number of other countries there have been similar developments.

At the present moment in world history nearly every nation must choose between alternative ways of life. The choice is too often not a free one.

One way of life is based upon the will of the majority, and is distinguished by free institutions, representative government, free elections, guarantees of individual liberty, freedom of speech and religion, and freedom from political oppression.

The second way of life is based upon the will of a minority forcibly imposed upon the majority. It relies upon terror and oppression, a controlled press and radio; fixed elections, and the suppression of personal freedoms.

I believe that it must be the policy of the United States to support free peoples who are resisting attempted subjugation by armed minorities or by outside pressures.

I believe that we must assist free peoples to work out their own destinies in their own way.

I believe that our help should be primarily through economic and financial aid which is essential to economic stability and orderly political processes.

The world is not static, and the status quo is not sacred. But we cannot allow changes in the status quo in violation of the Charter of the United Nations by such methods as coercion, or by such subterfuges as political infiltration. In helping free and independent nations to maintain their freedom, the United States will be giving effect to the principles of the Charter of the United Nations.

It is necessary only to glance at a map to realize that the survival and integrity of the Greek nation are of grave importance in a much wider situation. If Greece should fall under the control of an armed minority, the effect upon its neighbor, Turkey, would be immediate and serious. Confusion and disorder might well spread throughout the entire Middle East.

Moreover, the disappearance of Greece as an independent state would have a profound effect upon those countries in Europe whose peoples are struggling against great difficulties to maintain their freedoms and their independence while they repair the damages of war.

It would be an unspeakable tragedy if these countries, which have struggled so long against overwhelming odds, should lose that victory for which they sacrificed so much. Collapse of free institutions and loss of independence would be disastrous not only for them but for the world. Discouragement and possibly failure would quickly be the lot of neighboring peoples striving to maintain their freedom and independence.

Should we fail to aid Greece and Turkey in this fateful hour, the effect will be far reaching to the West as well as to the East.

We must take immediate and resolute action.

I therefore ask the Congress to provide authority for assistance to Greece and Turkey in the amount of $400,000,000 for the period ending June 30, 1948. In requesting these funds, I have taken into consideration the maximum amount of relief assistance which would be furnished to Greece out of the $350,000,000 which I recently requested that the Congress authorize for the prevention of starvation and suffering in countries devastated by the war.

In addition to funds, I ask the Congress to authorize the detail of American civilian and military personnel to Greece and Turkey, at the request of those countries, to assist in the tasks of recon-struction, and for the purpose of supervising the use of such financial and material assistance as may be furnished. I recom-mend that authority also be provided for the instruction and training of selected Greek and Turkish personnel.

Finally, I ask that the Congress provide authority which will permit the speediest and most effective use, in terms of needed commodities, supplies, and equipment, of such funds as may be authorized.

If further funds, or further authority, should be needed for purposes indicated in this message, I shall not hesitate to bring the situation before the Congress. On this subject the Executive and Legislative branches of the Government must work together.

This is a serious course upon which we embark.

I would not recommend it except that the alternative is much more serious. The United States contributed $341,000,000,000 toward winning World War II. This is an investment in world freedom and world peace.

The assistance that I am recommending for Greece and Turkey amounts to little more than 1 tenth of 1 per cent of this investment. It is only common sense that we should safeguard this investment and make sure that it was not in vain.

The seeds of totalitarian regimes are nurtured by misery and want. They spread and grow in the evil soil of poverty and strife. They reach their full growth when the hope of a people for a better life has died. We must keep that hope alive.

The free peoples of the world look to us for support in maintaining their freedoms.

If we falter in our leadership, we may endanger the peace of the world—and we shall surely endanger the welfare of our own nation.

Great responsibilities have been placed upon us by the swift movement of events.

I am confident that the Congress will face these responsibilities squarely.

McCarran Internal Security Act—1947

To protect the United States against certain Un American and subversive activities by requiring registration of Communist organizations, and for other purposes.

SEC. 2. As a result of evidence adduced before various committees of the Senate and House of Representatives, the Congress hereby finds that—

(I) There exists a world Communist movement which, in its origins, its development, and its present practice, is a world-wide revolutionary movement whose purpose it is, by treachery, deceit, infiltration into other groups (governmental and otherwise), espionage, sabotage, terrorism, and any other means deemed necessary, to establish a Communist totalitarian dictatorship in the countries throughout the world through the medium of a worldwide Communist organization....

(4) The direction and control of the world Communist movement is vested in and exercised by the Communist dictatorship of a foreign country.

(5) The Communist movement in the United States is an organization numbering thousands of adherents, rigidly and ruthlessly disciplined. Awaiting and seeking to advance a moment when the United States may be so far extended by foreign engagements, so far divided in counsel, or so far in industrial or financial straits, that overthrow of the Government of the United States by force and violence may seem possible of achievement, it seeks converts far and wide by an extensive system of schooling and indoctrination. Such preparations by Communist organizations in other countries have aided in supplanting existing governments. The Communist organization in the United States, pursuing its stated objectives, the recent successes of Communist methods in other countries, and the nature and control of the world Communist movement itself, present a clear and present danger to the security of the United States and to the existence of free American institutions, and make it necessary that Congress, in order to provide for the common defense, to preserve the sovereignty of the United States as an independent nation, and to guarantee to each State a republican form of government, enact appropriate legislation recognizing the existence of such world-wide conspiracy and designed to prevent it from accomplishing its purpose in the United States....

SEC. 4. (a) It shall be unlawful for any person knowingly to combine, conspire, or agree with any other person to perform any act which would substantially contribute to the establishment

within the United States of a totalitarian dictatorship, as defined
in paragraph (15) of section 3 of this title, the direction and control of which is to be vested in, or exercised by or under the
domination or control of, any foreign government, foreign
organization, or foreign individual: Provided, however, That this
subsection shall not apply to the proposal of a constitutional
amendment....

(f) Neither the holding of office nor membership in any
Communist organization by any person shall constitute per se a
violation of subsection (a) or subsection (c) of this section or of
any other criminal statute. The fact of the registration of any person under section 7 or section 8 of this title as an in officer or
member of any Communist organization shall not be received in
evidence against such person in any prosecution for a any alleged
violation of subsection (a) or subsection (c) of this section or for
any . alleged violation of any other criminal statue. . .

SEC. 7. (a) Each Communist action organization (including any
organization required, by a final order of the Board, to register as
a Communist-action organization) shall, within the time specified in subsection (c) of this section, register with the Attorney
General, or on a form prescribed by him by regulations, as a
Communist-action organize.

(b) Each Communist-front organization . . . shall . . register with
the Attorney General, on a form prescribed by him by regulations, as a Communist front organization....

(d) Upon the registration of each Communist organization under
the provisions of this title, the Attorney General shall publish in
the Federal Register the fact that such organization has registered as a Communist action organization, or as a Communist
front organization, as the case may be, and the publication
thereof shall constitute nor tice to all members of such organization that such organization has so registered.

SEC. 12. (a) There is hereby established a board, to be known as
the Subversive Ace tivities Control Board, which shall be cons
posed of five members, who shall be ap pointed by the President,
by and with the advice and consent of the Senate. Not more than
three members of the Board shall be members of the same political party. Two of the original members shall be appointed for a

term of one year, two for a term of two years, and one for a term of three years but their successors shall be appointed for terms of three years each, except that ale individual chosen to fill a vacancy shall be appointed only for the unexpired term of the member whom he shall succeed. The President shall designate one member to serve as Chairman of the Board. Any member of the Board may be removed by the President, upon notice and hearing, for neglect of duty or malfeasance in office, but for no other cause....

It shall be the duty of the Board— (I) upon application made by the Attorney General under section 13 (a) of this title, Or by any organization under section 13 (b) of this title, to determine whether any organization is a "Communist-action organization" within the meaning of paragraph (3) of section 3 of this title, or a "Communist-front organization" within the meaning of paragraph (4) of section 3 of this title; and

(2) upon application made by the Attorney General under section 13 (a) of this title, or by any individual under section 13 (b) of this title, to determine whether any individual is a member of any Communist-action organization registered, or by final order of the Board required to be registered, under section 7 (a) of this title....

Sec. 22. The Act of October 16, 191S . . . baby amended to read as follows: "That lien who is a member of any one of the following classes shall be excluded from adon into the United States: "(1) Aliens who seek to enter the United States whether solely, principally, or incidentally, to engage in activities which would be prejudicial to the public interest, or would endanger the welfare or safety of the United States;

"(2) Aliens who, at any time, shall be or shall have been members of any of the following classes:

"(A) Aliens who are anarchists;

"(B) Aliens who advocate or teach, or who are members of or affiliated with any organization that advocates or teaches, opposition to all organized government;

"(C) Aliens who are members of or affiliated with (i) the Communist Party of the United States; (ii) any other totalitarian party of the United States; (iii) the Communist Political Association; (iv) the Communist or other totalitarian party of any State of the United States, of any foreign state, or of any political or geographical subdivision of any foreign state; (v) any section, subsidiary, branch, affiliate, or subdivision of any such association or party; or (vi) the direct predecessors or successors of any such association or party, regardless of what name such group or organization may have used, may now bear, or may hereafter adopt;

"(D) Aliens not within any of the other provisions of this paragraph (2) who advocate the economic, international, and governmental doctrines of world communism or the economic and governmental doctrines of any other form of totalitarianism, or who are members of or affiliated with any organization that advocates the economic, international, and governmental doctrines of world communism, or the economic and governmental doctrines of any other form of totalitarianism, either through its own utterances or through any written or printed publications issued or published by or with the permission or consent of or under the authority of such organization or paid for by the funds of such organization....

"(F) Aliens who advocate or teach or who are members of or affiliated with any organization that advocates or teaches (i) the overthrow by force or violence or other unconstitutional means of the Government of the United States or of all forms of law; or (ii) the duty, necessity, or propriety of the unlawful assaulting or killing of any officer or officers (either of specific individuals or of officers generally) of the Government of the United States or of any other organized government, because of his or their official character; or (iii) the unlawful damage, injury, or destruction of property; or (iv) sabotage;

"(G) Aliens who write or publish, or cause to be written or published, or who knowingly circulate, distribute, print, or display, or knowingly cause to be circulated, distributed, printed, published, or displayed, or who knowingly have in their possession for the purpose of circulation, publications or display, any written or printed matter, advocating or teaching opposition to all organized government, or advocating (i) the overthrow by force or

violence or other unconstitutional means of the Government of
the United States or of ad forms of law, or (ii) the duty, necessity,
or propriety of the unlawful assaulting or killing of any officer or
officers (either of specific individuals or of officers generally) of
the Government of the United States or of any other organized
government; or (iii) the unlawful damage, injury, or destruction
of property; or (iv) sabotage; or (v) the economic, international,
and governmental doctrines of world communism or the economic and governmental doctrines of any other form of totalitarianism....

Sec 102. (a) In the event of any one of the following:

(1) Invasion of the territory of the United States or its possessions,

(2) Declaration of war by Congress, or

(3) Insurrection within the United

States in aid of a foreign enemy, a and if, upon the occurrence of
one or morel of the above, the President shall find that the
proclamation of an emergency pursuant to this section is essential
to the preservation, protection and defense of the Constitution,
and to the common defense and safety of the territory and people of the United States, the President is authorized to make
public proclamation of the existence of an "Internal Security
Emergency."

(b) A state of "Internal Security Emergency" (hereinafter referred
to as the "emergency") so declared shall continue in existence
until terminated by proclamation of the President or by concurrent resolution of the Congress....

SEC. 103. (a) Whenever there shall be in existence such an emergency, the President, acting through the Attorney General, is
hereby authorized to apprehend and by order detain, pursuant to
the provisions of this title, each person as to whom there is reasonable ground to believe that such person Probably will engage
in, or probably will con;pire with others to engage in, acts of
espionage or of sabotage....

Joseph McCarthy's speech on communists in the State Department (excerpt)

Ladies and Gentlemen:

Tonight as we celebrate the 141st birthday of one of the great men in American history, I would like to be able to talk about what a glorious day today is in the history of the world. As we celebrate the birth of this man, who with his whole heart and soul hated war, I would like to be able to speak of peace in our time, of war being outlawed, and of worldwide disarmament. These would be truly appropriate things to be able to mention as we celebrate the birthday of Abraham Lincoln.

Five years after a world war has been won, men's hearts should anticipate a long peace, and men's minds should be free from the heavy weight that comes with war. But this is not such a period—for this is not a period of peace. This is a time of the Cold War. This is a time when all the world is split into two vast, increasingly hostile armed camps—a time of a great armaments race. Today we can almost physically hear the mutterings and rumblings of an invigorated god of war. You can see it, feel it, and hear it all the way from the hills of Indochina, from the shores of Formosa right over into the very heart of Europe itself.

Today we are engaged in a final, all-out battle between communistic atheism and Christianity. The modern champions of communism have selected this as the time. And, ladies and gentlemen, the chips are down—they are truly down.

Lest there be any doubt that the time has been chosen, let us go directly to the leader of communism today—Joseph Stalin. Here is what he said—not back in 1928, not before the war, not during the war—but two years after the last war was ended: "To think that the communist revolution can be carried out peacefully, within the framework of a Christian democracy, means one has either gone out of one's mind and lost all normal understanding, or has grossly and openly repudiated the communist revolution."

And this is what was said by Lenin in 1919, which was also quoted with approval by Stalin in 1947: "We are living," said

Lenin, "not merely in a state but in a system of states, and the existence of the Soviet Republic side by side with Christian states for a long time is unthinkable. One or the other must triumph in the end. And before that end supervenes, a series of frightful collisions between the Soviet Republic and the bourgeois states will be inevitable."

Ladies and gentlemen, can there be anyone here tonight who is so blind as to say that the war is not on? Can there be anyone who fails to realize that the communist world has said, "The time is now"—that this is the time for the showdown between the democratic Christian world and the communist atheistic world? Unless we face this fact, we shall pay the price that must be paid by those who wait too long.

Six years ago, at the time of the first conference to map out peace—Dumbarton Oaks—there was within the Soviet orbit 180 million people. Lined up on the anti-totalitarian side there were in the world at that time roughly 1.625 billion people. Today, only six years later, there are 800 million people under the absolute domination of Soviet Russia—an increase of over 400 percent. On our side, the figure has shrunk to around 500 million. In other words, in less than six years the odds have changed from 9 to 1 in our favor to 8 to 5 against us. This indicates the swiftness of the tempo of communist victories and American defeats in the Cold War. As one of our outstanding historical figures once said, "When a great democracy is destroyed, it will not be because of enemies from without but rather because of enemies from within." The truth of this statement is becoming terrifyingly clear as we see this country each day losing on every front.

At war's end we were physically the strongest nation on Earth and, at least potentially, the most powerful intellectually and morally. Ours could have been the honor of being a beacon in the desert of destruction, a shining, living proof that civilization was not yet ready to destroy itself. Unfortunately, we have failed miserably and tragically to arise to the opportunity.

The reason why we find ourselves in a position of impotency is not because our only powerful, potential enemy has sent men to invade our shores, but rather because of the traitorous actions of those who have been treated so well by this nation. It has not been the less fortunate or members of minority groups who have been selling this nation out, but rather those who have had all the benefits that the wealthiest nation on earth has had to offer—the finest homes, the finest college education, and the finest jobs in government we can give.

This is glaringly true in the State Department. There the bright young men who are born with silver spoons in their mouths are the ones who have been worst.

Now I know it is very easy for anyone to condemn a particular bureau or department in general terms. Therefore, I would like to cite one rather unusual case—the case of a man who has done much to shape our foreign policy.

When Chiang Kai-shek was fighting our war, the State Department had in China a young man named John S. Service. His task, obviously, was not to work for the communization of China. Strangely, however, he sent official reports back to the State Department urging that we torpedo our ally Chiang Kai-shek and stating, in effect, that communism was the best hope of China.

Later, this man—John Service—was picked up by the Federal Bureau of Investigation for turning over to the communists secret State Department information. Strangely, however, he was never prosecuted. However, Joseph Grew, the undersecretary of state, who insisted on his prosecution, was forced to resign. Two days after, Grew's successor, Dean Acheson, took over as undersecretary of state, this man—John Service—who had been picked up by the FBI and who had previously urged that communism was the best hope of China, was not only reinstated in the State Department but promoted; and finally, under Acheson, placed in charge of all placements and promotions. Today, ladies and gentlemen, this man Service is on his way to represent the State Department and Acheson in Calcutta—by far and away the most important listening post in the Far East.

Now, let's see what happens when individuals with communist connections are forced out of the State Department. Gustave Duran, who was labeled as, I quote, "a notorious international communist," was made assistant secretary of state in charge of Latin American affairs. He was taken into the State Department from his job as a lieutenant colonel in the Communist International Brigade. Finally, after intense congressional pressure and criticism, he resigned in 1946 from the State Department— and, ladies and gentlemen, where do you think he is now? He took over a high-salaried job as chief of Cultural Activities Section in the office of the assistant secretary-general of the United Nations. ...

This, ladies and gentlemen, gives you somewhat of a picture of the type of individuals who have been helping to shape our foreign policy. In my opinion the State Department, which is one of the most important government departments, is thoroughly infested with communists.

I have in my hand 57 cases of individuals who would appear to be either card-carrying members or certainly loyal to the Communist Party, but who nevertheless are still helping to shape our foreign policy.

One thing to remember in discussing the communists in our government is that we are not dealing with spies who get 30 pieces of silver to steal the blueprints of new weapons. We are dealing with a far more sinister type of activity because it permits the enemy to guide and shape our policy.

This brings us down to the case of one Alger Hiss, who is important not as an individual anymore but rather because he is so representative of a group in the State Department. It is unnecessary to go over the sordid events showing how he sold out the nation which had given him so much. Those are rather fresh in all of our minds. However, it should be remembered that the facts in regard to his connection with this international communist spy ring were made known to the then-Undersecretary of State Berle three days after Hitler and Stalin signed the Russo-German Alliance Pact. At that time one Whittaker Chambers—who was also part of the spy ring—apparently decided that with Russia on Hitler's side, he could no longer betray our nation to Russia. He gave Undersecretary of State Berle—and this is all a matter of record—practically all, if not more, of the facts upon which Hiss' conviction was based.

Undersecretary Berle promptly contacted Dean Acheson and received word in return that Acheson, and I quote, "could vouch for Hiss absolutely"—at which time the matter was dropped. And this, you understand, was at a time when Russia was an ally of Germany. This condition existed while Russia and Germany were invading and dismembering Poland, and while the communist groups here were screaming "warmonger" at the United States for their support of the Allied nations.

Again in 1943, the FBI had occasion to investigate the facts surrounding Hiss' contacts with the Russian spy ring. But even after that FBI report was submitted, nothing was done.

Then, late in 1948—on August 5—when the Un-American Activities Committee called Alger Hiss to give an accounting, President Truman at once issued a presidential directive ordering all government agencies to refuse to turn over any information whatsoever in regard to the communist activities of any government employee to a congressional committee.

Incidentally, even after Hiss was convicted, it is interesting to note that the president still labeled the expose of Hiss as a "red herring."

If time permitted, it might be well to go into detail about the fact that Hiss was Roosevelt's chief adviser at Yalta when Roosevelt was admittedly in ill health and tired physically and mentally ... and when, according to the secretary of state, Hiss and Gromyko drafted the report on the conference.

According to the then-Secretary of State Stettinius, here are some of the things that Hiss helped to decide at Yalta: (1) the establishment of a European High Commission; (2) the treatment of Germany—this you will recall was the conference at which it was decided that we would occupy Berlin with Russia occupying an area completely encircling the city, which as you know, resulted in the Berlin airlift which cost 31 American lives; (3) the Polish question; (4) the relationship between UNRRA and the Soviet; (5) the rights of Americans on control commissions of Rumania, Bulgaria and Hungary; (6) Iran; (7) China—here's where we gave away Manchuria; (8) Turkish Straits question; (9) international trusteeships; (10) Korea.

Of the results of this conference, Arthur Bliss Lane of the State Department had this to say: "As I glanced over the document, I could not believe my eyes. To me, almost every line spoke of a surrender to Stalin."

As you hear this story of high treason, I know that you are saying to yourself, "Well, why doesn't the Congress do something about it?" Actually, ladies and gentlemen, one of the important reasons for the graft, the corruption, the dishonesty, the disloyalty, the treason in high government positions—one of the most important reasons why this continues—is a lack of moral uprising on the part of the 140 million American people. In the light of history, however, this is not hard to explain.

It is the result of an emotional hangover and a temporary moral lapse which follows every war. It is the apathy to evil which people who have been subjected to the tremendous evils of war feel. As the people of the world see mass murder, the destruction of defenseless and innocent people, and all of the crime and lack of morals which go with war, they become numb and apathetic. It has always been thus after war. However, the morals of our people have not been destroyed. They still exist. This cloak of numbness and apathy has only needed a spark to rekindle them. Happily, this spark has finally been supplied.

As you know, very recently the secretary of state proclaimed his loyalty to a man guilty of what has always been considered as the most abominable of all crimes—of being a traitor to the people who gave him a position of great trust. The secretary of state, in attempting to justify his continued devotion to the man who sold out the Christian world to the atheistic world, referred to Christ's Sermon on the Mount as a justification and reason therefore, and the reaction of the American people to this would have made the heart of Abraham Lincoln happy. When this pompous diplomat in striped pants, with a phony British accent, proclaimed to the American people that Christ on the Mount endorsed communism, high treason, and betrayal of a sacred trust, the blasphemy was so great that it awakened the dormant indignation of the American people.

He has lighted the spark which is resulting in a moral uprising and will end only when the whole sorry mess of twisted warped thinkers are swept from the national scene so that we may have a new birth of national honesty and decency in government.

Margaret Chase Smith: Declaration of Conscience

Mr. President:

I would like to speak briefly and simply about a serious national condition. It is a national feeling of fear and frustration that could result in national suicide and the end of everything that we Americans hold dear. It is a condition that comes from the lack of effective leadership in either the Legislative Branch or the Executive Branch of our Government.

That leadership is so lacking that serious and responsible proposals are being made that national advisory commissions be appointed to provide such critically needed leadership.

I speak as briefly as possible because too much harm has already been done with irresponsible words of bitterness and selfish political opportunism. I speak as briefly as possible because the issue is too great to be obscured by eloquence. I speak simply and briefly in the hope that my words will be taken to heart.

I speak as a Republican. I speak as a woman. I speak as a United States Senator. I speak as an American.

The United States Senate has long enjoyed worldwide respect as the greatest deliberative body in the world. But recently that deliberative character has too often been debased to the level of a forum of hate and character assassination sheltered by the shield of congressional immunity.

It is ironical that we Senators can in debate in the Senate directly or indirectly, by any form of words, impute to any American who is not a Senator any conduct or motive unworthy or unbecoming an American—and without that non-Senator American having any legal redress against us—yet if we say the same thing in the Senate about our colleagues we can be stopped on the grounds of being out of order.

It is strange that we can verbally attack anyone else without restraint and with full protection and yet we hold ourselves above the same type of criticism here on the Senate Floor. Surely the United States Senate is big enough to take self-criticism and self-appraisal. Surely we should be able to take the same kind of character attacks that we "dish out" to outsiders.

I think that it is high time for the United States Senate and its members to do some soul-searching—for us to weigh our consciences—on the manner in which we are performing our duty to the people of America—on the manner in which we are using or abusing our individual powers and privileges.

I think that it is high time that we remembered that we have sworn to uphold and defend the Constitution. I think that it is high time that we remembered that the Constitution, as amended, speaks not only of the freedom of speech but also of trial by jury instead of trial by accusation.

Whether it be a criminal prosecution in court or a character prosecution in the Senate, there is little practical distinction when the life of a person has been ruined.

Those of us who shout the loudest about Americanism in making character assassinations are all too frequently those who, by our own words and acts, ignore some of the basic principles of Americanism:

> The right to criticize;
>
> The right to hold unpopular beliefs;
>
> The right to protest;
>
> The right of independent thought.

The exercise of these rights should not cost one single American citizen his reputation or his right to a livelihood nor should he be in danger of losing his reputation or livelihood merely because he happens to know someone who holds unpopular beliefs. Who of us doesn't?   Otherwise none of us could call our souls our own. Otherwise thought control would have set in.

The American people are sick and tired of being afraid to speak their minds lest they be politically smeared as "Communists" or "Fascists" by their opponents.   Freedom of speech is not what it used to be in America.   It has been so abused by some that it is not exercised by others.

The American people are sick and tired of seeing innocent people smeared and guilty people whitewashed.   But there have been enough proved cases, such as the Amerasia case, the Hiss case, the Coplon case, the Gold case, to cause the nationwide distrust and strong suspicion that there may be something to the unproved, sensational accusations.

As a Republican, I say to my colleagues on this side of the aisle that the Republican Party faces a challenge today that is not unlike the challenge that it faced back in Lincoln's day. The Republican Party so successfully met that challenge that it emerged from the Civil War as the champion of a united nation—in addition to being a Party that unrelentingly fought loose spending and loose programs.

Today our country is being psychologically divided by the confusion and the suspicions that are bred in the United States Senate to spread like cancerous tentacles of "know nothing, suspect everything" attitudes. Today we have a Democratic Administration that has developed a mania for loose spending and loose programs. History is repeating itself—and the Republican Party again has the opportunity to emerge as the champion of unity and prudence.

The record of the present Democratic Administration has provided us with sufficient campaign issues without the necessity of resorting to political smears. America is rapidly losing its position as leader of the world simply because the Democratic Administration has pitifully failed to provide effective leadership.

The Democratic Administration has completely confused the American people by its daily contradictory grave warnings and optimistic assurances—that show the people that our Democratic Administration has no idea of where it is going.

The Democratic Administration has greatly lost the confidence of the American people by its complacency to the threat of communism here at home and the leak of vital secrets to Russia though key officials of the Democratic Administration. There are enough proved cases to make this point without diluting our criticism with unproved charges.

Surely these are sufficient reasons to make it clear to the American people that it is time for a change and that a Republican victory is necessary to the security of this country. Surely it is clear that this nation will continue to suffer as long as

it is governed by the present ineffective Democratic
Administration.

Yet to displace it with a Republican regime embracing a philosophy that lacks political integrity or intellectual honesty would
prove equally disastrous to this nation.   The nation sorely needs
a Republican victory.   But I don't want to see the Republican
Party ride to political victory on the Four Horsemen of
Calumny—Fear, Ignorance, Bigotry, and Smear.

I doubt if the Republican Party could—simply because I don't
believe the American people will uphold any political party that
puts political exploitation above national interest.   Surely we
Republicans aren't that desperate for victory.

I don't want to see the Republican Party win that way.   While it
might be a fleeting victory for the Republican Party, it would be
a more lasting defeat for the American people.   Surely it would
ultimately be suicide for the Republican Party and the two-party
system that has protected our American liberties from the dictatorship of a one party system.

As members of the Minority Party, we do not have the primary
authority to formulate the policy of our Government.   But we
do have the responsibility of rendering constructive criticism, of
clarifying issues, of allaying fears by acting as responsible citizens.

As a woman, I wonder how the mothers, wives, sisters, and
daughters feel about the way in which members of their families
have been politically mangled in the Senate debate—and I use
the word "debate" advisedly.

As a United States Senator, I am not proud of the way in which
the Senate has been made a publicity platform for irresponsible
sensationalism.   I am not proud of the reckless abandon in
which unproved charges have been hurled from the side of the
aisle.   I am not proud of the obviously staged, undignified coun-
tercharges that have been attempted in retaliation from the other
side of the aisle.

I don't like the way the Senate has been made a rendezvous for
vilification, for selfish political gain at the sacrifice of individual
reputations and national unity.   I am not proud of the way we
smear outsiders from the Floor of the Senate and hide behind the

cloak of congressional immunity and still place ourselves beyond criticism on the Floor of the Senate.

As an American, I am shocked at the way Republicans and Democrats alike are playing directly into the Communist design of "confuse, divide, and conquer." As an American, I don't want a Democratic Administration "whitewash" or "cover-up" any more than a want a Republican smear or witch hunt.

As an American, I condemn a Republican "Fascist" just as much I condemn a Democratic "Communist." I condemn a Democrat "Fascist" just as much as I condemn a Republican "Communist." They are equally dangerous to you and me and to our country. As an American, I want to see our nation recapture the strength and unity it once had when we fought the enemy instead of ourselves.

It is with these thoughts that I have drafted what I call a "Declaration of Conscience." I am gratified that Senator Tobey, Senator Aiken, Senator Morse, Senator Ives, Senator Thye, and Senator Hendrickson have concurred in that declaration and have authorized me to announce their concurrence.

Elizabeth Gurley Flynn:
Statement at the Smith Act Trial

MISS FLYNN: Your Honor, ladies and gentlemen, my name is Elizabeth Gurley Flynn. I am a defendant in this case, acting as my own attorney, and therefore have the opportunity to address you directly. It is unusual for a defendant to represent one's self, but my comrade, Mr. Pettis Perry and I have elected to do so. Neither of us is a lawyer. We will speak to you in the language of laymen and women, I should say.

We are both Communist leaders, proudly and avowedly. We are qualified to explain to you what the Communist Party of the U.S.A. really stands for, what it advocates, what its day-by-day activities are, and what are its ultimate aims. We will try to do so in simple, non-technical language. We will prove to you that we are not a criminal conspiracy but a 33-year-old working class political party, devoted to the immediate needs and aspirations of the American people, to the advancement of the workers, farmers and the Negro people, to the preservation of the democracy and culture, and to the advocacy of Socialism.

Our ideas may be new and strange to you. Probably you have never seen or met a Communist before. We don't ask you to agree with us but to listen with an open mind and not to accept as gospel truth the sensational tales of stool-pigeons and planted agents who will be the Government's chief, if not sole, witnesses.

Centuries ago, Judas became the symbol of such infamy, a forerunner of those who join a group of sincere and honest people, advocate its teachings, carry out its practices only to betray it.

★   ★   ★

MISS FLYNN: We will prove to you that we who stand ready to make extreme sacrifices for what we believe, are giving you a true picture of the purposes of the Communist Party. It is customary for a client to be introduced to the jury by his or her attorney. I am my own attorney. I must therefore, introduce myself. I am an American of Irish decent. My father, Thomas Flynn, was born in Maine. My mother, Anne Gurley, was born in Galway, Ireland. I was born in Concord, New Hampshire, 62 years ago. I married in 1908, separated from my husband shortly thereafter, and have always used my own name. My only son, Fred, died in 1940 at the age of 29 from a chest cancer. I reside with my sister, who is a retired school teacher. We have lived in New York City for the past 52 years. My mother was a skilled tailoress; my father a quarry worker who worked his way through the engineering school at Dartmouth College in New Hampshire. My father, grandfather, and all my uncles were members of labor unions.

★   ★   ★

MISS FLYNN: To continue, ladies and gentlemen, one of the essential issues in this case is my individual intent, the intent with which I joined the Communist Party and have remained a member of it, and the intent with which I have tried to carry out its program. My intent has been shaped out of my earlier experiences and my reaction   to the conditions of life, especially the conditions of the worker.

By showing you what my intent is and what in my life shaped the intent, I shall show you that never have I, and not now do I, intend to advocate the overthrow of government by force and violence, nor do I intend to bring about such overthrow.

I come from a family whose day-by-day diet included important social issues of the day, and form this I early learned to question things as they are and to seek improvements. Thus, my mother advocated Women's Suffrage, and my father and mother-

★   ★   ★

MISS FLYNN: -and my father and mother discussed with their children the campaigns of Debs, the Socialist candidate for President.

My father read aloud to me and to my brother and sisters such books as the Communist Manifesto and other writings of Marx and Engels, which the Government will use as evidence in this trial. I was a serious child, due probably to these childish impressions which are background to my affiliation in my extreme youth with the Socialist movement and in my mature years with the Communist Party.

Times were hard. We were poor. My first experience with discrimination was in Manchester, New Hampshire, when my father ran for city engineer about 1895. I heard it said he was defeated because he was Irish. He was very bitter on this subject and told us of signs on factories when he was a boy, "No Irish need apply."

Our parents opposed all forms of national, religious or color discrimination, which we will prove is identical with the position of the Communist Party today and form the basis of the position I take today in the Communist Party.

My first knowledge of the meaning of imperialism, which will be an issue in this case, was a vivid recollection of my father's opposition to the Spanish-American War and his insistence on the right of the Cuban and Philippine peoples to their independence. He joined an anti-imperialist league to protest against our country embarking on the evil path of imperialism, which we will prove began at that time.

The conditions in the textile towns of New Hampshire and Massachusetts contributed to my later joining the Communist Party, which, as Mr. Lane says, concentrates on the recruiting of workers in industry: huge gray mills, like prisons, barrack-like company boarding houses, long hours, low wages, long periods of slack; the prosperous owner lived in the center of Adams, Massachusetts, and rode around in his fine carriage with its beautiful horses. I saw lard instead of butter on neighbors' tables, children without underwear in cold New England winters, a girl scalped by an unguarded machine in a mill across the street from our school. I saw an old man weeping as they put him in the lock-up as a tramp.

Then we came to live in the drab South Bronx, near the New Haven Railroad's roundhouse, in a cold water, unheated, gas-lit flat. Casualties and accidents were high among the railroad workers. Children were maimed as they gathered coal in the yards in bad times. My mother helped women in the neighborhood who could not afford a doctor when a baby came.

★   ★   ★

MISS FLYNN: Yes, I was greatly troubled by all this. Why did good hard-working people suffer so? Why were men who were willing, able, and anxious to work, denied jobs? Why was there so much unemployment? Why were there rich people who apparently did little but enjoyed life? I hated poverty. I saw my mother humiliated when unpaid grocery bills could not be met and the landlord stood at the door demanding his rent.

★   ★   ★

MISS FLYNN: I joined a debating society in P.S. 9 in the lower Bronx. I won a medal in a debate on the subject, "Should the Government own the mines?" I said, "Yes, it should."

This was during the great anthracite coal strike in 1902. I attended Bronx Socialist meeting in 1905; later at the Harlem Socialist Club at 125th Street. My speaking career started in 1906 on the ambitious subject of women under socialism. Naturally, I drew heavily on authors, American women, like Charlotte Petingill and Susan B. Anthony, also on a book written

in 1872 by Augustus Bebel, a Socialist member of the German
Reichstag, written while he was in prison under Bismarck's anti-
Socialist law.   It was first published here by the Socialist Labor
Party in 1904.   I am puzzled to see it on the Government's list
of documents.   What relation it has to this indictment is hard to
fathom, unless to advocate the full political, economic, and social
emancipation of women has become a form of advocacy of the
overthrow of government by force and violence under the
Government's interpretation of the Smith Act.   But if this historic and economic study, which is very much out of date today,
is to be finely tooth-combed for sentences which torn out of
context can distort its meaning, this, we will prove, can be done
to any book, no matter what its purpose, even to the Bible,
Shakespeare, or Gray's Anatomy.

My youthful ambition, believe it or not, was to be a constitutional lawyer.   Instead, I became a labor organizer.   Then it was
call an agitator, or, by the press, one who stirred up the people.
I was determined to do something about the bad conditions
under which our family and all around us suffered.   I have stuck
to that purpose for 46 years.   I consider in so doing I have been
a good American.   I have spent my life among the American
workers all over this country, slept in their homes, eaten at their
tables.   They are the majority of the people who have the
inalienable right in our view to govern the country.   We mean
by workers, all who do useful work of hand or brain.   My life
work began when I joined the I.W.W., Industrial Workers of the
World, in 1906, a pioneer in industrial unions which flashed like
a great comet across the horizon of the American labor movement for nearly two decades.   I returned as an I.W.W. organizer
in 1912 to New England, my birthplace, where the I.W.W. led
historical textile strikes in Lawrence, Lowell, and New Bedford,
Massachusetts.   The strikes were unorganized, largely foreign-
born men and women whose wages were cut when their hours
were reduced by Massachusetts law.

★   ★   ★

MISS FLYNN: In 1913 I was a leader in the Paterson, New
Jersey silk strike; in 1916, in a strike of the iron ore miners on
the Mesaba range in Minnesota, where the mines are owned by

the U.S. Street trust, I will attempt to prove to you that it is not the Communists who advocate and use force and violence. I saw it used in all of these labor struggles, not by the workers but by police, company guards and State militia. I saw workers clubbed, beaten and shot down. I spoke-

★   ★   ★

MISS FLYNN: My travels as a Communist speaker have taken me all over the country. I saw the fruits of a lawless, aggressive, brutal and ruthless capitalism which garnered profits for a few at the expense of the many.

Our country is a rich and beautiful country, fully capable of producing plenty for all, educating its youth and caring for its aged. We believe it could do this under Socialism. I saw great forests cut down and the denuded land left with blackened stumps; miles of top soil blown and washed away, and fertile fields became like a desert.

I have seen textile workers who wove beautiful woolen fabrics shivering for lack of warm clothing, and coal miners living in cold shacks in company towns, and steel towns that were armed camps. I saw men black-listed, driven from town to town, forced to change their names because they had dared to try to organize a union.

We will prove to you that it is not the Communists who have advocated or practiced force and violence but that it is the employing class which has done both throughout the history of my life in the American labor movement, like General Sherman Bell who said in Colorado during a miner's strike "To Hell with habeas corpus; we'll give them post-mortems."

We will prove to you that-

★   ★   ★

MISS FLYNN: We will prove to you that it is nor we who flaunt the Constitution and the Bill of Rights, but that is has always been done by the employing class. We will prove that we are fighting here for our constitutional and democratic rights, not to advocate force and violence, but to expose and stop its use against the people.

We will demonstrate that in fighting for our rights, we believe we are defending the constitutional rights of all Americans. We believe we are acting as good Americans.

Since six out of eleven of my writings in Political Affairs listed by the Government deal with what is called defense, I will prove to you that this has been a part of my life work since 1907 before there was a Communist Party.

For example, I distributed thousands of copies of a famous document in the '20's called "Illegal Practices of the Department of Justice," which is not among the Government's exhibits of old-time documents, but which I would gladly offer to the jury. It was signed by twelve of the most prominent lawyers of that period, including Professors Frankfurter and Chafee of Harvard and Francis Fisher Kane, who resigned his post as United States Attorney in Philadelphia in protest against such proceedings.

I early engaged in struggles to win free speech on the streets and in halls. This early identification with civil liberties led to my becoming a charter member of the American Civil liberties Union in 1917, and later the organizer of the Workers Defense Union, a delegate body from unions and fraternal organizations which furnished legal defense in political and labor prosecutions.

We had plenty to do during the infamous 1920 Palmer Red Raids. We defended Socialist: I defended Socialists-

★   ★   ★

MISS FLYNN: I worked for seven years in the unsuccessful struggles to save the lives of Sacco and Vanzetti. In the Government's list of exhibits is an article I wrote in August, 1947 entitled "Sacco and Vanzetti-Twenty Years After," in which I pointed out the world-wide belief in their innocence.

★   ★   ★

MISS FLYNN: Now I will show how and why I left the I.W.W. and joined the Communist Party. This bears directly on the issue of forcible overthrow of the government that Mr. Lane spoke to you about this morning. After careful reflection, it became clear to me that the I.W.W. was an anarcho-syndicalist organization. The I.W.W. wanted to bring Socialism within

Capitalism and then break through the shell of Capitalism by the general strike and the seizing and possession of industry. Now, it was precisely this position that I rejected.

I came to the conclusion that Socialism could be achieved, not by one splurge of violence, but by the persistent political activities of the workers and the people. And so in order to participate in political activities in the effort to achieve Socialism, I joined the Communist Party. In doing this, I got back into the labor movement and stopped being what I then had decided was anarchistic.

★   ★   ★

MISS FLYNN: I have handbills, advertisements and press clipping relative to hundreds of public mass meetings arranged by the Communist Party at which I and other defendants have spoken in the past 15 years. We will prove that nowhere has there been any advocacy of force and violence. The subject matter of such meetings should interest this jury, I believe, however, as evidence of our intent.

Take some at random: "The Struggle Against the Taft-Hartley Law" - "The Rights of the Negro People" –

★   ★   ★

MISS FLYNN: We have believed that under the Bill of Rights we have a right to advocate our views, but since our ideas are here on trial we feel we have a sacred duty to ourselves and to our Party to adequately defend them from any slander or distortion.

We contend that Americans have a right to speak their minds out on any subject. We Communists have a right to defend socialism or the evolution of the capitalist system and economy and of the private ownership of the means of life of all the people.

We will prove that such a change can and will be achieved, only when the majority of the American people are ready and willing to make it, and that the Communist Party does not advocate force and violence to effect such a change.

We will try to prove to you during this trial the meaning of working class internationalism, which the Government will use to bolster up their theory of foreign agent.

Abraham Lincoln said: "The strongest bond of human sympathy, outside the family relation, should be one uniting all working people of all nations and tongues, and kindred." Both May Day and International Women's Day, we will prove, had their origin here in the United States even though they are now celebrated internationally.

We are here before you as defendants in the Smith Act case. We will prove to you that we are not conspirators, but that we are animated and united by common ideals and aspirations, with courage to affirm our beliefs, faith in the people and the future, and a willingness to sacrifice for a better world, which we are confident is in birth. Nevertheless, it is incumbent on the Government, regardless of our ideological unity, to deal with us as individuals, and not to lump us together as a conspiracy because of the identity of our political views. We will try to bring you a true and accurate picture of who we are, what our lives have been, what we say and mean, what we live by day by day and the relation of all this immediate activity to our ultimate aims. We will try to present to you during this trial our theories and work, our program, and our ultimate goal, the unity of theory and practice as it says in the books. We will not do this in a classroom atmosphere, but so that you can understand us, in terms of our own knowledge and experience, regardless of whether you agree with us. We expect to convince you that we are within our established constitutional rights to advocate change and progress, to advocate Socialism, which we are convinced will guarantee to all our people in our great and beautiful country the rights of life, liberty, and the pursuit of happiness. Whether we are right is no issue here, and no jury, in this or any other trial, but time alone, will decide. Let none of us forget, especially in this trial in dealing with new ideas and proposals for social change, the wise words of Abraham Lincoln:

"This country with its institutions belongs to the people who inhabit it."

We are asking you to decide this case on the evidence, or, more correctly, may I say, on the lack of evidence which we are confident will be glaringly revealed long before this trial is over, to decide this case on the exact issues, regardless of fear or favor or the hysteria or prejudice which we all know very well does exist among some groups in the community. We ask you to keep your minds open until all the evidence, including our own, is before you. Then you will be shown that we do not advocate the overthrow of the Government of the United States by force and violence.

"You Are the Un-Americans, and You Ought to be Ashamed of Yourselves": Paul Robeson Appears Before HUAC

Testimony of Paul Robeson before the House Committee on Un-American Activities, June 12, 1956

THE CHAIRMAN: The Committee will be in order. This morning the Committee resumes its series of hearings on the vital issue of the use of American passports as travel documents in furtherance of the objectives of the Communist conspiracy. . . .

Mr. ARENS: Now, during the course of the process in which you were applying for this passport, in July of 1954, were you requested to submit a non-Communist affidavit?

Mr. ROBESON: We had a long discussion—with my counsel, who is in the room, Mr. [Leonard B.] Boudin—with the State Department, about just such an affidavit and I was very precise not only in the application but with the State Department, headed by Mr. Henderson and Mr. McLeod, that under no conditions would I think of signing any such affidavit, that it is a complete contradiction of the rights of American citizens.

Mr. ARENS: Did you comply with the requests?

Mr. ROBESON: I certainly did not and I will not.

Mr. ARENS: Are you now a member of the Communist Party?

Mr. ROBESON: Oh please, please, please.

Mr. SCHERER: Please answer, will you, Mr. Robeson?

Mr. ROBESON: What is the Communist Party? What do you mean by that?

Mr. SCHERER: I ask that you direct the witness to answer the question.

Mr. ROBESON: What do you mean by the Communist Party? As far as I know it is a legal party like the Republican Party and the Democratic Party. Do you mean a party of people who have sacrificed for my people, and for all Americans and workers, that they can live in dignity? Do you mean that party?

Mr. ARENS: Are you now a member of the Communist Party?

Mr. ROBESON: Would you like to come to the ballot box when I vote and take out the ballot and see?

Mr. ARENS: Mr. Chairman, I respectfully suggest that the witness be ordered and directed to answer that question.

THE CHAIRMAN: You are directed to answer the question.

(The witness consulted with his counsel.)

Mr. ROBESON: I stand upon the Fifth Amendment of the American Constitution.

Mr. ARENS: Do you mean you invoke the Fifth Amendment?

Mr. ROBESON: I invoke the Fifth Amendment.

Mr. ARENS: Do you honestly apprehend that if you told this Committee truthfully—

Mr. ROBESON: I have no desire to consider anything. I invoke the Fifth Amendment, and it is none of your business what I would like to do, and I invoke the Fifth Amendment. And forget it.

THE CHAIRMAN: You are directed to answer that question.

MR, ROBESON: I invoke the Fifth Amendment, and so I am answering it, am I not?

Mr. ARENS: I respectfully suggest the witness be ordered and directed to answer the question as to whether or not he honestly apprehends, that if he gave us a truthful answer to this last principal question, he would be supplying information which might be used against him in a criminal proceeding.

(The witness consulted with his counsel.)

THE CHAIRMAN: You are directed to answer that question, Mr. Robeson.

Mr. ROBESON: Gentlemen, in the first place, wherever I have been in the world, Scandinavia, England, and many places, the first to die in the struggle against Fascism were the Communists and I laid many wreaths upon graves of Communists. It is not criminal, and the Fifth Amendment has nothing to do with criminality. The Chief Justice of the Supreme Court, Warren, has been very clear on that in many speeches, that the Fifth Amendment does not have anything to do with the inference of criminality. I invoke the Fifth Amendment.

Mr. ARENS: Have you ever been known under the name of "John Thomas"?

Mr. ROBESON: Oh, please, does somebody here want—are you suggesting—do you want me to be put up for perjury some place? "John Thomas"! My name is Paul Robeson, and anything I have to say, or stand for, I have said in public all over the world, and that is why I am here today.

Mr. SCHERER: I ask that you direct the witness to answer the question. He is making a speech.

Mr. FRIEDMAN: Excuse me, Mr. Arens, may we have the photographers take their pictures, and then desist, because it is rather nerve-racking for them to be there.

THE CHAIRMAN: They will take the pictures.

Mr. ROBESON: I am used to it and I have been in moving pictures. Do you want me to pose for it good? Do you want me to smile? I cannot smile when I am talking to him.

Mr. ARENS: I put it to you as a fact, and ask you to affirm or deny the fact, that your Communist Party name was "John Thomas."

Mr. ROBESON: I invoke the Fifth Amendment. This is really ridiculous.

Mr. ARENS: Now, tell this Committee whether or not you know Nathan Gregory Silvermaster.

Mr. SCHERER: Mr. Chairman, this is not a laughing matter.

Mr. ROBESON: It is a laughing matter to me, this is really complete nonsense.

Mr. ARENS: Have you ever known Nathan Gregory Silvermaster?

(The witness consulted with his counsel.)

Mr. ROBESON: I invoke the Fifth Amendment.

Mr. ARENS: Do you honestly apprehend that if you told whether you know Nathan Gregory Silvermaster you would be supplying information that could be used against you in a criminal proceeding?

Mr. ROBESON: I have not the slightest idea what you are talking about. I invoke the Fifth—

Mr. ARENS: I suggest, Mr. Chairman, that the witness be directed to answer that question.

THE CHAIRMAN: You are directed to answer the question.

Mr. ROBESON: I invoke the Fifth.

Mr. SCHERER: The witness talks very loud when he makes a speech, but when he invokes the Fifth Amendment I cannot hear him.

Mr. ROBESON: I invoked the Fifth Amendment very loudly. You know I am an actor, and I have medals for diction.

★   ★   ★

Mr. ROBESON: Oh, gentlemen, I thought I was here about some passports.

Mr. ARENS: We will get into that in just a few moments.

Mr. ROBESON: This is complete nonsense.

★   ★   ★

THE CHAIRMAN: This is legal. This is not only legal but usual. By a unanimous vote, this Committee has been instructed to perform this very distasteful task.

Mr. ROBESON: To whom am I talking?

THE CHAIRMAN: You are speaking to the Chairman of this Committee.

Mr. ROBESON: Mr. Walter?

THE CHAIRMAN: Yes.

Mr. ROBESON: The Pennsylvania Walter?

THE CHAIRMAN: That is right.

Mr. ROBESON: Representative of the steelworkers?

THE CHAIRMAN: That is right.

Mr. ROBESON: Of the coal-mining workers and not United States Steel, by any chance? A great patriot.

THE CHAIRMAN: That is right.

Mr. ROBESON: You are the author of all of the bills that are going to keep all kinds of decent people out of the country.

THE CHAIRMAN: No, only your kind.

Mr. ROBESON: Colored people like myself, from the West Indies and all kinds. And just the Teutonic Anglo-Saxon stock that you would let come in.

THE CHAIRMAN: We are trying to make it easier to get rid of your kind, too.

Mr. ROBESON: You do not want any colored people to come in?

THE CHAIRMAN: Proceed. . . .

Mr. ROBESON: Could I say that the reason that I am here today, you know, from the mouth of the State Department itself, is: I should not be allowed to travel because I have struggled for years for the independence of the colonial peoples of Africa. For many years I have so labored and I can say modestly that my name is very much honored all over Africa, in my struggles for their independence. That is the kind of independence like Sukarno got in Indonesia. Unless we are double-talking, then these efforts in the interest of Africa would be in the same context. The other reason that I am here today, again from the State Department and from the court record of the court of appeals, is that when I am abroad I speak out against the injustices against the Negro people of this land. I sent a message to the Bandung Conference and so forth. That is why I am here. This is the basis, and I am not being tried for whether I am a Communist, I am being tried for fighting for the rights of my people, who are still second-class citizens in this United States of America. My mother was born in your state, Mr. Walter, and my mother was a Quaker, and my ancestors in the time of Washington baked bread for George Washington's troops when they crossed the Delaware, and my own father was a slave. I stand here struggling for the rights of my people to be full citizens in this country. And they are not. They are not in Mississippi. And they are not in Montgomery, Alabama. And they are not in Washington. They are nowhere, and that is why I am here today. You want to shut up every Negro who has the courage to stand up and fight for the rights of his people, for the rights of workers, and I have been on many a picket line for the steelworkers too. And that is why I am here today. . . .

Mr. ARENS: Did you make a trip to Europe in 1949 and to the Soviet Union?

Mr. ROBESON: Yes, I made a trip. To England. And I sang.

Mr. ARENS: Where did you go?

Mr. ROBESON: I went first to England, where I was with the Philadelphia Orchestra, one of two American groups which was invited to England. I did a long concert tour in England and Denmark and Sweden, and I also sang for the Soviet people, one of the finest musical audiences in the world. Will you read what the Porgy and Bess people said? They never heard such applause in their lives. One of the most musical peoples in the world, and the great composers and great musicians, very cultured people, and Tolstoy, and—

THE CHAIRMAN: We know all of that.

Mr. ROBESON: They have helped our culture and we can learn a lot.

Mr. ARENS: Did you go to Paris on that trip?

Mr. ROBESON: I went to Paris.

Mr. ARENS: And while you were in Paris, did you tell an audience there that the American Negro would never go to war against the Soviet government?

Mr. ROBESON: May I say that is slightly out of context? May I explain to you what I did say? I remember the speech very well, and the night before, in London, and do not take the newspaper, take me: I made the speech, gentlemen, Mr. So-and-So. It happened that the night before, in London, before I went to Paris . . . and will you please listen?

Mr. ARENS: We are listening.

Mr. ROBESON: Two thousand students from various parts of the colonial world, students who since then have become very important in their governments, in places like Indonesia and India, and in many parts of Africa, two thousand students asked me and Mr. [Dr. Y. M.] Dadoo, a leader of the Indian people in South Africa, when we addressed this conference, and remember I was speaking to a peace conference, they asked me and Mr. Dadoo to say there that they were struggling for peace, that they did not want war against anybody. Two thousand students who came from populations that would range to six or seven hundred million people.

Mr. KEARNEY: Do you know anybody who wants war?

Mr. ROBESON: They asked me to say in their name that they did not want war. That is what I said. No part of my speech made in Paris says fifteen million American Negroes would do anything. I said it was my feeling that the American people would struggle for peace, and that has since been underscored by the President of these United States. Now, in passing, I said—

Mr. KEARNEY: Do you know of any people who want war?

Mr. ROBESON: Listen to me. I said it was unthinkable to me that any people would take up arms, in the name of an Eastland, to go against anybody. Gentlemen, I still say that. This United States Government should go down to Mississippi and protect my people. That is what should happen.

THE CHAIRMAN: Did you say what was attributed to you?

Mr. ROBESON: I did not say it in that context.

Mr. ARENS: I lay before you a document containing an article, "I Am Looking for Full Freedom," by Paul Robeson, in a publication called the Worker, dated July 3, 1949.

At the Paris Conference I said it was unthinkable that the Negro people of America or elsewhere in the world could be drawn into war with the Soviet Union.

Mr. ROBESON: Is that saying the Negro people would do anything? I said it is unthinkable. I did not say that there [in Paris]: I said that in the Worker.

Mr. ARENS:

I repeat it with hundredfold emphasis: they will not.

Did you say that?

Mr. ROBESON: I did not say that in Paris, I said that in America. And, gentlemen, they have not yet done so, and it is quite clear that no Americans, no people in the world probably, are going to war with the Soviet Union. So I was rather prophetic, was I not?

Mr. ARENS: On that trip to Europe, did you go to Stockholm?

Mr. ROBESON: I certainly did, and I understand that some people in the American Embassy tried to break up my concert. They were not successful.

Mr. ARENS: While you were in Stockholm, did you make a little speech?

Mr. ROBESON: I made all kinds of speeches, yes.

Mr. ARENS: Let me read you a quotation.

Mr. ROBESON: Let me listen.

Mr. ARENS: Do so, please.

Mr. ROBESON: I am a lawyer.

Mr. KEARNEY: It would be a revelation if you would listen to counsel.

Mr. ROBESON: In good company, I usually listen, but you know people wander around in such fancy places. Would you please let me read my statement at some point?

THE CHAIRMAN: We will consider your statement.

Mr. ARENS:

I do not hesitate one second to state clearly and unmistakably: I belong to the American resistance movement which fights against American imperialism, just as the resistance movement fought against Hitler.

Mr. ROBESON: Just like Frederick Douglass and Harriet Tubman were underground railroaders, and fighting for our freedom, you bet your life.

THE CHAIRMAN: I am going to have to insist that you listen to these questions.

MR, ROBESON: I am listening.

Mr. ARENS:

If the American warmongers fancy that they could win America's millions of Negroes for a war against those countries (i.e., the Soviet Union and the peoples' democracies) then they ought to understand that this will never be the case. Why should the Negroes ever fight against the only nations of the world where racial discrimination is prohibited, and where the people can live freely? Never! I can assure you, they will never fight against either the Soviet Union or the peoples' democracies.

Did you make that statement?

Mr. ROBESON: I do not remember that. But what is perfectly clear today is that nine hundred million other colored people have told you that they will not. Four hundred million in India, and millions everywhere, have told you, precisely, that the colored people are not going to die for anybody: they are going to die for their independence. We are dealing not with fifteen million colored people, we are dealing with hundreds of millions.

Mr. KEARNEY: The witness has answered the question and he does not have to make a speech. . . .

Mr. ROBESON: In Russia I felt for the first time like a full human being. No color prejudice like in Mississippi, no color prejudice like in Washington. It was the first time I felt like a human being. Where I did not feel the pressure of color as I feel [it] in this Committee today.

Mr. SCHERER: Why do you not stay in Russia?

Mr. ROBESON: Because my father was a slave, and my people died to build this country, and I am going to stay here, and have a part of it just like you. And no Fascist-minded people will drive me from it. Is that clear? I am for peace with the Soviet Union, and I am for peace with China, and I am not for peace or friendship with the Fascist Franco, and I am not for peace with Fascist Nazi Germans. I am for peace with decent people.

Mr. SCHERER: You are here because you are promoting the Communist cause.

Mr. ROBESON: I am here because I am opposing the neo-Fascist cause which I see arising in these committees. You are like the Alien [and] Sedition Act, and Jefferson could be sitting here, and Frederick Douglass could be sitting here, and Eugene Debs could be here.

★   ★   ★

THE CHAIRMAN: Now, what prejudice are you talking about? You were graduated from Rutgers and you were graduated from the University of Pennsylvania. I remember seeing you play football at Lehigh.

Mr. ROBESON: We beat Lehigh.

THE CHAIRMAN: And we had a lot of trouble with you.

Mr. ROBESON: That is right. DeWysocki was playing in my team.

THE CHAIRMAN: There was no prejudice against you. Why did you not send your son to Rutgers?

Mr. ROBESON: Just a moment. This is something that I challenge very deeply, and very sincerely: that the success of a few Negroes, including myself or Jackie Robinson can make up—and here is a study from Columbia University—for seven hundred dollars a year for thousands of Negro families in the South. My father was a slave, and I have cousins who are sharecroppers, and I do not see my success in terms of myself. That is the reason my own success has not meant what it should mean: I have sacrificed literally hundreds of thousands, if not millions, of dollars for what I believe in.

Mr. ARENS: While you were in Moscow, did you make a speech lauding Stalin?

Mr. ROBESON: I do not know.

Mr. ARENS: Did you say, in effect, that Stalin was a great man, and Stalin had done much for the Russian people, for all of the nations of the world, for all working people of the earth? Did you say something to that effect about Stalin when you were in Moscow?

Mr. ROBESON: I cannot remember.

Mr. ARENS: Do you have a recollection of praising Stalin?

Mr. ROBESON: I said a lot about Soviet people, fighting for the peoples of the earth.

Mr. ARENS: Did you praise Stalin?

Mr. ROBESON: I do not remember.

Mr. ARENS: Have you recently changed your mind about Stalin?

Mr. ROBESON: Whatever has happened to Stalin, gentlemen, is a question for the Soviet Union, and I would not argue with a representative of the people who, in building America, wasted sixty to a hundred million lives of my people, black people drawn from Africa on the plantations. You are responsible, and your forebears, for sixty million to one hundred million black people dying in the slave ships and on the plantations, and don't ask me about anybody, please.

Mr. ARENS: I am glad you called our attention to that slave problem. While you were in Soviet Russia, did you ask them there to show you the slave labor camps?

THE CHAIRMAN: You have been so greatly interested in slaves, I should think that you would want to see that.

Mr. ROBESON: The slaves I see are still in a kind of semiserfdom. I am interested in the place I am, and in the country that can do something about it. As far as I know, about the slave camps, they were Fascist prisoners who had murdered millions of the Jewish people, and who would have wiped out millions of the Negro people, could they have gotten a hold of them. That is all I know about that.

Mr. ARENS: Tell us whether or not you have changed your opinion in the recent past about Stalin.

Mr. ROBESON: I have told you, mister, that I would not discuss anything with the people who have murdered sixty million of my people, and I will not discuss Stalin with you.

Mr. ARENS: You would not, of course, discuss with us the slave labor camps in Soviet Russia.

Mr. ROBESON: I will discuss Stalin when I may be among the Russian people some day, singing for them, I will discuss it there. It is their problem.

★   ★   ★

Mr. ARENS: Now I would invite your attention, if you please, to the Daily Worker of June 29, 1949, with reference to a get-together with you and Ben Davis. Do you know Ben Davis?

Mr. ROBESON: One of my dearest friends, one of the finest Americans you can imagine, born of a fine family, who went to Amherst and was a great man.

THE CHAIRMAN: The answer is yes?

Mr. ROBESON: Nothing could make me prouder than to know him.

THE CHAIRMAN: That answers the question.

Mr. ARENS: Did I understand you to laud his patriotism?

Mr. ROBESON: I say that he is as patriotic an American as there can be, and you gentlemen belong with the Alien and Sedition Acts, and you are the nonpatriots, and you are the un-Americans, and you ought to be ashamed of yourselves.

THE CHAIRMAN: Just a minute, the hearing is now adjourned.

Mr. ROBESON: I should think it would be.

THE CHAIRMAN: I have endured all of this that I can.

Mr. ROBESON: Can I read my statement?

THE CHAIRMAN: No, you cannot read it. The meeting is adjourned.

Mr. ROBESON: I think it should be, and you should adjourn this forever, that is what I would say. . . .

Globalizing American Power

A Study of Assassination: A CIA Manual for Guatemala

DEFINITION

Assassination is a term thought to be derived from "Hashish", a drug similar to marijuana, said to have been used by Hasan-Dan-Sabah to induce motivation in his followers, who were assigned to carry out political and other murders, usually at the cost of their lives.

It is here used to describe the planned killing of a person who is not under the legal jurisdiction of the killer, who is not physically in the hands of the killer, who has been selected by a resistance organization for death, and who has been sele cted by a resistance organization for death, and whose death provides positive advantages to that organization.

EMPLOYMENT

Assassination is an extreme measure not normally used in clandestine operations. It should be assumed that it will never be ordered or authorized by any U.S. Headquarters, though the latter may in rare instances agree to its execution by members of an associated foreign service. This reticence is partly due to the necessity for committing communications to paper. No assassination instructions should ever be written or recorded. Consequently, the decision to employ this technique must nearly always be reached in the field, at the area where the act will take place. Decision and instructions should be confined to an absolute minimum of persons. Ideally, only one person will be involved. No report may be made, but usually the act will be pr operly covered by normal news services, whose output is available to all concerned.

JUSTIFICATION

Murder is not morally justifiable. Self-defense may be argued if the victim has knowledge which may destroy the resistance organization if divulged. Assassination of persons responsible for atrocities or reprisals may be regarded as just puni shment. Killing a political leader whose burgeoning career is a clear and present danger to the cause of freedom may be held necessary.

But assassination can seldom be employed with a clear conscience. Persons who are morally squeamish should not attempt it.

CLASSIFICATIONS

The techniques employed will vary according to whether the subject is unaware of his danger, aware but unguarded, or guarded. They will also be affected by whether or not the assassin is to be killed with the subject hereafter, assassinations in which the subject is unaware will be termed "simple"; those where the subject is aware but unguarded will be termed "chase"; those where the victim is guarded will be termed "guarded."

If the assassin is to die with the subject, the act will be called "lost." If the assassin is to escape, the adjective will be "safe." It should be noted that no compromises should exist here. The assassin must not fall alive into enemy hands.

A further type division is caused by the need to conceal the fact that the subject was actually the victim of assassination, rather than an accident or natural causes. If such concealment is desirable the operation will be called "secret" ;; if concealment is immaterial, the act will be called "open"; while if the assassination requires publicity to be effective it will be termed "terroristic."

Following these definitions, the assassination of Julius Caesar was safe, simple, and terroristic, while that of Huey Long was lost, guarded and open. Obviously, successful secret assassinations are not recorded as assassination at all. [Illeg] o f Thailand and Augustus Caesar may have been the victims of safe, guarded and secret assassination. Chase assassinations usually involve clandestine agents or members of criminal organizations.

THE ASSASSIN

In safe assassinations, the assassin needs the usual qualities of a clandestine agent. He should be determined, courageous, intelligent, resourceful, and physically active. If special equipment is to be used, such as firearms or drugs, it is clear that he must have outstanding skill with such equipment.

Except in terroristic assassinations, it is desirable that the assassin be transient in the area. He should have an absolute minimum of contact with the rest of the organization and his instructions should be given orally by one person only. His safe evacuation after the act is absolutely essential, but here again contact should be as limited as possible. It is preferable that the person issuing instructions also conduct any withdrawal or covering action which may be necessary.

In lost assassination, the assassin must be a fanatic of some sort. Politics, religion, and revenge are about the only feasible motives. Since a fanatic is unstable psychologically, he must be handled with extreme care. He must not know the iden tities of the other members of the organization, for although it is intended that he die in the act, something may go wrong. While the Assassin of Trotsky has never revealed any significant information, it was unsound to depend on this when the act was p lanned.

PLANNING

When the decision to assassinate has been reached, the tactics of the operation must be planned, based upon an estimate of the situation similar to that used in military operations. The preliminary estimate will reveal gaps in information and possibly indicate a need for special equipment which must be procured or constructed. When all necessary data has been collected, an effective tactical plan can be prepared. All planning must be mental; no papers should ever contain evidence of the oper ation.

In resistance situations, assassination may be used as a counter-reprisal. Since this requires advertising to be effective, the resistance organization must be in a position to warn high officials publicly that their lives will be the price of rep risal action against innocent people. Such a threat is of no value unless it can be carried out, so it may be necessary to plan the assassination of various responsible officers of the oppressive regime and hold such plans in readiness to be used only i f provoked by excessive brutality. Such plans must be modified frequently to meet changes in the tactical situation.

TECHNIQUES

The essential point of assassination is the death of the subject. A human being may be killed in many ways but sureness is often overlooked by those who may be emotionally unstrung by the seriousness of this act they intend to commit. The spe cific technique employed will depend upon a large number of variables, but should be constant in one point: Death must be absolutely certain. The attempt on Hitler's life failed because the conspiracy did not give this matter proper attention.

Techniques may be considered as follows:

1. Manual

It is possible to kill a man with the bare hands, but very few are skillful enough to do it well. Even a highly trained Judo expert will hesitate to risk killing by hand unless he has absolutely no alternative. However, the simplest local tools a re often much the most efficient means of assassination. A hammer, axe, wrench, screw driver, fire poker, kitchen knife, lamp stand, or anything hard, heavy and handy will suffice. A length of rope or wire or a belt will do if the assassin is strong and agile. All such improvised weapons have the important advantage of availability and apparent innocence. The obviously lethal machine gun failed to kill Trotsky where an item of sporting goods succeeded.

In all safe cases where the assassin may be subject to search, either before or after the act, specialized weapons should not be used. Even in the lost case, the assassin may accidentally be searched before the act and should not carry an incrimin ating device if any sort of lethal weapon can be improvised at or near the site. If the assassin normally carries weapons because of the nature of his job, it may still be desirable to improvise and implement at the scene to avoid disclosure of his ident ity.

2. Accidents

For secret assassination, either simple or chase, the contrived accident is the most effective technique. When successfully executed, it causes little excitement and is only casually investigated.

The most efficient accident, in simple assassination, is a fall of 75 feet or more onto a hard surface. Elevator shafts, stair wells, unscreened windows and bridges will serve. Bridge falls into water are not reliable. In simple cases a private meeting with the subject may be arranged at a properly-cased location. The act may be executed by sudden, vigorous [excised] of the ankles, tipping the subject over the edge. If the assassin immediately sets up an outcry, playing the "horrified wit ness", no alibi or surreptitious withdrawal is necessary. In chase cases it will usually be necessary to stun or drug the subject before dropping him. Care is required to insure that no wound or condition not attributable to the fall is discernible after death.

Falls into the sea or swiftly flowing rivers may suffice if the subject cannot swim. It will be more reliable if the assassin can arrange to attempt rescue, as he can thus be sure of the subject's death and at the same time establish a workable al ibi.

If the subject's personal habits make it feasible, alcohol may be used [2 words excised] to prepare him for a contrived accident of any kind.

Falls before trains or subway cars are usually effective, but require exact timing and can seldom be free from unexpected observation.

Automobile accidents are a less satisfactory means of assassination. If the subject is deliberately run down, very exact timing is necessary and investigation is likely to be thorough. If the subject's car is tampered with, reliability is very lo w. The subject may be stunned or drugged and then placed in the car, but this is only reliable when the car can be run off a high cliff or into deep water without observation.

Arson can cause accidental death if the subject is drugged and left in a burning building. Reliability is not satisfactory unless the building is isolated and highly combustible.

3. Drugs

In all types of assassination except terroristic, drugs can be very effective. If the assassin is trained as a doctor or nurse and the subject is under medical care, this is an easy and rare method. An overdose of morphine administered as a sedat ive will cause death without disturbance and is difficult to detect. The size of the dose will depend upon whether the subject has been using narcotics regularly. If not, two grains will suffice.

If the subject drinks heavily, morphine or a similar narcotic can be injected at the passing out stage, and the cause of death will often be held to be acute alcoholism.

Specific poisons, such as arsenic or strychine, are effective but their possession or procurement is incriminating, and accurate dosage is problematical. Poison was used unsuccessfully in the assassination of Rasputin and Kolohan, though the latte r case is more accurately described as a murder.

4. Edge Weapons

Any locally obtained edge device may be successfully employed. A certain minimum of anatomical knowledge is needed for reliability.

Puncture wounds of the body cavity may not be reliable unless the heart is reached. The heart is protected by the rib cage and is not always easy to locate.

Abdominal wounds were once nearly always mortal, but modern medical treatment has made this no longer true.

Absolute reliability is obtained by severing the spinal cord in the cervical region. This can be done with the point of a knife or a light blow of an axe or hatchet.

Another reliable method is the severing of both jugular and carotid blood vessels on both sides of the windpipe.

If the subject has been rendered unconscious by other wounds or drugs, either of the above methods can be used to insure death.

5. Blunt Weapons

As with edge weapons, blunt weapons require some anatomical knowledge for effective use. Their main advantage is their universal availability. A hammer may be picked up almost anywhere in the world. Baseball and [illeg] bats are very widely dist ributed. Even a rock or a heavy stick will do, and nothing resembling a weapon need be procured, carried or subsequently disposed of.

Blows should be directed to the temple, the area just below and behind the ear, and the lower, rear portion of the skull. Of course, if the blow is very heavy, any portion of the upper skull will do. The lower frontal portion of the head, from th e eyes to the throat, can withstand enormous blows without fatal consequences.

6. Firearms

Firearms are often used in assassination, often very ineffectively. The assassin usually has insufficient technical knowledge of the limitations of weapons, and expects more range, accuracy and killing power than can be provided with reliability. Since certainty of death is the major requirement, firearms should be used which can provide destructive power at least 100% in excess of that thought to be necessary, and ranges should be half that considered practical for the weapon.

Firearms have other drawbacks. Their possession is often incriminating. They may be difficult to obtain. They require a degree of experience from the user. They are [illeg]. Their [illeg] is consistently over-rated.

However, there are many cases in which firearms are probably more efficient than any other means. These cases usually involve distance between the assassin and the subject, or comparative physical weakness of the assassin, as with a woman.

(a) **The precision rifle.** In guarded assassination, a good hunting or target rifle should always be considered as a possibility. Absolute reliability can nearly always be achieved at a distance of one hundred yards. In ideal circumstances, t he range may be extended to 250 yards. The rifle should be a well made bolt or falling block action type, handling a powerful long-range cartridge. The .300 F.A.B. Magnum is probably the best cartridge readily available. Other excellent calibers are . 375 M.[illeg]. Magnum, .270 Winchester, .30 - 106 p.s., 8 x 60 MM Magnum, 9.3 x 62 kk and others of this type. These are preferable to ordinary military calibers, since ammunition available for them is usually of the expanding bullet type, whereas most ammunition for military rifles is full jacketed and hence not sufficiently let hal. Military ammunition should not be altered by filing or drilling bullets, as this will adversely affect accuracy.

The rifle may be of the "bull gun" variety, with extra heavy barrel and set triggers, but in any case should be capable of maximum precision. Ideally, the weapon should be able to group in one inch at one hundred yards, but 21/2" groups are adequa te. The sight should be telescopic, not only for accuracy, but because such a sight is much better in dim light or near darkness. As long as the bare outline of the target is discernable, a telescope sight will work, even if the rifle and shooter are in total darkness.

An expanding, hunting bullet of such calibers as described above will produce extravagant laceration and shock at short or mid-range. If a man is struck just once in the body cavity, his death is almost entirely certain.

Public figures or guarded officials may be killed with great reliability and some safety if a firing point can be established prior to an official occasion. The propaganda value of this system may be very high.

(b) **The machine gun.**

Machine guns may be used in most cases where the precision rifle is applicable. Usually, this will require the subversion of a unit of an official guard at a ceremony, though a skillful and determined team might conceivably dispose of a loyal gun crow without commotion and take over the gun at the critical time.

The area fire capacity of the machine gun should not be used to search out a concealed subject. This was tried with predictable lack of success on Trotsky. The automatic feature of the machine gun should rather be used to increase reliability by placing a 5 second burst on the subject. Even with full jacket ammunition, this will be absolute lethal is the burst pattern is no larger than a man. This can be accomplished at about 150 yards. In ideal circumstances, a properly padded and targeted ma chine gun can do it at 850 yards. The major difficulty is placing the first burst exactly on the target, as most machine gunners are trained to spot their fire on target by observation of strike. This will not do in assassination as the subject will not wait.

(c) **The Submachine Gun.**

This weapon, known as the "machine-pistol" by the Russians and Germans and "machine-carbine" by the British, is occasionally useful in assassination. Unlike the rifle and machine gun, this is a short range weapon and since it fires pistol ammu nition, much less powerful. To be reliable, it should deliver at least 5 rounds into the subject's chest, though the .45 caliber U.S. weapons have a much larger margin of killing efficiency than the 9 mm European arms.

The assassination range of the sub-machine gun is point blank. While accurate single rounds can be delivered by sub-machine gunners at 50 yards or more, this is not certain enough for assassination. Under ordinary circumstances, the 5MG should be used as a fully automatic weapon. In the hands of a capabl e gunner, a high cyclic rate is a distinct advantage, as speed of execution is most desirable, particularly in the case of multiple subjects.

The sub-machine gun is especially adapted to indoor work when more than one subject is to be assassinated. An effective technique has been devised for the use of a pair of sub-machine gunners, by which a room containing as many as a dozen subjects can be "purifico" in about twenty seconds with little or no risk to the gunners. It is illustrated below.

While the U.S. sub-machine guns fire the most lethal cartridges, the higher cyclic rate of some foreign weapons enable the gunner to cover a target quicker with acceptable pattern density. The Bergmann Model 1934 is particularly good in this way. The Danish Madman? SMG has a moderately good cyclic rate and is admirably compact and concealable. The Russian SHG's have a good cyclic rate, but are handicapped by a small, light protective which requires more kits for equivalent killing effect.

(d) The Shotgun.

A large bore shotgun is a most effective killing instrument as long as the range is kept under ten yards. It should normally be used only on single targets as it cannot sustain fire successfully. The barrel may be "sawed" off for convenience, but this is not a significant factor in its killi ng performance. Its optimum range is just out of reach of the subject. 00 buckshot is considered the best shot size for a twelve gage gun, but anything from single balls to bird shot will do if the range is right. The assassin should aim for the solar plexus as the shot pattern is small at close range and can easily [illeg] the head.

(e) The Pistol.

While the handgun is quite inefficient as a weapon of assassination, it is often used, partly because it is readily available and can be concealed on the person, and partly because its limitations are not widely appreciated. While many well kn own assassinations have been carried out with pistols (Lincoln, Harding, Ghandi), such attempts fail as often as they succeed, (Truman, Roosevelt, Churchill).

If a pistol is used, it should be as powerful as possible and fired from just beyond reach. The pistol and the shotgun are used in similar tactical situations, except that the shotgun is much more lethal and the pistol is much more easily conceale d.

In the hands of an expert, a powerful pistol is quite deadly, but such experts are rare and not usually available for assassination missions.

.45 Colt, .44 Special, .455 Kly, .45 A.S.[illeg] (U.S. Service) and .357 Magnum are all efficient calibers. Less powerful rounds can suffice but are less reliable. Sub-power cartridges such as the .32s and .25s should be avoided.

In all cases, the subject should be hit solidly at least three times for complete reliability.

(f) Silent Firearms

The sound of the explosion of the proponent in a firearm can be effectively silenced by appropriate attachments. However, the sound of the projective passing through the air cannot, since this sound is generated outside the weapon. In cases w here the velocity of the bullet greatly exceeds that of sound, the noise so generated is much louder than that of the explosion. Since all powerful rifles have muzzle velocities of over 2000 feet per second, they cannot be silenced.

Pistol bullets, on the other hand, usually travel slower than sound and the sound of their flight is negligible. Therefore, pistols, sub-machine guns and any sort of improvised carbine or rifle which will take a low velocity cartridge can be silenc ed. The user should not forget that the sound of the operation of a repeating action is considerable, and that the sound of bullet strike, particularly in bone is quite loud.

Silent firearms are only occasionally useful to the assassin, though they have been widely publicized in this connection. Because permissible velocity is low, effective precision range is held to about 100 yards with rifle or carbine type weapons, while with pistols, silent or otherwise, are most efficient just beyond arms length. The silent feature attempts to provide a degree of safety to the assassin, but mere possession of a silent firearm is likely to create enough hazard to counter the advantage of its silence. The silent pisto l combines the disadvantages of any pistol with the added one of its obviously clandestine purpose.

A telescopically sighted, closed-action carbine shooting a low velocity bullet of great weight, and built for accuracy, could be very useful to an assassin in certain situations. At the time of writing, no such weapon is known to exist.

7. Explosives.

Bombs and demolition charges of various sorts have been used frequently in assassination. Such devices, in terroristic and open assassination, can provide safety and overcome guard barriers, but it is curious that bombs have often been the imp lement of lost assassinations.

The major factor which affects reliability is the use of explosives for assassination. the charge must be very large and the detonation must be controlled exactly as to time by the assassin who can observe the subject. A small or moderate explosi ve charge is highly unreliable as a cause of death, and time delay or booby-trap devices are extremely prone to kill the wrong man. In addition to the moral aspects of indiscriminate killing, the death of casual bystanders can often produce public reacti ons unfavorable to the cause for which the assassination is carried out.

Bombs or grenades should never be thrown at a subject. While this will always cause a commotion and may even result in the subject's death, it is sloppy, unreliable, and bad propaganda. The charge must be too small and the assassin is never sure of: (1)reaching his attack position, (2) placing the charge close en ough to the target and (3) firing the charge at the right time.

Placing the charge surreptitiously in advance permits a charge of proper size to be employed, but requires accurate prediction of the subject's movements.

Ten pounds of high explosive should normally be regarded as a minimum, and this is explosive of fragmentation material. The latter can consist of any hard, [illeg] material as long as the fragments are large enough. Metal or rock fragments should be walnut-size rather than pen-size. If solid plates are used, to be ruptured by the explosion, cast iron, 1" thick, gives excellent fragmentation. Military or commercial high explosives are practical for use in assassination. Homemade or improvised e xplosives should be avoided. While possibly powerful, they tend to be dangerous and unreliable. Anti-personnel explosive missiles are excellent, provided the assassin has sufficient technical knowledge to fuse them properly. 81 or 82 mm mortar shells, or the 120 mm mortar shell, are particularly good. Anti-personnel shells for 85, 88, 90, 100 and 105 mm guns and howitzers are both large enough to be completely reliable and small enough to be carried by one man.

The charge should be so placed that the subject is not ever six feet from it at the moment of detonation.

A large, shaped charge with the [illeg] filled with iron fragments (such as 1" nuts and bolts) will fire a highly lethal shotgun-type [illeg] to 50 yards. This reaction has not been thoroughly tested, however, and an exact replica of the proposed device should be fired in advance to determine exact range, pattern-size, and penetration of fragments. Fragments should penetrate at lea st 1" of seasoned pine or equivalent for minimum reliability. Any firing device may be used which permits exact control by the assassin. An ordinary commercial or military explorer is efficient, as long as it is rigged for instantaneous action with no time fuse in the system. The wise [illeg] electric target can serve as the triggering device and provide exact timing from as far away as the assassin can reliably hit the target. This will avid the disadvantages olitary or commercial high explosives are practical for use in assassination. Homemade or improvised explosives should be avoided. While possibly powerful, they tend to be dangerous and unreliable. Anti-personnel explosive missiles are excellent, provided the assassin has sufficient techn ical knowledge to fuse them properly. 81 or 82 mm mortar shells, or the 120 mm mortar shell, are particularly good. Anti-personnel shells for 85, 88, 90, 100 and 105 mm guns and howitzers are both large enough to be completely reliable and small enough to be carried by one man.

The charge should be so placed that the subject is not ever six feet from it at the moment of detonation.

A large, shaped charge with the [illeg] filled with iron fragments (such as 1" nuts and bolts) will fire a highly lethal shotgun-type [illeg] to 50 yards. This reaction has not been thoroughly tested, however, and an exact replica of the proposed device should be fired in advance to determine exact range, pattern-size, and penetration of fragments. Fragments should penetrate at lea st 1" of seasoned pine or equivalent for minimum reliability.

Any firing device may be used which permits exact control by the assassin. An ordinary commercial or military explorer is efficient, as long as it is rigged for instantaneous action with no time fuse in the system.

The wise [illeg] electric target can serve as the triggering device and provide exact timing from as far away as the assassin can reliably hit the target. This will avid the disadvantages of stringing wire between the proposed positions of the ass assin and the subject, and also permit the assassin to fire the charge from a variety of possible positions.

The radio switch can be [illeg] to fire [illeg], though its reliability is somewhat lower and its procurement may not be easy.

EXAMPLES

([illeg] may be presented brief outlines, with critical evaluations of the following assassinations and attempts:

Marat	Benes
Hedrich	Rasputin
Lincoln	Aung Sang
Hitler	Madero
Harding	[illeg]
Roosevelt	Kirov
Grand Duke Sergei	Abdullah
Truman	Huey Long
Pirhivie	Ghandi
Mussolini	Alexander of Yugoslvia
Archduke Francis Ferdinand	Trotsky

CONFERENCE ROOM TECHNIQUE

(1) Enters room quickly but quietly

(2) Stands in doorway

(2) Opens fire on first subject to react. Swings across group toward center of mass. Times burst to empty magazine at end of swing.

(1) Covers group to prevent individual dangerous reactions, if necessary, fires individual bursts of 3 rounds.

(2) Finishes burst. Commands"Shift." Drops back thru [sic] door. Replaces empty magazine. Covers corridor.

(1) On command "shift", opens fire on opposite side of target, swings one burst across group.

(1) Finishes burst. Commands "shift". Drops back thru [sic] door. Replaces magazine. Covers corridor.

(2) On command, "shift", re-enters room. Covers group: kills survivors with two-round bursts. Leaves propaganda.

(2) Leaves room. Commands "GO". Covers rear with nearly full magazine.

(1) On command "GO", leads withdrawl, covering front with full magazine.

The Final Declaration of The Geneva Conference: On Indochina, July 21, 1954

Final declaration, dated July 21, 1954, of the Geneva Conference on the problem of restoring peace in Indochina, in which the representatives of Cambodia, the Democratic Republic of Viet-Nam, France, Laos, the People's Republic of China, the State of Viet-Nam, the Union of Soviet Socialist Republics, the United Kingdom and the United States of America took part.

1. The Conference takes note of the agreements ending hostilities in Cambodia, Laos, and Viet-Nam and organizing international control and the supervision of the execution of the provisions of these agreements.

2. The Conference expresses satisfaction at the ending of hostilities in Cambodia, Laos, and Viet-Nam. The Conference
expresses its conviction that the execution of the provisions set out in the present declaration and in the agreements on the cessation of hostilities will permit
Cambodia, Laos, and Viet-Nam henceforth to play their
part, in full independence and sovereignty, in the peaceful
community of nations.

3. The Conference takes note of the declarations made by the
Governments of Cambodia and of Laos of their intention
to adopt measures permitting all citizens to take their
place in the national community, in particular by participating in the next general elections, which, in conformity
with the constitution of each of these countries, shall take
place in the course of the year 1955, by secret ballot and in
conditions of respect for fundamental freedoms.

4. The Conference takes note of the clauses in the agreement
on the cessation of hostilities in Viet-Nam prohibiting the
introduction into Viet Nam of foreign troops and military
personnel as well as of all kinds of arms and munitions.
The Conference also takes note of the declarations made
by the Governments of Cambodia and Laos of their resolution not to request foreign aid, whether in war material,
in personnel, or in instructors except for the purpose of
effective defense of their territory and, in the case of
Laos, to the extent defined by the agreements on the cessation of hostilities in Laos.

5. The Conference takes note of the clauses in the agreement
on the cessation of hostilities in Viet-Nam to the effect
that no military base at the disposition of a foreign state
may be established in the regrouping zones of the two parties, the latter having the obligation to see that the zones
allotted to them shall not constitute part of any military
alliance and shall not be utilized for the resumption of
hostilities or in the service of an aggressive policy. The
Conference also takes note of the declarations of the
Governments of Cambodia and Laos to the effect that they
will not join in any agreement with other states if this
agreement includes the obligation to participate in a military alliance not in conformity with the principles of the
charter of the United Nations or, in the case of Laos, with

the principles of the agreement on the cessation of hostilities in Laos or, so long as their security is not threatened, the obligation to establish bases on Cambodian or Laotian territory for the military forces of foreign powers.

6. The Conference recognizes that the essential purpose of the agreement relating to Viet-Nam is to settle military questions with a view to ending hostilities and that the military demarcation line should not in any way be interpreted as constituting a political or territorial boundary. The Conference expresses its conviction that the execution of the provisions set out in the present declaration and in the agreement on the cessation of hostilities creates the necessary basis for the achievement in the near future of a political settlement in Viet-Nam.

7. The Conference declares that, so far as Viet-Nam is concerned, the settlement of political problems, effected on the basis of respect for the principles of independence, unity, and territorial integrity, shall permit the Vietnamese people to enjoy the fundamental freedoms, guaranteed by democratic institutions established as a result of free general elections by secret ballot.

In order to insure that sufficient progress in the restoration of peace has been made, and that all the necessary conditions obtain for free expression of the national will, general elections shall be held in July 1956, under the supervision of an international commission composed of representatives of the member states of the International Supervisory Commission referred to in the agreement on the cessation of hostilities. Consultations will be held on this subject between the competent representative authorities of the two zones from April 20, 1955, onwards.

8. The provisions of the agreements on the cessation of hostilities intended to insure the protection of individuals and of property must be most strictly applied and must, in particular, allow every one in Viet-Nam to decide freely in which zone he wishes to live.

9. The competent representative authorities of the northern and southern zones of Viet-Nam, as well as the authorities of Laos and Cambodia, must not permit any individual or collective reprisals against persons who have collaborated

in any way with one of the parties during the war, or against members of such persons' families.

10. The Conference takes note of the declaration of the French Government to the effect that it is ready to with-draw its troops from the territory of Cambodia, Laos, and Viet-Nam, at the request of the governments concerned and within a period which shall be fixed by agreement between the parties except in the cases where, by agree-ment between the two parties, a certain number of French troops shall remain at specified points and for a specified time.

11. The Conference takes note of the declaration of the French Government to the effect that for the settlement of all the problems connected with the reestablishment and consolidation of peace in Cambodia, Laos, and Viet-Nam, the French Government will proceed from the principle of respect for the independence and sovereignty, unity, and territorial integrity of Cambodia, Laos, and Viet-Nam.

12. In their relations with Cambodia, Laos, and Viet-Nam, each member of the Geneva Conference undertakes to respect the sovereignty, the independence, the unity, and the terri-torial integrity of the above-mentioned states, and to refrain from any interference in their internal affairs.

13. The members of the Conference agree to consult one another on any question which may be referred to them by the International Supervisory Commission, in order to study such measures as may prove necessary to insure that the agreements on the cessation of hostilities in Cambodia, Laos, and Viet-Nam are respected.

Plot to Kill Lumumba

Memorandum for the Record:

In November 1962 Mr. _____ advised Mr. Lyman Kirkpatrick that he had, at one time, been directed by Mr. Richard Bissell to assume responsibility for a project involving the assassination of Patrice Lumumba, then Premier, Republic of Congo. According to _____ poison was to have been the vehicle as he made ref-erence to having been instructed to see Dr. Sidney Gottlieb in order procure the appropriate vehicle.

V

The Heyday of the Liberals and the Fall

Throughout the 20th Century, the U.S. political economy was guided by ideology of "liberalism," an idea which stressed that the open door and relative democracy was essential for global prosperity. But liberalism had its inherent contradictions, as it was hard to reconcile the idea of free markets and self-determination with the growing nature of American imperialism abroad. One of the most acute, and surprising, critics of this was President, and General of the Army, Dwight Eisenhower.

Despite Eisenhower's warnings, the U.S. decided to ramp up its imperial ambitions, especially in Vietnam and Cuba, leading to failure on both fronts and a setback to American power and to American world leadership.

Meanwhile, the prosperity that was so evident after World War II began to fade, as the economic pie began to shrink and working people found it harder to make ends meet. Then, with Vietnam raging and civil rights declining, assassinations and political division brought the country to its knees, so much so that politicians such as Richard Nixon and Ronald Reagan were encouraged to declare the death of liberalism.

Limits of Power, or Pay Any Price?

Military-Industrial Complex Speech, Dwight D. Eisenhower, 1961

My fellow Americans:

Three days from now, after half a century in the service of our country, I shall lay down the responsibilities of office as, in traditional and solemn ceremony, the authority of the Presidency is vested in my successor.

This evening I come to you with a message of leave-taking and farewell, and to share a few final thoughts with you, my countrymen.

Like every other citizen, I wish the new President, and all who will labor with him, Godspeed. I pray that the coming years will be blessed with peace and prosperity for all.

Our people expect their President and the Congress to find essential agreement on issues of great moment, the wise resolution of which will better shape the future of the Nation.

My own relations with the Congress, which began on a remote and tenuous basis when, long ago, a member of the Senate appointed me to West Point, have since ranged to the intimate during the war and immediate post-war period, and, finally, to the mutually interdependent during these past eight years.

In this final relationship, the Congress and the Administration have, on most vital issues, cooperated well, to serve the national good rather than mere partisanship, and so have assured that the business of the Nation should go forward. So, my official relationship with the Congress ends in a feeling, on my part, of gratitude that we have been able to do so much together.

II.

We now stand ten years past the midpoint of a century that has witnessed four major wars among great nations. Three of these involved our own country. Despite these holocausts America is today the strongest, the most influential and most productive nation in the world. Understandably proud of this pre-eminence, we yet realize that America's leadership and prestige depend, not merely upon our unmatched material progress, riches and military strength, but on how we use our power in the interests of world peace and human betterment.

III.

Throughout America's adventure in free government, our basic purposes have been to keep the peace; to foster progress in human achievement, and to enhance liberty, dignity and integrity among people and among nations. To strive for less would be unworthy of a free and religious people. Any failure traceable to arrogance, or our lack of comprehension or readiness to sacrifice would inflict upon us grievous hurt both at home and abroad.

Progress toward these noble goals is persistently threatened by the conflict now engulfing the world. It commands our whole attention, absorbs our very beings. We face a hostile ideology—global in scope, atheistic in character, ruthless in purpose, and insidious in method. Unhappily the danger is poses promises to be of indefinite duration. To meet it successfully, there is called for, not so much the emotional and transitory sacrifices of crisis, but rather those which enable us to carry forward steadily, surely, and without complaint the burdens of a prolonged and complex struggle—with liberty the stake. Only thus shall we remain, despite every provocation, on our charted course toward permanent peace and human betterment.

Crises there will continue to be. In meeting them, whether foreign or domestic, great or small, there is a recurring temptation to feel that some spectacular and costly action could become the miraculous solution to all current difficulties. A huge increase in newer elements of our defense; development of unrealistic programs to cure every ill in agriculture; a dramatic expansion in basic and applied research—these and many other possibilities, each possibly promising in itself, may be suggested as the only way to the road we wish to travel.

But each proposal must be weighed in the light of a broader consideration: the need to maintain balance in and among national programs—balance between the private and the public economy, balance between cost and hoped for advantage—balance between the clearly necessary and the comfortably desirable; balance between our essential requirements as a nation and the duties imposed by the nation upon the individual; balance between actions of the moment and the national welfare of the future. Good judgment seeks balance and progress; lack of it eventually finds imbalance and frustration.

The record of many decades stands as proof that our people and their government have, in the main, understood these truths and have responded to them well, in the face of stress and threat. But threats, new in kind or degree, constantly arise. I mention two only.

IV.

A vital element in keeping the peace is our military establishment. Our arms must be mighty, ready for instant action, so that no potential aggressor may be tempted to risk his own destruction.

Our military organization today bears little relation to that known by any of my predecessors in peacetime, or indeed by the fighting men of World War II or Korea.

Until the latest of our world conflicts, the United States had no armaments industry. American makers of plowshares could, with time and as required, make swords as well. But now we can no longer risk emergency improvisation of national defense; we have been compelled to create a permanent armaments industry of vast proportions. Added to this, three and a half million men and women are directly engaged in the defense establishment. We annually spend on military security more than the net income of all United States corporations.

This conjunction of an immense military establishment and a large arms industry is new in the American experience. The total influence—economic, political, even spiritual—is felt in every city, every State house, every office of the Federal government. We recognize the imperative need for this development. Yet we must not fail to comprehend its grave implications. Our toil, resources and livelihood are all involved; so is the very structure of our society.

In the councils of government, we must guard against the acquisition of unwarranted influence, whether sought or unsought, by the militaryindustrial complex. The potential for the disastrous rise of misplaced power exists and will persist.

We must never let the weight of this combination endanger our liberties or democratic processes. We should take nothing for granted. Only an alert and knowledgeable citizenry can compel the proper meshing of the huge industrial and military machinery of defense with our peaceful methods and goals, so that security and liberty may prosper together.

Akin to, and largely responsible for the sweeping changes in our industrial-military posture, has been the technological revolution during recent decades.

In this revolution, research has become central; it also becomes more formalized, complex, and costly. A steadily increasing share is conducted for, by, or at the direction of, the Federal government.

Today, the solitary inventor, tinkering in his shop, has been overshadowed by task forces of scientists in laboratories and testing fields. In the same fashion, the free university, historically the fountainhead of free ideas and scientific discovery, has experienced a revolution in the conduct of research. Partly because of the huge costs involved, a government contract becomes virtually a substitute for intellectual curiosity. For every old blackboard there are now hundreds of new electronic computers.

The prospect of domination of the nation's scholars by Federal employment, project allocations, and the power of money is ever present and is gravely to be regarded. Yet, in holding scientific research and discovery in respect, as we should, we must also be alert to the equal and opposite danger that public policy could itself become the captive of a scientifictechnological elite.

It is the task of statesmanship to mold, to balance, and to integrate these and other forces, new and old, within the principles of our democratic system—ever aiming toward the supreme goals of our free society.

V.

Another factor in maintaining balance involves the element of time. As we peer into society's future, we—you and I, and our government—must avoid the impulse to live only for today, plundering, for our own ease and convenience, the precious resources of tomorrow. We cannot mortgage the material assets of our grandchildren without risking the loss also of their political and spiritual heritage. We want democracy to survive for all generations to come, not to become the insolvent phantom of tomorrow.

VI.

Down the long lane of the history yet to be written America knows that this world of ours, ever growing smaller, must avoid becoming a community of dreadful fear and hate, and be instead, a proud confederation of mutual trust and respect.

Such a confederation must be one of equals. The weakest must come to the conference table with the same confidence as do we, protected as we are by our moral, economic, and military strength. That table, though scarred by many past frustrations, cannot be abandoned for the certain agony of the battlefield.

Disarmament, with mutual honor and confidence, is a continuing imperative. Together we must learn how to compose differences, not with arms, but with intellect and decent purpose. Because this need is so sharp and apparent I confess that I lay down my official responsibilities in this field with a definite sense of disappointment. As one who has witnessed the horror and the lingering sadness of war—as one who knows that another war could utterly destroy this civilization which has been so slowly and painfully built over thousands of years—I wish I could say tonight that a lasting peace is in sight.

Happily, I can say that war has been avoided. Steady progress toward our ultimate goal has been made. But, so much remains to be done. As a private citizen, I shall never cease to do what little I can to help the world advance along that road.

VII.

So—in this my last good night to you as your President—I thank you for the many opportunities you have given me for public service in war and peace. I trust that in that service you find some things worthy; as for the rest of it, I know you will find ways to improve performance in the future.

You and I—my fellow citizens—need to be strong in our faith that all nations, under God, will reach the goal of peace with justice. May we be ever unswerving in devotion to principle, confident but humble with power, diligent in pursuit of the Nation's great goals.

To all the peoples of the world, I once more give expression to America's prayerful and continuing aspiration:

We pray that peoples of all faiths, all races, all nations, may have their great human needs satisfied; that those now denied opportunity shall come to enjoy it to the full; that all who yearn for freedom may experience its spiritual blessings; that those who have freedom will understand, also, its heavy responsibilities; that all who are insensitive to the needs of others will learn charity; that the scourges of poverty, disease and ignorance will be made to disappear from the earth, and that, in the goodness of time, all peoples will come to live together in a peace guaranteed by the binding force of mutual respect and love.

Inaugural Address of John F. Kennedy

FRIDAY, JANUARY 20, 1961

Vice President Johnson, Mr. Speaker, Mr. Chief Justice, President Eisenhower, Vice President Nixon, President Truman, reverend clergy, fellow citizens, we observe today not a victory of party, but a celebration of freedom—symbolizing an end, as well as a beginning—signifying renewal, as well as change. For I have sworn before you and Almighty God the same solemn oath our forebears prescribed nearly a century and three quarters ago.

The world is very different now. For man holds in his mortal hands the power to abolish all forms of human poverty and all forms of human life. And yet the same revolutionary beliefs for which our forebears fought are still at issue around the globe—the belief that the rights of man come not from the generosity of the state, but from the hand of God.

We dare not forget today that we are the heirs of that first revolution. Let the word go forth from this time and place, to friend and foe alike, that the torch has been passed to a new generation of Americans—born in this century, tempered by war, disciplined by a hard and bitter peace, proud of our ancient heritage—and unwilling to witness or permit the slow undoing of those human rights to which this Nation has always been committed, and to which we are committed today at home and around the world.

Let every nation know, whether it wishes us well or ill, that we shall pay any price, bear any burden, meet any hardship, support any friend, oppose any foe, in order to assure the survival and the success of liberty.

This much we pledge—and more.

To those old allies whose cultural and spiritual origins we share, we pledge the loyalty of faithful friends. United, there is little we cannot do in a host of cooperative ventures. Divided, there is little we can do—for we dare not meet a powerful challenge at odds and split asunder.

To those new States whom we welcome to the ranks of the free, we pledge our word that one form of colonial control shall not have passed away merely to be replaced by a far more iron tyranny. We shall not always expect to find them supporting our view. But we shall always hope to find them strongly supporting their own freedom—and to remember that, in the past, those who foolishly sought power by riding the back of the tiger ended up inside.

To those peoples in the huts and villages across the globe struggling to break the bonds of mass misery, we pledge our best efforts to help them help themselves, for whatever period is required—not because the Communists may be doing it, not because we seek their votes, but because it is right. If a free society cannot help the many who are poor, it cannot save the few who are rich.

To our sister republics south of our border, we offer a special pledge—to convert our good words into good deeds—in a new alliance for progress—to assist free men and free governments in casting off the chains of poverty. But this peaceful revolution of hope cannot become the prey of hostile powers. Let all our neighbors know that we shall join with them to oppose aggression or subversion anywhere in the Americas. And let every other power know that this Hemisphere intends to remain the master of its own house.

To that world assembly of sovereign states, the United Nations, our last best hope in an age where the instruments of war have far outpaced the instruments of peace, we renew our pledge of support—to prevent it from becoming merely a forum for invective—to strengthen its shield of the new and the weak—and to enlarge the area in which its writ may run.

Finally, to those nations who would make themselves our adversary, we offer not a pledge but a request: that both sides begin anew the quest for peace, before the dark powers of destruction unleashed by science engulf all humanity in planned or accidental self-destruction.

We dare not tempt them with weakness. For only when our arms are sufficient beyond doubt can we be certain beyond doubt that they will never be employed.

But neither can two great and powerful groups of nations take comfort from our present course—both sides overburdened by the cost of modern weapons, both rightly alarmed by the steady spread of the deadly atom, yet both racing to alter that uncertain balance of terror that stays the hand of mankind's final war.

So let us begin anew—remembering on both sides that civility is not a sign of weakness, and sincerity is always subject to proof. Let us never negotiate out of fear. But let us never fear to negotiate.

Let both sides explore what problems unite us instead of belaboring those problems which divide us.

Let both sides, for the first time, formulate serious and precise proposals for the inspection and control of arms—and bring the absolute power to destroy other nations under the absolute control of all nations.

Let both sides seek to invoke the wonders of science instead of its terrors. Together let us explore the stars, conquer the deserts, eradicate disease, tap the ocean depths, and encourage the arts and commerce.

Let both sides unite to heed in all corners of the earth the command of Isaiah—to "undo the heavy burdens ... and to let the oppressed go free."

And if a beachhead of cooperation may push back the jungle of suspicion, let both sides join in creating a new endeavor, not a new balance of power, but a new world of law, where the strong are just and the weak secure and the peace preserved.

All this will not be finished in the first 100 days. Nor will it be finished in the first 1,000 days, nor in the life of this Administration, nor even perhaps in our lifetime on this planet. But let us begin.

In your hands, my fellow citizens, more than in mine, will rest the final success or failure of our course. Since this country was founded, each generation of Americans has been summoned to give testimony to its national loyalty. The graves of young Americans who answered the call to service surround the globe.

Now the trumpet summons us again—not as a call to bear arms, though arms we need; not as a call to battle, though embattled we are—but a call to bear the burden of a long twilight struggle, year in and year out, "rejoicing in hope, patient in tribulation"— a struggle against the common enemies of man: tyranny, poverty, disease, and war itself.

Can we forge against these enemies a grand and global alliance, North and South, East and West, that can assure a more fruitful life for all mankind? Will you join in that historic effort?

In the long history of the world, only a few generations have been granted the role of defending freedom in its hour of maximum danger. I do not shrink from this responsibility—I welcome it. I do not believe that any of us would exchange places with any other people or any other generation. The energy, the faith, the devotion which we bring to this endeavor will light our country and all who serve it—and the glow from that fire can truly light the world.

And so, my fellow Americans: ask not what your country can do for you—ask what you can do for your country.

My fellow citizens of the world: ask not what America will do for you, but what together we can do for the freedom of man.

Finally, whether you are citizens of America or citizens of the world, ask of us the same high standards of strength and sacrifice which we ask of you. With a good conscience our only sure reward, with history the final judge of our deeds, let us go forth to lead the land we love, asking His blessing and His help, but knowing that here on earth God's work must truly be our own.

Kennedy's Radio and Television Address on the Cuban Missile Crisis

President John F. Kennedy: October 22, 1962

Good Evening, My Fellow Citizens:

This government, as promised, has maintained the closest surveillance of the Soviet military buildup on the island of Cuba. Within the past week, unmistakable evidence has established the fact that a series of offensive missile sites is now in preparation on that imprisoned island. The purpose of these bases can be none other than to provide a nuclear strike capability against the Western Hemisphere.

Upon receiving the first preliminary hard information of this nature last Tuesday morning at 9 a.m., I directed that our surveillance be stepped up. And having now confirmed and completed our evaluation of the evidence and our decision on a course of action, this government feels obliged to report this new crisis to you in fullest detail.

The characteristics of these new missile sites indicate two distinct types of installations. Several of them include medium range ballistic missiles, capable of carrying a nuclear warhead for a distance of more than 1,000 nautical miles. Each of these missiles, in short, is capable of striking Washington, D.C., the Panama Canal, Cape Canaveral, Mexico City, or any other city in the southeastern part of the United States, in Central America or in the Caribbean area.

Additional sites not yet completed appear to be designed for intermediate range ballistic missiles—capable of traveling more than twice as far—and thus capable of striking most of the major cities in the Western Hemisphere, ranging as far north as Hudson Bay, Canada, and as far south as Lima, Peru. In addition, jet bombers capable of carrying nuclear weapons are now being uncrated and assembled in Cuba while the necessary air bases are being prepared.

This urgent transformation of Cuba into an important strategic base—by the presence of these large, long-range, and clearly offensive weapons of sudden mass destruction—constitutes an explicit threat to the peace and security of all Americas, in flagrant and deliberate defiance of the Rio Pact of 1947, the traditions of this nation and hemisphere, the joint resolution of the 87th Congress, the Charter of the United Nations, and my own public warnings to the Soviets on September 4 and 13. This action also contradicts the repeated assurances of Soviet spokesmen, both publicly and privately delivered, that the arms buildup in Cuba would retain its original defensive character, and that the Soviet Union had no need or desire to station strategic missiles on the territory of any other nation. ...

But this secret, swift and extraordinary buildup of communist missiles—in an area well known to have a special and historical relationship to the United States and the nations of the Western Hemisphere, in violation of Soviet assurances, and in defiance of American and hemispheric policy—the sudden, clandestine decision to station strategic weapons for first time outside of Soviet soil—is a deliberately provocative and unjustified change in the status quo which cannot be accepted by this country, if our courage and our commitments are ever to be trusted again by either friend or foe. ...

Acting, therefore, in the defense of our own security and of the entire Western Hemisphere, and under the authority entrusted to me by the Constitution as endorsed by the resolution of the Congress, I have directed that the following initial steps be taken immediately:

First: To halt this offensive buildup, a strict quarantine on all offensive military equipment under shipment to Cuba is being initiated. All ships of any kind bound for Cuba from whatever nation and port will, if found to contain cargoes of offensive weapons, be turned back. This quarantine will be extended, if needed, to other types of cargo and carriers. We are not at this time, however, denying the necessities of life as the Soviets attempted to do in their Berlin blockade of 1948.

Second: I have directed the continued and increased close surveillance of Cuba and its military buildup. The foreign ministers of the OAS, in their communique of October 6, rejected secrecy on such matters in this hemisphere. Should these offensive military preparations continue, thus increasing the threat to the hemisphere, further action will be justified. I have directed the Armed Forces to prepare for any eventualities; and I trust that in the interest of both the Cuban people and the Soviet technicians at the sites, the hazards to all concerned of continuing the threat will be recognized.

Third: It shall be the policy of this nation to regard any nuclear missile launched from Cuba against any nation in the Western Hemisphere as an attack on the United States, requiring a full retaliatory response upon the Soviet Union.

Fourth: As a necessary military precaution, I have reinforced our base at Guantanamo, evacuated today the dependents of our personnel there, and ordered additional military units to be on a standby alert status.

Fifth: We are calling tonight for an immediate meeting of the Organ of Consultation under the Organization of American States, to consider this threat to hemispheric security and to invoke articles 6 and 8 of the Rio Treaty in support of all necessary action. The United Nations Charter allows for regional security arrangements—and the nations of this hemisphere decided long ago against the military presence of outside powers. Our other allies around the world have also been alerted.

Sixth: Under the Charter of the United Nations, we are asking tonight that an emergency meeting of the Security Council be convoked without delay to take action against this latest Soviet threat to world peace. Our resolution will call for the prompt dismantling and withdrawal of all offensive weapons in Cuba, under the supervision of U.N. observers, before the quarantine can be lifted.

Seventh and finally: I call upon Chairman Khrushchev to halt and eliminate this clandestine, reckless, and provocative threat to world peace and to stable relations between our two nations. I call upon him further to abandon this course of world domination, and to join in an historic effort to end the perilous arms race and to transform the history of man. He has an opportunity now to move the world back from the abyss of destruction—by returning to his government's own words that it had no need to station missiles outside its own territory, and withdrawing these weapons from Cuba—by refraining from any action which will widen or deepen the present crisis—and then by participating in a search for peaceful and permanent solutions. ...

My fellow citizens: let no one doubt that this is a difficult and dangerous effort on which we have set out. No one can foresee precisely what course it will take or what costs or casualties will be incurred. Many months in which both our patience and our will will be tested—months in which many threats and denunciations will keep us aware of our dangers. But the greatest danger of all would be to do nothing. ...

Our goal is not the victory of might, but the vindication of right—not peace at the expense of freedom, but both peace and freedom, here in this hemisphere, and we hope, around the world. God willing, that goal will be achieved.

Thank you and good night.

Gulf of Tonkin Resolution

Joint Resolution of Congress: H.J. RES 1145 August 7, 1964

Resolved by the Senate and House of Representatives of the United States of America in Congress assembled,

That the Congress approves and supports the determination of the President, as Commander in Chief, to take all necessary measures to repel any armed attack against the forces of the United States and to prevent further aggression.

Section 2. The United States regards as vital to its national interest and to world peace the maintenance of international peace and security in southeast Asia. Consonant with the Constitution of the United States and the Charter of the United Nations and in accordance with its obligations under the Southeast Asia Collective Defense Treaty, the United States is, therefore, prepared, as the President determines, to take all necessary steps, including the use of armed force, to assist any member or protocol state of the Southeast Asia Collective Defense Treaty requesting assistance in defense of its freedom.

Section 3. This resolution shall expire when the President shall determine that the peace and security of the area is reasonably assured by international conditions created by action of the United Nations or otherwise, except that it may be terminated earlier by concurrent resolution of the Congress.

The End of Hope?

Mexican-American Migrant Farmworkers Testify before Congress

STATEMENT OF RUDOLFO JUAREZ, OF OKEECHOBEE, FLA.

Mr. JUAREZ. Mr. Chairman, members of the subcommittee, I have prepared a statement that I would like to present to you. This statement is based on what I myself lived through since I was old enough to work and became a migrant at the age of 5. Based on my experience and how I continue to see the way my people suffer, in this statement I would like to express my feelings, as well as my opinions, and the feeling and opinions of others that I have worked with side by side in the fields.

Of all the groups living in poverty, the migrant farmworker and his family in general suffer the greatest socioeconomic deprivation. The migrant farmworker and his family travels throughout the Nation, living from day to day, depending upon his luck that the crops are good and that nothing happens, for instance, while he travels on the road.

Him and his family will eat as little and as cheap as he can, for he has very little money to get there. If his car breaks down, the mechanics overcharge him as much as they feel they can get away with. Because of bad weather and the time that laps between each crop, it is impossible for him to save any money—plus the high cost of living, plus the excessive amount of rent that he has to pay for the rat and roach infested pigpen that him and his family are forced to live in while he lives in Florida.

So when crops are over in the State of Florida, there is no way that he can continue to survive, so he migrates. And because of that the migrant farmworkers have had great difficulties in their employment relationships, much of this arising out of exploitation and abuse by irresponsible farmers and crew leaders who sometimes underpay them, short count them, and overcharge them for transportation. Crew leaders on occasions, collect wages from the employers and then abandon the workers without paying them.

His mobility deprives the migrant of many of the basic social services that are available to the local poor such as welfare, medical coverage and care, vocational rehabilitation, and day care for children. More than often his housing does not meet code standards.

Our children are pulled out of schools so that they may help provide for the family in the fields or at home taking care of smaller children so that mothers can work. . . .

Our children suffer regardless of what you do. If he goes to school, often he goes without breakfast—and if you are able to find out about the free lunch program and was able to take the insults or had the courage to fight for it, and find someone to fill out the forms, then your child might get lunch. For there are very few schools who have people who will search for ways to help you and many persons who will search for as many ways possible to keep you from getting such services.

This is also true in some of the Federal and State local agencies. For we have a very discriminatory and humiliating welfare system and unconstitutional residency requirements for receiving welfare and health services. Some of those people, when not able to deprive us from such services on terms of residency, plainly tell us we have no right and that we don't belong—thus making most of my people mad, never to return.

What this system and our society is going to have to know and understand is that the migrant farmworker, even though tired, uneducated, hungry, and sick, have contributed and sacrificed just as much as anyone else and more than most to this Nation. We have cultivated this earth, planted and harvested all crops for generations in order to provide all the luxuries in food, clothing, and many other items that those of society which surrounds us enjoy today.

My people, the migrants in general, composed of all types of Americans, regardless of race, color, or religion, our fathers, our sons, our kin, have died in wars fighting for the security and peace of this Nation as well as in the fields while harvesting the crops because of irresponsible farmers and their insecticides sprayed in the fields.

Gentlemen, bad working conditions and low wages for generations have maintained a slave labor system which insures that the migrant farmworker's children will have to live the same way he did and will continue to be slaves to agriculture and business.

Hunger, malnutrition, sickness, and lack of education will continue to exist. Our children will continue to suffer because children cannot study if they are hungry, always ill, and trying to do homework in hot and crowded shacks. And our men today will continue to lack the initiative and power because a hungry man with children who are sick and suffering from malnutrition, who must be constantly struggling to live and keep his family alive will soon tire and if he continues to seek assistance in the traditional government-processed way, and makes no headway, God knows how long he will be patient in his struggle to get his children out of the cycle of poverty that this system, through discriminatory legislation, has kept.

Mr. Chairman, members of this subcommittee, of all things I have said I hope you have paid attention. With all my heart I have presented some of the problems that have existed since past generations and continue to exist to this day. I have lived them, experienced them, and suffered them. This is not hearsay.

I am sure that others have told you the same things I have spoke about. Some of you have seen them with your own eyes. We have no reason to lie for we have nothing to lose for we have never had anything.

Those who have spoken against us, have because of profits, others for their own person gain, some have, because they, too, suffer and really don't understand who is to blame and because they misinterpret our needs to charity they tend to be against us.

But more and more people are joining together and soon there will be enough people to keep men in power who will make, pass, and enforce laws that will be fair and equal to all Americans, just as there will be enough people to bring down those in power who are favorable to one group only because of personal gain.

Therefore, discriminary legislation practices should continue no more. The migrant worker should be covered by the National Labor Relations Act with additional favorable rights as well as workman's compensation laws, unemployment compensation, insurance laws, social security codes must be enforced to improve the conditions of housing provided to him. Programs such as housing loans, small business loans which the migrant has never heard about until others who have recently come into this Nation.

Let's stop worrying about other nations and do something about our own. Do something about the migrant so he can pull himself out of this repeating cycle.

The men who are in power must fight hard to make real changes in society and society's laws. Change all discriminatory laws and attitudes. The men who are in power must help the powerless to gain power and all rights entitled to him. Bad programs of the establishment must be eliminated for good programs. Those which dispute the powers that be and fight for the poor must be maintained and encouraged in their activities.

If the poor are not given extra encouragement and help in gaining power over their own lives and influence into the general society in order to eliminate poverty; if the governments, local and national, do not respond to the real needs of the poor through traditional processes, the poor will find other ways to make their needs known and to gain power. . . .

Senator BELLMON. You mentioned you were sold to a sugar beet company?

Mr. JUAREZ. Yes, sir.

Senator BELLMON. How? Can you explain?

Mr. JUAREZ. Well, through our crew leader, through a person who had a truck who recruited labor who found out that the sugar beet company in Ohio happened to be in need of labor and so he just went around and since he was known to most of the people there, even to my father, these families were talked into coming to Ohio where the word that he gave was you can sweep money with a broom. So this is the way we were sold in the State of Ohio. I remember that it was a little town called Metamora, Ohio. From there, because of the rains we didn't get to even know what the sugar beets looked like. Then I didn't even know what sugar beets were. But we were kept there anyway because the man who brought us there just brought us there for what he got and he returned. We never seen him no more.

Senator BELLMON. So you were left in Ohio and it was raining and you weren't able to work in the sugar beets, right?

Mr. JUAREZ. Yes, and we created a big debt. My father and all the rest of the families got in real bad debt. They split up the families, the company did, and found other various jobs so that they could pay for the food that they had eaten, my father. And my cousin, which was the oldest one in our family, was the one who worked along with him. The job that they got was the railroad company, railroad tracks, working on the railroad. After he paid, after they paid the debt and we were able to make enough money to try to return to Texas, we only made it as far as Osceola, Ark., because while we were there waiting to transfer on the bus, one of my sisters was very sick and then we met another Mexican-American fellow there that told us about the good cotton that was being raised there and we had picked cotton before.

So therefore we decided to end our journey there and maybe try to make a little more money and give my sister a chance to get well. So that is where we stopped and then from Arkansas then we traveled into Missouri and from Arkansas and Missouri we started migrating into Durand, Wis., to work with the pea viner- ies. The only reason we went to Wisconsin was because when I was about, 1 year, there was 1 year, way after we had already started migrating back into Ohio to pick tomatoes and Indiana to pick tomatoes and Michigan to pick cherries. When we went to Duran, it was because I stowed away in a crew leader's truck and I ran away from home. I was 12 years then. I was able after being tested by the foreman to prove my ability to do the job. I was given a job and was able to save about $200 to bring back to my father and thus told him about the good work over there. Then we started going into Wisconsin.

President Johnson Announces Steps To Limit the War in Vietnam Decides Not To Seek Reelection. March 30, 1968

Good evening,my fellow Americans:

Tonight I want to speak to you of peace in Vietnam and Southeast Asia.

No other question so preoccupies our people. No other dream so absorbs the 250 million human beings who live in that part of the world. No other goal motivates American policy in Southeast Asia.

For years, representatives of our Government and others have traveled the world— seeking to find a basis for peace talks.

Since last September, they have carried the offer that I made public at San Antonio.

That offer was this:

That the United States would stop its bombardment of North Vietnam when that would lead promptly to productive discus- sions—and that we would assume that North Vietnam would not take military advantage of our restraint.

Hanoi denounced this offer, both privately and publicly. Even while the search for peace was going on, North Vietnam rushed their preparations for a savage assault on the people, the government, and the allies of South Vietnam.

Their attack—during the Tet holidays— failed to achieve its principal objectives.

It did not collapse the elected government of South Vietnam or shatter its army—as the Communists had hoped.

It did not produce a "general uprising" among the people of the cities as they had predicted.

The Communists were unable to maintain control of any of the more than 30 cities that they attacked. And they took very heavy casualties.

But they did compel the South Vietnamese and their allies to move certain forces from the countryside into the cities.

They caused widespread disruption and suffering. Their attacks, and the battles that followed, made refugees of half a million human beings.

The Communists may renew their attack any day.

They are, it appears, trying to make 1968 the year of decision in South Vietnam—the year that brings, if not final victory or defeat, at least a turning point in the struggle.

This much is clear:

If they do mount another round of heavy attacks, they will not succeed in destroying the fighting power of South Vietnam and its allies.

But tragically, this is also clear: Many men—on both sides of the struggle—will be lost. A nation that has already sudered 20 years of warfare will suffer once again. Armies on both sides will take new casualties. And the war will go on.

There is no need for this to be so.

There is no need to delay the talks that could bring an end to this long and this bloody war.

Tonight, I renew the offer I made last August—to stop the bombardment of North Vietnam. We ask that talks begin promptly, that they be serious talks on the substance of peace. We assume that during those talks Hanoi will not take advantage of our restraint.

We are prepared to move immediately toward peace through negotiations.

So, tonight, in the hope that this action will lead to early talks, I am taking the first step to deescalate the conflict. We are reducing—substantially reducing—the present level of hostilities.

And we are doing so unilaterally, and at once.

Tonight, I have ordered our aircraft and our naval vessels to make no attacks on North Vietnam, except in the area north of the demilitarized zone where the continuing enemy buildup directly threatens allied forward positions and where the movements of their troops and supplies are clearly related to that threat.

The area in which we are stopping our attacks includes almost go percent of North Vietnam's population, and most of its territory. Thus there will be no attacks around the principal populated areas, or in the foodproducing areas of North Vietnam.

Even this very limited bombing of the North could come to an early end—if our restraint is matched by restraint in Hanoi. But I cannot in good conscience stop all bombing so long as to do so would immediately and directly endanger the lives of our men and our allies. Whether a complete bombing halt becomes possible in the future will be determined by events.

Our purpose in this action is to bring about a reduction in the level of violence that now exists.

It is to save the lives of brave men—and to save the lives of innocent women and children. It is to permit the contending forces to move closer to a political settlement.

And tonight, I call upon the United Kingdom and I call upon the Soviet Union—as cochairmen of the Geneva Conferences, and as permanent members of the United Nations Security Council—to do all they can to move from the unilateral act of deescalation that I have just announced toward genuine peace in Southeast Asia.

Now, as in the past, the United States is ready to send its representatives to any forum, at any time, to discuss the means of bringing this ugly war to an end.

I am designating one of our most distin. guished Americans, Ambassador Averell Harriman, as my personal representative for such talks. In addition, I have asked Ambassador Llewellyn Thompson, who returned from Moscow for consultation, to be available to join Ambassador Harriman at Geneva or any other suitable place—just as soon as Hanoi agrees to a conference.

I call upon President Ho Chi Minh to respond positively, and favorably, to this new step toward peace.

But if peace does not come now through negotiations, it will come when Hanoi understands that our common resolve is unshakable, and our common strength is invincible.

Tonight, we and the other allied nations are contributing 600,000 fighting men to assist 700,000 South Vietnamese troops in defending their little country.

Our presence there has always rested on this basic belief: The main burden of preserving their freedom must be carried out by them—by the South Vietnamese themselves.

We and our allies can only help to provide a shield behind which the people of South Vietnam can survive and can grow and develop. On their efforts—on their determination and resourcefulness—the outcome will ultimately depend.

That small, beleaguered nation has suffered terrible punishment for more than 20 years.

I pay tribute once again tonight to the great courage and endurance of its people. South Vietnam supports armed forces tonight of almost 700,000 men—and I call your attention to the fact that this is the equivalent of more than 10 million in our own population. Its people maintain their firm determination to be free of domination by the North.

There has been substantial progress, I think, in building a durable government during these last 3 years. The South Vietnam of 1965 could not have survived the enemy's Tet offensive of 1968. The elected government of South Vietnam survived that attack—and is rapidly repairing the devastation that it wrought.

In order that these forces may reach maximum combat effectiveness, the Joint Chiefs of Staff have recommended to me that we should prepare to send—during the next 5 months—support troops totaling approximately 13,500 men.

A portion of these men will be made available from our active forces. The balance will come from reserve component units which will be called up for service.

The actions that we have taken since the beginning of the year

- to reequip the South Vietnamese forces,

- to meet our responsibilities in Korea, as well as our responsibilities in Vietnam, ~i)

- to meet price increases and the cost of activating and deploying reserve forces,

- to replace helicopters and provide the other military supplies we need, all of these actions are going to require additional expenditures.

The tentative estimate of those additional expenditures is $2.5 billion in this fiscal year, and $2.6 billion in the next fiscal year.

These projected increases in expenditures for our national security will bring into sharper focus the Nation's need for immediate action: action to protect the prosperity of the American people and to protect the strength and the stability of our American dollar.

On many occasions I have pointed out that, without a tax bill or decreased expenditures, next year's deficit would again be around $20 billion. I have emphasized the need to set strict priorities in our spending. I have stressed that failure to act and to act promptly and decisively would raise very strong doubts throughout the world about America's willingness to keep its financial house in order.

Yet Congress has not acted. And tonight we face the sharpest financial threat in the postwar era—a threat to the dollar's role as the keystone of international trade and finance in the world.

Last week, at the monetary conference in Stockholm, the major industrial countrie, decided to take a big step toward creating a new international monetary asset that will strengthen the international monetary system. I am very proud of the very able work done by Secretary Fowler and Chairman Martin of the Federal Reserve Board.

But to make this system work the United States just must bring its balance of payments to—or very close to—equilibrium. We must have a responsible fiscal policy in this country. The passage of a tax bill now, together with expenditure control that the Congress may desire and dictate, is absolutely necessary to protect this Nation's security, to continue our prosperity, and to meet the needs of our people.

What is at stake is 7 years of unparalleled prosperity. In those 7 years, the real income of the average American, after taxes, rose by almost 30 percent—a gain as large as that of the entire preceding 19 years.

So the steps that we must take to convince the world are exactly the steps we must take to sustain our own economic strength here at home. In the past 8 months, prices and interest rates have risen because of our inaction.

We must, therefore, now do everything we can to move from debate to action—from talking to voting. There is, I believe—I hope there is—in both Houses of the Congress—a growing sense of urgency that this situation just must be acted upon and must be corrected.

My budget in January was, we thought, a tight one. It fully reflected our evaluation of most of the demanding needs of this Nation.

But in these budgetary matters, the President does not decide alone. The Congress has the power and the duty to determine appropriations and taxes.

The Congress is now considering our proposals and they are considering reductions in the budget that we submitted.

As part of a program of fiscal restraint that includes the tax surcharge, I shall approve appropriate reductions in the January budget when and if Congress so decides that that should be done.

One thing is unmistakably clear, however: Our deficit just must be reduced. Failure to act could bring on conditions that would strike hardest at those people that all of us are trying so hard to help:`

These times call for prudence in this land of plenty. I believe that we have the character to provide it, and torught I plead with the Congress and with the people to act promptly to serve the national interest, and thereby serve all of our people.

So, I repeat on behalf of the United States again tonight what I said at Johns Hopkins—that North Vietnam could take its place in this common effort just as soon as peace comes.

Over time, a wider framework of peace and security in Southeast Asia may become possible. The new cooperation of the nations of the area could be a foundation- stone. Certainly friendship with the nations of such a Southeast Asia is what the United States seeks—and that is all that the United States seeks.

One day, my fellow citizens, there will be peace in Southeast Asia.

It will come because the people of Southeast Asia want it—those whose armies are at war tonight, and those who, though threatened, have thus far been spared.

Peace will come because Asians were willing to work for it—and to sacrifice for it— and to die by the thousands for it.

But let it never be forgotten: Peace will come also because America sent her sons to help secure it.

It has not been easy~far from it. During the past 4~/2 years, it has been my fate and my responsibility to be Commander in Chief. I have lived—daily and nightly—with the cost of this war. I know the pain that it has inflicted. I know, perhaps better than anyone, the misgivings that it has aroused.

Throughout this entire, long period, I have been sustained by a single principle: that what we are doing now, in Vietnam, is vital not only to the security of Southeast Asia, but it is vital to the security of every American.

There is division in the American house now. There is divisiveness among us all tonight. And holding the trust that is mine, as President of all the people, I cannot disregard the peril to the progress of the American people and the hope and the prospect of peace for all peoples.

So, I would ask all Americans, ~ whatever their personal interests or concern, to guard against divisiveness and all its ugly consequences.

Fifty-two months and io days ago, in a moment of tragedy and trauma, the duties of this office fell upon me. I asked then for your help and God's, that we might continue America on its course, binding up our wounds, healing our history, moving forward in new unity, to clear the American agenda and to keep the American commitment for all of our people.

United we have kept that commitment. United we have enlarged that commitment.

Through all time to come, I think America will be a stronger nation, a more just society, and a land of greater opportunity and fulfillment because of what we have all done together in these years of unparalleled achievement.

Our reward will come in the life of freedom, peace, and hope that our children will enjoy through ages ahead.

What we won when all of our people united just must not now be lost in suspicion, distrust, selfishness, and politics among any of our people.

Believing this as I do, I have concluded that I should not permit the Presidency to become involved in the partisan divisions that are developing in this political year.

With America's sons in the fields far away, with America's future under challenge right here at home, with our hopes and the world's hopes for peace in the balance every day, I do not believe that I should devote an hour or a day of my time to any personal partisan causes or to any duties other than the awesome duties of this office—the Presidency of your country.

Accordingly, I shall not seek, and I will not accept, the nomination of my party for another term as your Prcsident.

But let men everywhere know, however, that a strong, a confident, and a vigilant America stands ready tonight to seek an honorable peace—and stands ready tonight to defend an honored cause—whatever the price, whatever the burden, whatever the sacrifice that duty may require.

Thank you for listening.

Good night and God bless all of you.

Robert F. Kennedy: Remarks on the Assassination of Martin Luther King, Jr., April 4, 1968

Ladies and Gentlemen,

I'm only going to talk to you just for a minute or so this evening, because I have some—some very sad news for all of you—Could you lower those signs, please?—I have some very sad news for all of you, and, I think, sad news for all of our fellow citizens, and people who love peace all over the world; and that is that Martin Luther King was shot and was killed tonight in Memphis, Tennessee.

Martin Luther King dedicated his life to love and to justice between fellow human beings. He died in the cause of that effort. In this difficult day, in this difficult time for the United States, it's perhaps well to ask what kind of a nation we are and what direction we want to move in. For those of you who are black—considering the evidence evidently is that there were white people who were responsible—you can be filled with bitterness, and with hatred, and a desire for revenge.

We can move in that direction as a country, in greater polarization—black people amongst blacks, and white amongst whites, filled with hatred toward one another. Or we can make an effort, as Martin Luther King did, to understand, and to comprehend, and replace that violence, that stain of bloodshed that has spread across our land, with an effort to understand, compassion, and love.

For those of you who are black and are tempted to fill with—be filled with hatred and mistrust of the injustice of such an act, against all white people, I would only say that I can also feel in my own heart the same kind of feeling. I had a member of my family killed, but he was killed by a white man.

But we have to make an effort in the United States. We have to make an effort to understand, to get beyond, or go beyond these rather difficult times.

My favorite poem, my—my favorite poet was Aeschylus. And he once wrote:

> Even in our sleep, pain which cannot forget
>
> falls drop by drop upon the heart,
>
> until, in our own despair,
>
> against our will,
>
> comes wisdom
>
> through the awful grace of God.

What we need in the United States is not division; what we need in the United States is not hatred; what we need in the United States is not violence and lawlessness, but is love, and wisdom, and compassion toward one another, and a feeling of justice toward those who still suffer within our country, whether they be white or whether they be black.

So I ask you tonight to return home, to say a prayer for the family of Martin Luther King—yeah, it's true—but more importantly to say a prayer for our own country, which all of us love—a prayer for understanding and that compassion of which I spoke.

We can do well in this country. We will have difficult times. We've had difficult times in the past, but we—and we will have difficult times in the future. It is not the end of violence; it is not the end of lawlessness; and it's not the end of disorder.

But the vast majority of white people and the vast majority of black people in this country want to live together, want to improve the quality of our life, and want justice for all human beings that abide in our land.

And let's dedicate ourselves to what the Greeks wrote so many years ago: to tame the savageness of man and make gentle the life of this world. Let us dedicate ourselves to that, and say a prayer for our country and for our people.

Thank you very much.

President Reagan's "Evil Empire" Speech: Orlando, Florida; March 8, 1983.

President Ronald Reagan

Those of you in the National Association of Evangelicals are known for you spiritual and humanitarian work. And I would be especially remiss if I didn't discharge right now one personal debt of gratitude. Thank you for your prayers. Nancy and I have felt their presence many times in many years. And believe me, for us they've made all the difference.

The other day in the East Room of the White House at a meeting there, someone asked me whether I was aware of all the people out there who were praying for the President. And I had to say, "Yes, I am. I've felt it. I believe in intercessionary prayer." But I couldn't help but say to that questioner after he'd asked the question that - or at least say to them that if sometimes when he was praying he got a busy signal, it was just me in there ahead of him. I think I understand how Abraham Lincoln felt when he said, "I have been driven many times to my knees by the overwhelming conviction that I had nowhere else to go." From the joy and the good feeling of this conference, I go to a political reception. Now, I don't know why, but that bit of scheduling reminds me of a story - - which I'll share with you.

An evangelical minister and a politician arrived at Heaven's gate one day together. And St. Peter, after doing all the necessary formalities, took them in hand to show them where their quarters would be. And he took them to a small, single room with a bed, a chair, and a table and said this was for the clergyman. And the politician was a little worried about what might be in store for him. And he couldn't believe it then when St. Peter stopped in front of a beautiful mansion with lovely grounds, many servants, and told him that these would be his quarters.

And he couldn't help but ask, he said, "But wait, how-there's something wrong - how do I get this mansion while that good and holy man only gets a single room?" And St. Peter said, "You have to understand how things are up here. We've got thousands and thousands of clergy. You're the first politician who ever made it."

But I don't want to contribute to a stereotype. So I tell you there are a great many God-fearing, dedicated, noble men and women in public life, present company included. And yes, we need your help to keep us ever mindful of the ideas and the principles that brought us into the public arena in the first place. The basis of those ideals and principles is a commitment to freedom and personal liberty that, itself, is grounded in the much deeper realization that freedom prospers only where the blessings of God are avidly sought and humbly accepted.

The American experiment in democracy rests on this insight. Its discovery was the great triumph of our Founding Fathers, voiced by William Penn when he said: "If we will not be governed by God, we must be governed by tyrants." Explaining the inalienable rights of men, Jefferson said, "The God who gave us life, gave us liberty at the same time." And it was George Washington who said that "of all the disposition and habits which lead to political prosperity, religion and morality are indispensable supporters."

And finally, that shrewdest of all observers of American democracy, Alexis de Tocqueville, put it eloquently after he had gone on a search for the secret of America's greatness and genius - and he said: "Not until I went into the churches of America and heard her pulpits aflame with righteousness did I understand the greatness and the genius of America . . . America is good. And if America ever ceases to be good, America will cease to be great."

Well, I'm pleased to be here today with you who are keeping America great by keeping her good. Only through your work and prayers and those of millions of others cans we hope to survive this perilous century and keep alive this experiment in liberty, this last, best hope of man.

I want you to know that this administration is motivated by a political philosophy that sees the greatness of America in you, here people, and in your families, churches, neighborhoods, communities – the institutions that foster and nourish values like concern for others and respect for the rule of law under God.

Now, I don't have to tell you that this puts us in opposition to, or at least out of step with, a prevailing attitude of many who have turned to a modern-day secularism, discarding the tried and time-tested values upon which our very civilization is based. No matter how well intentioned, their value system is radically different from that of most Americans. And while they proclaim that they're freeing us from superstitions of the past, they've taken upon themselves the job of superintending us by government rule and regulation. Sometimes their voices are louder than ours, but they are not yet a majority.

An example of that vocal superiority is evident in a controversy now going on in Washington. And since I'm involved I've been waiting to hear from the parents of young America. How far are they willing to go in giving to government their prerogatives as parents?

Let me state the case as briefly and simply as I can. An organization of citizens, sincerely motivated and deeply concerned about the increase in illegitimate births and abortions involving girls well below the age of consent, some time ago established a nationwide network of clinics to offer help to these girls and, hopefully, alleviate this situation. Now, again, let me say, I do not fault their intent. However, in their well-intentioned effort, these clinics have decided to provide advice and birth control drugs and devices to underage girls without the knowledge of their parents.

For some years now, the federal government has helped with funds to subsidize these clinics. In providing for this, the Congress decreed that every effort would be made to maximize parental participation. Nevertheless, the drugs and devices are prescribed without getting parental consent or giving notification after they've done so. Girls termed "sexually active" – and that has replaced the word "promiscuous" – are given this help in order to prevent illegitimate birth or abortion.

Well, we have ordered clinics receiving federal funds to notify the parents such help has been given. One of the nation's leading newspapers has created the term "squeal rule" in editorializing against us for doing this, and we're being criticized for violating the privacy of young people. A judge has recently granted an injunction against an enforcement of our rule. I've watched TV panel shows discuss the issue, seen columnists pontificating on our error, but no one seems to mention morality as playing a part in the subject of sex.

Is all of Judeo-Christian tradition wrong? Are we to believe that something so sacred can be looked upon as a purely physical thing with no potential for emotional and psychological harm? And isn't it the parents' right to give counsel and advice to keep their children from making mistakes that may affect their entire lives?

Many of us in government would like to know what parents think about this intrusion in their family by government. We're going to fight in the courts. The right of parents and the rights of family take precedence over those of Washington-based bureaucrats and social engineers.

But the fight against parental notification is really only one example of many attempts to water down traditional values and even abrogate the original terms of American democracy. Freedom prospers when religion is vibrant and the rule of law under God is acknowledged. When our Founding Fathers passed the First Amendment, they sought to protect churches from government interference. They never intended to construct a wall of hostility between government and the concept of religious belief itself.

The evidence of this permeates our history and our government. The Declaration of Independence mentions the Supreme Being no less than four times. "In God We Trust" is engraved on our coinage. The Supreme Court opens its proceedings with a religious invocation. And the members of Congress open their sessions with a prayer. I just happen to believe the schoolchildren of the United States are entitled to the same privileges as Supreme Court justices and congressmen.

Last year, I sent the Congress a constitutional amendment to restore prayer to public schools. Already this session, there's growing bipartisan support for the amendment, and I am calling on the Congress to act speedily to pass it and to let our children pray.

Perhaps some of you read recently about the Lubbock school case, where a judge actually ruled that it was unconstitutional for a school district to give equal treatment to religious and nonreligious student groups, even when the group meetings were being held during the students' own time. The First Amendment never intended to require government to discriminate against religious speech.

Senators Denton and Hatfield have proposed legislation in the Congress on the whole question of prohibiting discrimination against religious forms of student speech. Such legislation could go far to restore freedom of religious speech for public school students. And I hope the Congress considers these bills quickly. And with you help, I think it's possible we could also get the constitutional amendment through the Congress this year.

More than a decade ago, a Supreme Court decision literally wiped off the books of fifty states statutes protecting the rights of unborn children. Abortion on demand now takes the lives of up to one and a half million unborn children a year. Human life legislation ending this tragedy will someday pass the Congress, and you and I must never rest until it does. Unless and until it can be proven that the unborn child is not a living entity, then its right to life, liberty, and the pursuit of happiness must be protected.

You may remember that when abortion on demand began, many, and indeed, I'm sure many of you, warned that the practice would lead to a decline in respect for human life, that the philosophical premises used to justify abortion on demand would ultimately be used to justify other attacks on the sacredness of human life;infanticide or mercy killing. Tragically enough, those warnings proved all too true. Only last year a court permitted the death by starvation of a handicapped infant.

I have directed the Health and Human Services Department to make clear to every health care facility in the United States that the Rehabilitation Act of 1973 protects all handicapped persons against discrimination based on handicaps, including infants. And we have taken the further step of requiring that each and every recipient of federal funds who provides health care services to infants must post and keep posted in a conspicuous place a notice stating that "discriminatory failure to feed and care for handicapped infants in this facility is prohibited by federal law." It also lists a twenty-four-hour, toll-free number so that nurses and others may report violations in time to save the infant's life.

In addition, recent legislation introduced in the Congress by Representative Henry Hyde of Illinois not only increases restrictions on publicly financed abortions, it also addresses this whole problem of infanticide. I urge the Congress to begin hearings and to adopt legislation that will protect the right of life to all children, including the disabled or handicapped.

Now, I'm sure that you must get discouraged at times, but you've done better than you know, perhaps. There's a great spiritual awakening in America, a renewal of the traditional values that have been the bedrock of America's goodness and greatness.

One recent survey by a Washington-based research council concluded that Americans were far more religious than the people of other nations; 95 percent of those surveyed expressed a belief in God and a huge majority believed the Ten Commandments had real meaning in their lives. And another study has found that an overwhelming majority of Americans disapprove of adultery, teenage sex, pornography, abortion, and hard drugs. And this same study showed a deep reverence for the importance of family ties and religious belief.

I think the items that we've discussed here today must be a key part of the nation's political agenda. For the first time the Congress is openly and seriously debating and dealing with the prayer and abortion issues;and that's enormous progress right there. I repeat: America is in the midst of a spiritual awakening and a moral renewal. And with your biblical keynote, I say today, "Yes, let justice roll on like a river, righteousness like a never-failing stream."

Now, obviously, much of this new political and social consensus I've talked about is based on a positive view of American history, one that takes pride in our country's accomplishments and record. But we must never forget that no government schemes are going to perfect man. We know that living in this world means dealing with what philosophers would call the phenomenology of evil or, as theologians would put it, the doctrine of sin.

There is sin and evil in the world, and we're enjoined by Scripture and the Lord Jesus to oppose it with all our might. Our nation, too, has a legacy of evil with which it must deal. The glory of this land has been its capacity for transcending the moral evils of our past. For example, the long struggle of minority citizens for equal rights, once a source of disunity and civil war, is now a point of pride for all Americans. We must never go back. There is no room for racism, anti-Semitism, or other forms of ethnic and racial hatred in this country.

I know that you've been horrified, as have I, by the resurgence of some hate groups preaching bigotry and prejudice. Use the mighty voice of your pulpits and the powerful standing of your churches to denounce and isolate these hate groups in our midst. The commandment given us is clear and simple: "Thou shalt love thy neighbor as thyself."

But whatever sad episodes exist in our past, any objective observer must hold a positive view of American history, a history that has been the story of hopes fulfilled and dreams made into reality. Especially in this century, America has kept alight the torch of freedom, but not just for ourselves but for millions of others around the world.

And this brings me to my final point today. During my first press conference as president, in answer to a direct question, I point out that, as good Marxist-Leninists, the Soviet leaders have openly and publicly declared that the only morality they recognize is that which will further their cause, which is world revolution. I think I should point out I was only quoting Lenin, their guiding spirit, who said in 1920 that they repudiate all morality that proceeds from supernatural ideas - that's their name for religion - or ideas that are outside class conceptions. Morality is entirely subordinate to the interests of class war. And everything is moral that is necessary for the annihilation of the old, exploiting social order and for uniting the proletariat.

Well, I think the refusal of many influential people to accept this elementary fact of Soviet doctrine illustrates a historical reluctance to see totalitarian powers for what they are. We saw this phenomenon in the 1930s. We see it too often today.

This doesn't mean we should isolate ourselves and refuse to seek an understanding with them. I intend to do everything I can to persuade them of our peaceful intent, to remind them that it was the West that refused to use its nuclear monopoly in the forties and fifties for territorial gain and which now proposes a 50-percent cut in strategic ballistic missiles and the elimination of an entire class of land-based, intermediate-range nuclear missiles.

At the same time, however, they must be made to understand we will never compromise our principles and standards. We will never give away our freedom. We will never abandon our belief in God. And we will never stop searching for a genuine peace. But we can assure none of these things America stands for through the so-called nuclear freeze solutions proposed by some.

The truth is that a freeze now would be a very dangerous fraud, for that is merely the illusion of peace. The reality is that we must find peace through strength.

I would agree to freeze if only we could freeze the Soviets' global desires. A freeze at current levels of weapons would remove any incentive for the Soviets to negotiate seriously in Geneva and virtually end our chances to achieve the major arms reductions which we have proposed. Instead, they would achieve their objectives through the freeze.

A freeze would reward the Soviet Union for its enormous and unparalleled military buildup. It would prevent the essential and long overdue modernization of United States and allied defenses and would leave our aging forces increasingly vulnerable. And an honest freeze would require extensive prior negotiations on the systems and numbers to be limited and on the measures to ensure effective verification and compliance. And the kind of a freeze that has been suggested would be virtually impossible to verify. Such a major effort would divert us completely from our current negotiations on achieving substantial reductions.

A number of years ago, I heard a young father, a very prominent young man in the entertainment world, addressing a tremendous gathering in California. It was during the time of the cold war, and communism and our own way of life were very much on people's minds. And he was speaking to that subject. And suddenly, though, I heard him saying, "I love my little girls more than anything -" And I said to myself, "Oh, no, don't. You can't - don't say that." But I had underestimated him. He went on: "I would rather see my little girls die now, still believing in God, than have them grow up under communism and one day die no longer believing in God."

There were thousands of young people in that audience. They came to their feet with shouts of joy. They had instantly recognized the profound truth in what he had said, with regard to the physical and the soul and what was truly important.

Yes, let us pray for the salvation of all of those who live in that totalitarian darkness - pray they will discover the joy of knowing God. But until they do, let us be aware that while they preach the supremacy of the state, declare its omnipotence over individual man, and predict its eventual domination of all peoples on the earth, they are the focus of evil in the modern world.

It was C.S. Lewis who, in his unforgettable Screwtape Letters, wrote: "The greatest evil is not done now in those sordid 'dens of rime' that Dickens loved to paint. It is not even done in concentration camps and labor camps. In those we see its final result. But it is conceived and ordered (moved, seconded, carried and minuted) in clean, carpeted, warmed, and well-lighted offices, by quiet men with white collars and cut fingernails and smooth-shaven cheeks who do no need to raise their voice."

Well, because these "quiet men" do no "raise their voices," because they sometimes speak in soothing tones of brotherhood and peace, because, like other dictators before them, they're always making "their final territorial demand," some would have us accept them as their word and accommodate ourselves to their aggressive impulses. But if history teaches anything, it teaches that simpleminded appeasement or wishful thinking about our adversaries is folly. It means the betrayal of our past, the squandering of our freedom.

So, I urge you to speak our against those who would place the United States in a position of military and moral inferiority. You know, I've always believed that old Screwtape reserved his best efforts for those of you in the church. So, in your discussions of the nuclear freeze proposals, I urge you to beware the temptation of pride – the temptation of blithely declaring yourselves above it all and label both sides equally at fault, to ignore the facts of history and the aggressive impulses of an evil empire, to simply call the arms race a giant misunderstanding and thereby remove yourself from the struggle between right and wrong and good and evil.

I ask you to resist the attempts of those who would have you withhold your support for our efforts, this administration's efforts, to keep America strong and free, while we negotiate real and verifiable reductions in the world's nuclear arsenals and one day, with God's help, their total elimination.

While America's military strength is important, let me add here that I've always maintained that the struggle now going on for the world will never be decided by bombs or rockets, by armies or military might. The real crisis we face today is a spiritual one; at root, it is a test of moral will and faith.

Whittaker Chambers, the man whose own religious conversion made him a witness to one of the terrible traumas of our time, the Hiss–Chambers case, wrote that the crisis of the Western world exists to the degree in which the West is indifferent to God, the degree to which it collaborates in communism's attempt to make man stand alone without God. And then he said, for Marxism-Leninism is actually the second-oldest faith, first proclaimed in the Garden of Eden with the words of temptation, "Ye shall be as gods."

The Western world can answer this challenge, he wrote, "but only provided that its faith in God and the freedom He enjoins is as great as communism's faith in Man."

I believe we shall rise to the challenge. I believe that communism is another sad, bizarre chapter in human history whose last pages even now are being written. I believe this because the source of our strength in the quest for human freedom is not material, but spiritual. And because it knows no limitation, it must terrify and ultimately triumph over those who would enslave their fellow man. For in the words of Isaiah: "He giveth power to the faint; and to them that have no might He increased strength . . . But they that wait upon the Lord shall renew their strength; they shall mount up with wings as eagles; they shall run, and not be weary . . . "

Yes, change your world. One of our Founding Fathers, Thomas Paine, said, "We have it within our power to begin the world over again." We can do it, doing together what no one church could do by itself.

God bless you, and thank you very much.

Senator Byron Dorgan's Anti-Deregulation Speech: November 4, 1999.

Mr. President, we are debating a piece of legislation in the Senate that is called the Financial Services Modernization Act of 1999.

I come today with the confession I am probably hopelessly old fashioned on this issue. For those who have a vision of re-landscaping the financial system in this country with different parts operating with each other in different ways and saying that represents modernization, then I am just hopelessly old fashioned, and there is probably nothing that can be said or done that will march me towards the future.

I want to sound a warning call today about this legislation. I think this legislation is just fundamentally terrible. I hear all these words about the industry remaking itself--banks, security firms and insurance companies, and that we'd better catch up and put a fence around where they are or at least build a pasture in the vicinity of where they are grazing. What a terrible idea.

What is it that sparks this need to modernize our financial system? And what does modernization mean? This chart shows bank mergers in 1998, in just 1 year, last year, the top 10 bank mergers. We have discovered all these corporations have fallen in love and decided to get married. Citicorp, with an insurance company--that is a big one--$698 billion in combined assets; NationsBank--BankAmerica, $570 million; and the list goes on. This is a massive concentration through mergers.

Is it good for the consumers? I don't think so. Better service, lower prices, lower fees? I don't think so. Bigger profits? You bet.

What about the banking industry concentration? The chart shows the number of banks with 25 percent of the domestic deposits. In 1984, 42 of the biggest banks had 25 percent of the biggest deposits. Now only six banks have the biggest deposits. That is a massive concentration.

I didn't bring the chart out about profits, but it will show --this is an industry that says it needs to be modernized--banks have record-breaking profits, security firms have very healthy profits, and most insurance companies are doing just fine. Why is there a need to modernize them?

So we must ask the question, what about the customer? What impact on the economy will all of this so-called modernization have?

It is interesting to me that the bill brought to the floor that says, ``Let's modernize this," is a piece of legislation that doesn't do anything about a couple of areas which I think pose very serious problems. I want to mention a couple of these problems because I want to offer a couple of amendments on them.

I begin by reading an article that appeared in the Wall Street Journal, November 16, 1998. This is a harbinger of things to come, just as something I will read that happened in 1994 is a harbinger of things to come, especially as we move in this direction of modernization.

It was Aug. 21, a sultry Friday, and nearly half the partners at Long-Term Capital Management LP [that's LTCM, a company] were out of the office. Outside the fund's glass-and-granite headquarters, a fountain languidly streamed over a copper osprey clawing its prey.

Inside, the associates logged on to their computers and saw something deeply disturbing: U.S. Treasurys were skyrocketing, throwing their relationship to other securities out of whack. The Dow Jones Industrial Average was swooning--by noon, down 283 points. The European bond market was in shambles. LTCM's biggest bets were blowing up, and no one could do anything about it.

This was a private hedge funding.

By 11 a.m., the [hedge] fund had lost $150 million in a wager on the prices of two telecommunications stocks involved in a takeover. Then, a single bet tied to the U.S. bond market lost $100 million [by the same company]. Another $100 million evaporated in a similar trade in Britain. By day's end, LTCM [this hedge fund in New York] had hemorrhaged half a billion dollars. Its equity had sunk to $3.1 billion--down a third for the year.

This company had made bets over $1 trillion.

Now, what happened? They lost their silk shirts. But of course, they were saved because a Federal Reserve Board official decided we can't lose a hedge fund like this; it would be catastrophic to the marketplace. So on Sunday night they convened a meeting with an official of the Federal Reserve Board, and a group of banks came in as a result of that meeting and used bank funds to shore up a private hedge fund that was capitalized in the Caymen Islands for the purpose, I assume, of avoiding taxes. Bets of over $1 trillion in hedges--they could have set up a casino in their lobby, in my judgment, the way they were doing business. But they got bailed out.

This was massive exposure. The exposure on the hedge fund was such that the failure of the hedge fund would have had a significant impact on the market.

And so we modernize our banking system. This is unregulated. This isn't a bank; it is an unregulated hedge fund, except the banks have massive quantities of money in the hedge fund now in order to bail it out.

What does modernization say about this? Nothing, nothing. It says let's pretend this doesn't exist, this isn't a problem, let's not deal with it.

So we will modernize our financial institutions and we will say about this problem--nothing? Don't worry about it?

I find it fascinating that about 70 years ago in this country we had examples of institutions the futures of which rested on not just safety and soundness of the institutions themselves but the perception of safety and soundness, that is, banks. Those institutions, the future success and stability of which is only guaranteed by the perception that they are safe and sound, were allowed, 70

years ago, to combine with other kinds of risk enterprises--
notably securities underwriting and some other activities--and
that was going to be all right. That was back in the Roaring
Twenties when we had this go-go economy and the stock market
was shooting up like a Roman candle and banks got involved in
securities and all of a sudden everybody was doing well and
everybody was making massive amounts of money and the country was delirious about it.

Then the house of cards started to fall . As investigations began
and bank failures occurred and bank holidays were declared, from
that rubble came a description of a future that would separate
banking institutions from inherently risky enterprises. A piece of
legislation called the Glass-Steagall Act was written, saying maybe
we should learn from this, that we should not fuse inherently
risky enterprises with institutions whose perception of safety and
soundness is the only thing that can guarantee their future success. So we created circumstances that prevented certain institutions like banks from being involved in other activities such as
securities underwriting.

Over the years that has all changed. Banks have said, because
everybody else has decided they want to intrude into our busi-
ness--and that is right, a whole lot of folks now set themselves
up in a lobby someplace and say we are appearing to be like a
bank or want to behave like a bank--the banks say if that is the
case, we want to get into their business. So now we have the
kind of initiative here in the Congress that says: Let's forget the
lessons of the past; let's believe the 1920s did not happen; let's
not worry about Glass-Steagall. In fact, let's repeal Glass-Steagall;
let's decide we can merge once again or fuse together banking
enterprises and more risky enterprises, and we can go down the
road just as happy as clams and everything will be just great. And
of course it will not.

I mentioned hedge funds--talk about risk. How about derivatives? Incidentally, those who vote for this bill will remember this
at some point in the future when we have the next catastrophic
event that goes with the risks in derivatives. Fortune magazine
wrote an article, ``The Risk That Won't Go Away; Financial
Derivatives Are Tightening Their Grip on the World Economy
and No One Knows How to Control Them." Somewhere around
$70- to $80 trillion in derivatives.

I wrote an article in 1994 for the Washington Monthly magazine and derivatives at that point were $35 trillion. You know something, today in this country banks are trading derivatives on their own proprietary accounts. They could just as well put a roulette wheel in the lobby. They could just as well call it a casino. Banks ought not be trading derivatives on their proprietary accounts. I have an amendment to prohibit that. I don't suppose it would get more than a handful of votes, but I intend to offer it.

Is it part of financial modernization to say this sort of nonsense ought to stop; that banks ought not to be able to trade derivatives on their own proprietary accounts because that is inherently gambling? It does not fit with what we know to be the fundamental nature of banking and the requirement of the perception of safety and soundness of these institutions. Does anybody here think this makes any sense, that we have banks involved in derivatives, trading on their own proprietary accounts? Does anybody think it makes any sense to have hedge funds out there with trillions of dollars of derivatives, losing billions of dollars and then being bailed out by a Federal Reserve-led bailout because their failure would be so catastrophic to the rest of the market that we cannot allow them to fail?

And as banks get bigger, of course, we also have another doctrine. The doctrine in banking at the Federal Reserve Board is called, ``too big to fail.'' Remember that term, ``too big to fail.'' It means at a certain level, banks get too big to fail. They cannot be allowed to fail because the consequence on the economy is catastrophic and therefore these banks are too big to fail. Virtually every single merger you read about in the newspapers these days means we simply have more banks that are too big to fail. That is no-fault capitalism; too big to fail. Does anybody care about that? Does the Fed? Apparently not.

Of course the Fed has an inherent conflict of interest. I think, if the Congress were thinking very clearly about the Federal

Reserve Board, they would decide immediately that the Federal Reserve Board is not the locus of supervision of banks. The Federal Reserve Board is in charge of monetary policy. It is fundamentally a conflict of interest to be listening to the Fed about what is good for banks when they are involved in running the monetary policy of this country. If the Federal Reserve Board were, in my judgment, doing what it ought to be doing, it would be leading the charge, saying we need to regulate risky hedge funds because banks are involved in substantial risk on these hedge funds. Apparently hedge funds have become too big to fail. Then there needs to be some regulation.

The Fed, if it were thinking, would say we need to deal with derivatives, and that bank trading on proprietary accounts in derivatives is absurd and ought not happen. Some will remember in 1994 the collapse in the derivative area. You might remember the stories. ``Piper's Managers' Losses May Total $700 Million.'' ``Corporation After Corporation Had to Write Off Huge Losses Because They Were Involved in the Casino Game on Derivatives.'' ``Bankers Trust Thrives on Pitching Derivatives But Climate Is Shifting.'' ``Losses By P&G May Clinch Plan to Change.''

The point is, we have massive amounts of risk in all of these areas. The bill brought to the floor today does nothing to address these risks, nothing at all, but goes ahead and creates new risks by saying we will fuse and merge the opportunities for inherently risky economic activity to be combined with banking which requires the perception of safety and soundness.

We have all these folks here who know a lot more about this than I do, I must admit, who say: Except we are creating firewalls. We have subsidiaries, we have affiliates, we have firewalls. They have everything except common sense; everything, apparently, except a primer on history. I just wish, before people would vote for this bill, they would be forced to read just a bit of the financial history of this country to understand how consequential this decision is going to be.

I, obviously, am in a minority here. We have people who dressed in their best suits and they just think this is the greatest piece of legislation that has ever been given to Congress. We have choruses of folks standing outside this Chamber who spent their lifetimes working to get this done, to say: Would you just forget all that nonsense back in the 1930s about bank failures and Glass-Steagall and the requirement to separate risk from banking enterprises; just forget all that. Time has moved on. Let's understand that. Change with the times.

We have folks outside who have worked on this very hard and who very much want this to happen. We have a lot of folks in here who are very compliant to say: Absolutely, let me be the lead singer. And here we are. We have this bill, which I will bet, in 5, 10, 15 years from now, we will be back thinking of this bill like we thought of the bill passed in the late 1970s and early 1980s, in which this Congress unhitched the savings and loans so some sleepy little Texas institution could gather brokered deposits from all around America and, like a giant rocket, become a huge enterprise. And guess what. With all the speculation in the S&Ls and brokered deposits and all the things that went with it that this Congress allowed, what did it cost the American taxpayer to bail out that bunch of failures? What did it cost? Hundreds of billions of dollars. I will bet one day somebody is going to look back at this and they are going to say: How on Earth could we have thought it made sense to allow the banking industry to concentrate, through merger and acquisition, to become bigger and bigger and bigger; far more firms in the category of too big to fail? How did we think that was going to help this country? Then to decide we shall fuse it with inherently risky enterprises, how did we think that was going to avoid the lessons of the past?

Then the one question that bothers me, I guess, is--I understand what is in this for banks. I understand what is in it for the security firms. I understand what is in it for all the enterprises. What is in this for the American people? What is in it for the American people? Higher charges, higher fees? Do you know that some banks these days are charging people to see their money? We know that because we pay fees, obviously, to access our money at bank machines. But credit card companies, most of them through banks, are charging people who pay their bills on time because you cannot make money off somebody who wants to pay their bill every month.

If you have a credit card balance--incidentally, you need a credit card these days, because it is pretty hard to do business in cash in some places. You know with all the bills, everybody wants to use credit cards . Many businesses want you to use credit cards . So you use credit cards , then you pay off the entire balance at the end of every month because you don't want to pay the interest. Some companies have decided you should be penalized for paying off your whole balance. Isn't that interesting? You talk about turning logic on its head, suggesting we don't make money on people who pay off their credit card balance every month, so let us decide that our approach to banking is to say those who pay their credit card bill off every month shall be penalized.

Turning logic on its head? I think so. As I said when I started , I am likely to be branded as hopelessly old fashioned on these issues, and I accept that. I suspect that some day in some way others will scratch their heads and say, ``I wish we had been a bit more old fashioned in the way we assessed risk and the way we read history and the way we evaluated what would have made sense going forward in modernizing our financial institutions.''

Oh, there is a way to modernize them all right, but it is not to be a parrot and say because the industry has moved in this direction, we must now move in this direction and catch them and circle them to say it is fine that you are here now. That is not the appropriate way to address the fundamental challenges we have in the financial services industry.

I am not anti-bank, anti-security or anti-insurance. All of them play a constructive role and important role in this country. But this country will be better served with aggressive antitrust enforcement, with, in my judgment, fewer mergers, with fewer companies moving in to the ``too big to fail'' category of the Federal Reserve Board, with less concentration.

This country will be better served if we have tighter controls, not firewalls that allow these companies to come together and do inherently risky things adjacent to banking enterprises, but to decide the lessons of the 1930s are indelible transcendental lessons we ought to learn and ought to remember.

Mr. President, I have more to say, but I understand my time is about to expire.

VI

"Culture" Wars

At the same time that America's global power was being challenged and the domestic front was in turmoil, a series of "culture wars" began to rage. To the political right, liberalism had devalued American traditions and unleashed an immoral new culture of sexual permissiveness, lewd public behavior, and anti-American ideas.

Sex, Drugs, Rock & Roll

Elvis to Nixon

Dear Mr. President

First I would like to introduce myself. I am Elvis Presley and admire you and Have Great Respect for your office. I talked to Vice President Agnew in Palm Springs a week ago and expressed my concern for our country. The Drug Culture, The Hippie Elements, the SDS, Black Panthers, etc do not consider me as their enemy or as they call it The Establishment. I call it America and I Love it. Sir I can and will be of any Service that I can to help the country out. I have no concerns or motives other than helping the country out. So I wish not to be given a title or an appointed position, I can and will do more good if I were made a Federal Agent at Large, and I will help out by doing it my way through my communications with people of all ages. First and Foremost I am an entertainer but all I need is the Federal credentials. I am on the Plane with Sen. George Murphy and We have been discussing the problems that our country is faced with. Sir I am Staying at the Washington hotel Room 505-506-507. I have 2 men who work with me by the name of Jerry Schilling and Sonny West. I am registered under the name of Jon Burrows. I will be here for as long as it takes to get the credentials of a Federal Agent. I have done in depth study of Drug Abuse and Communist Brainwashing Techniques and I am right in the middle of the whole thing, where I can and will do the most good. I am Glad to help just so long as it is kept very Private. You can have your staff or whomever call me anytime today tonight or Tomorrow. I was nominated the coming year one of America's Ten Most outstanding young men. That will be in January 18 in my Home Town of Memphis Tenn. I am sending you the short autobiography about myself so you can better understand this approach. I would love to meet you just to say hello if you're not too busy.

Respectfully,

Elvis Presley

P.S. I believe that you Sir were one of the Top Ten Outstanding Men of America also.

I have a personal gift for you also which I would like to present to you and you can accept it or I will keep it for you until you can take it.

Roe v. Wade: Decided January 22, 1973

A pregnant single woman (Roe) brought a class action challenging the constitutionality of the Texas criminal abortion laws, which proscribe procuring or attempting an abortion except on medical advice for the purpose of saving the mother's life. A licensed physician (Hallford), who had two state abortion prosecutions pending against him, was permitted to intervene. A childless married couple (the Does), the wife not being pregnant, separately attacked the laws, basing alleged injury on the future possibilities of contraceptive failure, pregnancy, unpreparedness for parenthood, and impairment of the wife's health. A three-judge District Court, which consolidated the actions, held that Roe and Hallford, and members of their classes, had standing to sue and presented justiciable controversies. Ruling that declaratory, though not injunctive, relief was warranted, the court declared the abortion statutes void as vague and overbroadly infringing those plaintiffs' Ninth and Fourteenth Amendment rights. The court ruled the Does' complaint not justiciable. Appellants directly appealed to this Court on the injunctive rulings, and appellee cross-appealed from the District Court's grant of declaratory relief to Roe and Hallford. Held:

1. While 28 U. S. C. § 1253 authorizes no direct appeal to this Court from the grant or denial of declaratory relief alone, review is not foreclosed when the case is properly before the Court on appeal from specific denial of injunctive relief and the arguments as to both injunctive and declaratory relief are necessarily identical. P. 123.

2. Roe has standing to sue; the Does and Hallford do not. Pp. 123-129.

(a) Contrary to appellee's contention, the natural termination of Roe's pregnancy did not moot her suit.
Litigation involving pregnancy, which is "capable of
repetition, yet evading review," is an exception to the
usual federal rule that an actual controversy must exist
at review stages and not simply when the action is
initiated. Pp. 124–125.

(b) The District Court correctly refused injunctive, but
erred in granting declaratory, relief to Hallford, who
alleged no federally protected right not assertable as a
defense against the good-faith state prosecutions
pending against him. Samuels v. Mackell, 401 U.S. 66.
Pp. 125–127.

(c) The Does' complaint, based as it is on contingencies,
any one or more of which may not occur, is too speculative to present an actual case or controversy. Pp.
127–129.

3. State criminal abortion laws, like those involved here, that
except from criminality only a life-saving procedure on the
mother's behalf without regard to the stage of her pregnancy and other interests involved violate the Due Process
Clause of the Fourteenth Amendment, which protects
against state action the right to privacy, including a
woman's qualified right to terminate her pregnancy.
Though the State cannot override that right, it has legitimate interests in protecting both the pregnant woman's
health and the potentiality of human life, each of which
interests grows and reaches a "compelling" point at various
stages of the woman's approach to term. Pp. 147–164.

(a) For the stage prior to approximately the end of the
first trimester, the abortion decision and its effectua-
tion must be left to the medical judgment of the
pregnant woman's attending physician. Pp. 163, 164.

(b) For the stage subsequent to approximately the end of
the first trimester, the State, in promoting its interest
in the health of the mother, may, if it chooses, regulate the abortion procedure in ways that are reasonably related to maternal health. Pp. 163, 164.

(c) For the stage subsequent to viability the State, in promoting its interest in the potentiality of human life, may, if it chooses, regulate, and even proscribe, abortion except where necessary, in appropriate medical judgment, for the preservation of the life or health of the mother. Pp. 163-164; 164-165.

4. The State may define the term "physician" to mean only a physician currently licensed by the State, and may proscribe any abortion by a person who is not a physician as so defined. P. 165.

5. It is unnecessary to decide the injunctive relief issue since the Texas authorities will doubtless fully recognize the Court's ruling that the Texas criminal abortion statutes are unconstitutional. P. 166.

MR. JUSTICE BLACKMUN delivered the opinion of the Court.

This Texas federal appeal and its Georgia companion, Doe v. Bolton, post, p. 179, present constitutional challenges to state criminal abortion legislation. The Texas statutes under attack here are typical of those that have been in effect in many States for approximately a century. The Georgia statutes, in contrast, have a modern cast and are a legislative product that, to an extent at least, obviously reflects the influences of recent attitudinal change, of advancing medical knowledge and techniques, and of new thinking about an old issue.

We forthwith acknowledge our awareness of the sensitive and emotional nature of the abortion controversy, of the vigorous opposing views, even among physicians, and of the deep and seemingly absolute convictions that the subject inspires. One's philosophy, one's experiences, one's exposure to the raw edges of human existence, one's religious training, one's attitudes toward life and family and their values, and the moral standards one establishes and seeks to observe, are all likely to influence and to color one's thinking and conclusions about abortion.

In addition, population growth, pollution, poverty, and racial overtones tend to complicate and not to simplify the problem.

Our task, of course, is to resolve the issue by constitutional measurement, free of emotion and of predilection. We seek earnestly to do this, and, because we do, we have inquired into, and in this opinion place some emphasis upon, medical and medical-legal history and what that history reveals about man's attitudes toward the abortion procedure over the centuries. We bear in mind, too, Mr. Justice Holmes' admonition in his now-vindicated dissent in Lochner v. New York, 198 U.S. 45, 76 (1905):

"[The Constitution] is made for people of fundamentally differing views, and the accident of our finding certain opinions natural and familiar or novel and even shocking ought not to conclude our judgment upon the question whether statutes embodying them conflict with the Constitution of the United States."

I

The Texas statutes that concern us here are Arts. 1191–1194 and 1196 of the State's Penal Code. 1 These make it a crime to "procure an abortion," as therein defined, or to attempt one, except with respect to "an abortion procured or attempted by medical advice for the purpose of saving the life of the mother." Similar statutes are in existence in a majority of the States. 2

Texas first enacted a criminal abortion statute in 1854. Texas Laws 1854, c. 49, § 1, set forth in 3 H. Gammel, Laws of Texas 1502 (1898). This was soon modified into language that has remained substantially unchanged to the present time. See Texas Penal Code of 1857, c. 7, Arts. 531–536; G. Paschal, Laws of Texas, Arts. 2192–2197 (1866); Texas Rev. Stat., c. 8, Arts. 536–541 (1879); Texas Rev. Crim. Stat., Arts. 1071–1076 (1911). The final article in each of these compilations provided the same exception, as does the present Article 1196, for an abortion by "medical advice for the purpose of saving the life of the mother."

II

Jane Roe, 4 a single woman who was residing in Dallas County, Texas, instituted this federal action in March 1970 against the District Attorney of the county. She sought a declaratory judgment that the Texas criminal abortion statutes were unconstitutional on their face, and an injunction restraining the defendant from enforcing the statutes.

Roe alleged that she was unmarried and pregnant; that she wished to terminate her pregnancy by an abortion "performed by a competent, licensed physician, under safe, clinical conditions"; that she was unable to get a "legal" abortion in Texas because her life did not appear to be threatened by the continuation of her pregnancy; and that she could not afford to travel to another jurisdiction in order to secure a legal abortion under safe conditions. She claimed that the Texas statutes were unconstitutionally vague and that they abridged her right of personal privacy, protected by the First, Fourth, Fifth, Ninth, and Fourteenth Amendments. By an amendment to her complaint Roe purported to sue "on behalf of herself and all other women" similarly situated.

James Hubert Hallford, a licensed physician, sought and was granted leave to intervene in Roe's action. In his complaint he alleged that he had been arrested previously for violations of the Texas abortion statutes and that two such prosecutions were pending against him. He described conditions of patients who came to him seeking abortions, and he claimed that for many cases he, as a physician, was unable to determine whether they fell within or outside the exception recognized by Article 1196. He alleged that, as a consequence, the statutes were vague and uncertain, in violation of the Fourteenth Amendment, and that they violated his own and his patients' rights to privacy in the doctor-patient relationship and his own right to practice medicine, rights he claimed were guaranteed by the First, Fourth, Fifth, Ninth, and Fourteenth Amendments.

John and Mary Doe, 5 a married couple, filed a companion complaint to that of Roe. They also named the District Attorney as defendant, claimed like constitutional deprivations, and sought declaratory and injunctive relief. The Does alleged that they were a childless couple; that Mrs. Doe was suffering from a "neural-chemical" disorder; that her physician had "advised her to avoid pregnancy until such time as her condition has materially improved" (although a pregnancy at the present time would not present "a serious risk" to her life); that, pursuant to medical advice, she had discontinued use of birth control pills; and that if she should become pregnant, she would want to terminate the pregnancy by an abortion performed by a competent, licensed physician under safe, clinical conditions. By an amendment to their complaint, the Does purported to sue "on behalf of themselves and all couples similarly situated."

The two actions were consolidated and heard together by a duly convened three-judge district court. The suits thus presented the situations of the pregnant single woman, the childless couple, with the wife not pregnant, and the licensed practicing physician, all joining in the attack on the Texas criminal abortion statutes. Upon the filing of affidavits, motions were made for dismissal and for summary judgment. The court held that Roe and members of her class, and Dr. Hallford, had standing to sue and presented justiciable controversies, but that the Does had failed to allege facts sufficient to state a present controversy and did not have standing. It concluded that, with respect to the requests for a declaratory judgment, abstention was not warranted. On the merits, the District Court held that the "fundamental right of single women and married persons to choose whether to have children is protected by the Ninth Amendment, through the Fourteenth Amendment," and that the Texas criminal abortion statutes were void on their face because they were both unconstitutionally vague and constituted an overbroad infringement of the plaintiffs' Ninth Amendment rights. The court then held that abstention was warranted with respect to the requests for an injunction. It therefore dismissed the Does' complaint, declared the abortion statutes void, and dismissed the application for injunctive relief. 314 F.Supp. 1217, 1225 (ND Tex. 1970).

The plaintiffs Roe and Doe and the intervenor Hallford, pursuant to 28 U. S. C. § 1253, have appealed to this Court from that part of the District Court's judgment denying the injunction. The defendant District Attorney has purported to cross-appeal, pursuant to the same statute, from the court's grant of declaratory relief to Roe and Hallford. Both sides also have taken protective appeals to the United States Court of Appeals for the Fifth Circuit. That court ordered the appeals held in abeyance pending decision here. We postponed decision on jurisdiction to the hearing on the merits. 402 U.S. 941 (1971).

V

The principal thrust of appellant's attack on the Texas statutes is that they improperly invade a right, said to be possessed by the pregnant woman, to choose to terminate her pregnancy. Appellant would discover this right in the concept of personal "liberty" embodied in the Fourteenth Amendment's Due Process

Clause; or in personal, marital, familial, and sexual privacy said to be protected by the Bill of Rights or its penumbras, see Griswold v. Connecticut, 381 U.S. 479 (1965); Eisenstadt v. Baird, 405 U.S. 438 (1972); id., at 460 (WHITE, J., concurring in result); or among those rights reserved to the people by the Ninth Amendment, Griswold v. Connecticut, 381 U.S., at 486 (Goldberg, J., concurring). Before addressing this claim, we feel it desirable briefly to survey, in several aspects, the history of abortion, for such insight as that history may afford us, and then to examine the state purposes and interests behind the criminal abortion laws.

VI

It perhaps is not generally appreciated that the restrictive criminal abortion laws in effect in a majority of States today are of relatively recent vintage. Those laws, generally proscribing abortion or its attempt at any time during pregnancy except when necessary to preserve the pregnant woman's life, are not of ancient or even of common-law origin. Instead, they derive from statutory changes effected, for the most part, in the latter half of the 19th century.

> **5.** The American law. In this country, the law in effect in all but a few States until mid-19th century was the pre-existing English common law. Connecticut, the first State to enact abortion legislation, adopted in 1821 that part of Lord Ellenborough's Act that related to a woman "quick with child." 29 The death penalty was not imposed. Abortion before quickening was made a crime in that State only in 1860. 30 In 1828, New York enacted legislation 31 that, in two respects, was to serve as a model for early anti-abortion statutes. First, while barring destruction of an unquickened fetus as well as a quick fetus, it made the former only a misdemeanor, but the latter second-degree manslaughter. Second, it incorporated a concept of therapeutic abortion by providing that an abortion was excused if it "shall have been necessary to preserve the life of such mother, or shall have been advised by two physicians to be necessary for such purpose." By 1840, when Texas had received the common law, 32 only eight American States had statutes dealing with abortion. 33 It was not until after

the War Between the States that legislation began generally to replace the common law. Most of these initial statutes dealt severely with abortion after quickening but were lenient with it before quickening. Most punished attempts equally with completed abortions. While many statutes included the exception for an abortion thought by one or more physicians to be necessary to save the mother's life, that provision soon disappeared and the typical law required that the procedure actually be necessary for that purpose.

Gradually, in the middle and late 19th century the quickening distinction disappeared from the statutory law of most States and the degree of the offense and the penalties were increased. By the end of the 1950's, a large majority of the jurisdictions banned abortion, however and whenever performed, unless done to save or preserve the life of the mother. 34 The exceptions, Alabama and the District of Columbia, permitted abortion to preserve the mother's health. 35 Three States permitted abortions that were not "unlawfully" performed or that were not "without lawful justification," leaving interpretation of those standards to the courts. 36 In the past several years, however, a trend toward liberalization of abortion statutes has resulted in adoption, by about one-third of the States, of less stringent laws, most of them patterned after the ALI Model Penal Code, § 230.3, 37 set forth as Appendix B to the opinion in Doe v. Bolton, post, p. 205.

It is thus apparent that at common law, at the time of the adoption of our Constitution, and throughout the major portion of the 19th century, abortion was viewed with less disfavor than under most American statutes currently in effect. Phrasing it another way, a woman enjoyed a substantially broader right to terminate a pregnancy than she does in most States today. At least with respect to the early stage of pregnancy, and very possibly without such a limitation, the opportunity to make this choice was present in this country well into the 19th century. Even later, the law continued for some time to treat less punitively an abortion procured in early pregnancy.

Frank Zappa: Statement To Congress, September 19, 1985

STATEMENT OF FRANK ZAPPA. ACCOMPANIED BY LARRY STEIN, COUNSEL

Mr. ZAPPA. My name is Frank Zappa. This is my attorney Larry Stein from Los Angeles. Can you hear me?

The CHAIRMAN. If you could speak very directly and clearly into the microphone, I would appreciate it.

Mr. ZAPPA. My name is Frank Zappa. This is my attorney Larry Stein.

The statement that I prepared, that I sent you 100 copies of, is five pages long, so I have shortened it down and am going to read a condensed version of it.

Certain things have happened. I have been listening to the event in the other room and have heard conflicting reports as to whether or not people in this committee want legislation. I under- stand that Mr. Hollings does from his comments. Is that correct?

The CHAIRMAN. I think you had better concentrate on your testimony, rather than asking questions.

Mr. ZAPPA. The reason I need to ask it, because I have to change something in my testimony if there is not a clearcut version of whether or not legislation is what is being discussed here.

The CHAIRMAN. Do the best you can, because I do not think anybody here can characterize Senator Hollings' position.

Mr. ZAPPA. I will carry on with the issue, then.

Senator EXON. Mr. Chairman, I might help him out just a little bit. I might make a statement. This is one Senator that might be interested in legislation and/or regulation to some extent, recognizing the problems with the right of free expression.

I have previously expressed views that I do not believe I should be telling other people what they have to listen to. I really believe that the suggestion made by the original panel was some kind of an arrangement for voluntarily policing this in the music industry as the correct way to go.

If it will help you out in your testimony, I might join Senator Hollings or others in some kind of legislation and/or regulation, unless the free enterprise system, both the producers and you as the performers, see fit to clean up your act.

Mr. ZAPPA. OK, thank you.

The First thing I would like to do, because I know there is some foreign press involved here and they might not understand what the issue is about, one of the things the issue is about is the First Amendment to the Constitution, and it is short and I would like to read it so they will understand. It says:

Congress shall make no law respecting an establishment of religion or prohibiting the free exercise thereof, or abridging the freedom of speech or of the press or the right of the people peaceably to assemble and to petition the government for a redress of grievances.

That is for reference.

These are my personal observations and opinions. They are addressed to the [Parents' Music Resource Centre] as well as this committee. I speak on behalf of no group or professional organization.

The PMRC proposal is an ill-conceived piece of nonsense which fails to deliver any real benefits to children, infringes the civil liberties of people who are not children, and promises to keep the courts busy for years, dealing with the interpretational and enforcement problems inherent in the proposal's design.

It is my understanding that, in law, First Amendment Issues are decided with a preference for the least restrictive alternative. In this context, the PMRC's demands are the equivalent of treating dandruff by decapitation.

No one has forced Mrs. Baker or Mrs. Gore to bring Prince or Sheena Easton into their homes. Thanks to the Constitution, they are free to buy other forms of music for their children.

Apparently, they insist on purchasing the works of contemporary recording artists in order to support a personal illusion of aerobic sophistication. Ladies, please be advised: The $8.98 purchase price does not entitle you to a kiss on the foot from the composer or performer in exchange for a spin on the family Victrola. Taken as a whole, the complete list of PMRC demands reads like an instruction manual for some sinister kind of "toilet training program" to house-break all composers and performers because of the lyrics of a few. Ladies, how dare you?

The ladies' shame must be shared by the bosses at the major labels who, through the RIAA, chose to bargain away the rights of composers, performers, and retailers in order to pass H.R. 2911, The Blank Tape Tax: A private tax levied by an industry on consumers for the benefit of a select group within that industry.

Is this a consumer issue? You bet it is. PMRC spokesperson, Kandy Stroud, announced to millions of fascinated viewers on last Friday's ABC Nightline debate that Senator Gore, a man she described as "A friend of the music industry," is co-sponsor of something she referred to as "anti-piracy legislation". Is this the same tax bill with a nicer name?

The major record labels need to have H.R. 2911 whiz through a few committees before anybody smells a rat. One of them is chaired by Senator Thurmond. Is it a coincidence that Mrs. Thurmond is affiliated with the PMRC?

I cannot say she's a member, because the PMRC has no members. Their secretary told me on the phone last Friday that the PMRC has no members, only founders. I asked how many other District of Columbia wives are nonmembers of an organization that raises money by mail, has a tax-exempt status, and seems intent on running the Constitution of the United States through the family paper-shredder. I asked her if it was a cult. Finally, she said she couldn't give me an answer and that she had to call their lawyer.

While the wife of the Secretary of the Treasury recites "Gonna drive my love inside you" and Senator Gore's wife talks about "Bondage!" and "oral sex at gunpoint" on the CBS Evening News, people in high places work on a tax bill that is so ridiculous, the only way to sneak it through is to keep the public's mind on something else: 'Porn rock'.

Is the basic issue morality? Is it mental health? Is it an issue at all? The PMRC has created a lot of confusion with improper comparisons between song lyrics, videos, record packaging, radio broadcasting, and live performances. These are all different mediums, and the people who work in them have the right to conduct their business without trade-restraining legislation, whipped up like an instant pudding by The Wives of Big Brother.

Is it proper that the husband of a PMRC nonmember/founder/person sits on any committee considering business pertaining to the Blank Tape Tax or his wife's lobbying organization? Can any committee thus constituted 'find facts' in a fair and unbiased manner? This committee has three that we know about: Senator Danforth, Senator Packwood, and Senator Gore. For some reason, they seem to feel there is no conflict of interest involved.

The PMRC promotes their program as a harmless type of consumer information service providing 'guidelines' which will assist baffled parents in the determination of the 'suitability' of records listened to by 'very young children'. The methods they propose have several unfortunately [sic] side effects, not the least of which is the reduction of all American Music, recorded and live, to the intellectual level of a Saturday morning cartoon show.

Children in the vulnerable age bracket have a natural love for music. If, as a parent, you believe they should be exposed to something more uplifting than "Sugar Walls," support Music Appreciation programs in schools. Why have you not considered your child's need for consumer information? Music Appreciation costs very little compared to sports expenditures. Your children have a right to know that something besides pop music exists.

It is unfortunate that the PMRC would rather dispense governmentally sanitized heavy metal music than something more uplifting. Is this an indication of PMRC's personal taste, or just another manifestation of the low priority this administration has placed on education for the arts in America?

The answer, of course, is neither. You cannot distract people from thinking about an unfair tax by talking about Music Appreciation. For that you need sex, and lots of it.

The establishment of a rating system, voluntary or otherwise, opens the door to an endless parade of Moral Quality Control Programs based on "Things Certain Christians Don't Like". What if the next bunch of Washington Wives demands a large yellow "J" on all material written or performed by Jews, in order to save helpless children from exposure to concealed Zionist doctrine?

Record ratings are frequently compared to film ratings. Apart from the quantitative difference, there is another that is more important: People who act in films are hired to pretend. No matter how the film is rated, it won't hurt them personally.

Since many musicians write and perform their own material and stand by it as their art (whether you like it or not), an imposed rating will stigmatize them as individuals. How long before composers and performers are told to wear a festive little PMRC arm band with their scarlet letter on it?

Bad facts make bad law, and people who write bad laws are, in my opinion, more dangerous than songwriters who celebrate sexuality. Freedom of Speech, Freedom of Religious Thought, and the Right to Due Process for composers, performers and retailers are imperiled if the PMRC and the major labels consummate this nasty bargain.

Are we expected to give up article 1 so the big guys can collect an extra dollar on every blank tape and 10 to 25% on tape recorders? What is going on here? Do we get to vote on this tax? Do we get to vote on this tax? I think that this whole matter has gotten completely blown out of proportion, and I agree with Senator Exon that there is a very dubious reason for having this event. I also agree with Senator Exon that you should not be wasting time on stuff like this, because from the beginning I have sensed that it is somebody's hobby project.

Now, I have done a number of interviews on television. People keep saying, can you not take a few steps in their direction, can you not sympathize, can you not empathize? I do more than that at this point. I have got an idea for a way to stop all this stuff and a way to give parents what they really want, which is information, accurate information as to what is inside the album, without providing a stigma for the musicians who have played on the album or the people who sing it or the people who wrote it. And I think that if you 'listen carefully to this idea that it might just get by all of the constitutional problems and everything else.

As far as I am concerned, I have no objection to having all of the lyrics placed on the album routinely, all the time. But there is a little problem. Record companies do not own the right automatically to take these lyrics, because they are owned by a publishing company.

So, just as all the rest of the PMRC proposals would cost money, this would cost money too, because the record companies would need—they should not be forced to bear the cost, the extra expenditure to the publisher, to print those lyrics.

If you consider that the public needs to be warned about the contents of the records, what better way than to let them see exactly what the songs say? That way you do not have to put any kind of subjective rating on the record. You do not have to call it R, X, D/A, anything. You can read it for yourself.

But in order for it to work properly, the lyrics should be on a uniform kind of a sheet. Maybe even the Government could print those sheets. Maybe it should even be paid for by the Government, if the Government is interested in making sure that people have consumer information in this regard.

And you also have to realize that if a person buys the record and takes it out of the store, once it is out of the store you can't return it if you read the lyrics at home and decide that little Johnny is not supposed to have it.

I think that that should at least be considered, and the idea of imposing these ratings on live concerts, on the albums, asking record companies to reevaluate or drop or violate contracts that they already have with artists should be thrown out.

That is all I have to say.

The CHAIRMAN. Thank you very much, Mr. Zappa. You understand that the previous witnesses were not asking for legislation. And I do not know, I cannot speak for Senator Hollings, but I think the prevailing view here is that nobody is asking for legislation.

The question is just focusing on what a lot of people perceive to be a problem, and you have indicated that you at least understand that there is another point of view. But there are people that think that parents should have some knowledge of what goes into their home.

Mr. ZAPPA. All along my objection has been with the tactics used by these people in order to achieve the goal. I just think the tactics have been really bad, and the whole premise of their pro- posal- they were badly advised in terms of record business law, they were badly advised in terms of practicality. or they would have known that certain things do not work mechanically with what they suggest.

The CHAIRMAN. Senator Gore.

Senator GORE. Thank you very much, Mr. Chairman.

I found your statement very interesting and, although I disagree with some of the statements that you make and have made on other occasions, I have been a fan of your music, believe it or not. I respect you as a true original and a tremendously talented musician.

Your suggestion of printing the lyrics on the album is a very interesting one. The PMRC at one point said they would propose either a rating or warning, or printing all the lyrics on the album. The record companies came back and said they did not want to do that.

I think a lot of people agree with your suggestion that one easy way to solve this problem for parents would be to put the actual words there, so that parents could see them. In fact, the National Association of Broadcasters made exactly the same request of the record companies.

I think your suggestion is an intriguing one and might really be a solution for the problem.

Mr. ZAPPA. You have to understand that it does cost money, because you cannot expect publishers to automatically give up that right, which is a right for them. Somebody is going to have to reimburse the publishers, the record industry.

Without trying to mess up the album jacket art, it should be a sheet of paper that is slipped inside the shrink-wrap, so that when you take it out you can still have a complete album package. So there is going to be some extra cost for printing it.

But as long as people realize that for this kind of consumer safety you are going to spend some money and as long as you can find a way to pay for it, I think that would be the best way to let people know.

Senator GORE. I do not disagree with that at all. And the separate sheet would also solve the problem with cassettes as well, because you do not have the space for words on the cassette packs.

Mr. ZAPPA. There would have to be a little accordion-fold.

Senator GORE. I have listened to you a number of times on this issue, and I guess the statement that I want to get from you is whether or not you feel this concern is legitimate.

You feel very strongly about your position, and I understand that. You are very articulate and forceful.

But occasionally you give the impression that you think parents are just silly to be concerned at all.

Mr. ZAPPA. No; that is not an accurate impression.

Senator GORE. Well, please clarify it, then.

Mr. ZAPPA. First of all, I think it is the parents' concern; it is not the Government's concern.

Senator GORE. The PMRC agrees with you on that.

Mr. ZAPPA. Well. that does not come across in the way they have been speaking. The whole drift that I have gotten, based upon the media blitz that has attended the PMRC and its rise to infamy, is that they have a special plan, and it has smelled like legislation up until now.

There are too many things that look like hidden agendas involved with this. And I am a parent. I have got four children.

Two of them are here. I want them to grow up in a country where they can think what they want to think, be what they want to be, and not what somebody's wife or somebody in Government makes them be.

I do not want to have that and I do not think you do either.

Senator GORE. OK. But now you are back on the issue of Government involvement. Let me say briefly on this point that the PMRC says repeatedly no legislation, no regulation, no Governnient action. It certainly sounded clear to me.

And as far as a hidden agenda, I do not see one, hear one, or know of one.

Mr. ZAPPA. OK, let me tell you why I have drawn these conclusions. First of all, they may say, we are not interested in legislation. But there are others who are, and because of their project bad things have happened in this country in the industry.

I believe there is actually some liability. Look at this. You have a situation where, even if you go for the lyric printed thing in the record, because of the tendency among Americans to be copy-cats- one guy commits a murder, you get a copycat murder-now you've got copycat censors.

You get a very bad situation in San Antonio, TX, right now where they are trying to pass PMRC-type individual ratings and attach them to live concerts, with the mayor down there trying to make a national reputation by putting San Antonio on the map as the first city in the United States to have these regulations, against the suggestion of the city attorney, who says, I do not think this is constitutional.

But you know, there is this fervor to get in and do even more and even more.

And the other thing, the PMRC starts off talking about lyrics, but when they take it over into other realms they start talking about the videos. In fact, you misspoke yourself at the beginning in your introduction when you were talking about the music does this, the music does that. There is a distinct difference

between those notes and chords and the baseline [sic - error in
Congressional report] and the rhythm that support the words and
the lyrics.

I do not know whether you really are talking about controlling
the type of music.

The CHAIRMAN. The lyrics.

Mr. ZAPPA. So specifically we are talking about lyrics. It began
with lyrics. But even loo@ng at the PMRC fundraising letter, in
the last paragraph at the bottom of the page it starts looking like
it is branching into other areas, when it says: "We realize that this
material has pervaded other aspects of society." And it is like
what, you are going to fix it all for me?

Senator GORE. No. I think the PMRC's acknowledging some
of the statements by some of their critics who say: Well, why single out the music industry.

Do I understand that you do believe that there is a legitimate
concern here?

Mr. ZAPPA. But the legitimate concern is a matter of taste for
the individual parent and how much sexual information that parent wants to give their child, at what age, at what time, in what
quantity, OK. And I think that, because there is a tendency in the
United States to hide sex, which I think is an unhealthy thing to
do. and many parents do not give their children good sexual education, in spite of the fact that little books for kids are available,
and other parents demand that sexual education be taken out of
school, it makes the child vulnerable, because if you do not have
something rational to compare it to when you see or hear about
something that is aberrated you do not perceive it as an aberra-
tion.

Senator GORE. OK, I have run out of time.

Thank vou, Mr. Chairman.

The CHAIRMAN. Senator Rockefeller.

Senator ROCKEFELLER. No questions, Mr. Chairnan.

The CHAIRMAN. Senator Gorton.

Senator GORTON. Mr. Zappa, I am astounded at the courtesy and soft-voiced nature of the comments of my friend, the Senator from Tennessee. I can only say that I found your statement to be boorish, incredibly and insensitively insulting to the people that were here previously; that you could manage to give the first amendment of the Constitution of the United States a bad name, if I felt that you had the slightest understanding of it, which I do not.

You do not have the slightest understanding of the difference between Government action and private action, and you have certainly destroyed any case you might otherwise have had with this Senator.

Thank you, Mr. Chairman.

Mr. ZAPPA. Is this private action?

The CHAIRMAN. Senator Exon.

Senator EXON. Mr. Chairman, thank you very much.

Mr. Zappa, let me say that I was surprised that Senator Gore knew and liked your music. I must confess that I have never heard any of your music, to my knowledge.

Mr. ZAPPA. I would be more than happy to recite my lyrics to you.

Senator EXON. Can we forgo that?

Senator GORE. You have probably never heard of the Mothers of Invention.

Senator EXON. I have heard of Glen Miller and Mitch Miller. Did you ever perform with them?

Mr. ZAPPA. As a matter of fact, I took music lessons in grade school from Mitch Miller's brother.

Senator EXON. That is the first sign of hope we have had in this hearing.

Let us try and get down to a fundamental question here that I would like to ask you, Mr. Zappa. Do you believe that parents have the right and the obligation to mold the psychological development of their children?

Mr. ZAPPA. Yes, I think they have that right, and I also think they have that obligation.

Senator EXON. Do you see any extreme difficulty in carrying out those obligations for a parent by material falling into the hands of their children over which thely have little or no control?

Mr. ZAPPA. Well, one of the things that has been brought up before is talking about very young children getting access to the material that they have been showing here today. And what I have said to that in the past is a teenager may go into a record store unescorted with $8.98 in his pocket, but very young children do not.

If they go into a record store, the $8.98 is in mom or dad's pocket, and they can always say, Johnny, buy a book. They can say, Johnny, buy instrumental music; there is some nice classical music for you here; why do you not listen to that.

The parent can ask or guide the child in another direction, away from Sheena Easton, Prince, or whoever else you have been complaining about. There is always that possibility.

Senator EXON. As I understand it from your testimony—and once again, I want to emphasize that I see nothing wrong whatsoever; in fact, I salute the ladies for bringing this to the attention of the public as best they see fit. I think you could tell from my testimony that I tend to agree with them.

I want to be very careful that we do not overstep our bounds and try and—and I emphasize once again—tell somebody else what they should see. I am primarily worried about children.

It seems to me from your statement that you have no obligation—or no objection whatsoever to printing lyrics, if that would be legally possible, or from a standpoint of having the room to do that, on records or tapes. Is that not what you said?

Mr. ZAPPA. I think it would be advisable for two reasons. One, it gives people one of the things that they have been asking for. It gives them that type of consumer protection because, if you can read the English language and you can see the lyrics on the back, you have no excuse for complaning if you take the record out of the store.

And also, I think that the record industry has been damaged and it has been given a very bad rap by this whole situation because it has been indicated, or people have attempted to indicate, that there is so much of this kind of material that people object to in the industry, that that is what the industry is.

It is not bad at all. Some of the albums that have been selected for abuse here are obscure. Some of them are already several years old. And I think that a lot of deep digging was done in order to come up with the song about anal vapors or whatever it was that they were talking about before.

Senator EXON. If I understand you, you would be in support of printing the lyrics, but you are adamantly opposed to any kind of a rating system?

Mr. ZAPPA. I am opposed to the rating system because, as I said, if you put a rating on the record it goes directly to the character of the person who made the record, whereas if you rate a film, a guy who is in the film has been hired as an actor. He is pretending. You rate the film, whatever it is, it does not hurt him.

But whether you like what is on the record or not, the guy who made it, that is his art and to stigmatize him is unfair.

Senator EXON. Well, likewise, if you are primarily concerned about the artists, is it not true that for many many years, we have had ratings of movies with indications as to the sexual content of movies and that has been, as near as I can tell, a voluntary action on the part of the actors in the movies and the producers of the movies and the distributors?

That seems to have worked reasonably well. What is wrong with that?

Mr. ZAPPA. Well, first of all, it replaced something that was far more restrictive, which was the Hayes Office. And as far as that being voluntary, there are people who wish they did not have to rate their films. They still object to rating their films, but the reason the ratings go on is because if they are not rated they will not get distributed or shown in theaters. So there is a little bit of pressure involved, but still there is no stigma.

Senator EXON. The Government does not require that. The point I am trying to make is – and while I think these hearings should not have been held if we are not considering legislation or regulations at this time, I emphasized earlier that they might follow.

I simply want to say to you that I suspect that, unless the industry "clears up their act" – and I use that in quotes again – there is likely to be legislation. And it seems to me that it would not be too far removed from reality or too offensive to anyone if you could follow the general guidelines, right, wrong, or indifferent, that are now in place with regard to the movie industry.

Mr. ZAPPA. Well, I would object to that. I think first of all, I believe it was you who asked the question of Mrs. Gore whether there was any other indication on the album as to the contents. And I would say that a buzzsaw blade between a guy's legs on the album cover is a good indication that it is not for little Johnny.

Senator EXON. I do not believe I asked her that question, but the point you made is a good one, because if that should not go to little minds I think there should be at least some minimal activity or attempt on the part of the producers and distributors, and indeed possibly the performers, to see that that does not get to that little mind.

Mr. Chairman, thank you very much.

The CHAIRMAN. Senator Hollings.

Senator HOLLINGS. Mr. Zappa, I apologize for coming back in late, but I am just hearing the latter part of it. I hear that you say that perhaps we could print the words, and I think that is a good suggestion, but it is unfair to have albums rated.

Now, it is not considered unfair in the movie industry, and I want you to elaborate. I do not want to belabor you, but why is it unfair? I mean, it is accurate, is it not?

Mr. ZAPPA. Well, I do not know whether it is accurate, because sometimes they have trouble deciding how a film gets to be an X or an R or whatever. And you have two problems. One is the quantity of material, 325 films per year versus 25,000 4-minute songs per year, OK.

You also have a problem that an album is a compilation of different types of cuts. If one song on the album is sexually explicit and all the rest of it sounds like Pat Boone, what do you get on the album? How are you going to rate it?

There are little technical difficulties here, and and you have the problem of having somebody in the position of deciding what's good, what's bad, what's talking about the devil, what is too violent, and the rest of that stuff.

But the point I made before is that when you rate the album you are rating the individual, because he takes personal responsibility for the music; and in the movies, the actors who are performing in the movie, it does not hurt them.

Senator HOLLINGS. Well, very good. I think the actual printing of the content itself is perhaps even better than the rating. Let everyone else decide.

Mr. ZAPPA. I think you should leave it up to the parents, because not all parents want to keep their children totally ignorant.

Senator HOLLINGS. Well, you and I would differ on what is ignorance and education, I can see that. But if it was there, they could see what they were buying and I think that is a step in the right direction.

As Senator Exon has pointed out, the primary movers in this particular regard are not looking for legislation or regulations, which is our function. To be perfectly candid with you, I would look for regulations or some kind of legislation, if it could be constitutionally accomplished, unless of course we have these initiatives from the industry itself.

I think your suggestion is a good one. If you print those words, that would go a long way toward satisfying everyone's objections.

Mr. ZAPPA. All we have to do is find out how it is going to be paid for.

Senator HOLLINGS. Thank you, Mr. Chairman.

The CHAIRMAN. Senator Hawkins.

Senator HAWKINS. Mr. Zappa, you suy you have four children?

Mr. ZAPPA. Yes, four children.

Senator HAWKINS. Have you ever purchased toys for those children?

Mr. ZAPPA. No; my wife does.

Senator HAWKINS. Well, I might tell you that if you were to go in a toy store - which is very educational for fathers, by the way; it is not a maternal responsibility to buy toys for children - that you may look on the box and the box says, this is suitable for 5 to 7 years of age, or 8 to 15, or 15 and above, to give you some guidance for a toy for a child.

Do you object to that?

Mr. ZAPPA. In a way I do, because that means that somebody in an office someplace is making a decision about how smart my child is.

Senator HAWKINS. I would be interested to see what toys your kids ever had.

Mr. ZAPPA. Why would you be interested?

Senator HAWKINS. Just as a point of interest.

Mr. ZAPPA. Well, come on over to the house. I will show them to you.

Senator HAWKINS. I might do that.

Do you make a profit from sales of rock records?

Mr. ZAPPA. Yes.

Senator HAWKINS. So you do make a profit from the sales of rock records?

Mr. ZAPPA. Yes.

Senator HAWKINS. Thank you. I think that statement tells the story to this committee. Thank you.

The CHAIRMAN. Mr. Zappa, thank you very much for your testimony.

Mr. ZAPPA. Thank you.

Mary Fisher: 1992 Republication National Convention Address

Less than three months ago at platform hearings in Salt Lake City, I asked the Republican Party to lift the shroud of silence which has been draped over the issue of HIV and AIDS. I have come tonight to bring our silence to an end. I bear a message of challenge, not self-congratulation. I want your attention, not your applause.

I would never have asked to be HIV positive, but I believe that in all things there is a purpose; and I stand before you and before the nation gladly. The reality of AIDS is brutally clear. Two hundred thousand Americans are dead or dying. A million more are infected. Worldwide, forty million, sixty million, or a hundred million infections will be counted in the coming few years. But despite science and research, White House meetings, and congressional hearings, despite good intentions and bold initiatives, campaign slogans, and hopeful promises, it is—despite it all—the epidemic which is winning tonight.

In the context of an election year, I ask you, here in this great hall, or listening in the quiet of your home, to recognize that AIDS virus is not a political creature. It does not care whether you are Democrat or Republican; it does not ask whether you are black or white, male or female, gay or straight, young or old.

Tonight, I represent an AIDS community whose members have been reluctantly drafted from every segment of American society. Though I am white and a mother, I am one with a black infant struggling with tubes in a Philadelphia hospital. Though I am female and contracted this disease in marriage and enjoy the warm support of my family, I am one with the lonely gay man sheltering a flickering candle from the cold wind of his family's rejection.

This is not a distant threat. It is a present danger. The rate of infection is increasing fastest among women and children. Largely unknown a decade ago, AIDS is the third leading killer of young adult Americans today. But it won't be third for long, because unlike other diseases, this one travels. Adolescents don't give each other cancer or heart disease because they believe they are in love, but HIV is different; and we have helped it along. We have killed each other with our ignorance, our prejudice, and our silence.

We may take refuge in our stereotypes, but we cannot hide there long, because HIV asks only one thing of those it attacks. Are you human? And this is the right question. Are you human? Because people with HIV have not entered some alien state of being. They are human. They have not earned cruelty, and they do not deserve meanness. They don't benefit from being isolated or treated as outcasts. Each of them is exactly what God made: a person; not evil, deserving of our judgment; not victims, longing for our pity—people, ready for support and worthy of compassion.

My call to you, my Party, is to take a public stand, no less compassionate than that of the President and Mrs. Bush. They have embraced me and my family in memorable ways. In the place of judgment, they have shown affection. In difficult moments, they have raised our spirits. In the darkest hours, I have seen them reaching not only to me, but also to my parents, armed with that stunning grief and special grace that comes only to parents who have themselves leaned too long over the bedside of a dying child.

With the President's leadership, much good has been done. Much of the good has gone unheralded, and as the President has insisted, much remains to be done. But we do the President's cause no good if we praise the American family but ignore a virus that destroys it.

We must be consistent if we are to be believed. We cannot love justice and ignore prejudice, love our children and fear to teach them. Whatever our role as parent or policymaker, we must act as eloquently as we speak—else we have no integrity. My call to the nation is a plea for awareness. If you believe you are safe, you are in danger. Because I was not hemophiliac, I was not at risk. Because I was not gay, I was not at risk. Because I did not inject drugs, I was not at risk.

My father has devoted much of his lifetime guarding against another holocaust. He is part of the generation who heard Pastor Nemoellor come out of the Nazi death camps to say,

 "They came after the Jews, and I was not a Jew, so, I did not protest. They came after the trade unionists, and I was not a trade unionist, so, I did not protest. Then they came after the Roman Catholics, and I was not a Roman Catholic, so, I did not protest. Then they came after me, and there was no one left to protest."

The—The lesson history teaches is this: If you believe you are safe, you are at risk. If you do not see this killer stalking your children, look again. There is no family or community, no race or religion, no place left in America that is safe. Until we genuinely embrace this message, we are a nation at risk.

Tonight, HIV marches resolutely toward AIDS in more than a million American homes, littering its pathway with the bodies of the young—young men, young women, young parents, and young children. One of the families is mine. If it is true that HIV inevitably turns to AIDS, then my children will inevitably turn to orphans. My family has been a rock of support.

My 84-year-old father, who has pursued the healing of the nations, will not accept the premise that he cannot heal his daughter. My mother refuses to be broken. She still calls at midnight to tell wonderful jokes that make me laugh. Sisters and friends, and my brother Phillip, whose birthday is today, all have helped carry me over the hardest places. I am blessed, richly and deeply blessed, to have such a family.

But not all of you—But not all of you have been so blessed. You are HIV positive, but dare not say it. You have lost loved ones, but you dare not whisper the word AIDS. You weep silently. You grieve alone. I have a message for you. It is not you who should feel shame. It is we—we who tolerate ignorance and practice prejudice, we who have taught you to fear. We must lift our shroud of silence, making it safe for you to reach out for compassion. It is our task to seek safety for our children, not in quiet denial, but in effective action.

Someday our children will be grown. My son Max, now four, will take the measure of his mother. My son Zachary, now two, will sort through his memories. I may not be here to hear their judgments, but I know already what I hope they are. I want my children to know that their mother was not a victim. She was a messenger. I do not want them to think, as I once did, that courage is the absence of fear. I want them to know that courage is the strength to act wisely when most we are afraid. I want them to have the courage to step forward when called by their nation or their Party and give leadership, no matter what the personal cost.

I ask no more of you than I ask of myself or of my children. To the millions of you who are grieving, who are frightened, who have suffered the ravages of AIDS firsthand: Have courage, and you will find support. To the millions who are strong, I issue the plea: Set aside prejudice and politics to make room for compassion and sound policy.

To my children, I make this pledge: I will not give in, Zachary, because I draw my courage from you. Your silly giggle gives me hope; your gentle prayers give me strength; and you, my child, give me the reason to say to America, "You are at risk." And I will not rest, Max, until I have done all I can to make your world safe. I will seek a place where intimacy is not the prelude to suffering. I will not hurry to leave you, my children, but when I go, I pray that you will not suffer shame on my account.

To all within the sound of my voice, I appeal: Learn with me the lessons of history and of grace, so my children will not be afraid to say the word "AIDS" when I am gone. Then, their children and yours may not need to whisper it at all.

God bless the children, and God bless us all.

Good night.

Patrick J. Buchanan: Address to the Republican National Convention, 1992

What a terrific crowd this is. What a terrific crowd.

This may even be larger than the crowd I had in Ellijay, Georgia. Don't laugh. We carried Ellijay.

Listen, my friends, we may have taken the long way home, but we finally got here to Houston. And the first thing I want to do tonight is to congratulate President George Bush and to remove any doubt about where we stand. The primaries are over; the heart is strong again; and the Buchanan brigades are enlisted—all the way to a great Republican comeback victory in November.

My friends—My friends, like many of you—like many of you last month, I watched that giant masquerade ball up at Madison Square Garden, where 20,000 liberals and radicals came dressed up as moderates and centrists in the greatest single exhibition of cross-dressing in American political history.

You know, one—one by one—one by one the prophets of doom appeared at the podium. The Reagan decade, they moaned, was a terrible time in America, and they said the only way to prevent worse times is to turn our country's fate and our country's future over to the Party that gave us McGovern, Mondale, Carter, and Michael Dukakis. Where do they find these leaders? No way, my friends. The American people are not going to go back to the discredited liberalism of the 1960s and the failed liberalism of the 1970s, no matter how slick the package in 1992.

(Hold it, my friends.)

You know, the malcontents—the malcontents of Madison Square Garden notwithstanding, the 1980s were not terrible years in America. They were great years. You know it. And I know it. And everyone knows it except for the carping critics who sat on the sidelines of history, jeering at one of the great statesmen of modern time: Ronald Reagan. You know out of—Remember that time out of Jimmy Carter's days of malaise, Ronald Reagan crafted—Ronald Reagan crafted the greatest peacetime economic recovery in history: three million new businesses, and 20 million new jobs. Under the Reagan Doctrine, one by one, it was the Communist dominos that began to fall. First, Grenada was liberated by U.S. airborne troops of the U.S. Marine Corps. Then, the mighty Red Army was driven out of Afghanistan with American weapons. And then in Nicaragua, that squalid Marxist regime was forced to hold free elections by Ronald Reagan's Contra army, and the Communists were thrown out of power. Fellow Americans you ought to remember, it was under our Party that

the Berlin Wall came down and Europe was reunited. It was
under our Party that the Soviet Empire collapsed, and the captive
nations broke free.

You know it is said that every American President will be
remembered in history with but a single sentence. George
Washington was the father of his country. Abraham Lincoln freed
the slaves and saved the Union. And Ronald Reagan won the
Cold War. And it is time—And it is just about time—It is just
about time that my old colleagues, the columnists and commentators, looking down on us tonight from their sky boxes and
anchor booths, gave Ronald Reagan the full credit he deserves
for leading America to victory in the Cold War. Most of all, my
friends—Most of all, Ronald Reagan made us proud to be
Americans again. We never felt better about our country; and we
never stood taller in the eyes of the world than when "the
Gipper" was at the helm.

But we are here tonight, my friends, not only to celebrate, but to
nominate. An American President has many roles. He is our first
diplomat, the architect of American foreign policy. And which of
these two men is more qualified for that great role? George Bush
has been U.N. Ambassador, Director of the CIA, envoy to China.
As Vice President, George Bush co-authored and cosigned the
policies that won the Cold War. As President, George Bush
presided over the liberation of Eastern Europe and the termination of the Warsaw Pact. And what about Mr. Clinton? Well, Bill
Clinton—Bill Clinton couldn't find 150 words to discuss foreign
policy in an acceptance speech that lasted almost an hour. You
know, as was said—as was said of another Democratic candidate,
Bill Clinton's foreign policy experience is pretty much confined
to having had breakfast once at the International House of
Pancakes.

You know, let's recall what happened—let us look at the record
and recall what happened. Under President George Bush, more
human beings escaped from the prison house of tyranny to freedom than in any other four-year period in history. And for any
man—let me tell you—for any man to call this a record of failure
is the cheap political rhetoric of politicians who only know how
to build themselves up by tearing America down—and we don't
want that kind of leadership in the United States.

The presidency, my friends—The presidency is also an office that Theodore Roosevelt called America's "bully pulpit." Harry Truman said it was "preeminently a place of moral leadership." George Bush is a defender of right-to-life, and a champion of the Judeo-Christian values and beliefs upon which America was founded.

Mr. Clinton—Mr. Clinton however, has a different agenda. At its top is unrestricted—unrestricted abortion on demand. When the Irish-Catholic Governor of Pennsylvania, Robert Casey, asked to say a few words on behalf of the 25 million unborn children destroyed since Roe v Wade, Bob Casey was told there was no room for him at the podium at Bill Clinton's convention, and no room at the inn. Yet—Yet a militant leader of the homosexual rights movement could rise at that same convention and say: "Bill Clinton and Al Gore represent the most pro-lesbian and pro-gay ticket in history." And so they do. Bill Clinton says he supports "school choice"—but only for state-run schools. Parents who send their children to Christian schools, or private schools, or Jewish schools, or Catholic schools, need not apply.

Elect me, and you get "two for the price of one," Mr. Clinton says of his lawyer-spouse. And what—And what does Hillary believe? Well, Hillary believes that 12-year-olds should have the right to sue their parents. And Hillary has compared marriage and the family, as institutions, to slavery and life on an Indian reservation. Well, speak for yourself, Hillary.

Friends—Friends, this—This, my friends—This is radical feminism. The agenda that Clinton & Clinton would impose on America: abortion on demand, a litmus test for the Supreme Court, homosexual rights, discrimination against religious schools, women in combat units. That's change, all right. But that's not the kind of change America needs. It's not the kind of change America wants. And it's not the kind of change we can abide in a nation we still call "God's country."

The President—The President of the United States is also—The President of the United States is also America's Commander-in-Chief. He's the man we authorize to send fathers and sons and brothers and friends into battle. George Bush was 17 years old when they bombed Pearl Harbor. He left his high school graduation; he walked down to the recruiting office; and he signed up to become the youngest fighter pilot in the Pacific war.

And Mr. Clinton? And Bill Clinton? I'll tell you where he was. I'll tell you where he was. I'll tell you where he was. Let me tell you where he was. I'll tell you—I'll tell you where he was. When Bill Clinton's time came in Vietnam, he sat up in a dormitory room in Oxford, England, and figured out how to dodge the draft.

Let me ask the question to this convention: Which of these two men has won the moral authority to send young Americans into battle? I suggest respectfully—I suggest respectfully, it is the American patriot and war hero, Navy Lieutenant J. G. George Herbert Walker Bush! My fellow Americans—My fellow Americans, this campaign is about philosophy, and it is about character; and George Bush wins hands down on both counts. And it is time all of us came home and stood beside him.

As his running mate, Mr. Clinton chose Albert Gore. But just how moderate is Prince Albert? Well according to the National Taxpayers Union, Al Gore beat out Teddy Kennedy, two straight years, for the title of "biggest spender in the U.S. Senate" and Teddy Kennedy isn't moderate about anything. I'm not kidding. I'm not kidding about Teddy. How many 60-year-olds do you know who still go to Florida for spring break?

You know up at that great—at that great big costume party they held up in New York, Mr. Gore made a startling declaration. Henceforth, Albert Gore said, the "central organizing principle" of governments everywhere must be: the environment. Wrong, Albert. The central organizing principle of this republic is: freedom. And from the ancient—And from the ancient forests—from the ancient forests of Oregon and Washington, to the Inland Empire of California, America's great middle class has got to start standing up to these environmental extremists who put birds and rats and insects ahead of families, workers, and jobs.

One year ago—You know, one year ago, my friends—One year ago I could not have dreamt I would be here tonight. I was just one of many panelists on what President Bush calls "those crazy Sunday talk shows." But I disagreed with the President and so we challenged the President in the Republican primaries, and we fought as best we could. From February to June, President Bush won 33 of those primaries. I can't recall exactly how many we won. I'll get you the figure tomorrow.

But tonight I do want to speak from the heart to the 3 million people who voted for Pat Buchanan for President. I will never—I will never—I will never forget you, or the great honor you have done me. But I do believe—I do believe deep in my heart that the right place for us to be now, in this presidential campaign, is right beside George Bush. This Party—This Party is my home. This Party is our home and we've got to come home to it. And don't let anyone tell you any different.

Yes, we disagreed with President Bush, but we stand with him for the freedom to choose religious schools, and we stand with him against the amoral idea that gay and lesbian couples should have the same standing in law as married men and women. We stand with President Bush—We stand with President Bush for right-to-life and for voluntary prayer in the public schools. And we stand against putting our wives and daughters and sisters into combat units of the United States Army. And we stand, my—my friends— We also stand with President Bush in favor of the right of small towns and communities to control the raw sewage of pornography that so terribly pollutes our popular culture. We stand with President Bush in favor of federal judges who interpret the law as written, and against would-be Supreme Court justices like Mario Cuomo who think they have a mandate to rewrite the Constitution.

Friends, this election is about more than who gets what. It is about who we are. It is about what we believe and what we stand for as Americans. There is a religious war going on in this country. It is a cultural war, as critical to the kind of nation we shall be as the Cold War itself. For this war is for the soul of America. And in that struggle for the soul of America, Clinton & Clinton are on the other side, and George Bush is on our side. And so to the Buchanan Brigades out there, we have to come home and stand beside George Bush.

In these six months of campaigning from Concord, New Hampshire to California, I came to know our country better than I have known it ever before in my life, and I gathered up memories that are going to be with me the rest of my days.

There was that day-long ride through the great state of Georgia in a bus Vice President Bush himself had used in 1988 called Asphalt One. The ride ended in a 9:00 PM speech in a tiny town in southern Georgia called Fitzgerald.

There were those workers at the James River Paper Mill, in Northern New Hampshire in a town called Groveton—tough, hearty men. None of them would say a word to me as I came down the line, shaking their hands one by one. They were under a threat of losing their jobs at Christmas. And as I moved down the line, one tough fellow about my age just looked up and said to me, "Save our jobs."

Then there was the legal secretary that I met at the Manchester airport on Christmas Day who came running up to me and said, "Mr. Buchanan, I'm going to vote for you." And then she broke down weeping, and she said, "I've lost my job; I don't have any money, and they're going to take away my little girl. What am I going to do?"

My friends, these people are our people. They don't read Adam Smith or Edmund Burke, but they come from the same school-yards and the same playgrounds and towns as we came from. They share our beliefs and our convictions, our hopes and our dreams. These are the conservatives of the heart. They are our people. And we need to reconnect with them. We need to let them know we know how bad they're hurting. They don't expect miracles of us, but they need to know we care.

There were the people—There were the people that, my friends—There were the people of Hayfork, a tiny town up in California's Trinity Alps, a town that is now under a sentence of death because a federal judge has set aside nine million acres for the habitat of the spotted owl—forgetting about the habitat of the men and women who live and work in Hayfork.

And there were the brave people—And there were the brave people of Koreatown who took the worst of those L.A. riots, but still live the family values we treasure, and who still deeply believe in the American dream.

Friends, in these wonderful—In these wonderful 25 weeks of our campaign, the saddest days were the days of that riot in L.A., the worst riot in American history. But out of that awful tragedy can come a message of hope. Hours after that riot ended, I went down to the Army compound in South Los Angeles, where I met the troopers of the 18th Cavalry who had come to save the city of Los Angeles. An officer of the 18th Cav said, "Mr. Buchanan, I want you to talk to a couple of our troopers. And I went over and I met these young fellows. They couldn't have been 20 years old. They could not have been 20 years old. And they recounted their story.

They had come into Los Angeles late in the evening of the second day, and the rioting was still going on. And two of them walked up a dark street, where the mob had burned and looted every single building on the block but one, a convalescent home for the aged. And the mob was headed in, to ransack and loot the apartments of the terrified old men and women inside. The troopers came up the street, M-16s at the ready. And the mob threatened and cursed, but the mob retreated because it had met the one thing that could stop it: force, rooted in justice, and backed by moral courage.

Now, Greater—Greater love than this—"Greater love than this hath no man than that he lay down his life for his friend."? Here were 19-year-old boys ready to lay down their lives to stop a mob from molesting old people they did not even know. And as those boys took back the streets of Los Angeles, block by block, my friends, we must take back our cities, and take back our culture, and take back our country.

God bless you, and God bless America.

The Emergence of Gay Politics

William J. Clinton: Remarks Announcing the New Policy on Homosexuals in the Military

Thank you very much. Secretary Aspin, General Powell, members of the Joint Chiefs, Admiral Kime, to our host, Admiral Smith, ladies and gentlemen, I have come here today to discuss a difficult challenge and one which has received an enormous amount of publicity and public and private debate over the last several months: our Nation's policy toward homosexuals in the military.

I believe the policy I am announcing today represents a real step forward, but I know it will raise concerns in some of your minds. So I wanted you to hear my thinking and my decision directly and in person because I respect you, and because you are among the elite who will lead our Armed Forces into the next century, and because you will have to put this policy into effect and I expect your help in doing it.

The policy I am announcing today is, in my judgment, the right thing to do and the best way to do it. It is right because it provides greater protection to those who happen to be homosexual and want to serve their country honorably in uniform, obeying all the military's rules against sexual misconduct. It is the best way to proceed because it provides a sensible balance between the rights of the individual and the needs of our military to remain the world's number one fighting force. As President of all the American people, I am pledged to protect and to promote individual rights. As Commander in Chief, I am pledged to protect and advance our security. In this policy, I believe we have come close to meeting both objectives.

Let me start with this clear fact: Our military is one of our greatest accomplishments and our most valuable assets. It is the world's most effective and powerful fighting force, bar none. I have seen proof of this fact almost every day since I became President. I saw it last week when I visited Camp Casey, along the DMZ in Korea. I witnessed it at our military academies at Annapolis and West Point when I visited there. And I certainly relied on it 3 weeks ago when I ordered an attack on Iraq after that country's leadership attempted to assassinate President Bush.

We owe a great deal to the men and women who protect us through their service, their sacrifice, and their dedication. And we owe it to our own security to listen hard to them and act carefully as we consider any changes in the military. A force ready to fight must maintain the highest priority under all circumstances.

Let me review the events which bring us here today. Before I ran for President, this issue was already upon us. Some of the members of the military returning from the Gulf war announced their homosexuality in order to protest the ban. The military's policy has been questioned in college ROTC programs. Legal challenges have been filed in court, including one that has since succeeded. In 1991, the Secretary of Defense, Dick Cheney, was asked about reports that the Defense Department spent an alleged $500 million to separate and replace about 17,000 homosexuals from the military service during the 1980's, in spite of the findings of a Government report saying there was no reason to believe that they could not serve effectively and with distinction. Shortly thereafter, while giving a speech at the Kennedy School of Government at Harvard, I was asked by one of the students what I thought of this report and what I thought of lifting the ban. This question had never before been presented to me, and I had never had the opportunity to discuss it with anyone. I stated then what I still believe, that I thought there ought to be a presumption that people who wish to do so should be able to serve their country if they are willing to conform to the high standards of the military and that the emphasis should be always on people's conduct, not their status.

For me, and this is very important, this issue has never been one of group rights but rather of individual ones, of the individual opportunity to serve and the individual responsibility to conform to the highest standards of military conduct. For people who are willing to play by the rules, able to serve and make a contribution, I believed then and I believe now we should give them the chance to do so.

The central facts of this issue are not much in dispute. First, notwithstanding the ban, there have been and are homosexuals in the military service who serve with distinction. I have had the privilege of meeting some of these men and women, and I have been deeply impressed by their devotion to duty and to country.

Second, there is no study showing them to be less capable or more prone to misconduct than heterosexual soldiers. Indeed, all the information we have indicates that they are not less capable or more prone to misbehavior.

Third, misconduct is already covered by the laws and rules which also cover activities that are improper by heterosexual members of the military.

Fourth, the ban has been lifted in other nations and in police and fire departments in our country with no discernible negative impact on unit cohesion or capacity to do the job, though there is admittedly no absolute analogy to the situation we face and no study bearing on this specific issue.

Fifth, even if the ban were lifted entirely, the experience of other nations and police and fire departments in the United States indicates that most homosexuals would probably not declare their sexual orientation openly, thereby making an already hard life even more difficult in some circumstances.

But as the sociologist Charles Moskos noted after spending many years studying the American military, the issue may be tougher to resolve here in the United States than in Canada, Australia, and in some other nations because of the presence in our country of both vocal gay rights groups and equally vocal antigay rights groups, including some religious groups who believe that lifting the ban amounts to endorsing a lifestyle they strongly disapprove of.

Clearly the American people are deeply divided on this issue, with most military people opposed to lifting the ban because of the feared impact on unit cohesion, rooted in disapproval of homosexual lifestyles and the fear of invasion of privacy of heterosexual soldiers who must live and work in close quarters with homosexual military people. However, those who have studied this issue extensively have discovered an interesting fact. People in this country who are aware of having known homosexuals are far more likely to support lifting the ban. In other words, they are likely to see this issue in terms of individual conduct and individual capacity instead of the claims of a group with which they do not agree and also to be able to imagine how this ban could be lifted without a destructive impact on group cohesion and morale.

Shortly after I took office and reaffirmed my position, the foes of lifting the ban in the Congress moved to enshrine the ban in law. I asked that congressional action be delayed for 6 months while the Secretary of Defense worked with the Joint Chiefs to come up with a proposal for changing our current policy. I then met with the Joint Chiefs to hear their concerns and asked them to try to work through the issue with Secretary Aspin. I wanted to handle the matter in this way on grounds of both principle and practicality.

As a matter of principle, it is my duty as Commander in Chief to uphold the high standards of combat readiness and unit cohesion of the world's finest fighting force, while doing my duty as President to protect the rights of individual Americans and to put to use the abilities of all the American people. And I was determined to serve this principle as fully as possible through practical action, knowing this fact about our system of government: While the Commander in Chief and the Secretary of Defense can change military personnel policies, Congress can reverse those changes by law in ways that are difficult, if not impossible, to veto.

For months now, the Secretary of Defense and the Service Chiefs have worked through this issue in a highly charged, deeply emotional environment, struggling to come to terms with the competing consideration and pressures and, frankly, to work through their own ideas and deep feelings.

During this time many dedicated Americans have come forward to state their own views on this issue. Most, but not all, of the military testimony has been against lifting the ban. But support for changing the policy has come from distinguished combat veterans, including Senators Bob Kerrey, Chuck Robb, and John Kerry in the United States Congress. It has come from Lawrence Korb, who enforced the gay ban during the Reagan administration, and from former Senator Barry Goldwater, a distinguished veteran, former chairman of the Senate Armed Services Committee, founder of the Arizona National Guard, and patron saint of the conservative wing of the Republican Party.

Senator Goldwater's statement, published in the Washington Post recently, made it crystal clear that when this matter is viewed as an issue of individual opportunity and responsibility rather than one of alleged group rights, this is not a call for cultural license but rather a reaffirmation of the American value of extending opportunity to responsible individuals and of limiting the role of Government over citizens' private lives.

On the other hand, those who oppose lifting the ban are clearly focused not on the conduct of individual gay service members but on how nongay service members feel about gays in general and in particular those in the military service.

These past few days I have been in contact with the Secretary of Defense as he has worked through the final stages of this policy with the Joint Chiefs. We now have a policy that is a substantial advance over the one in place when I took office. I have ordered Secretary Aspin to issue a directive consisting of these essential elements: One, service men and women will be judged based on their conduct, not their sexual orientation. Two, therefore the practice, now 6 months old, of not asking about sexual orientation in the enlistment procedure will continue. Three, an open statement by a service member that he or she is a homosexual will create a rebuttable presumption that he or she intends to engage in prohibited conduct, but the service member will be given an opportunity to refute that presumption; in other words, to demonstrate that he or she intends to live by the rules of conduct that apply in the military service. And four, all provisions of the Uniform Code of Military Justice will be enforced in an even-handed manner as regards both heterosexuals and homosexuals. And thanks to the policy provisions agreed to by the Joint Chiefs, there will be a decent regard to the legitimate privacy and associational rights of all service members.

Just as is the case under current policy, unacceptable conduct, either heterosexual or homosexual, will be unacceptable 24 hours a day, 7 days a week from the time a recruit joins the service until the day he or she is discharged. Now, as in the past, every member of our military will be required to comply with the Uniform Code of Military Justice, which is Federal law, and military regulations at all times and in all places.

Let me say a few words now about this policy. It is not a perfect solution. It is not identical with some of my own goals. And it certainly will not please everyone, perhaps not anyone, and clearly not those who hold the most adamant opinions on either side of this issue.

But those who wish to ignore the issue must understand that it is already tearing at the cohesion of the military and it is today being considered by the Federal courts in ways that may not be to the liking of those who oppose any change. And those who want the ban to be lifted completely on both status and conduct must understand that such action would have faced certain and decisive reversal by the Congress and the cause for which many have fought for years would be delayed, probably for years.

Thus, on grounds of both principle and practicality, this is a major step forward. It is, in my judgment, consistent with my responsibilities as President and Commander in Chief to meet the need to change current policy. It is an honorable compromise that advances the cause of people who are called to serve our country by their patriotism, the cause of our national security, and our national interest in resolving an issue that has divided our military and our Nation and diverted our attention from other matters for too long.

The time has come for us to move forward. As your Commander in Chief, I charge all of you to carry out this policy with fairness, with balance, and with due regard for the privacy of individuals. We must and will protect unit cohesion and troop morale. We must and will continue to have the best fighting force in the world. But this is an end to witch hunts that spend millions of taxpayer dollars to ferret out individuals who have served their country well. Improper conduct, on or off base, should remain grounds for discharge. But we will proceed with an even hand against everyone, regardless of sexual orientation.

Such controversies as this have divided us before. But our Nation and our military have always risen to the challenge before. That was true of racial integration of the military and changes in the role of women in the military. Each of these was an issue, because it was an issue for society as well as for the military. And in each case our military was a leader in figuring out how to respond most effectively.

In the early 1970's, when President Nixon decided to transform our military into an all volunteer force, many argued that it could not work. They said it would ruin our forces. But the leaders of our military not only made it work, they used the concept of an all-volunteer force to build the very finest fighting force our Nation and the world have ever known.

Ultimately, the success of this policy will depend in large measure on the commitment it receives from the leaders of the military services. I very much respect and commend the Joint Chiefs for the good-faith effort they have made through this whole endeavor. And I thank General Powell, the Joint Chiefs, and the Commandant of the Coast Guard for joining me here today and for their support of this policy.

I would also like to thank those who lobbied aggressively in behalf of changing the policy, including Congressman Barney Frank; Congressman Gerry Studds; and the Campaign for Military Service, who worked with us and who clearly will not agree with every aspect of the policy announced today, but who should take some solace in knowing that their efforts have helped to produce a strong advance for the cause they seek to serve.

I must now look to General Powell, to the Joint Chiefs, to all the other leaders in our military to carry out this policy through effective training and leadership. Every officer will be expected to exert the necessary effort to make this policy work. That has been the key every time the military has successfully addressed a new challenge, and it will be key in this effort, too.

Our military is a conservative institution, and I say that in the very best sense, for its purpose is to conserve the fighting spirit of our troops, to conserve the resources and the capacity of our troops, to conserve the military lessons acquired during our Nation's existence, to conserve our very security, and yes, to conserve the liberties of the American people. Because it is a conservative institution, it is right for the military to be wary of sudden changes. Because it is an institution that embodies the best of America and must reflect the society in which it operates, it is also right for the military to make changes when the time for change is at hand.

I strongly believe that our military, like our society, needs the talents of every person who wants to make a contribution and who is ready to live by the rules. That is the heart of the policy that I have announced today. I hope in your heart you will find the will and the desire to support it and to lead our military in incorporating it into our Nation's great asset and the world's best fighting force.

Thank you very much.

1996 Republican Party Platform

Families and Society

Stronger Families

Our agenda for more secure families runs throughout this platform. Here we take special notice of the way congressional
Republicans have advanced adoption assistance, promoted foster
care reform, and fought the marriage penalty in the tax code.
They have worked to let parents have flex-time and comp-time in
private industry, and have safeguarded family choice in child care
against the Democrats' attempts to control it. They passed the
Defense of Marriage Act, which defines "marriage" for purposes
of federal law as the legal union of one man and one woman and
prevents federal judges and bureaucrats from forcing states to recognize other living arrangements as "marriages." Further, they
have advanced the Family Rights and Privacy Act - a bill of rights
against the intrusions of big government and its grantees.

Restoring American World Leadership

The Men and Women of Defense

We oppose Bill Clinton's assault on the culture and traditions of
the Armed Forces, especially his attempt to lift the ban on homosexuals in the military. We affirm that homosexuality is incompatible with military service.

U.S. Supreme Court: BOWERS v. HARDWICK, 478 U.S. 186 (1986)

478 U.S. 186

BOWERS, ATTORNEY GENERAL OF GEORGIA v. HARDWICK ET AL.

CERTIORARI TO THE UNITED STATES COURT OF APPEALS FOR THE ELEVENTH CIRCUIT

No. 85-140.

Argued March 31, 1986

Decided June 30, 1986

After being charged with violating the Georgia statute criminalizing sodomy by committing that act with another adult male in the bedroom of his home, respondent Hardwick (respondent) brought suit in Federal District Court, challenging the constitutionality of the statute insofar as it criminalized consensual sodomy. The court granted the defendants' motion to dismiss for failure to state a claim. The Court of Appeals reversed and remanded, holding that the Georgia statute violated respondent's fundamental rights.

Held:

The Georgia statute is constitutional. Pp. 190-196.

> (a) The Constitution does not confer a fundamental right upon homosexuals to engage in sodomy. None of the fundamental rights announced in this Court's prior cases involving family relationships, marriage, or procreation bear any resemblance to the right asserted in this case. And any claim that those cases stand for the proposition that any kind of private sexual conduct between consenting adults is constitutionally insulated from state proscription is unsupportable. Pp. 190-191.

> (b) Against a background in which many States have criminalized sodomy and still do, to claim that a right to engage in such conduct is "deeply rooted in this Nation's history and tradition" or "implicit in the concept of ordered liberty" is, at best, facetious. Pp. 191-194.

> (c) There should be great resistance to expand the reach of the Due Process Clauses to cover new fundamental rights. Otherwise, the Judiciary necessarily would take upon itself further authority to govern the country without constitutional authority. The claimed right in this case falls far short of overcoming this resistance. Pp. 194-195.

(d) The fact that homosexual conduct occurs in the privacy of the home does not affect the result. Stanley v. Georgia, 394 U.S. 557 , distinguished. Pp. 195–196.

(e) Sodomy laws should not be invalidated on the asserted basis that majority belief that sodomy is immoral is an inadequate rationale to support the laws. P. 196.

760 F.2d 1202, reversed. [478 U.S. 186, 187]

WHITE, J., delivered the opinion of the Court, in which BURGER, C. J., and POWELL, REHNQUIST, and O'CONNOR, JJ., joined. BURGER, C. J., post, p. 196, and POWELL, J., post, p. 197, filed concurring opinions. BLACKMUN, J., filed a dissenting opinion, in which BRENNAN, MARSHALL, and STEVENS, JJ., joined, post, p. 199. STEVENS, J., filed a dissenting opinion, in which BRENNAN and MARSHALL, JJ., joined, post, p. 214.

Michael E. Hobbs, Senior Assistant Attorney General of Georgia, argued the cause for petitioner. With him on the briefs were Michael J. Bowers, Attorney General, pro se, Marion O. Gordon, First Assistant Attorney General, and Daryl A. Robinson, Senior Assistant Attorney General.

Laurence H. Tribe argued the cause for respondent Hardwick. With him on the brief were Kathleen M. Sullivan and Kathleen L. Wilde.

JUSTICE WHITE delivered the opinion of the Court.

In August 1982, respondent Hardwick (hereafter respondent) was charged with violating the Georgia statute criminalizing [478 U.S. 186, 188]   sodomy 1 by committing that act with another adult male in the bedroom of respondent's home. After a preliminary hearing, the District Attorney decided not to present the matter to the grand jury unless further evidence developed.

Respondent then brought suit in the Federal District Court, challenging the constitutionality of the statute insofar as it criminalized consensual sodomy. 2 He asserted that he was a practicing homosexual, that the Georgia sodomy statute, as administered by the defendants, placed him in imminent danger of arrest, and that the statute for several reasons violates the Federal Constitution. The District Court granted the defendants' motion to dismiss for failure to state a claim, relying on Doe v. Commonwealth's Attorney for the City of Richmond, 403 F. Supp. 1199 (ED Va. 1975), which this Court summarily affirmed, 425 U.S. 901 (1976). [478 U.S. 186, 189]

A divided panel of the Court of Appeals for the Eleventh Circuit reversed. 760 F.2d 1202 (1985). The court first held that, because Doe was distinguishable and in any event had been undermined by later decisions, our summary affirmance in that case did not require affirmance of the District Court. Relying on our decisions in Griswold v. Connecticut, 381 U.S. 479 (1965); Eisenstadt v. Baird, 405 U.S. 438 (1972); Stanley v. Georgia, 394 U.S. 557 (1969); and Roe v. Wade, 410 U.S. 113 (1973), the court went on to hold that the Georgia statute violated respondent's fundamental rights because his homosexual activity is a private and intimate association that is beyond the reach of state regulation by reason of the Ninth Amendment and the Due Process Clause of the Fourteenth Amendment. The case was remanded for trial, at which, to prevail, the State would have to prove that the statute is supported by a compelling interest and is the most narrowly drawn means of achieving that end.

Because other Courts of Appeals have arrived at judgments contrary to that of the Eleventh Circuit in this case, 3 we granted the Attorney General's petition for certiorari questioning the holding that the sodomy statute violates the fundamental rights of homosexuals. We agree with petitioner that the Court of Appeals erred, and hence reverse its judgment. 4 [478 U.S. 186, 190]

This case does not require a judgment on whether laws against sodomy between consenting adults in general, or between homosexuals in particular, are wise or desirable. It raises no question about the right or propriety of state legislative decisions to repeal their laws that criminalize homosexual sodomy, or of state-court decisions invalidating those laws on state constitutional grounds. The issue presented is whether the Federal Constitution confers a fundamental right upon homosexuals to engage in sodomy and hence invalidates the laws of the many States that still make such conduct illegal and have done so for a very long time. The case also calls for some judgment about the limits of the Court's role in carrying out its constitutional mandate.

We first register our disagreement with the Court of Appeals and with respondent that the Court's prior cases have construed the Constitution to confer a right of privacy that extends to homosexual sodomy and for all intents and purposes have decided this case. The reach of this line of cases was sketched in Carey v. Population Services International, 431 U.S. 678, 685 (1977). Pierce v. Society of Sisters, 268 U.S. 510 (1925), and Meyer v. Nebraska, 262 U.S. 390 (1923), were described as dealing with child rearing and education; Prince v. Massachusetts, 321 U.S. 158 (1944), with family relationships; Skinner v. Oklahoma ex rel. Williamson, 316 U.S. 535 (1942), with procreation; Loving v. Virginia, 388 U.S. 1 (1967), with marriage; Griswold v. Connecticut, supra, and Eisenstadt v. Baird, supra, with contraception; and Roe v. Wade, 410 U.S. 113 (1973), with abortion. The latter three cases were interpreted as construing the Due Process Clause of the Fourteenth Amendment to confer a fundamental individual right to decide whether or not to beget or bear a child. Carey v. Population Services International, supra, at 688-689.

Accepting the decisions in these cases and the above description of them, we think it evident that none of the rights announced in those cases bears any resemblance to the [478 U.S. 186, 191] claimed constitutional right of homosexuals to engage in acts of sodomy that is asserted in this case. No connection between family, marriage, or procreation on the one hand and homosexual activity on the other has been demonstrated, either by the Court of Appeals or by respondent. Moreover, any claim that these cases nevertheless stand for the proposition that any kind of private sexual conduct between consenting adults is constitutionally insulated from state proscription is unsupportable. Indeed, the Court's opinion in Carey twice asserted that the privacy right, which the Griswold line of cases found to be one of the protections provided by the Due Process Clause, did not reach so far. 431 U.S., at 688 , n. 5, 694, n. 17.

Precedent aside, however, respondent would have us announce, as the Court of Appeals did, a fundamental right to engage in homosexual sodomy. This we are quite unwilling to do. It is true that despite the language of the Due Process Clauses of the Fifth and Fourteenth Amendments, which appears to focus only on the processes by which life, liberty, or property is taken, the cases are legion in which those Clauses have been interpreted to have substantive content, subsuming rights that to a great extent are immune from federal or state regulation or proscription. Among such cases are those recognizing rights that have little or no textual support in the constitutional language. Meyer, Prince, and Pierce fall in this category, as do the privacy cases from Griswold to Carey.

Striving to assure itself and the public that announcing rights not readily identifiable in the Constitution's text involves much more than the imposition of the Justices' own choice of values on the States and the Federal Government, the Court has sought to identify the nature of the rights qualifying for heightened judicial protection. In Palko v. Connecticut, 302 U.S. 319, 325 , 326 (1937), it was said that this category includes those fundamental liberties that are "implicit in the concept of ordered liberty," such that "neither [478 U.S. 186, 192]   liberty nor justice would exist if [they] were sacrificed." A different description of fundamental liberties appeared in Moore v. East Cleveland, 431 U.S. 494, 503 (1977) (opinion of POWELL, J.), where they are characterized as those liberties that are "deeply rooted in this Nation's history and tradition." Id., at 503 (POWELL, J.). See also Griswold v. Connecticut, 381 U.S., at 506 .

It is obvious to us that neither of these formulations would extend a fundamental right to homosexuals to engage in acts of consensual sodomy. Proscriptions against that conduct have ancient roots. See generally Survey on the Constitutional Right to Privacy in the Context of Homosexual Activity, 40 U. Miami L. Rev. 521, 525 (1986). Sodomy was a criminal offense at common law and was forbidden by the laws of the original 13 States when they ratified the Bill of Rights. 5 In 1868, when the Fourteenth Amendment was [478 U.S. 186, 193]   ratified, all but 5 of the 37 States in the Union had criminal sodomy laws. 6 In fact, until 1961, 7 all 50 States outlawed sodomy, and today, 24 States and the District of Columbia [478 U.S. 186, 194] continue to provide criminal penalties for sodomy performed in private and between consenting adults. See Survey, U. Miami L. Rev., supra, at 524, n. 9. Against this background, to claim that a right to engage in such conduct is "deeply rooted in this Nation's history and tradition" or "implicit in the concept of ordered liberty" is, at best, facetious.

Nor are we inclined to take a more expansive view of our authority to discover new fundamental rights imbedded in the Due Process Clause. The Court is most vulnerable and comes nearest to illegitimacy when it deals with judge-made constitutional law having little or no cognizable roots in the language or design of the Constitution. That this is so was painfully demonstrated by the face-off between the Executive and the Court in the 1930's, which resulted in the repudiation [478 U.S. 186, 195] of much of the substantive gloss that the Court had placed on the Due Process Clauses of the Fifth and Fourteenth Amendments. There should be, therefore, great resistance to expand the substantive reach of those Clauses, particularly if it requires redefining the category of rights deemed to be fundamental. Otherwise, the Judiciary necessarily takes to itself further authority to govern the country without express constitutional authority. The claimed right pressed on us today falls for short of overcoming this resistance.

Respondent, however, asserts that the result should be different where the homosexual conduct occurs in the privacy of the home. He relies on Stanley v. Georgia, 394 U.S. 557 (1969), where the Court held that the First Amendment prevents conviction for possessing and reading obscene material in the privacy of one's home: "If the First Amendment means anything, it means that a State has no business telling a man, sitting alone in his house, what books he may read or what films he may watch." Id., at 565.

Stanley did protect conduct that would not have been protected outside the home, and it partially prevented the enforcement of state obscenity laws; but the decision was firmly grounded in the First Amendment. The right pressed upon us here has no similar support in the text of the Constitution, and it does not qualify for recognition under the prevailing principles for construing the Fourteenth Amendment. Its limits are also difficult to discern. Plainly enough, otherwise illegal conduct is not always immunized whenever it occurs in the home. Victimless crimes, such as the possession and use of illegal drugs, do not escape the law where they are committed at home. Stanley itself recognized that its holding offered no protection for the possession in the home of drugs, firearms, or stolen goods. Id., at 568, n. 11. And if respondent's submission is limited to the voluntary sexual conduct between consenting adults, it would be difficult, except by fiat, to limit the claimed right to homosexual conduct [478 U.S. 186, 196]   while leaving exposed to prosecution adultery, incest, and other sexual crimes even though they are committed in the home. We are unwilling to start down that road.

Even if the conduct at issue here is not a fundamental right, respondent asserts that there must be a rational basis for the law and that there is none in this case other than the presumed belief of a majority of the electorate in Georgia that homosexual sodomy is immoral and unacceptable. This is said to be an inadequate rationale to support the law. The law, however, is constantly based on notions of morality, and if all laws representing essentially moral choices are to be invalidated under the Due Process Clause, the courts will be very busy indeed. Even respondent makes no such claim, but insists that majority sentiments about the morality of homosexuality should be declared inadequate. We do not agree, and are unpersuaded that the sodomy laws of some 25 States should be invalidated on this basis. 8

Accordingly, the judgment of the Court of Appeals is

Reversed.

LAWRENCE et al. v. TEXAS

certiorari to the court of appeals of texas, fourteenth district

No. 02-102. Argued March 26, 2003—Decided June 26, 2003

Responding to a reported weapons disturbance in a private residence, Houston police entered petitioner Lawrence's apartment and saw him and another adult man, petitioner Garner, engaging in a private, consensual sexual act. Petitioners were arrested and convicted of deviate sexual intercourse in violation of a Texas

statute forbidding two persons of the same sex to engage in certain intimate sexual conduct. In affirming, the State Court of
Appeals held, inter alia, that the statute was not unconstitutional
under the Due Process Clause of the Fourteenth Amendment.
The court considered Bowers v. Hardwick, 478 U. S. 186, controlling on that point.

Held: The Texas statute making it a crime for two persons of the
same sex to engage in certain intimate sexual conduct violates
the Due Process Clause. Pp. 3-18.

(a) Resolution of this case depends on whether petitioners
were free as adults to engage in private conduct in the
exercise of their liberty under the Due Process Clause. For
this inquiry the Court deems it necessary to reconsider its
Bowers holding. The Bowers Court's initial substantive
statement—"The issue presented is whether the Federal
Constitution confers a fundamental right upon homosexuals to engage in sodomy ... ," 478 U. S., at 190—discloses
the Court's failure to appreciate the extent of the liberty at
stake. To say that the issue in Bowers was simply the right
to engage in certain sexual conduct demeans the claim the
individual put forward, just as it would demean a married
couple were it said that marriage is just about the right to
have sexual intercourse. Although the laws involved in
Bowers and here purport to do not more than prohibit a
particular sexual act, their penalties and purposes have
more far-reaching consequences, touching upon the most
private human conduct, sexual behavior, and in the most
private of places, the home. They seek to control a personal
relationship that, whether or not entitled to formal recognition in the law, is within the liberty of persons to choose
without being punished as criminals. The liberty protected
by the Constitution allows homosexual persons the right to
choose to enter upon relationships in the confines of their
homes and their own private lives and still retain their dignity as free persons. Pp. 3-6.

(b) Having misapprehended the liberty claim presented to it,
the Bowers Court stated that proscriptions against sodomy
have ancient roots. 478 U. S., at 192. It should be noted,
however, that there is no longstanding history in this country of laws directed at homosexual conduct as a distinct

matter. Early American sodomy laws were not directed at homosexuals as such but instead sought to prohibit non-procreative sexual activity more generally, whether between men and women or men and men. Moreover, early sodomy laws seem not to have been enforced against consenting adults acting in private. Instead, sodomy prosecutions often involved predatory acts against those who could not or did not consent: relations between men and minor girls or boys, between adults involving force, between adults implicating disparity in status, or between men and animals. The longstanding criminal prohibition of homosexual sodomy upon which Bowers placed such reliance is as consistent with a general condemnation of nonprocreative sex as it is with an established tradition of prosecuting acts because of their homosexual character. Far from possessing "ancient roots," ibid., American laws targeting same-sex couples did not develop until the last third of the 20th century. Even now, only nine States have singled out same-sex relations for criminal prosecution. Thus, the historical grounds relied upon in Bowers are more complex than the majority opinion and the concurring opinion by Chief Justice Burger there indicated. They are not without doubt and, at the very least, are overstated. The Bowers Court was, of course, making the broader point that for centuries there have been powerful voices to condemn homosexual conduct as immoral, but this Court's obligation is to define the liberty of all, not to mandate its own moral code, Planned Parenthood of Southeastern Pa. v. Casey, 505 U. S. 833, 850. The Nation's laws and traditions in the past half century are most relevant here. They show an emerging awareness that liberty gives substantial protection to adult persons in deciding how to conduct their private lives in matters pertaining to sex. See County of Sacramento v. Lewis, 523 U. S. 833, 857. Pp. 6-12.

(c) Bowers' deficiencies became even more apparent in the years following its announcement. The 25 States with laws prohibiting the conduct referenced in Bowers are reduced now to 13, of which 4 enforce their laws only against homosexual conduct. In those States, including Texas, that still proscribe sodomy (whether for same-sex or heterosexual conduct), there is a pattern of nonenforcement with respect to consenting adults acting in private. Casey, supra, at 851—which confirmed that the Due Process Clause protects personal decisions relating to marriage, procreation, contraception, family relationships, child rearing, and education—and Romer v. Evans, 517 U. S. 620, 624—which struck down class-based legislation directed at homosexuals—cast Bowers' holding into even more doubt. The stigma the Texas criminal statute imposes, moreover, is not trivial. Although the offense is but a minor misdemeanor, it remains a criminal offense with all that imports for the dignity of the persons charged, including notation of convictions on their records and on job application forms, and registration as sex offenders under state law. Where a case's foundations have sustained serious erosion, criticism from other sources is of greater significance. In the United States, criticism of Bowers has been substantial and continuing, disapproving of its reasoning in all respects, not just as to its historical assumptions. And, to the extent Bowers relied on values shared with a wider civilization, the case's reasoning and holding have been rejected by the European Court of Human Rights, and that other nations have taken action consistent with an affirmation of the protected right of homosexual adults to engage in intimate, consensual conduct. There has been no showing that in this country the governmental interest in circumscribing personal choice is somehow more legitimate or urgent. Stare decisis is not an inexorable command. Payne v. Tennessee, 501 U. S. 808, 828. Bowers' holding has not induced detrimental reliance of the sort that could counsel against overturning it once there are compelling reasons to do so. Casey, supra, at 855-856. Bowers causes uncertainty, for the precedents before and after it contradict its central holding. Pp. 12-17.

(d) Bowers' rationale does not withstand careful analysis. In his dissenting opinion in Bowers Justice Stevens concluded that (1) the fact a State's governing majority has traditionally viewed a particular practice as immoral is not a sufficient reason for upholding a law prohibiting the practice, and (2) individual decisions concerning the intimacies of physical relationships, even when not intended to produce offspring, are a form of "liberty" protected by due process. That analysis should have controlled Bowers, and it controls here.

Bowers was not correct when it was decided, is not correct today, and is hereby overruled. This case does not involve minors, persons who might be injured or coerced, those who might not easily refuse consent, or public conduct or prostitution. It does involve two adults who, with full and mutual consent, engaged in sexual practices common to a homosexual lifestyle. Petitioners' right to liberty under the Due Process Clause gives them the full right to engage in private conduct without government intervention. Casey, supra, at 847. The Texas statute furthers no legitimate state interest which can justify its intrusion into the individual's personal and private life. Pp. 17–18.

41 S. W. 3d 349, reversed and remanded.

Kennedy, J., delivered the opinion of the Court, in which Stevens, Souter, Ginsburg, and Breyer, JJ., joined. O'Connor, J., filed an opinion concurring in the judgment. Scalia, J., filed a dissenting opinion, in which Rehnquist, C. J., and Thomas, J., joined. Thomas, J., filed a dissenting opinion.

JOHN GEDDES LAWRENCE and TYRON GARNER, PETITIONERS v. TEXAS

on writ of certiorari to the court of appeals of texas, fourteenth district

Justice Kennedy delivered the opinion of the Court.

Liberty protects the person from unwarranted government intrusions into a dwelling or other private places. In our tradition the State is not omnipresent in the home. And there are other spheres of our lives and existence, outside the home, where the State should not be a dominant presence. Freedom extends beyond spatial bounds. Liberty presumes an autonomy of self that includes freedom of thought, belief, expression, and certain intimate conduct. The instant case involves liberty of the person both in its spatial and more transcendent dimensions.

I

The question before the Court is the validity of a Texas statute making it a crime for two persons of the same sex to engage in certain intimate sexual conduct.

In Houston, Texas, officers of the Harris County Police Department were dispatched to a private residence in response to a reported weapons disturbance. They entered an apartment where one of the petitioners, John Geddes Lawrence, resided. The right of the police to enter does not seem to have been questioned. The officers observed Lawrence and another man, Tyron Garner, engaging in a sexual act. The two petitioners were arrested, held in custody over night, and charged and convicted before a Justice of the Peace.

The complaints described their crime as "deviate sexual intercourse, namely anal sex, with a member of the same sex (man)." App. to Pet. for Cert. 127a, 139a. The applicable state law is Tex. Penal Code Ann. §21.06(a) (2003). It provides: "A person commits an offense if he engages in deviate sexual intercourse with another individual of the same sex." The statute defines "[d]eviate sexual intercourse" as follows:

> "(A) any contact between any part of the genitals of one person and the mouth or anus of another person; or

> "(B) the penetration of the genitals or the anus of another person with an object." §21.01(1).

The petitioners exercised their right to a trial de novo in Harris County Criminal Court. They challenged the statute as a violation of the Equal Protection Clause of the Fourteenth Amendment and of a like provision of the Texas Constitution. Tex. Const., Art. 1, §3a. Those contentions were rejected. The petitioners, having entered a plea of nolo contendere, were each fined $200 and assessed court costs of $141.25. App. to Pet. for Cert. 107a–110a.

The Court of Appeals for the Texas Fourteenth District considered the petitioners' federal constitutional arguments under both the Equal Protection and Due Process Clauses of the Fourteenth

Amendment. After hearing the case en banc the court, in a divided opinion, rejected the constitutional arguments and affirmed the convictions. 41 S. W. 3d 349 (Tex. App. 2001). The majority opinion indicates that the Court of Appeals considered our decision in Bowers v. Hardwick, 478 U. S. 186 (1986), to be controlling on the federal due process aspect of the case. Bowers then being authoritative, this was proper.

We granted certiorari, 537 U. S. 1044 (2002), to consider three questions:

> "1. Whether Petitioners' criminal convictions under the Texas "Homosexual Conduct" law—which criminalizes sexual intimacy by same-sex couples, but not identical behavior by different-sex couples—violate the Fourteenth Amendment guarantee of equal protection of laws?

> "2. Whether Petitioners' criminal convictions for adult consensual sexual intimacy in the home violate their vital interests in liberty and privacy protected by the Due Process Clause of the Fourteenth Amendment?

> "3. Whether Bowers v. Hardwick, 478 U. S. 186 (1986), should be overruled?" Pet. for Cert. i.

The petitioners were adults at the time of the alleged offense. Their conduct was in private and consensual.

★   ★   ★

The rationale of Bowers does not withstand careful analysis. In his dissenting opinion in Bowers Justice Stevens came to these conclusions:

> "Our prior cases make two propositions abundantly clear. First, the fact that the governing majority in a State has traditionally viewed a particular practice as immoral is not a sufficient reason for upholding a law prohibiting the practice; neither history nor tradition could save a law prohibiting miscegenation from constitutional attack. Second, individual decisions by married persons, concerning the intimacies of their physical relationship, even when not intended to produce offspring, are a form of "liberty" protected by the Due Process Clause of the Fourteenth

Amendment. Moreover, this protection extends to intimate choices by unmarried as well as married persons." 478 U. S., at 216 (footnotes and citations omitted).

Justice Stevens' analysis, in our view, should have been controlling in Bowers and should control here.

Bowers was not correct when it was decided, and it is not correct today. It ought not to remain binding precedent. Bowers v. Hardwick should be and now is overruled.

The present case does not involve minors. It does not involve persons who might be injured or coerced or who are situated in relationships where consent might not easily be refused. It does not involve public conduct or prostitution. It does not involve whether the government must give formal recognition to any relationship that homosexual persons seek to enter. The case does involve two adults who, with full and mutual consent from each other, engaged in sexual practices common to a homosexual lifestyle. The petitioners are entitled to respect for their private lives. The State cannot demean their existence or control their destiny by making their private sexual conduct a crime. Their right to liberty under the Due Process Clause gives them the full right to engage in their conduct without intervention of the government. "It is a promise of the Constitution that there is a realm of personal liberty which the government may not enter." Casey, supra, at 847. The Texas statute furthers no legitimate state interest which can justify its intrusion into the personal and private life of the individual.

Had those who drew and ratified the Due Process Clauses of the Fifth Amendment or the Fourteenth Amendment known the components of liberty in its manifold possibilities, they might have been more specific. They did not presume to have this insight. They knew times can blind us to certain truths and later generations can see that laws once thought necessary and proper in fact serve only to oppress. As the Constitution endures, persons in every generation can invoke its principles in their own search for greater freedom.

The judgment of the Court of Appeals for the Texas Fourteenth District is reversed, and the case is remanded for further proceedings not inconsistent with this opinion.

It is so ordered.

VII

The Problem of the Color Line

The brilliant African-American social Critic W.E. B. DuBois wrote, around 1900, that the problem of the 20th Century would be the "problem of the color line," meaning America's racist past and failure to give blacks political and social equality. This chapter looks at the problem of the color line from the Civil War to the present, since it makes more sense to approach it in its totality than in chronological segments.

After the Civil War, politicians argued that giving Blacks political rights would create equality, but violence against African-Americans persisted while the legal system maintained a segregated society.

Only at the end of the Second World War did American leaders begin to seriously address this crisis, because of the need to expand economic democracy and because of the protests of African-Americans themselves, and this led to important laws guaranteeing civil rights to Blacks.

Laws, however, did not eliminate racism, and the problem continues today, but, with the candidacy and election of America's first Black president, Barack Obama, new opportunities to confront a racist past have emerged.

Background: From Hope to Reaction

Amendments 13, 14, and 15

Amendment 13 - Slavery Abolished. Ratified 12/6/1865.

1. Neither slavery nor involuntary servitude, except as a punishment for crime whereof the party shall have been duly convicted, shall exist within the United States, or any place subject to their jurisdiction.

2. Congress shall have power to enforce this article by appropriate legislation.

Amendment 14 - Citizenship Rights. Ratified 7/9/1868.

1. All persons born or naturalized in the United States, and subject to the jurisdiction thereof, are citizens of the United States and of the State wherein they reside. No State shall make or enforce any law which shall abridge the privileges or immunities of citizens of the United States; nor shall any State deprive any person of life, liberty, or property, without due process of law; nor deny to any person within its jurisdiction the equal protection of the laws.

2. Representatives shall be apportioned among the several States according to their respective numbers, counting the whole number of persons in each State, excluding Indians not taxed. But when the right to vote at any election for the choice of electors for President and Vice-President of the United States, Representatives in Congress, the Executive and Judicial officers of a State, or the members of the Legislature thereof, is denied to any of the male inhabitants of such State, being twenty-one years of age, and citizens of the United States, or in any way abridged,

except for participation in rebellion, or other crime, the basis of representation therein shall be reduced in the proportion which the number of such male citizens shall bear to the whole number of male citizens twenty-one years of age in such State.

3. No person shall be a Senator or Representative in Congress, or elector of President and Vice-President, or hold any office, civil or military, under the United States, or under any State, who, having previously taken an oath, as a member of Congress, or as an officer of the United States, or as a member of any State legislature, or as an executive or judicial officer of any State, to support the Constitution of the United States, shall have engaged in insurrection or rebellion against the same, or given aid or comfort to the enemies thereof. But Congress may by a vote of two-thirds of each House, remove such disability.

4. The validity of the public debt of the United States, authorized by law, including debts incurred for payment of pensions and bounties for services in suppressing insurrection or rebellion, shall not be questioned. But neither the United States nor any State shall assume or pay any debt or obligation incurred in aid of insurrection or rebellion against the United States, or any claim for the loss or emancipation of any slave; but all such debts, obligations and claims shall be held illegal and void.

5. The Congress shall have power to enforce, by appropriate legislation, the provisions of this article.

Amendment 15 - Race No Bar to Vote. Ratified 2/3/1870.

1. The right of citizens of the United States to vote shall not be denied or abridged by the United States or by any State on account of race, color, or previous condition of servitude.

2. The Congress shall have power to enforce this article by appropriate legislation.

Murder Records for the State of Georgia

Report of Persons Murdered in the District of Savannah, Ga. 1865 - 1866

Name of Person Murdered: Simpson Whitfield (colored); County: Cass; Names of Supposed Murderers: John Allen (white); Date of killing: August 1866; Remarks: murderer acquitted by civil court.

Name of Person Murdered: Peter (colored); County: Effingham; Name of supposed murderer: Mr. Fox (white); Date of killing:20 September 1866; Remarks: a verdict of justifiable homicide was rendered by jury on coroners inquest, the man was set at liberty.

Name of person murdered: Charles Smith (colored); County: Tattnall; Names of Supposed Murderers: Regulators; Date of killing: August 1866; Remarks: a guard was sent and arrested several parties who were turned over to the civil authorities to be tried for assault with intent to kill. Mr. E. Yuler, Agt. For B of R. F. And A. L. For Liberty County has all the necessary papers in the case.

Name of Person Murdered: John Allford (white); County: Chatham; Name of Supposed Murderers: Smart Cummings (colored); Date of Killing: September 1865; Remarks: is now in jail and has confessed the deed.

Report of Freedpeople Murdered and Assaulted with intent to kill in the Sub District of Thomasville

Brooks Co., Oct. 7, John Tellmar was shot and killed by Alfred Kelton (white). No action by authorities.

Thomas Co., Nov. 8, 1868, McCullough assaulted and severely beaten by John Lyn (white). No action taken by Civil Authorities.

Thomas Co., Nov. 12, 1868, Isaac Beard kidnapped by Ed Stearns and others (white). No action.

Thomas Co., Jany. 20, 1868, Primus Hatch was kidnapped and murdered by Jarrett Hanley and others (white). No action.

Thomas Co., June, John Platt and his wife were kidnapped and murdered by Ed Stearns (white). No action.

Report of Freedmen who have been murdered and assaulted with intent to kill in the Sub District of Macon, Ga. During the year 1868 up to 31 Oct. 1868

Victim: Ned Hardeman. Attacker: W. Ross (white). Date: 4 March. County: Bibb. Injuries: received gun shot in face. Cause: altercation. Remarks: warrant issued, case settled.

Victim: Abram Blount. Attacker: Thos. James (white). Date: 27 April. County: Jones. Injury: Badly cut and stabbed. Cause: altercation about work. Remarks: settled by parties.

Victim: Edmund Patterson. Attacker: Henry Patterson (white). Date: 20 July. County: Jones. Injury: shot in leg with pistol ball. Cause: altercation about work. Remarks: Patterson bound over.

Victim: Andrew Cook. Attacker: Mike Bird, et. al. (white). Date: 2 Oct. County: Jones. Injuries: swing by neck three times. Cause: suspicion of arson. Remarks: no action by civil authorities. Brought before Grand Jury. Anderson (Andrew?) failing to appear through fear.

Victim: Moses Siah. Attacker: William Oxford (white). Date: 30 Jul. County: Washington. Injuries: killed, struck on head with revolver. Cause: unprovoked. Remarks: warrant issued. Party escaped.

Victim: James Douglass. Attacker: Wm. Downs (white). Date: May. County: Washington. Remarks: warrant issued. Party escaped.

Victim: freedboy. Attacker: Bush (white). Date: 20 May. County: Washington. Cause: instigation of Frank Brantley. Remarks: warrant issued. Party escaped.

Victim: David Bryant. Attacker: Wm. Lucas (col'd). Date: 28 May. County: Monroe. Injury: shot dead in house. Cause: jealousy. Remarks: warrant issued; Lucas awaiting trial.

Victim: Sallie Butler. Attacker: Alfred Butler (col'd). Date: 19 August. County: Spalding. Injuries: killed. Cause: not known. Remarks: warrant issued; sentenced to be hung Dec. 11, 1868.

Victim: Warwick Birdsong: Attacker: Wm. H. Reever (white). Date: April. County: Pike. Injuries: badly beaten. Remarks: no bill found. Report forwarded May 22, 1868.

Victim: Benjamin Thomas. Attacker: unknown (white). Date: 24 April. County: Spalding. Injury: badly cut. Remarks: nothing done by civil authorities. Assaulted by a party of whites.

Victim: Wyatt Williams & wife. Attackers: Green ?Risbn and A. Pritchard (white). Date: 6 July. County: Spalding. Injuries: tied up and whipped. Remarks: nothing done. Report of investigation for Jul. 18.

Victim: Elbert Proiton. Attacker: Capt. Johns (white). Date: 15 Feb. County: Pulaski. Injury: wounded in arm. Cause: dispute about wages. Remarks: warrant issued, settled.

Victim: Alex Jennings. Attacker: Jno. A. Sonders (white). Date: 1 June. County: Pulaski. Injury: killed. Cause: (blank). Remarks: warrant issued, no arrest.

Victim: Joshua. Attacker: unknown. Date: June. County: Wilcox. Injury: burned in jail in Abbeville. Cause: killed a man in self defense.

Victim: Joseph Troup. Attacker: unknown (white). Date: August. County: Montgomery. Injury: killed in his own house at night. Cause: were radical leaders. Remarks: killed by a party of disguised whites.

Victim: Frank John. Attacker: John Finley (white). Date: 22 July. County: Houston. Injury: (blank). Cause: (blank). Remarks: (blank).

Victim: Henry Boon. Attacker: unknown. Date: July. County: Houston. Remarks: attempt to murder by persons unknown.

Victim: Jeff Hughes. Attacker: Larogia Lamar (white). Date: 18 Feb. County: Houston. Injury: shot dead with pistol. Cause: dispute about wages. Remarks: warrant issued, party escaped.

Victim: Freedmen. Attacker: Henry Moyatt (white). Date: 7 April. County: Houston. Injuries: shot dead with pistols. Remarks: Moyatt was a private Co. B, 17 U. S. Infantry. Report 11 April 1868.

Victim: Carolina. Attacker: Nelson Oliver (col'd). Date: 15 August. County: Twiggs. Injuries: shot dead. Cause: political dispute. Remarks: warrant issued. Oliver escaped.

Victim: Thos. Brocket. Attacker: Sheriff's party. Date: 24 August. County: Twiggs. Injuries: shot and killed. Cause: said to be resisting authorities. Remarks: Verdict - justifiable homicide. Brocket had no arms of any kind.

Victim: Benj. Hill. Attackers: Sheriff's party. Date:: 29 August. County: Twiggs. Injuries: shot and killed. Cause: said to be resisting authorities. Remarks: justifiable homicide.

Victim: John Fleetwood. Attacker: Chas. E. Fraser (white). Date: 26 August. County: Wilkinson. Injuries: shot and killed. Cause: President Loyal League. Remarks: no bill found by G. Jury.

Victim: George Solomon. Attacker: John B. Glover (white). Date: 21 Oct. County: Twiggs. Injuries: shot and killed. Cause: dispute. Remarks: warrant issued. Escaped. Glover was allowed to be at liberty some two weeks after the shooting and escaped.

Victim: freedman wife of John Brown. Attacker: Homer Barnes (white). Date: January. County: Jasper. Injuries: shot and killed. Cause: (blank). Remarks: bound over to appear.

Victim: Emanuel Tripp. Attacker: unknown. Date: 16 October. County: Jasper. Injuries: shot and killed. Remarks: shot by a party of disguised men at night, called up from bed.

Victim: Gabriel Singleterry. Attacker: J. W. Weeks (white). Date: Feb. County: Telfair. Injury: shot and killed. Cause: revenge of injuries. Remarks: warrant issued; Weeks not arrested.

Bureau of Refugees, Freedmen and Abandoned Lands, 1865 - 1869

Bureau R. F. & A. L.

Office Asst. Comr. State Office

Augusta, Ga.

March 13, 1866

State of Georgia

Wilkes County

This agreement entered into this the 9th day of January 1866 between Clark Anderson & Co. of the State of Mississippi, County of (blank) of the first part and the Freedmen whose names are annexed of the State and County aforesaid of the second part. Witnesseth that the said Clark Anderson & Co. agrees to furnish to the Freed Laborers whose names are annexed quarters, fuel and healthey rations. Medical attendance and supplies in case of sickness, and the amount set opposite their respective names per month during the continuation of this contract paying one third of the wages each month, and the amount in full at the end of the year before the final disposal of the crop which is to be raised by them on said Clark Anderson & Co. Plantation in the County of (blank) and State aforesaid. The said Clark Anderson & Co. further agree to give the female laborers one half day in each week to do their washing &c.

The Laborers on their part agree to work faithfully and diligently on the Plantation of the said Clark Anderson & Co. for six days in the week and to do all necessary work usually done on a plantation on the Sabbath, during this year 1866 commencing with this date and ending 1st January 1867, that we will be respectful and obedient to said Clark Anderson & Co. or their agents, and that we will in all respects endeavor to promote their interests, and we further bind ourselves to treat with humanity and kindness the stock entrusted to our care and will be responsible for such stock as die through out inhumanity or carelessness and we further agree to deduct for time lost by our own fault one dollar per day during the Spring and two dollars during cotton picking season, also that the Father & Mother should pay for board of children, also for lost time by protracted sickness and we further agree to have deducted from our respective wages the expense of medical attendance and supplies during sickness.

Plessy vs. Ferguson—1896

BROWN, J. This case turns upon the constitutionality of an act of the general assembly of the state of Louisiana, passed in 1890, providing for separate railway carriages for the white and colored races....

The constitutionality of this act is attacked upon the ground that it conflicts both with the 13th Amendment of the Constitution, abolishing slavery, and the 14th Amendment, which prohibits certain restrictive legislation on the part of the states.

1. That it does not conflict with the 13th Amendment, which abolished slavery and involuntary servitude, except as a punishment for crime, is too clear for argument....

A statute which implies merely a legal distinction between the white and colored races—a distinction which is founded in the color of the two races, and which must always exist so long as white men are distinguished from the other race by color— has no tendency to destroy the legal equality of the two races, or re-establish a state of involuntary servitude. Indeed, we do not understand that the 13th Amendment is strenuously relied upon by the plaintiff in, error in this connection.... '

The object of the amendment was undoubtedly to enforce the absolute equality of the two races before the law, but in the nature of things it could not have been intended to abolish distinctions based upon color, or to enforce social, as distinguished from political, equality, or a commingling of the two races upon terms unsatisfactory to either. Laws permitting, and even requiring their separation in places where they are liable to be brought into contact do not necessarily imply the inferiority of either race to the other, and have been generally, if not universally, recognized as within the competency of the state legislatures in the exercise of their police power. The most common instance of this is connected with the establishment of separate schools for white and colored children, which have been held to be a valid exercise of the legislative power even by courts of states where the political rights of the colored race have been longest and most earnestly enforced....

It is claimed by the plaintiff in error that, in any mixed community, the reputation of belonging to the dominant race, in this instance the white race is property, in the same sense that a right of action, or of inheritance, is property. Conceding this to be so for the purposes of this case, we are unable to see how this statute deprives him of, or in any way affects his right to, such property. If he be a white man and assigned to a colored coach, he may have his action for damages against the company for being deprived of his so-called property . Upon the other hand, if he be a colored man and be, so assigned, he has been deprived of no property, since he is not lawfully entitled . . to the reputation of being a white man....

So far, then. as a conflict with the 14th

Amendment is concerned, the case reduces itself to the question whether the statute of Louisiana is a reasonable regulation, and with respect to this there must necessarily be a large discretion on the part of the legislature. In determining the question of reasonableness it is at liberty to act with reference to the established usages, customs, and traditions of the people, and with a view to the promotion of their comfort, and the preservation of the public peace and good order. Gauged by this standard, we cannot say that a law which authorizes or even requires the separation of the two races in public conveyances is unreasonable or more obnoxious to the 14th Amendment than the acts of Congress requiring separate schools for colored children in the District of Columbia, the constitutionality of which does not seem to have been questioned, or the corresponding acts of state legislatures.

Die consider the underlying fallacy of the plaintiffs argument to consist in the assumption that the enforced separation of the two races stamps the colored race with a badge of inferiority. If this be so, it is not by reason of anything found in the act, but solely because the colored race chooses to put that construction upon it. The argument necessarily assumes that if, as has been more than once the case, and is not unlikely to be so again, the colored race should become the dominant power in the state legislature, and should enact a law in precisely similar terms. it would thereby relegate the white race to an inferior position. We imagine that the white race, at least, would not acquiesce in this assumption. The argument also assumes that social prejudice may be overcome by legislation, and that equal rights cannot be secured to the Negro except by an enforced commingling of the two races. We cannot accept this proposition. If the two races are to meet on terms of social equality wit must be the result of natural affinities, a mutual appreciation of each other's merits and a voluntary consent of individuals.... Legislation is powerless to eradicate racial instincts or to abolish distinctions based upon physical differences, and the attempt to do so can only result in accentuating the difficulties of the present situation. If the civil right of both races be equal, one cannot be inferior (552) to the other civilly or politically. If one race be inferior to the other socially, the Constitution of the United States cannot put them upon the same plane.

Justice HARLAN, dissenting.... In respect of civil rights, common to all citizens, the Constitution of the United States does not, I think, permit any public authority to know the race of those entitled to be protected in the enjoyment of such rights. Every true man has pride of race, and under appropriate circumstances, when the rights of others, his equals before the law, are not to be affected, it is his privilege to express such pride and to take such action based upon it as to him seems proper. But I deny that any legislative body or judicial tribunal may have regard to the race of citizens when the civil rights of those citizens are involved. Indeed such legislation as that here in question is inconsistent, not only with that equality of rights which pertains to citizenship, national and state, but with the personal liberty enjoyed by every one within the United States....

In my opinion, the judgment this day rendered will, in time, prove to be quite as pernicious as the decision made by this tribunal in the Dred Scott Case. It was adjudged in that case that the descendants of Africans who were imported into this country and sold as slaves were not included nor intended to be included under the word "citizens" in the Constitution, and could not claim any of the rights and privileges which that instrument provided for and secured to citizens of the United States; that at the time of the adoption of the Constitution they were "considered as a subordinate and inferior class of beings, who had been subjugated by the dominant race, and, whether emancipated or not, yet remained subject to their authority, and had no rights or privileges but such as those who held the power and the government might choose to grant them." The recent amendments of the Constitution, it was supposed, had eradicated these principles from our institutions. But it seems that we have yet, in some of the states, a dominant race, a superior class of citizens, which assumes to regulate the enjoyment of civil rights, common to all citizens, upon the basis of race. The present decision, it may well be apprehended, will not only stimulate aggressions, more or less brutal and irritating, upon the admitted rights of colored citizens, but will encourage the belief that it is possible, by means of state enactments, to defeat the beneficent purposes which the people of the United States had in view when they adopted the recent amendments of the Constitution, by one of which the blacks of this country were made citizens of the United States and of the states in which they respectively reside and whose privileges and immunities, as citizens, the states are forbidden to abridge. Sixty millions of whites are in no danger from the presence here of eight millions of blacks. The destinies of the two races in this country are indissolubly linked together, and the interests of both require that the common government of all shall not permit the seeds of race hate to be planted under the sanction of law. What can more certainly arouse race hate, what more certainly create and perpetuate a feeling of distrust between these races, than state enactments which in fact proceed on the ground that colored citizens are so inferior and degraded that they cannot be allowed to sit in public coaches occupied by white citizens? That, as all will admit, is the real meaning of such legislation as was enacted in Louisiana....

If evils will result from the commingling of the two races upon public highways established for the benefit of all, they will be infinitely less than those that will surely come from state legislation regulating the enjoyment of civil rights upon the basis of race. Ale boast of the freedom enjoyed by our People above all other peoples. But it is difficult to reconcile that boast with a state of the law which, practically, puts the brand of servitude and degradation upon a large class of our fellow citizens, our equals before the law. The thin disguise of "equal" accommodations for passengers in railroad coaches will not mislead anyone, or atone for the wrong this day done....

I am of opinion that the statute of Louisiana is inconsistent with the personal liberty of citizens, white and black, in that state, and hostile to both the spirit and letter of the Constitution of the United States. If laws of like character should be enacted in the several states of the Union, the effect would be in the highest degree mischievous. Slavery as an institution tolerated by law would, it is true, have disappeared from our country, but there would remain a power in the states, by sinister legislation, to interfere with the full enjoyment of the blessings of freedom; to regulate civil rights, common to all citizens, upon the basis of race; and to place in a condition of legal inferiority a large body of American citizens, now constituting a part of the political community, called the people of the United States, for whom and by whom, through representatives, our government is administered. Such a system is inconsistent with the guarantee given by the Constitution of each state of a republican form of government, and may be stricken down by Congressional action, or by the courts in the dissupreme law charge of their solemn duty to maintain the supreme law of the land, anything in the constitution or laws of any state to the conrary notwithstanding.

For the reasons stated, I am constrained to withhold my assent from the opinion and judgment of the majority.

Ida Wells-Barnett on Lynching, 1898

Mr. President, the colored citizens of this country in general, and Chicago in particular, desire to respectfully urge that some action be taken by you as chief magistrate of this great nation, first for the apprehension and punishment of the lynchers of Postmaster Baker, of Lake City, S.C.; second, we ask indemnity for the widow and children, both for the murder of the husband and father, and for injuries sustained by themselves; third, we most earnestly desire that national legislation be enacted for the suppression of the national crime of lynching.

For nearly twenty years lynching crimes, which stand side by side with Armenian and Cuban outrages, have been committed and permitted by this Christian nation. Nowhere in the civilized world save the United States of America do men, possessing all civil and political power, go out in bands of 50 and 5,000 to hunt down, shoot, hang or burn to death a single individual, unarmed and absolutely powerless. Statistics show that nearly 10,000 American citizens have been lynched in the past 20 years. To our appeals for justice the stereotyped reply has been that the government could not interfere in a state matter. Postmaster Baker's case was a federal matter, pure and simple. He died at his post of duty in defense of his country's honor, as truly as did ever a soldier on the field of battle. We refuse to believe this country, so powerful to defend its citizens abroad, is unable to protect its citizens at home. Italy and China have been indemnified by this government for the lynching of their citizens. We ask that the government do as much for its own.

Senator Benjamin R. "Pitchfork Ben" Tillman on Violence Against Southern Blacks

. . . And he [Senator John C. Spooner, of Wisconsin] said we had taken their rights away from them. He asked me was it right to murder them in order to carry the elections. I never saw one murdered. I never saw one shot at an election. It was the riots before the elections precipitated by their own hot-headedness in attempting to hold the government, that brought on conflicts between the races and caused the shotgun to be used. That is what I meant by saying we used the shotgun.

I want to call the Senator's attention to one fact. He said that the Republican party gave the negroes the ballot in order to protect themselves against the indignities and wrongs that were attempted to be heaped upon them by the enactment of the black code. I say it was because the Republicans of that day, led by Thad Stevens, wanted to put white necks under black heels and to get revenge. There is a difference of opinion. You have your opinion about it, and I have mine, and we can never agree.

I want to ask the Senator this proposition in arithmetic: In my State there were 135,000 negro voters, or negroes of voting age, and some 90,000 or 95,000 white voters. General Canby set up a carpetbag government there and turned our State over to this majority. Now, I want to ask you, with a free vote and a fair count, how are you going to beat 135,000 by 95,000? How are you going to do it? You had set us an impossible task. You had handcuffed us and thrown away the key, and you propped your carpetbag negro government with bayonets. Whenever it was necessary to sustain the government you held it up by the Army.

Mr. President, I have not the facts and figures here, but I want the country to get the full view of the Southern side of this question and the justification for anything we did. We were sorry we had the necessity forced upon us, but we could not help it, and as white men we are not sorry for it, and we do not propose to apologize for anything we have done in connection with it. We took the government away from them in 1876. We did take it. If no other Senator has come here previous to this time who would acknowledge it, more is the pity. We have had no fraud in our elections in South Carolina since 1884. There has been no organized Republican party in the State.

We did not disfranchise the negroes until 1895. Then we had a constitutional convention convened which took the matter up calmly, deliberately, and avowedly with the purpose of disfranchising as many of them as we could under the fourteenth and fifteenth amendments. We adopted the educational qualification as the only means left to us, and the negro is as contented and as prosperous and as well protected in South Carolina to-day as in any State of the Union south of the Potomac. He is not meddling with politics, for he found that the more he meddled with them the worse off he got. As to his "rights"—I will not discuss them now. We of the South have never recognized the right of the negro to govern white men, and we never will. We have never believed him to be equal to the white man, and we will not submit to his gratifying his lust on our wives and daughters without lynching him. I would to God the last one of them was in Africa and that none of them had ever been brought to our shores. But I will not pursue the subject further.

I want to ask permission in this connection to print a speech which I made in the constitutional convention of South Carolina when it convened in 1895, in which the whole carpetbag regime and the indignities and wrongs heaped upon our people, the robberies which we suffered, and all the facts and figures there brought out are incorporated, and let the whole of the facts go to the country. I am not ashamed to have those facts go to the country. They are our justification for the present situation in our State. If I can get it, I should like that permission; otherwise I shall be forced to bring that speech here and read it when I can put my hand on it. I will then leave this matter and let the dead past bury its dead.

Movement, at Last, and Backlash

Negro March-on-Washington Committee

June 4th, 1941

Honorable Henry L. Stimson

Secretary of War

War Department

Washington, D.C.

My dear Secretary Stimson:

Because the Negro people have not received their just shared of jobs in national defense, and our young men have not been integrated into the armed forces of the Nation, including the Army, Navy, Air Corps and Marine, on a basis of equality, including the Army, leaders have formulated plans and set up the necessary machinery in the various sections of the country for the purpose of mobilizing from ten to fifty thousand Negroes to march on Washington in the interest of securing jobs and justice in national defense and fair participation and equal integration into the Nation's military and naval forces.

This movement has been initiated by the officers of the National Association for the Advancement of Colored People, the National Urban League, the Brotherhood of Sleeping Car Porters, the Young Men's Christian Association's branch of the Harlem

Community, the Negro Labor Committee of New York, the Elks and a number of other groups.

A Call for the march, to take place July 1st, is singed by Walter White of the National Association for the Advancement of Colored People, Reverend William Lloyd Imes of the Presbyterian Church of Harlem, Frank R. Crosswaith, Chairman of the Negro Labor Committee of New York, Layle Lane, Vice-President of the American Federation of Teachers, Dr. Rayford Logan, Chairman of the National and State Committee for the Participation of Negroes in National Defense, Henry K. Craft, Secretary of the 135th Street branch of the YMCA, J. Finley Wilson, Grand Exalted Ruler of the Independent Benevolent Order of Elks of the World, Reverend Adam C. Powell, Jr. of the Abyssinian Baptist Church of Harlem and the undersigned.

March-on-Washington local committees are being set up throughout the country with a view to recruiting the marchers and carrying out the general program in the interest of developing an all-out total demonstration of the Negro people for full participation in the national defense program.

A week prior to the march on Washington, plans have been developed to stage marches in various cities in the interest of urging the Mayors and City Councils to memorialize President Roosevelt to issue an executive order to abolish discrimination in national defense and all departments of the Federal Government.

Following the march in Washington, the program includes a great rally at the Monument of Abraham Lincoln, because of its historical symbolism in relation to the issuance of the Emancipation Proclamation for the liberation of the Negroes from chattel salvery.

Because of your commanding and strategic position, as Secretary of War, in the whole program of national defense, I, in the name of the National Defense, wish to request you to address the Rally from the Monument of Abraham Lincoln where a great throng of Negroes from all parts of the country will be gathered.

I want to assure you that the Negroes of America are deeply stirred over the question of their receiving equal opportunity to share in the benefits and responsibilities and duties and sacrifices incident to this great and tremendous national effort to build a defense machinery for the protection of our own country and to safe-guard the cause of democracy.

I am sure that nothing has arisen in the life of the Negro since Emancipation which has gripped their hearts and caught their interest and quickened their imagination more than the girding of our country for national defense without according them the recognition and opportunity as citizens, consumers and workers they feel justified in expecting.

I assure you, Mr. Secretary, the hearts of the Negro people will be grateful to you for your speech on the "Policy of the War Department on the Negroes' Participation and Integration in the Army, Marine and Air Corps in National Defense."

Kindly accept assurance of my high personal esteem and appreciation for your interest and cooperation for the cause of the advancement of the Negro people of America.

Respectfully yours,

A. Philip Randolph, Director

Causative Factors of Detroit Race Riot

June 20, 1943

The Detroit Race Riot, which began on Belle Isle Bridge on the evening of June 20, 1943, occurred spontaneously. It started as an individual altercation and resulted in unorganized, group fighting between negro and white civilians. Reports of the incident on the Bridge spread throughout the city and other unorganized gangs of both negroes and whites rioted under individual leadership at scattered points in the city.

The principle underlying causes are mismanagement, economic insecurity of the negro as a group, and the action of militant and subversive groups.

Mismanagement has been evident in several instances. One was the handling of the Sojourner Truth Housing Proect (named for a Negro Civil War abolitionist). Objection was raised by white people in the neighborhood when they learned that the project was to be occupied by negro families. The Federal Housing

Administration issued conflicting orders concerning the occupancy of this property by white and colored families and feeling ran so high as to cause some violence in February and March, 1942. A similar situation existed with reference to the housing project at the Willow Run Bomber Plant due to the failure of Federal authorities to state their position with reference to colored occupancy.

The increase in production due to the demands of war time economy have resulted in an infux of labor into the Detroit area. The importation of a large number of Southern workers, both white and colored, has caused considerable increase in tension between these groups due to the traditional racial prejudices which have long existed in the South. The colored workers have continually requested equality in working conditions and facilities, and some of these requests have been opposed strenuously by white employees. Other serious disturbances have resulted where white employees have rested the upgrading of colored workers (such as recently occurred at the Packard Motor Company plant) and where skilled colored labor was employed in unskilled positions (such as recently occurred at the Briggs Mfg. Co.) This latter practice has been seriously objected to by colored leaders and workers and in numerous instances strikes have resulted.

Both the WPA and NYA instituted industrial training programs which were open to both white and colored. However, upon completion of this training, many colored individuals found that it was difficult or impossible to secure employment on an equal footing with white persons who had completed the same training. As a result of these conditions the colored people organized for the purpose of exerting pressure upon employees, the public, and the government in order to improve their situation. Because many of these organizations deliberately embarked on a program of race antagonism they contributed to the growing tension between colored and white.

The Reverend Charles Hill was the leader of one such organization. Originally organized for the purpose of pressing colored demands at the time of the Sojourner Truth difficulty, it later transferred its funds and personnel to a new organization to press colored economic and social demands. On the other hand, the whites organized themselves to resist the influx and upgrading of colored labor. Strife of this nature has had two recent manifestations in Detroit: At the Hudson Motor Company, white employees walked out in protest against the importation of colored labor, and at the Packard Motor Company white employees stopped work in protest against the upgrading of colored employees.

The economic situation in Detroit and the incident arising from it have served to further inflame the racial prejudices existing between the colored and white population to a point where violence was apt to be cause by any small incident.

There are a number of national negro organizations which have actively championed the cause of negroes in the Detroit area. Although these organizations have different leadership, they are united in protesting discrimination and segregation in war industry and in housing and take a definite stand in situations which involve these principles. Perhaps the most active of this group at the present time is the March on Washington Movement. The national director, A. Phillip Randolph, is also the president of the International Brotherhood of Sleeping Car Porters, which was the first negro organization to band together and to attain success as a labor union.

Randolph organized his March on Washington Movement in protest against segregation and discrimination of negroes. This organization planned an actual march on Washington to press the negro demands for equality. The President of the United States stopped the proposed march by conferring with Randolph and other negro leaders. From the conference resulted Executive Order 8802 which stipulates that any employer holding a defense contract must hire labor regardless of race or color. To insure the proper execution of the Order the President's Fair Employment Practices Committee was established. The March on Washington Movement claims complete credit for obtaining this concession.

The March on Washington Movement and other negro movements, organized originally to safeguard Negro rights, have been subject to infiltration by Communist and Japanese groups which desire to direct the Negro minority in a subversive effort against the United States. Among the organizations in which the greatest Communist influence has been felt are the March on Washington Movement, the National Association for the Advancement of

Colored People, the National Urban League, the National Negro Congress, the Universal Negro Improvement Association.

The most important of the pro-Japanese organizations are the Pacific Movement of the Eastern World, the Allah Temple of Islam, and the Moorish Science Temple. These latter organizations are based upon an implied racial affinity between the Japanese, the "American" negro and other colored peoples. The Japanese have fostered this feeling, and have promised the negroes complete equality in the event that Japan wins the war.

All of the negro organizations, regardless of their affiliations, state that the discrimination which the negro has suffered in the past must cease. The gains made by the negroes since the beginning of the war have given them a taste of equality which they openly state they will never relinguish. Many negro leaders, thinking of the conditions which will result with the return to a peacetime economy, believe that unless negroes successfully complete their fight for equality before the war ends there will never be another chance.

It is believed that two of the basic underlying causes of the Detroit riot (economic insecurity of the negro and the action of subversive groups) also exist, in an equal degree, in other cities of the Service Command which contains large segments of Negro population, particularly Chicago, East St. Louis, and the Gary-Indiana Harbor District. A race riot in any of these cities at any time is a distinct possibility.

Racial animosity has been brought to such a high pitch that a race riot can occur without any further active intervention on the part of any subversive groups. All of the evidence points to the fact that the Detroit riot was not engineered by any subversive group, Communist, Nazi, Negro or Japanese; and that it was not a part of any plan to foment nationwide race riots at this particular time; but, rather that tension was so great in Detroit that the riot resulted from a fist fight between one white and two negro individuals. It is believed that in other sections of the Service Command similar riots may result from similar causes, and that relations between the whites and negroes are so tense that any of the usual incidents of normal business and social contacts between negro and white are apt to constitute the incident which supplies the needed spark.

February 9, 1942

Memorandum

To: The Adjutant General

Mr. John H. Thompson, representative of the Associated Negro Press in Houston, Texas, whose office is at 419 _ Milan Street, Room 14, has submitted the following report on conditions of racial tension involving Negro soldiers and military and civilian policemen in Houston, Texas.

"This past Saturday night while a group of soldiers from Ellington Field and Camp Wallace were seated in a tavern in the heart of the Negro section of the Third Ward, a policeman (white) came into the place and ordered 'you nigger soldiers' to listen to him while he delivered a lecture to them on their iniquities. One intelligent sergeant, resenting the appellation, told the policeman that he was 'not a Nigger solder, we are American soldiers.' The policeman answered him by saying 'you are a nigger soldier if I say so and if you don't like it I will kill you.'

"When he saw the temper of the soldier rising, he sent in a riot call and several squad cars responded. From each car came several policemen and some white MPs. When they saw and heard what was going on they backed the officer up in what he said, the white MP telling them they were in the South and were niggers and that they would be treated as such as long as they were there. To give the boys credit they did not back up an inch. They reiterated they were not Niggers and that since they were American soldiers they were as good as the policemen or the MPs. The policemen then told the colored lads to take off their hats while talking to them and the white MP tried to knock off the uniform cap with is billy but did not succeed. The colored soldiers did not take off their hats. Several threats were heard to kill the colored lads.

"One Negro civilian who tried to intervene by saying that he as a civilian resented being called a Nigger and he knew these boys, fresh from the North, also hated it, was arrested and thrown into jail on a charge of 'inciting to riot'. He was held under $1,000 bond on this charge for three days before local citizens, coming to his rescue, had his bail reduced and released on bond.

"There are no colored MPs in this city and when one is seen he has no side arms nor billy. White MPs come into the Negro sections, whenever a call for police is issued. They always carry sidearms and a billy, jump out ready for trouble. They usually have their hands on their pistols. Head whipping by police officers is the usual thing. But for the courageous attitude of the sergeant and his comrades, there would have been some head whipping at this time.

"We in this city, remindful of the terrible riot back in 1919, are fearful that another one will occur soon, for the present day soldier which we see here, is not taking the abuse the white people are placing on them.

"Seemingly the white officers are resentful of the uniform the Negroes are wearing. No provisions are made for soldier recreation here except that which is provided by the Houston Negro Chamber of Commerce and that is very small. They must have some pleasure when they come to town. There are several camps in and about this section, all having Negro soldiers, Ellington Field, an advanced aviation training camp, has a few companies of Negroes who are doing menial work. There are some soldiers at Camp Wallace, a replacement center.

"I and the Houston Press Club feel that the War Department should be told of the danger of another riot if police are not made to respect the United States uniform even though it is worn by a Negro. Telling soldiers that they are inferior to whites does nothing to increase their morale. If Negro soldiers are taught to fear white faces, then they are likely to go into battle with this same fear. Psychologically, fear is usually a recurrent thing and soon becomes a habit. What is to prevent Negro soldiers, trained in the Southern tradition to fear a white man, from throwing down their arms on the battlefield if a white German or Italian tells then not to fight the white man?

"And if the civilians who take the soldiers part in these conflicts with police, are arrested and charged with inciting to riot, where will this section of the country end up. This civilian is to go to trial soon. He is afraid, not that the Negro newspapers have gotten hold of the story. He is afraid that they will either make him close up his little business or have him bumped off or arrest him on every occasion. They do that in the South, you know.

"These soldiers have told me and other newsmen that they are not going to stand for a lot of 'foolishness' by whites as long as they are in uniforms. 'I would rather die fighting for my race and my rights in this country than to die fight for a false democracy in a foreign land,' one lad told me in a bitter interview.

"The Negro Labor News and The Houston Informer will carry the story of this latest persecution in this week's papers. Read the stories – then act. I am correspondent for the Associated Negro Press and also a photographer for the Negro Labor News here in Houston.

"Finally, getting in touch with Major Smith over the telephone, who is in charge of the Military Police in Houston, he told this reporter angrily, 'The Army policy is to permit civil authorities and police to treat Negro soldiers as they see fit. They may talk to them in any way they wish. This case has been investigated by military authorities and it is settled. Negro soldiers when off military reservations are subject to civil laws and authorities. It is not the policy of the Army to have white MPs call Negro soldiers 'Niggers'. I don't mean to be cross examined by you on this case and it is best that you do not stir up any trouble over it.'

"It is a dangerous situation here and Major Smith was terribly angry. We newsmen look for some reprisals on us for publishing the story. It should be looked into."

Since receiving the above report, Mr. Thompson has sent in the following additional statement.

"Since writing you a few days ago, the Negro soldiers at Camp Wallace who had the trouble with the police and MPs here have had much trouble over that and other incidents.

"Three of the soldiers were arrested that Saturday night and thrown into jail, I have since learned. They were charged with inciting a riot because they openly resented being called Nigger soldiers rather than American soldiers. One of the lads, who because of his determined and courageous attitude on that night, was said to have been told by an MP that everytime he came into the city he was going to be arrested, was turned loose early Sunday morning, arrested again that day. When he got out on Monday morning (payday) he received his pay, borrowed some money from friends, changed to civilian clothes and went AWOL. He is reported to have gone back to his induction center to tell his stories of abuse and terror while in Texas.

"His name is Ivan H. Whitaker, Co. E, 34th Quartermaster Regiment, Ellington Field, Texas. He is supposed to have returned to Langley Field, Virginia. You might check on his destination from the Eastern end. The names of the three soldiers arrested and charged with inciting riot are Whitaker, Sgt. Vasco Edmunds and J.C. Stevenson, all of Co. E.

"There are two Lieutenants in the Company who are exceedingly nice to their troops but their hands are practically tied because of red tape. Both are from the North according to numerous men in the company who are all doing menial work or nursemaid word for the officers although they are entitled to Army training.

"The enlisted men charge that they have not had any drill, rifles have been taken away from them, non-coms continually tell them that they are in the South and are Niggers and would be as long as they were in the South and therefore they must expect to be treated like niggers.

"Please do something about this situation here before it is too late."

In view of the riot in Houston in 1919, I believe it is important that the Commanding General of the Eighth Corps Area be advised of this report and requested to inquire as expeditiously as possible into the matter of military and civilian police control of soldiers in Negro neighborhoods in Houston.

I believe the record will show that when a somewhat similar situation in Galveston was brought to the attention of Major General Donovan, he dealt with the matter promptly and effectively.

Civilian Aide to the Secretary of War

Congress of the United States House of Representatives

Washington, D. C.

February 14, 1942

Hon Henry L. Stimson, Sec. of War,

War Department,

Washington, D. C.

My dear Mr. Secretary:

I am sending herewith a copy of an important letter which I have written Major General Robert Donovan, commander in charge of the 8th Corps Area, Fort Sam Houston, Texas. I regard this matter as being most important at this time, and feel that it is my duty to bring it to your attention as well as to the attention of General Donovan.

I cannot emphasize too strongly the importance of the high command of the army taking a special interest in what I am sure is a very grave situation.

I am,

Very sincerely yours,

Arthur W. Mitchell

★　　★　　★

February 13, 1942
Major General Robert Donovan,
Fort Sam Houston, Texas

My dear General:

During this crucial crisis through which the world and particularly the United States are now passing, nothing is more important than complete unity and cooperation in our own land and country. Success in this struggle is possible only through full cooperation of all of our citizens, particularly our armed forces.

Recently there have occurred several uprisings in the South
between white civilians and uniformed Negro soldiers. The
morale of the Negro has been tremendously lowered by the
treatment of the white civilian population toward Negro soldiers
in some the camps in North Carolina, Lousiana, Arkansas, and
Texas, and other southern states. Hundreds of complaints have
come to me from these places. In some of these states there has
already been the shedding of blood and the destruction of life. In
others the threat is imminent. I am writing to call you attention
particularly to the situation in the 8th Corps Area, and quote
from a confidential report which I have dealing with the situation at Houston, Texas.

> "This past Saturday night while a group of soldiers from
> Ellington Field and Camp Wallace were seated in a tavern
> in the heart of the Negro section of the Third Ward, a
> policeman (white) came into the place and ordered "you
> nigger soldiers" to listen to him while he delivered a lec-
> ture to them on their iniquities. One intelligent sergeant,
> resenting the appellation, told the policeman that he was
> "not a Nigger soldier, we are American soldiers." The
> policeman answered him by saying "you are a nigger sol-
> dier if I say so and if you don't like it I will kill you."

> "When he saw the temper of the soldier rising he sent in a
> riot call and several squad cars responded. From each car
> came several policement and some white MPs. When they
> saw and heard what was going on they backed up the offi-
> cer in what he said, the white MP telling them they were
> in the South and were niggers and that they would be
> treated as such as long as they were there. To give the boys
> credit they did not back up an inch. They reiterated they
> were not Niggers and that since they were American sol-
> diers they were as good as the policeman or the MPs. The
> policemen then told the colored lads to take off their hats
> while talking to them and the white MP tried to knock off
> the uniform cap with is billy but did not succeed. The col-
> ored soldiers did not take off their hats. Several threats
> were heards to kill the colored lads."

> "One Negro civilian who tried to intervene by saying that
> he as a civilian resented being called a Nigger and he knew
> these boys, fresh from the North, also hated it, was arrested

and thrown into jail on a charge of "inciting to riot". He
was held under $1,000 bond on this charge for three days
before local citizens, coming to his rescue, had his bail
reduced and released on bond."

"One Negro civilian who tried to intervene by saying that
he as a civilian resented being called a Nigger and he knew
these boys, fresh from the North, also hated it, was arrested
and thrown into jail on a charge of 'inciting to riot'. He
was held under $1,000 bond on this charge for three days
before local citizens, coming to his rescue, had his bail
reduced and released on bond."

"There are no colored MPs in this city and when one is
seen he has no side arms nor billy. White MPs come into
the Negro sections, whenever a call for police is issued.
They always carry sidearms and a billy, jump out ready for
trouble. They usually have their hands on their pistols.
Head whipping by police officers is the usual thing. But
for the courageous attitude of the sergeant and his comrades, there would have been some head whipping at this
time."

"We in this city, remindful of the terrible riot back in
1919, are fearful that another one will occur soon, for the
present day soldier which we see here, is not taking the
abuse the white people are placing on them."

"Seemingly the white officers are resentful of the uniform
the Negroes are wearing. No provisions are made for soldier recreation here except that which is provided by the
Houston Negro Chamber of Commerce and that is very
small. They must have some pleasure when they come to
town. There are several camps in and about this section, all
having Negro soldiers, Ellington Field, an advanced aviation training camp, has a few companies of Negroes who
are doing menial work. There are some soldiers at Camp
Wallace, a replacement center."

"Finally, getting in touch with Major Smith over the telephone, who is in charge of the Military Police in Houston,
he told this reporter angrily, 'The Army policy is to permit
civil authorities and police to treat Negro soldiers as they
see fit. They may talk to them in any way they wish. This
case has been investigated by military authorities and it is

settled. Negro soldiers when off military reservations are subject to civil laws and authorities. It is not the policy of the Army to have white MPs call Negro soldiers "Niggers". I don't mean to be cross examined by you on this case and it is best that you do not stir up any trouble over it."

"It is a dangerous situation here and Major Smith was terribly angry. We newsmen look for some reprisals on us for publishing the story. It should be looked into."

"Since writing you a few days ago, the Negro soldiers at Camp Wallace who had the trouble with the police and MPs here have had much trouble over that and other incidents."

"Three of the soldiers were arrested that Saturday night and thrown into jail, I have since learned. They were charged with inciting a riot because they openly resented being called Nigger soldiers rather than American soldiers. One of the lads, who because of his determined and courageous attitude on that night, was said to have been told by an MP that everytime he came into the city he was going to be arrested, was turned loose early Sunday morning, arrested again that day. When he got out on Monday morning (payday) he received his pay, borrowed some money from friends, changed to civilian clothes and went AWOL. He is reported to have gone back to his induction center to tell his stories of abuse and terror while in Texas."

"His name is Ivan H. Whitaker, Co. E, 34th Quartermaster Regiment, Ellington Field, Texas. He is supposed to have returned to Langley Field, Virginia. You might check on his destination from the Eastern end. The names of the three soldiers arrested and charged with inciting riot are Whitaker, Sgt. Vasco Edmunds and J.C. Stevenson, all of Co. E."

"There are two Lieutenants in the Company who are exceedingly nice to their troops but their hands are practically tied because of red tape. Both are from the North according to numerous men in the company who are all doing menial work or nursemaid word for the officers although they are entitled to Army training."

"The enlisted men charge that they have not had any drill, rifles have been taken away from them, non-coms continually tell them that they are in the South and are Niggers and would be as long as they were in the South and therefore they must expect to be treated like niggers."

In my judgement the United States Negro soldier in uniform is receiving treatment from American citizens such as not other country in the world would impose upon its uniformed soldiers. Why are there soldiers being treated thus? There is only one answer, race prejudice.

The treatment of the Negro soldier by the civilian population and by the War Department itself constitute one of the greatest, if not the greatest menace to our success in this conflict. I have discussed this matter at length with Congressman Albert Thomas of Houston, Texas, representative of the 8th district, who thinks as I do that you should take some action immediately to prevent a race riot in Houston. It seems to us that the army officers who are in immediate charge of the colored soldiers should have a conference with the civilian authorities in Houston and in other cities where race trouble is brewing, and the civilian authorities should be informed that those in charge of the United States Army will not further tolerate this unnecessary prevoking of trouble by civilian officers.

I am bringing the matter to your attention with the hpe that we can get immediate action by you, as I am sure you have not been fully informed in the premises.

Thanking you for your attention to this matter. I am,

Very sincerely and gratefully yours,

Arthur W. Mitchell

233rd AAF Base Unit (CCTS(H))

Section C

Davis-Monthan Field

Tucson, Arizona

9 May 1944

President Franklin Delano Roosevelt

White House

Washington, D. C.

Dear President Roosevelt:

It was with extreme pride that I, a soldier in the Armed Forces of our country, read the following affirmation of our war aims, pronounced by you at a recent press conference:

> "The United Nations are fighting to make a world in which tyranny, and aggression cannot exist; a world based upon freedom, equality, and justice; a world in which all persons, regardless of race, color and creed, may live in peace, honor and dignity."

Your use of the word "world" means that we are fighting for "freedom, equality, and justice" for "all persons, regardless of race, color and creed" in our own part of the world, the United States of America, as well as all other countries where such a fight is needed to be carried through. Your use of the words "all persons, regardless of race, color and creed" means that we are fighting for "freedom, equality, and justice" for our Negro Americans, no less than for our white Americans, or our Jewish, Protestant and Catholic Americans, or for the subjugated peoples in Europe and China and all other lands.

And the part that our country is playing in the United Nations world struggle against "tyranny and aggression" and for "a world based upon freedom, equality and justice", although lacking in many respects, is certainly not one to be ashamed of.

Our driving back of the Japanese fascists in the Pacific; our driving back of the German fascists in North Africa, Sicily, and Italy, in conjunction with our British and French Allies, freeing that part of the world from "tyranny and aggression" as the prerequisite for bringing "freedom, equality and justice" to the North African and Italian peoples; the tremendous preparations and planning that we as part of the United Nations have carried out so that we now stand on the eve of the invasion, and in conjunction with our Allies, the British, Russian, French and European Underground, on the eve of freeing the subjugated peoples of Europe from the German fascist tyranny; the glorious part that we played in the decisions reached at Teheran; these are vivid records of the manner in which the war aims of the United Nations, as pronounced by you, are being fought for by us, throughout the world.

On the home front there are vivid examples also: your issuance of Executive Order 8802, which established the Fair Employment Practices Committee, to fight against the discriminatory employment practices being used against Negroes and other minority groups in the war industries; the precedent-smashing decision of the United States Supreme Court, upholding the right of Negroes to vote in the Texas Democratic Primaries; the April 10th decision of the United States Supreme Court, against peonage, which voided a Florida statute which makes it a crime to obtain a wage advance with intent to defraud an employer. The court held that the statute was a violation of the 13th Amendment and the Federal Antipeonage Act; Attorney General Biddle's clearing of the CIO Political Action Committee, against the attempts on the part of Representative Smith of Virginia to destroy it; the establishment on the part of our government of mixed housing projects like the Mother Cabrini Housing Project in Chicago, where segregation because of "race, color and creed" was done away with; the cleansing of our home front of the out and out fascists, such as Elizabeth Dilling, Lawrence Dennis, George Sylvester Viereck, Kunze, Pelley, and the other twenty five, who are being brought to trial by our Justice Department; the support which you have given to the fight against the flagrantly undemocratic poll tax as reported in the Afro American of April the 8th: "President Roosevelt told his press conference last week that he feels the poll tax is undemocratic."; the production by the U. S. Army Signal Corps, as authorized by the War Department, of the film "The Negro Soldier"; these are but a few of the many examples of the fight that the democratic forces in our government, with you leadership, is carrying on in our country as part of the world struggle against "tyranny" and for a "world based upon freedom, equality and justice; a world in which all person, regardless of race, color and creed, may live in peace, honor and dignity".

But the picture in our country is marred by one of the strangest paradoxes in our whole fight against world fascism. The very instrument which our government has organized and built, the United States Armed Forces, to fight for World Democracy, is within itself undemocratic. The undemocratic policy of jim-crow and segregation is practiced by our Armed Forces against its Negro members. Totally inadequate opportunities are given to the Negro members of our Armed Forces, nearly one tenth of the whole, to participate with "equality"… "regardless of race and color" in the fight for our war aims. In fact it appears that the army intends to follow the very policy that the FEPC is battling against in civilian life, the pattern of assigning Negroes to the lowest types of work.

Let me give you an example of this lack of democracy in our Armed Forces as it reflects itself at the Air Base, Davis-Monthan Field, where I am now stationed. Negro soldiers are completely segregated from the white soldiers on the base. And to make doubly sure that not mistake is made about this, the barracks and other housing facilities (supply room, mess hall, etc.) of the Negro Section C are covered with black tar paper, while all other barracks and housing facilities on the base are painted white.

It is the stated policy of the Second Air Force that "every potential fighting man must be used as a fighting man. If you have such a man in a base job, you have no choice. His job must be eliminated or be filled by a limited service man, WAC, or civilian". And yet, leaving out the Negro soldiers working with the Medical Section, fully 50% of the Negro soldiers are working in base jobs, such as, for example, at the Resident Officers' Mess, Bachelor Officers' Quarters, and Officers' Club, as mess personnel, BOQ orderlies, and bar tenders. Leaving out the medical men again, based on the Section C average only 4% of this 50% would not be "potential fighting men".

It is also a fact that "…the employment of enlisted men as attendants at officers' clubs, whether officially designated as "Officers' Mess" or "Officers' Club" is not sanctioned by…" the Headquarters of the Army Air Forces.

Leaving out the medical men again, at least 50% of the members of the Negro Section C are being used for decidedly menial work, such as BOQ orderlies, janitors, permanent KP's and the like.

Let us assume as a basis for discussion that there are no civilians or limited servicemen to do the menial work on the base. The democratic way, based upon "equality and justice" would be to assign this work to both Negro and white. Instead the discriminatory and undemocratic method is used whereby all of this work is assigned to the Negro soldiers.

On the other hand suppose civilians were found to take over all of the base jobs and thus free the Negro soldiers for use as fighting men. They would not be given "on-the-job-training" to become members of the ground crew, such as is being done for the WAC members on the base, because there is no such program for Negroes at Davis-Monthan Field. They would not be trained to become aerial gunners, or bombardiers, or navigators, or pilots, or bombsight mechanics, or any of the many other specialists at Davis-Monthan Field, because there is no authorization in the Second Air Force for this training to be given to Negroes.

About 15% of the soldiers of Section C are in fighting jobs, and about another 5% are receiving "on-the-job-training" in Vehicle Maintenance. Thus we see that the maintenance of the ideology of "white supremacy" resulting in the undemocratic practices of jim-crow and segregation of the Negro members of the Armed Forces brings about the condition on Davis-Monthan Field whereby 80% of the whole Section is removed from the fighting activities on the base.

From what I read in the Newspapers, the above example from my own experience at Davis-Monthan Field, is typical of the situation throughout the Armed Forces. There is the report in an editorial on page five of the March 25th edition of the Pittsburgh Courier which states that: "Negro combat untis are being constantly broken up and transferred to service units".

How can we convince nearly one tenth of the Armed Forces, the Negro members, that your pronouncement of the war aims of the United States means what it says, when their experience with one of the United Nations, the United States of America, is just the opposite?

Are the Chinese people to believe that we are fighting to bring them "freedom, equality, and justice", when they can see that in our Armed Forces we are not even practicing ourselves what we are preaching?

Moveover, we leave ourselves wide open for sowers of disunity. Nothing would suit Hitler, Tojo, and our own native fascists better, than disunity. The lead editorial in the Afro American of April the 1st, entitled "Soldiers or Sissies" is a tragic example of this. The editorial after relating two cases of tyranny against two Negro soldiers: one in Alabama where the "civil police lynched a handcuffed, defenseless soldier when they were moving from one prison to another", and another case in Louisiana, where a "Bus driver shot and killed a New York soldier who refused to move to a rear seat", goes on to say: "This is terrorism, and the army has no answer for it. Have the soldiers themselves an answer? There are thousands of them and only a few police or bus drivers". If the advice of that editorial were followed it could only lead to disunity and civil strife. We know that isn't the answer. Disunity and civil strife would only weaken our fight against the German and Japanese fascists, or more than that result in our defeat. A victory for the German and Japanese fascists would mean a victory for our own native fascists, who are at the bottom of this whole program of "white supremacy", race hatred, jim-crowism, and segregation. It would mean victory, not defeat for the Rankins, Bilbos, Smiths, Hearsts, McCormicks, Peglers, and Dies.

Such an editorial is totally irresponsible. But decrying such an editorial will get us nowhere. The only answer is to remove the conditions which give rise to such as editorial. That means fighting for the war aims of the United Nations in our own country as well as throughout the rest of the world. That means that we must fight against the fascist shouters of "white supremacy", against the labor baiters, against segregation and jim-crowism, wherever these evils show their fangs, whether in the Armed Forces, or in the civilian population.

The Public Affairs Pamphlet "The Races of Mankind" by Ruth Benedict and Gene Weltfish, as well as many other scientific writings have exploded the anti-democratic doctrine of "race-superiority" or "white-supremacy".

The achievements of heroes like Dorie Miller; the record of the 99th Pursuit Squadron in Italy; the records of the 24th Infantry and 93rd Infantry in Bougainfille, disprove Secretary of War Stimson's statement in a recent letter: "Negro units…have been unable to master efficiently the techniques of modern weapons".

The experience in training Negro and white, on a mixed basis, in the Officer's Candidate Schools, and the Army Technical Training Schools, is proof enough, if proof is needed, that there is no justification for the present policy of jim-crow and segregation in the Armed Forces. The Navy can look to the Merchant Marine for an example of democracy in action, in which the crews are organized on a mixed basis, with Negroes and whites from North and South eating and sleeping, working and fighting together.

Just as our government in civilian life, is carrying on a fight for the full integration of the Negro and all other minority groups into the war effort, with the result that Negro men and women are producing the implements of war, in jobs from the unskilled to the most highly skilled, side by side with their white brothers and sisters, so in the Armed Forces our government must take up the same fight for the full integration of the Negro into all phases of our fighting forces from the lowest to the highest.

President Roosevelt, in the interest of the war effort you issued Executive Order 8802, which established the Fair Employment Practices Committee. Although there is still much to be done, nevertheless this committee, against heavy opposition, has played, and is playing a gallant role in fighting for democracy for the men and women behind the liens, in the industries that produe the guns, and tanks, and bombers for victory over world fascism.

With your issuance of Executive Order 8802, and the setting up of the Fair Employment Practices Committee, you established the foundation for fighting for democracy in the industrial forces of our country, in the interest of victory for the United Nations. In the interest of victory for the United Nations, another Executive Order is now needed. An Executive Order which will lay the base for fighting for democracy in the Armed Forces of our country. An Executive Order which would bring about the result here at Davis-Monthan Field whereby the Negro soldiers would be integrated into all of the Sections on the base, as fighting men, instead of in the segregated Section C as housekeepers.

Then and only then can your pronouncement of the war aims of the United Nations mean to mean to all that we "are fighting to make a world in which tyranny, and aggression cannot exist; a world based upon freedom, equality and justice; a world in which all person, regardless of race, color and creed, may live in peace, honor dignity".

Respectfully yours,

Charles F. Wilson, 36794590

Private, Air Corps.

Private Charles F. Wilson

233rd AAF Base Unit CCTS (H)

Section C

Davis-Monthan Field

Tucson, Arizona

Dear Private Wilson:

Your letter of May 9, 1944, addressed to the President, has been referred to me for reply.

You interpretation of the war aims of the United States, and your recital of acts to effect those aims, are well correlated, but I cannot agree with the dark and opaque picture you paint of the Negro in the Army. Indeed, your mention of the documented film, "The Negro Soldier," made by the United States Army Signal Corps, contradicts you in this respect.

Military leaders believe that organization of enlisted personnel in the Army in separate units based on race is the most effective method and that the present is not time to experience with other methods. Such a method of organization does not mean, however, that Negro and white troops cannot work and fight together in a common cause. I believe there is abundant evidence to the contrary. For example, both the Ninety-ninth Fighter Squadron and the Fighter Group commanded by Colonel Benjamin O. Davis, Jr., have been escorting bombers in the

Mediterranean theater of operations. Moreover, pilots of the Ninety-ninth have flown with white units and pilots of white units have flown with the Ninety-ninth. I may also cite the Ninety-third Infantry Division, which you also mention in your letter. This organization has been fighting with units of the American Division on Bougainville Island in the South Pacific, and if the reports passed by the censors are correct, it has given a good account of itself and won the respect of their white comrades-in-arms.

The policy of the Army is not to discriminate against any soldier.

I make this general observation with regard to the utilization of Negro troops. The Army has been faced with the fact that in civilian life large numbers of Negro inductees had inadequate educational opportunities. In a recent study of all men processed at reception centers from June through December 1943, 20 percent.

★   ★   ★

The Adjutant General

> Let us assume as a basis for discussion that there are no civilians or limited service men to do the menial work on the base. The democratic way, based upon "equality and justice" would be to assign this work to both Negro and white. Instead the discriminatory and undemocratic method is used whereby all of this work is assigned to the Negro soldiers.
>
> On the other hand suppose civilians were found to take over all of the base jobs and thus free the Negro soldiers for use as fighting men. They would not be given "on-the-job-training" to become members of the ground crew, such as is being done for the WAC members on the base, because there is not such program for Negroes at Davis-Monthan Field. They would not be trained to become aerial gunners, or bombardiers, or navigators, or pilots, or bombsight mechanics, or any of the many other specialists at Davis-Monthan Field, because there is not authorization in the Second Air Force for this training to be given to Negroes.

About 15% of the soldiers of Section C are in fighting jobs and about another 5% are receiving "on-the-job-training" in Vehicle Maintenance. Thus we see that the maintenance of the ideology of "white supremacy" resulting in the undemocratic practices of jim-crow and segregation of the Negro members of the Armed Forces brings about the condition on Davis-Monthan Field whereby 80% of the whole Section is removed from the fighting activities on the base.

May these matters be investigated and a copy of the report furnished this office.

Executive Order 9981: Establishing the President's Committee on Equality of Treatment and Opportunity in the Armed Services

WHEREAS it is essential that there be maintained in the armed services of the United States the highest standards of democracy, with equality of treatment and opportunity for all those who serve in our country's defense:

NOW, THEREFORE, by virtue of the authority vested in me as President of the United States, by the Constitution and the statutes of the United States, and as Commander in Chief of the armed services, it is hereby ordered as follows:

1. It is hereby declared to be the policy of the President that there shall be equality of treatment and opportunity for all persons in the armed services without regard to race, color, religion or national origin. This policy shall be put into effect as rapidly as possible, having due regard to the time required to effectuate any necessary changes without impairing efficiency or morale.

2. There shall be created in the National Military Establishment an advisory committee to be known as the President's Committee on Equality of Treatment and Opportunity in the Armed Services, which shall be composed of seven members to be designated by the President.

3. The Committee is authorized on behalf of the President to examine into the rules, procures and practices of the armed services in order to determine in what respect such rules, procedures and practices may be altered or improved with a view to carrying out the policy of this order. The Committee shall confer and advise with the Secretary of Defense, the Secretary of the Army, the Secretary of the Navy, and the Secretary of the Air Force, and shall make such recommendations to the President and to said Secretaries as in the judgment of the Committee will effectuate the policy hereof.

4. All executive departments and agencies of the Federal Government are authorized and directed to cooperate with the Committee in its work, and to furnish the Committee such information or the services of such persons as the Committee may require in the performance of its duties.

5. When requested by the Committee to do so, persons in the armed services or in any of the executive departments and agencies of the Federal Government shall testify before the Committee and shall make available for the use of the Committee such documents and other information as the Committee may require.

6. The Committee shall continue to exist until such time as the President shall terminate its existence by Executive order.

HARRY S. TRUMAN
THE WHITE HOUSE,
July 26, 1948.

Brown vs. Board of Education—1954

WARREN, C. J. These cases come to us from the States of Kansas, South Carolina, Virginia, and Delaware. They are premised on different facts and different local conditions, but a common legal question justifies their consideration together in this consolidated opinion.

In each of the cases, minors of the Negro race, through their legal representatives, seek the aid of the courts in obtaining admission to the public schools of their community on a nonsegregated basis. In each instance, they have been denied admission to schools attended by white children under laws requiring or permitting segregation according to race. This segregation was alleged to deprive the plaintiffs of the equal protection of the laws under the Fourteenth Amendment. In each of the cases other than the Delaware case, a three-judge federal district court denied relief to the plaintiffs on the so-called "separate but equal" doctrine announced by this Court in Plessy v. Ferguson, 163 IJ. S. 537. Under that doctrine, equality of treatment is accorded when the races are provided substantially equal facilities, even though these facilities be separate. In the Delaware case, the Supreme Court of Delaware adhered to that doctrine, but ordered that the plaintiffs be admitted to the white schools because of their superiority to the Negro schools.

The plaintiffs contend that segregated public schools are not "equal" and cannot be made "equal," and that hence they are deprived of the equal protection of the laws. Because of the obvious importance of the question presented, the Court took jurisdiction. Argument was heard in the 1952 Term, and re argument was heard this Term on certain questions propounded by the Court.

Reargument was largely devoted to the circumstances surrounding the adoption of the Fourteenth Amendment in 1868. It covered exhaustively consideration of the Amendment in Congress, ratification by the states, then existing practices in racial segregation, and the views of proponents and opponents of the Amendment. This discussion and our own investigation convince us that, although these sources cast some light, it is not enough to resolve the problem with which we are faced. At best, they are inconclusive. The most avid proponents of the post–War Amendments undoubtedly intended them to remove all legal distinctions among "all persons born or naturalized in the United States." Their opponents, just as certainly, were antagonistic to both the letter and the spirit of the Amendments and wished them to have the most limited effect. What others in Congress and the state legislatures had in mind cannot be determined with any degree of certainty.

An additional reason for the inconclusive nature of the Amendment's history, with respect to segregated schools, is the status of public education at that time. In the South, the movement toward free common schools, supported by general taxation, had not yet taken hold. Education of white children was largely in the hands of private groups. Education of Negroes was almost nonexistent, and practically all of the race were illiterate. In fact, any education of Negroes was forbidden by law in some states. Today, in contrast, many Negroes have achieved outstanding success in the arts and sciences as well as in the business and professional world. It is true that public education had already advanced further in the North, but the effect of the Amendment on Northern States was generally ignored in the congressional debates. Even in the North, the conditions of public education did not ad proximate those existing today. The curriculum was usually rudimentary; ungraded schools were common in rural areas; the school term was but three months a year in many states; and compulsory school attendance was virtually unknown. As a consequence, it is not surprising that there should be so little in the history of the Fourteenth Amendment relating to its intended effect on public education.

In the first cases in this Court construing the Fourteenth Amendment, decided shortly after its adoption, the Court interpreted it as proscribing all state-imposed discriminations against the Negro race. The doctrine of separate but equal" did not make its appearance in this Court until 1896 in the case of Plessy v. Ferguson, supra, involving not education but transportation. American courts have since labored with the doctrine br over half a century. In this Court, there have been six cases involving the "separate but equal" doctrine in the field of public education. In Cumming v. Board of Education of Richmond County, 175 U. S. 528, d Gong Lum v. Rice, 275 U. S. 78, the Validity of the doctrine itself was not challenged. In more recent cases, all on the school level, inequality was found in that specific benefits enjoyed by white students were denied to Negro students of the same educational qualifications. State of Missouri ex ret. Gaines v. Canada, 305 U. S. 337# Sipuel v. Board of Regents of University of Oklahoma, 332 U. S. 631; Sweatt v. Painter, 339 U. S. 629; McLaurin v. Oklahoma State Regents, 339 U. S. 637. In none of these cases was it necessary to reexamine the doctrine to grant relief to the Negro plaintiff. And in Sweatt v. Painter, supra, the Court expressly reserved decision on the question whether Plessy v. Ferguson should j be held inapplicable to public education.

In the instant cases, that question is directly presented. Here, unlike Sweatt v. Painter, there are findings below that the Negro and white schools involved have been equalized, or are being equalized, with respect to buildings, curricula, qualifications and salaries of teachers, and other "tangible" factors. Our decision, therefore, cannot turn merely a comparison of these tangible Actors in the Negro and white schools involved in each of the cases. We must look Stead to the effect of segregation itself on public education.

In approaching this problem, we cannot turn the clock back to 1868 when the Amendment was adopted, or even to 1896 hen Plessy v. Ferguson was written. We must consider public education in the light of its full development and its present place E American life throughout the Nation. puly in this way can it be determined if segregation in public schools deprives these plaintiffs of the equal protection of the laws. Today, education is perhaps the most important function of state and local governments. Compulsory school attendance law sand the great expenditures for education both demonstrate our recognition of the importance of education to our democratic society. It is required in the performance of our most basic public responsibilities, even service in the armed forces. It is the very foundation of good citizenship. Today it is a principal instrument in awakening the child to cultural values, in preparing him for later professional training, and in helping him to adjust normally to his environment. In these days, it is doubtful that any child may reasonably be expected to succeed in life if he is denied the opportunity of an education. Such an opportunity, where the state has undertaken to provide it, is a right which must be made available to all on equal terms.

We come then to the question presented: Does segregation of children in public schools solely on the basis of race, even though the physical facilities and other "tangible" factors may be equal, deprive the children of the minority group of equal educational opportunities ? We believe that it does.

In Sweatt v. Painter, supra [339 U. S. 629, 70 S.Ct. 850] in finding that a segregated law school for Negroes could not provide
them equal educational opportunities, this Court relied in
large part on "those qualities which are incapable of objective
measurement but which make for greatness in a law school." In
McLaurin v. Oklahoma State Regents, supra [339 U. S. 637, 70
S.Ct. 853], the Court, in requiring that a Negro admitted to a
white graduate school be treated like all other students, again
resorted to intangible considerations: ". . . his ability to study, to
engage in discussions and exchange views with other students,
and, in general, to learn his profession." Such considerations
apply with added force to children in grade and high schools. To
separate them from others of similar age and qualifications solely
because of their race generates a feeling of inferiority as to their
status in the community that may affect their hearts and minds in
a way unlikely ever to be undone. The effect of this separation
on their educational opportunities was well stated by a finding in
the Kansas case by a court which nevertheless felt compelled to
rule against the Negro plaintiffs:

> "Segregation of white and colored children in public schools
> has a detrimental effect upon the colored children. The
> impact is greater when it has the sanction of the law; for the
> policy of separating the races is usually interpreted as denot-
> ing the inferiority of the Negro group A sense of inferiority
> affects the motivation of a child to learn. Segregation with
> the sanction of law, therefore, has a tendency to retard the
> educational and mental development of Negro children and
> to deprive them of some of the benefits they would receive
> in a racially integrated school system."

Whatever may have been the extent of psychological knowledge
at the time of Plessy v. Ferguson, this finding is amply supported
by modern authority. Any language in Plessy v. Ferguson contrary
to this finding is rejected.

We conclude that in the field of public education the doctrine of
"separate but equal" has no place. Separate educational facilities
are inherently unequal. Therefore, we hold that the plaintiffs and
others similarly situated for whom the actions have been brought
are, by reason of the segregation complained of, deprived of the

equal protection of the laws guaranteed by the Fourteenth Amendment. This deposition makes unnecessary any discussion whether such segregation also violates the Due Process Clause of the Fourteenth Amendment.

Because these are class actions, because of the wide applicability of this decision, and because of the great variety of local conditions, the formulation of decrees in these cases presents problems of considerable complexity. On re argument, the consideration of appropriate relief was necessarily subordinated to the primary question—the constitutionality of segregation in public education. We have now announced that such segregation is a denial of the equal protection of the laws. In order that we may have the full assistance of the parties in formulating decrees, the cases will be restored to the docket, and the parties are requested to present further argument.... The Attorney General of the United States is again invited to participate. The Attorneys General of the states requiring or permitting segregation in public education will also be permitted to appear as amici curiae upon request to do so by September 15, 1954, and submission of briefs by October 1,1954.

It is so ordered.

George C. Wallace, Inaugural Address as Governor of Alabama

January 14, 1963
Montgomery, Alabama

For Release
Monday P.M. January 14, 1963

OPENING REMARKS

Governor Patterson, Governor Barnette, from one of the greatest states in this nation, Mississippi, Judge Brown, representing Governor Hollings of South Carolina, _, members of the Alabama Congressional Delegation, members of the Alabama Legislature, distinguished guests, fellow Alabamians:

Before I begin my talk with you, I want to ask you for a few minutes patience while I say something that is on my heart: I want to thank those home folks of my county who first gave an anxious country boy his opportunity to serve in State politics. I shall always owe a lot to those who gave me that first opportunity to serve.

I will never forget the warm support and close loyalty at the folks of Suttons, Haigler's Mill, Eufaula, Beat 6 and Beat 14, Richards Cross Roads and Gammage Beat . . . at Baker Hill, Beat 8, and Comer, Spring Hill, Adams Chapel and Mount Andrew . . . White Oak, Baxter's Station, Clayton, Louisville and Cunnigham Place; Horns Crossroads, Texasville and Blue Springs, where the vote was 304 for Wallace and 1 for the opposition . . . and the dear little lady whom I heard had made that one vote against me . . by mistake . . because she couldn't see too well . . and she had pulled the wrong lever . . . Bless her heart. At Clio, my birthplace, and Elamville. I shall never forget them. May God bless them.

And I shall forever remember that election day morning as I waited . . . and suddenly at ten o'clock that morning the first return of a box was flashed over this state: it carried the message . . . . Wallace 15, opposition zero; and it came from the Hamrick Beat at Putman's Mountain where live the great hill people of our state. May God bless the mountain man . . his loyalty is unshakeable, he'll do to walk down the road with.

I hope you'll forgive me these few moments of remembering . . . but I wanted them . . and you . . to know, that I shall never forget.

And I wish I could shake hands and thank all of you in this state who voted for me . . and those of you who did not . . for I know you voted your honest convictions . . . and now, we must stand together and move the great State of Alabama forward.

I would be remiss, this day, if I did not thank my wonderful wife and fine family for their patience, support and loyalty . . . . and there is no man living who does not owe more to his mother than he can ever repay, and I want my mother to know that I realize my debt to her.

This is the day of my Inauguration as Governor of the State of Alabama. And on this day I feel a deep obligation to renew my pledges, my covenants with you . . . the people of this great state.

General Robert E. Lee said that "duty" is the sublimest word on the English language and I have come, increasingly, to realize what he meant. I SHALL do my duty to you, God helping . . . to every man, to every woman . . . yes, to every child in this state. I shall fulfill my duty toward honesty and economy in our State government so that no man shall have a part of his livelihood cheated and no child shall have a bit of his future stolen away.

I have said to you that I would eliminate the liquor agents in this state and that the money saved would be returned to our citizens . . . I am happy to report to you that I am now filling orders for several hundred one-way tickets and stamped on them are these words . . . "for liquor agents . . . destination: . . . out of Alabama." I am happy to report to you that the big-wheeling cocktail-party boys have gotten the word that their free whiskey and boat rides are over . . . that the farmer in the field, the worker in the factory, the businessman in his office, the housewife in her home, have decided that the money can be better spent to help our children's education and our older citizens . . . and they have put a man in office to see that it is done. It shall be done. Let me say one more time . . . . no more liquor drinking in your governor's mansion.

I shall fulfill my duty in working hard to bring industry into our state, not only by maintaining an honest, sober and free-enterprise climate of government in which industry can have confidence . . but in going out and getting it . . . so that our people can have industrial jobs in Alabama and provide a better life for their children.

I shall not forget my duty to our senior citizens . . . so that their lives can be lived in dignity and enrichment of the golden years, nor to our sick, both mental and physical . . . and they will know we have not forsaken them. I want the farmer to feel confident that in this State government he has a partner who will work with him in raising his income and increasing his markets. And I want the laboring man to know he has a friend who is sincerely striving to better his field of endeavor.

I want to assure every child that this State government is not afraid to invest in their future through education, so that they will not be handicapped on every threshold of their lives.

Today I have stood, where once Jefferson Davis stood, and took an oath to my people. It is very appropriate then that from this Cradle of the Confederacy, this very Heart of the Great Anglo-Saxon Southland, that today we sound the drum for freedom as have our generations of forebears before us done, time and time again through history. Let us rise to the call of freedom-loving blood that is in us and send our answer to the tyranny that clanks its chains upon the South. In the name of the greatest people that have ever trod this earth, I draw the line in the dust and toss the gauntlet before the feet of tyranny . . . and I say . . . segregation today . . . segregation tomorrow . . . segregation forever.

The Washington, D.C. school riot report is disgusting and revealing. We will not sacrifice our children to any such type school system—and you can write that down. The federal troops in Mississippi could be better used guarding the saftey of the citizens of Washington, D.C., where it is even unsafe to walk or go to a ballgame—and that is the nation's capitol. I was safer in a B-29 bomber over Japan during the war in an air raid, than the people of Washington are walking to the White House neighborhood. A closer example is Atlanta. The city officials fawn for political reasons over school integration and THEN build barricades to stop residential integration—what hypocrisy!

Let us send this message back to Washington by our representatives who are with us today . . that from this day we are standing up, and the heel of tyranny does not fit the neck of an upright man . . . that we intend to take the offensive and carry our fight for freedom across the nation, wielding the balance of power we know we possess in the Southland . . . . that WE, not the insipid bloc of voters of some sections . . will determine in the next election who shall sit in the White House of these United States . . . That from this day, from this hour . . . from this minute . . . we give the word of a race of honor that we will tolerate their boot in our face no longer . . . . and let those certain judges put that in their opium pipes of power and smoke it for what it is worth.

Hear me, Southerners! You sons and daughters who have moved north and west throughout this nation . . . . we call on you from

your native soil to join with us in national support and vote . .
and we know . . . wherever you are . . away from the hearths of
the Southland . . . that you will respond, for though you may live
in the fartherest reaches of this vast country . . . . your heart has
never left Dixieland.

And you native sons and daughters of old New England's
rock-ribbed patriotism . . . and you sturdy natives of the great
Mid-West . . and you descendants of the far West flaming spirit of
pioneer freedom . . we invite you to come and be with us . . for
you are of the Southern spirit . . and the Southern philosophy . .
. you are Southerners too and brothers with us in our fight.

What I have said about segregation goes double this day . . . and
what I have said to or about some federal judges goes TRIPLE
this day.

Alabama has been blessed by God as few states in this Union
have been blessed. Our state owns ten percent of all the natural
resources of all the states in our country. Our inland waterway
system is second to none . . . and has the potential of being the
greatest waterway transport system in the entire world. We possess over thirty minerals in usable quantities and our soil is rich
and varied, suited to a wide variety of plants. Our native pine
and forestry system produces timber faster than we can cut it and
yet we have only pricked the surface of the great lumber and
pulp potential.

With ample rainfall and rich grasslands our live stock industry is
in the infancy of a giant future that can make us a center of the
big and growing meat packing and prepared foods marketing.
We have the favorable climate, streams, woodlands, beaches, and
natural beauty to make us a recreational mecca in the booming
tourist and vacation industry. Nestled in the great Tennessee
Valley, we possess the Rocket center of the world and the keys to
the space frontier.

While the trade with a developing Europe built the great port cities
of the east coast, our own fast developing port of Mobile faces as a
magnetic gateway to the great continent of South America, well
over twice as large and hundreds of times richer in resources, even
now awakening to the growing probes of enterprising capital with a

potential of growth and wealth beyond any present dream for our port development and corresponding results throughout the connecting waterways that thread our state.

And while the manufacturing industries of free enterprise have been coming to our state in increasing numbers, attracted by our bountiful natural resouces, our growing numbers of skilled workers and our favorable conditions, their present rate of settlement here can be increased from the trickle they now represent to a stream of enterprise and endeavor, capital and expansion that can join us in our work of development and enrichment of the educational futures of our children, the opportunities of our citizens and the fulfillment of our talents as God has given them to us. To realize our ambitions and to bring to fruition our dreams, we as Alabamians must take cognizance of the world about us. We must re-define our heritage, re-school our thoughts in the lessons our forefathers knew so well, first hand, in order to function and to grow and to prosper. We can no longer hide our head in the sand and tell ourselves that the ideology of our free fathers is not being attacked and is not being threatened by another idea . . . for it is. We are faced with an idea that if a centralized government assume enough authority, enough power over its people, that it can provide a utopian life . . that if given the power to dictate, to forbid, to require, to demand, to distribute, to edict and to judge what is best and enforce that will produce only "good" . . and it shall be our father . . . . and our God. It is an idea of government that encourages our fears and destroys our faith . . . for where there is faith, there is no fear, and where there is fear, there is no faith. In encouraging our fears of economic insecurity it demands we place that economic management and control with government; in encouraging our fear of educational development it demands we place that education and the minds of our children under management and control of government, and even in feeding our fears of physical infirmities and declining years, it offers and demands to father us through it all and even into the grave. It is a government that claims to us that it is bountiful as it buys its power from us with the fruits of its rapaciousness of the wealth that free men before it have produced and builds on crumbling credit without responsibilities to the debtors . . . our children. It is an ideology of government erected on the encouragement of fear and fails to recognize the

basic law of our fathers that governments do not produce wealth
. . . people produce wealth . . . free people; and those people
become less free . . . as they learn there is little reward for ambition . . . that it requires faith to risk . . . and they have none . . as
the government must restrict and penalize and tax incentive and
endeavor and must increase its expenditures of bounties . . . then
this government must assume more and more police powers and
we find we are become government-fearing people . . . not
God-fearing people. We find we have replaced faith with fear . . .
and though we may give lip service to the Almighty . . in reality,
government has become our god. It is, therefore, a basically
ungodly government and its appeal to the psuedo-intellectual and
the politician is to change their status from servant of the people
to master of the people . . . to play at being God . . . without
faith in God . . . and without the wisdom of God. It is a system
that is the very opposite of Christ for it feeds and encourages
everything degenerate and base in our people as it assumes the
responsibilities that we ourselves should assume. Its psuedo-lib-
eral spokesmen and some Harvard advocates have never examined
the logic of its substitution of what it calls "human rights" for
individual rights, for its propaganda play on words has appeal for
the unthinking. Its logic is totally material and irresponsible as it
runs the full gamut of human desires . . . including the theory
that everyone has voting rights without the spiritual responsibility of preserving freedom. Our founding fathers recognized those
rights . . . but only within the framework of those spiritual
responsiblities. But the strong, simple faith and sane reasoning of
our founding fathers has long since been forgotten as the so-
called "progressives" tell us that our Constitution was written for
"horse and buggy" days . . . so were the Ten Commandments.

Not so long ago men stood in marvel and awe at the cities, the
buildings, the schools, the autobahns that the government of
Hitler's Germany had built . . . just as centuries before they stood
in wonder of Rome's building . . . but it could not stand . . . for
the system that built it had rotted the souls of the builders . . .
and in turn . . . rotted the foundation of what God meant that
men should be. Today that same system on an international scale
is sweeping the world. It is the "changing world" of which we
are told . . . it is called "new" and "liberal". It is as old as the
oldest dictator. It is degenerate and decadent. As the national

racism of Hitler's Germany persecuted a national minority to the whim of a national majority . . . so the international racism of the liberals seek to persecute the international white minority to the whim of the international colored majority . . . so that we are footballed about according to the favor of the Afro-Asian bloc. But the Belgian survivors of the Congo cannot present their case to a war crimes commission . . . nor the Portuguese of Angola . . . nor the survivors of Castro . . . nor the citizens of Oxford, Mississippi.

It is this theory of international power politic that led a group of men on the Supreme Court for the first time in American history to issue an edict, based not on legal precedent, but upon a volume, the editor of which said our Constitution is outdated and must be changed and the writers of which, some had admittedly belonged to as many as half a hundred communist-front organizations. It is this theory that led this same group of men to briefly bare the ungodly core of that philosophy in forbidding little school children to say a prayer. And we find the evidence of that ungodliness even in the removal of the words "in God we trust" from some of our dollars, which was placed there as like evidence by our founding fathers as the faith upon which this system of government was built. It is the spirit of power thirst that caused a President in Washington to take up Caesar's pen and with one stroke of it make a law. A Law which the law making body of Congress refused to pass . . . a law that tells us that we can or cannot buy or sell our very homes, except by his conditions . . . and except at HIS descretion. It is the spirit of power thirst that led the same President to launch a full offensive of twenty-five thousand troops against a university . . . of all places . . . in his own country . . . and against his own people, when this nation maintains only six thousand troops in the beleagured city of Berlin. We have witnessed such acts of "might makes right" over the world as men yielded to the temptation to play God . . . but we have never before witnessed it in America. We reject such acts as free men. We do not defy, for there is nothing to defy . . . since as free men we do not recognize any government right to give freedom . . . or deny freedom. No government erected by man has that right. As Thomas Jefferson said, "The God who gave us life, gave us liberty at the same time; no King holds the right of liberty in his hands." Nor does any ruler in American government.

We intend, quite simply, to practice the free heritage as
bequeathed to us as sons of free fathers. We intend to re-vitalize
the truly new and progressive form of government that is less
that two hundred years old . . . a government first founded in this
nation simply and purely on faith . . . that there is a personal
God who rewards good and punishes evil . . . that hard work will
receive its just deserts . . . that ambition and ingenuity and incen-
tiveness . . . and profit of such . . are admirable traits and goals . .
that the individual is encouraged in his spiritual growth and from
that growth arrives at a character that enhances his charity
toward others and from that character and that charity so is
influenced business, and labor and farmer and government. We
intend to renew our faith as God-fearing men . . . not government-fearing men nor any other kind of fearing-men. We intend
to roll up our sleeves and pitch in to develop this full bounty
God has given us . . . to live full and useful lives and in absolute
freedom from all fear. Then can we enjoy the full richness of the
Great American Dream.

We have placed this sign, "In God We Trust," upon our State
Capitol on this Inauguration Day as physical evidence of determination to renew the faith of our fathers and to practice the
free heritage they bequeathed to us. We do this with the clear
and solemn knowledge that such physical evidence is evidently a
direct violation of the logic of that Supreme Court in
Washington D.C., and if they or their spokesmen in this state
wish to term this defiance . . . I say . . . then let them make the
most of it.

This nation was never meant to be a unit of one . . . but a united
of the many . . . . that is the exact reason our freedom loving
forefathers established the states, so as to divide the rights and
powers among the states, insuring that no central power could
gain master government control.

In united effort we were meant to live under this government . . .
whether Baptist, Methodist, Presbyterian, Church of Christ, or
whatever one's denomonation or religious belief . . . each respecting the others right to a separate denomination . . . each, by
working to develop his own, enriching the total of all our lives
through united effort. And so it was meant in our political lives .
. . whether Republican, Democrat, Prohibition, or whatever

political party . . . each striving from his separate political station
. . . respecting the rights of others to be separate and work from
within their political framework . . . and each separate political
station making its contribution to our lives . . . .

And so it was meant in our racial lives . . . each race, within its
own framework has the freedom to teach . . to instruct . . to
develop . . to ask for and receive deserved help from others of
separate racial stations. This is the great freedom of our American
founding fathers . . . but if we amalgamate into the one unit as
advocated by the communist philosophers . . then the enrichment
of our lives . . . the freedom for our development . . . is gone forever. We become, therefore, a mongrel unit of one under a single
all powerful government . . . and we stand for everything . . . and
for nothing.

The true brotherhood of America, of respecting the separateness
of others . . and uniting in effort . . has been so twisted and distorted from its original concept that there is a small wonder that
communism is winning the world.

We invite the negro citizens of Alabama to work with us from
his separate racial station . . as we will work with him . . to
develop, to grow in individual freedom and enrichment. We want
jobs and a good future for BOTH races . . the tubercular and the
infirm. This is the basic heritage of my religion, if which I make
full practice . . . . for we are all the handiwork of God.

But we warn those, of any group, who would follow the false
doctrine of communistic amalgamation that we will not surrender
our system of government . . . our freedom of race and religion . .
. that freedom was won at a hard price and if it requires a hard
price to retain it . . we are able . . and quite willing to pay it.

The liberals' theory that poverty, discrimination and lack of
opportunity is the cause of communism is a false theory . . . if it
were true the South would have been the biggest single communist bloc in the western hemisphere long ago . . . for after the
great War Between the States, our people faced a desolate land of
burned universities, destroyed crops and homes, with manpower
depleted and crippled, and even the mule, which was required to
work the land, was so scarce that whole communities shared one

animal to make the spring plowing. There were no government handouts, no Marshall Plan aid, no coddling to make sure that our people would not suffer; instead the South was set upon by the vulturous carpetbagger and federal troops, all loyal Southerners were denied the vote at the point of bayonet, so that the infamous, illegal 14th Amendment might be passed. There was no money, no food and no hope of either. But our grandfathers bent their knee only in church and bowed their head only to God.

Not for a single instant did they ever consider the easy way of federal dictatorship and amalgamation in return for fat bellies. They fought. They dug sweet roots from the ground with their bare hands and boiled them in iron pots .... they gathered poke salad from the woods and acorns from the ground. They fought. They followed no false doctrine . . . they knew what the wanted . . and they fought for freedom! They came up from their knees in the greatest disply of sheer nerve, grit and guts that has ever been set down in the pages of written history . . . and they won! The great writer, Rudyard Kipling wrote of them, that: "There in the Southland of the United States of America, lives the greatest fighting breed of man . . . in all the world!"

And that is why today, I stand ashamed of the fat, well-fed whimperers who say that it is inevitable . . . that our cause is lost. I am ashamed of them . . . . and I am ashamed for them. They do not represent the people of the Southland.

And may we take note of one other fact, with all trouble with communists that some sections of this country have . . . there are not enough native communists in the South to fill up a telephone booth . . . . and THAT is a matter of public FBI record.

We remind all within hearing of this Southland that a Southerner, Peyton Randolph, presided over the Continental Congress in our nation's beginning . . . that a Southerner, Thomas Jefferson, wrote the Declaration of Independence, that a Southerner, George Washington, is the Father of our country . . . that a Southerner, James Madison, authored our Constitution, that a Southerner, George Mason, authored the Bill of Rights and it was a Southerner who said, "Give me liberty . . . . . . or give me death," Patrick Henry.

Southerners played a most magnificent part in erecting this great divinely inspired system of freedom . . and as God is our witnesses, Southerners will save it.

Let us, as Alabamians, grasp the hand of destiny and walk out of the shadow of fear . . . and fill our divine destination. Let us not simply defend . . but let us assume the leadership of the fight and carry our leadership across this nation. God has placed us here in this crisis . . . let is not fail in this . . our most historical moment.

You are here today, present in this audience, and to you over this great state, wherever you are in sound of my voice, I want to humbly and with all sincerity, thank you for your faith in me.

I promise you that I will try to make you a good governor. I promise you that, as God gives me the wisdom and the strength, I will be sincere with you. I will be honest with you.

I will apply the old sound rule of our fathers, that anything worthy of our defense is worthy of one hundred percent of our defense. I have been taught that freedom meant freedom from any threat or fear of government. I was born in that freedom, I was raised in that freedom . . . I intend to live live in that freedom . . . and God willing, when I die, I shall leave that freedom to my children . . . as my father left it to me.

My pledge to you . . . to "Stand up for Alabama," is a stronger pledge today than it was the first day I made that pledge. I shall "Stand up for Alabama," as Governor of our State . . . you stand with me . . . and we, together, can give courageous leadership to millions of people throughout this nation who look to the South for their hope in this fight to win and preserve our freedoms and liberties.

So help me God.

And my prayer is that the Father who reigns above us will bless all the people of this great sovereign State and nation, both white and black.

I thank you.

Civil Rights Act: July 2, 1964

An Act

To enforce the constitutional right to vote, to confer jurisdiction upon the district courts of the United States to provide injunctive relief against discrimination in public accommodations, to authorize the Attorney General to institute suits to protect constitutional rights in public facilities and public education, to extend the Commission on Civil Rights, to prevent discrimination in federally assisted programs, to establish a Commission on Equal Employment Opportunity, and for other purposes.

Be it enacted by the Senate and House of Representatives of the United States of America in Congress assembled, That this Act may be cited as the "Civil Rights Act of 1964".

TITLE II—INJUNCTIVE RELIEF AGAINST DISCRIMINATION IN PLACES OF PUBLIC ACCOMMODATION

SEC. 201. (a) All persons shall be entitled to the full and equal enjoyment of the goods, services, facilities, and privileges, advantages, and accommodations of any place of public accommodation, as defined in this section, without discrimination or segregation on the ground of race, color, religion, or national origin.

(b) Each of the following establishments which serves the public is a place of public accommodation within the meaning of this title if its operations affect commerce, or if discrimination or segregation by it is supported by State action:

(1) any inn, hotel, motel, or other establishment which provides lodging to transient guests, other than an establishment located within a building which contains not more than five rooms for rent or hire and which is actually occupied by the proprietor of such establishment as his residence;

(2) any restaurant, cafeteria, lunchroom, lunch counter, soda fountain, or other facility principally engaged in selling food for consumption on the premises, including, but not limited to, any

such facility located on the premises of any retail establishment; or any gasoline station;

(3) any motion picture house, theater, concert hall, sports arena, stadium or other place of exhibition or entertainment; and

(4) any establishment (A)(i) which is physically located within the premises of any establishment otherwise covered by this subsection, or (ii) within the premises of which is physically located any such covered establishment, and (B) which holds itself out as serving patrons of such covered establishment.

(c) The operations of an establishment affect commerce within the meaning of this title if (1) it is one of the establishments described in paragraph (1) of subsection (b); (2) in the case of an establishment described in paragraph (2) of subsection (b), it serves or offers to serve interstate travelers or a substantial portion of the food which it serves, or gasoline or other products which it sells, has moved in commerce; (3) in the case of an establishment described in paragraph (3) of subsection (b), it customarily presents films, performances, athletic teams, exhibitions, or other sources of entertainment which move in commerce; and (4) in the case of an establishment described in paragraph (4) of subsection (b), it is physically located within the premises of, or there is physically located within its premises, an establishment the operations of which affect commerce within the meaning of this subsection. For purposes of this section, "commerce" means travel, trade, traffic, commerce, transportation, or communication among the several States, or between the District of Columbia and any State, or between any foreign country or any territory or possession and any State or the District of Columbia, or between points in the same State but through any other State or the District of Columbia or a foreign country.

(d) Discrimination or segregation by an establishment is supported by State action within the meaning of this title if such discrimination or segregation (1) is carried on under color of any law, statute, ordinance, or regulation; or (2) is carried on under color of any custom or usage required or enforced by officials of the State or political subdivision thereof; or (3) is required by action of the State or political subdivision thereof.

(e) The provisions of this title shall not apply to a private club or other establishment not in fact open to the public, except to the extent that the facilities of such establishment are made available to the customers or patrons of an establishment within the scope of subsection (b).

SEC. 202. All persons shall be entitled to be free, at any establishment or place, from discrimination or segregation of any kind on the ground of race, color, religion, or national origin, if such discrimination or segregation is or purports to be required by any law, statute, ordinance, regulation, rule, or order of a State or any agency or political subdivision thereof.

SEC. 203. No person shall (a) withhold, deny, or attempt to withhold or deny, or deprive or attempt to deprive, any person of any right or privilege secured by section 201 or 202, or (b) intimidate, threaten, or coerce, or attempt to intimidate, threaten, or coerce any person with the purpose of interfering with any right or privilege secured by section 201 or 202, or (c) punish or attempt to punish any person for exercising or attempting to exercise any right or privilege secured by section 201 or 202.

SEC. 204. (a) Whenever any person has engaged or there are reasonable grounds to believe that any person is about to engage in any act or practice prohibited by section 203, a civil action for preventive relief, including an application for a permanent or temporary injunction, restraining order, or other order, may be instituted by the person aggrieved and, upon timely application, the court may, in its discretion, permit the Attorney General to intervene in such civil action if he certifies that the case is of general public importance. Upon application by the complainant and in such circumstances as the court may deem just, the court may appoint an attorney for such complainant and may authorize the commencement of the civil action without the payment of fees, costs, or security.

(b) In any action commenced pursuant to this title, the court, in its discretion, may allow the prevailing party, other than the United States, a reasonable attorney's fee as part of the costs, and the United States shall be liable for costs the same as a private person.

(c) In the case of an alleged act or practice prohibited by this title which occurs in a State, or political subdivision of a State, which has a State or local law prohibiting such act or practice and establishing or authorizing a State or local authority to grant or seek relief from such practice or to institute criminal proceedings with respect thereto upon receiving notice thereof, no civil action may be brought under subsection (a) before the expiration of thirty days after written notice of such alleged act or practice has been given to the appropriate State or local authority by registered mail or in person, provided that the court may stay proceedings in such civil action pending the termination of State or local enforcement proceedings.

(d) In the case of an alleged act or practice prohibited by this title which occurs in a State, or political subdivision of a State, which has no State or local law prohibiting such act or practice, a civil action may be brought under subsection (a): Provided, That the court may refer the matter to the Community Relations Service established by title X of this Act for as long as the court believes there is a reasonable possibility of obtaining voluntary compliance, but for not more than sixty days: Provided further, That upon expiration of such sixty-day period, the court may extend such period for an additional period, not to exceed a cumulative total of one hundred and twenty days, if it believes there then exists a reasonable possibility of securing voluntary compliance.

SEC. 205. The Service is authorized to make a full investigation of any complaint referred to it by the court under section 204(d) and may hold such hearings with respect thereto as may be necessary. The Service shall conduct any hearings with respect to any such complaint in executive session, and shall not release any testimony given therein except by agreement of all parties involved in the complaint with the permission of the court, and the Service shall endeavor to bring about a voluntary settlement between the parties.

SEC. 206. (a) Whenever the Attorney General has reasonable cause to believe that any person or group of persons is engaged in a pattern or practice of resistance to the full enjoyment of any of the rights secured by this title, and that the pattern or practice is of such a nature and is intended to deny the full exercise of the rights herein described, the Attorney General may bring a civil action in the appropriate district court of the United States by filing with it a complaint (1) signed by him (or in his absence the Acting Attorney General), (2) setting forth facts pertaining to such pattern or practice, and (3) requesting such preventive relief, including an application for a permanent or temporary injunction, restraining order or other order against the person or persons responsible for such pattern or practice, as he deems necessary to insure the full enjoyment of the rights herein described.

TITLE III—DESEGREGATION OF PUBLIC FACILITIES

SEC. 301. (a) Whenever the Attorney General receives a complaint in writing signed by an individual to the effect that he is being deprived of or threatened with the loss of his right to the equal protection of the laws, on account of his race, color, religion, or national origin, by being denied equal utilization of any public facility which is owned, operated, or managed by or on behalf of any State or subdivision thereof, other than a public school or public college as defined in section 401 of title IV hereof, and the Attorney General believes the complaint is meritorious and certifies that the signer or signers of such complaint are unable, in his judgment, to initiate and maintain appropriate legal proceedings for relief and that the institution of an action will materially further the orderly progress of desegregation in public facilities, the Attorney General is authorized to institute for or in the name of the United States a civil action in any appropriate district court of the United States against such parties and for such relief as may be appropriate, and such court shall have and shall exercise jurisdiction of proceedings instituted pursuant to this section. The Attorney General may implead as defendants such additional parties as are or become necessary to the grant of effective relief hereunder.

(b) The Attorney General may deem a person or persons unable to initiate and maintain appropriate legal proceedings within the meaning of subsection

(a) of this section when such person or persons are unable, either directly or through other interested persons or organizations, to bear the expense of the litigation or to obtain effective legal representation; or whenever he is satisfied that the institution of such litigation would jeopardize the personal safety, employment, or economic standing of such person or persons, their families, or their property.

SEC. 302. In any action or proceeding under this title the United States shall be liable for costs, including a reasonable attorney's fee, the same as a private person.

SEC. 303. Nothing in this title shall affect adversely the right of any person to sue for or obtain relief in any court against discrimination in any facility covered by this title.

SEC. 304. A complaint as used in this title is a writing or document within the meaning of section 1001, title 18, United States Code.

TITLE IV—DESEGREGATION OF PUBLIC EDUCATION

SUITS BY THE ATTORNEY GENERAL

SEC. 407. (a) Whenever the Attorney General receives a complaint in writing—

(1) signed by a parent or group of parents to the effect that his or their minor children, as members of a class of persons similarly situated, are being deprived by a school board of the equal protection of the laws, or

(2) signed by an individual, or his parent, to the effect that he has been denied admission to or not permitted to continue in attendance at a public college by reason of race, color, religion, or national origin, and the Attorney General believes the complaint is meritorious and certifies that the signer or signers of such complaint are unable, in his judgment, to initiate and maintain appropriate legal proceedings for relief and that the institution of an action will materially further the orderly achievement of desegregation in public education, the Attorney General is authorized, after giving notice of such complaint to the appropriate school board or college authority and after certifying that he is satisfied that such board or authority has had a reasonable

time to adjust the conditions alleged in such complaint, to institute for or in the name of the United States a civil action in any appropriate district court of the United States against such parties and for such relief as may be appropriate, and such court shall have and shall exercise jurisdiction of proceedings instituted pursuant to this section, provided that nothing herein shall empower any official or court of the United States to issue any order seeking to achieve a racial balance in any school by requiring the transportation of pupils or students from one school to another or one school district to another in order to achieve such racial balance, or otherwise enlarge the existing power of the court to insure compliance with constitutional standards. The Attorney General may implead as defendants such additional parties as are or become necessary to the grant of effective relief hereunder.

(b) The Attorney General may deem a person or persons unable to initiate and maintain appropriate legal proceedings within the meaning of subsection

(a) of this section when such person or persons are unable, either directly or through other interested persons or organizations, to bear the expense of the litigation or to obtain effective legal representation; or whenever he is satisfied that the institution of such litigation would jeopardize the personal safety, employment, or economic standing of such person or persons, their families, or their property.

(c) The term "parent" as used in this section includes any person standing in loco parentis. A "complaint" as used in this section is a writing or document within the meaning of section 1001, title 18, United States Code.

SEC. 408. In any action or proceeding under this title the United States shall be liable for costs the same as a private person.

SEC. 409. Nothing in this title shall affect adversely the right of any person to sue for or obtain relief in any court against discrimination in public education.

SEC. 410. Nothing in this title shall prohibit classification and assignment for reasons other than race, color, religion, or national origin.

Voting Rights Act of 1965; August 6, 1965

AN ACT To enforce the fifteenth amendment to the Constitution of the United States, and for other purposes.

Be it enacted by the Senate and House of Representatives of the United States of America in Congress [p★338] assembled, That this Act shall be known as the "Voting Rights Act of 1965."

SEC. 2. No voting qualification or prerequisite to voting, or standard, practice, or procedure shall be imposed or applied by any State or political subdivision to deny or abridge the right of any citizen of the United States to vote on account of race or color.

SEC. 3.

(a) Whenever the Attorney General institutes a proceeding under any statute to enforce the guarantees of the fifteenth amendment in any State or political subdivision the court shall authorize the appointment of Federal examiners by the United States Civil Service Commission in accordance with section 6 to serve for such period of time and for such political subdivisions as the court shall determine is appropriate to enforce the guarantees of the fifteenth amendment (1) as part of any interlocutory order if the court determines that the appointment of such examiners is necessary to enforce such guarantees or (2) as part of any final judgment if the court finds that violations of the fifteenth amendment justifying equitable relief have occurred in such State or subdivision: Provided, That the court need not authorize the appointment of examiners if any incidents of denial or abridgement of the right to vote on account of race or color (1) have been few in number and have been promptly and effectively corrected by State or local action, (2) the continuing effect of such incidents has been eliminated, and (3) there is no reasonable probability of their recurrence in the future. (b) If in a proceeding instituted by the Attorney General under any statute to enforce the guarantees of the fifteenth amendment in any State or political subdivision the court finds that a test or device has been used for the purpose or with the effect of denying or abridging the right of any citizen of the United States to vote on account of race or color, it shall suspend the use of [p★339] tests and devices in such State or political subdivisions as the court shall determine is appropriate and for such period as it deems necessary.

(c) If in any proceeding instituted by the Attorney General under any statute to enforce the guarantees of the fifteenth amendment in any State or political subdivision the court finds that violations of the fifteenth amendment justifying equitable relief have occurred within the territory of such State or political subdivision, the court, in addition to such relief as it may grant, shall retain jurisdiction for such period as it may deem appropriate and during such period no voting qualification or prerequisite to voting, or standard, practice, or procedure with respect to voting different from that in force or effect at the time the proceeding was commenced shall be enforced unless and until the court finds that such qualification, prerequisite, standard, practice, or procedure does not have the purpose and will not have the effect of denying or abridging the right to vote on account of race or color: Provided, That such qualification, prerequisite, standard, practice, or procedure may be enforced if the qualification, prerequisite, standard, practice, or procedure has been submitted by the chief legal officer or other appropriate official of such State or subdivision to the Attorney General and the Attorney General has not interposed an objection within sixty days after such submission, except that neither the court's finding nor the Attorney General's failure to object shall bar a subsequent action to enjoin enforcement of such qualification, prerequisite, standard, practice, or procedure.

SEC. 4. (a) To assure that the right of citizens of the United States to vote is not denied or abridged on account of race or color, no citizen shall be denied the right to vote in any Federal, State, or local election because of his failure to comply with any test or device in any State with respect to which the determinations have been made under subsection (b) or in any political subdivision with respect to which such determinations have been made as a separate unit, unless the United States District Court for the District of Columbia in an action for a declaratory judgment brought by such State or subdivision against the United States has determined that no such test or device has been used during the five years preceding the filing of the action for the purpose or with the effect of denying or abridging the right to vote on account of race or color: Provided, That no such declaratory judgment shall issue with respect to any plaintiff for a period of five years after the entry of a final judgment of any court of the United States, other than the denial of a declaratory judgment under this section, whether entered prior to or after the enactment of this Act, determining that denials or abridgments of the right to vote on account of race or color through the use of such tests or devices have occurred anywhere in the territory of such plaintiff. An action pursuant to this subsection shall be heard and determined by a court of three judges in accordance with the provisions of section 2284 of title 28 of the United States Code and any appeal shall lie to the Supreme Court. The court shall retain jurisdiction of any action pursuant to this subsection for five years after judgment and shall reopen the action upon motion of the Attorney General alleging that a test or device has been used for the purpose or with the effect of denying or abridging the right to vote on account of race or color.

If the Attorney General determines that he has no reason to believe that any such test or device has been used during the five years preceding the filing of the action for the purpose or with the effect of denying or abridging the right to vote on account of race or color, he shall consent to the entry of such judgment

(b) The provisions of subsection (a) shall apply in any State or in any political subdivision of a state which (1) the Attorney General determines maintained on November 1, 1964, any test or device, and with respect to which (2) the Director of the Census determines that less than 50 percentum of the persons of voting age residing therein were registered on November 1, 1964, or that less than 50 percentum of such persons voted in the presidential election of November 1964.

A determination or certification of the Attorney General or of the Director of the Census under this section or under section 6 or section 13 shall not be reviewable in any court and shall be effective upon publication in the Federal Register.

(c) The phrase "test or device" shall mean any requirement that a person as a prerequisite for voting or registration for voting (1) demonstrate the ability to read, write, understand, or interpret any matter, (2) demonstrate any educational achievement or his knowledge of any particular subject, (3) possess good moral character, or (4) prove his qualifications by the voucher of registered voters or members of any other class.

(d) For purposes of this section no State or political subdivision shall be determined to have engaged in the use of tests or devices for the purpose or with the effect of denying or abridging the right to vote on account of race or color if (1) incidents of such use have been few in number and have been promptly and effectively corrected by State or local action, (2) the continuing effect of such incidents has been eliminated, and (3) there is no reasonable probability of their recurrence in the future.

(e)(1) Congress hereby declares that to secure the rights under the fourteenth amendment of persons educated in American-flag schools in which the predominant classroom language was other than English, it is necessary to prohibit the States from conditioning the right to vote of such persons on ability to read, write, understand, or interpret any matter in the English language. (2) No person who demonstrates that he has successfully completed the sixth primary grade in a public school in, or a private school accredited by, any State or territory, the District of Columbia, or the Commonwealth of Puerto Rico in which the predominant classroom language was other than English, shall be denied the right to vote in any Federal, State, or local election because of his inability to read, write, understand, or interpret any matter in the English language, except that, in States in which State law provides that a different level of education is presumptive of literacy, he shall demonstrate that he has successfully completed an equivalent level of education in a public school in, or a private school accredited by, any State or territory, the District of Columbia, or the Commonwealth of Puerto Rico in which the predominant classroom language was other than English.

COINTELPRO

SAC, Albany   August 25, 1967

PERSONAL ATTENTION TO ALL OFFICES

[From] Director, FBI

COUNTERINTELLIGENCE PROGRAM
BLACK NATIONALIST - HATE GROUPS
INTERNAL SECURITY

[...] The purpose of this new counterintelligence endeavor is to expose, disrupt, misdirect, discredit, or OTHERWISE NEU-TRALIZE [emphasis added] the activities of black nationalist hate-type organizations and groupings, their leadership, spokes-men, membership, and supporters, and to counter their propen-sity for violence and civil disorder. The activities of all such groups of intelligence interest to the Bureau must be followed on a continuous basis so we will be in a position to promptly take advantage of all opportunities for counterintelligence and inspire action in instances where circumstances warrant. The pernicious background of such groups, their duplicity, and devious maneu-vers must be exposed to public scrutiny where such publicity will have a neautralizing effect. Efforts of the various groups to con-solidate their forces or to recruit new or youthful adherents must be frustrated. NO OPPORTUNITY SHOULD BE MISSED TO EXPLOIT THROUGH COUNTERINTELLIGENCE TECH-NIQUES THE ORGANIZATIONAL AND PERSONAL CON-FLICTS OF THE LEADERSHIPS OF THE GROUPS AND WHERE POSSIBLE AN EFFORT SHOULD BE MADE TO CAPITALIZE UPON EXISTING CONFLICTS BETWEEN COMPETING BLACK NATIONALIST ORGANIZATIONS. [emphasis added] When an opportunity is apparent to disrupt or NEUTRALIZE [emphasis added] black nationalist, hate-type organizations through the cooperation of established local news media contacts or through such contact with sources available to the Seat of Government [Hoover's office], in every instance care-ful attention must be given to the proposal to insure the target-ted group is disrupted, ridiculed, or discredited through the publicity and not merely publicized...

You are also cautioned that the nature of this new endeavor is such that UNDER NO CIRCUMSTANCES SHOULD THE EXISTENCE OF THE PROGRAM BE MADE KNOWN OUT-SIDE THE BUREAU [emphasis added] and appropriate within-office security should be afforded to sensitive operations and techniques considered under the program.

No counterintelligence action under this program may be initiated by the field without specific prior Bureau authorization. [Emphasis in orig.]

★   ★   ★

COUNTERINTELLIGENCE PROGRAM
BLACK NATIONALIST - HATE GROUPS
RACIAL INTELLIGENCE

GOALS

For maximum effectiveness of the Counterintelligence Program, and to prevent wasted effort, long-range goals are being set.

1. Prevent the COALITION of militant black nationalist groups. In unity there is strength; a truism that is no less valid for all its triteness. An effective coalition of black nationalist groups might be the first step toward a real "Mau Mau" [Black revolutionary army] in America, the beginning of a true black revolution.

2. Prevent the RISE OF A "MESSIAH" who could unify, and electrify, the militant black nationalist movement. Malcolm X might have been such a "messiah;" he is the martyr of the movement today. Martin Luther King, Stokely Carmichael and Elijah Muhammed all aspire to this position. Elijah Muhammed is less of a threat because of his age. King could be a very real contender for this position should he abandon his supposed "obedience" to "white, liberal doctrines" (nonviolence) and embrace black nationalism. Carmichael has the necessary charisma to be a real threat in this way.

3. Prevent VIOLENCE on the part of black nationalist groups. This is of primary importance, and is, of course, a goal of our investigative activity; it should also be a goal of the Counterintelligence Program to pinpoint potential troublemakers and neutralize them before they exercise their potential for violence.

4. Prevent militant black nationalist groups and leaders from gaining RESPECTABILITY, by discrediting them to three

separate segments of the community. The goal of discrediting black nationalists must be handled tactically in three ways. You must discredit those groups and individuals to, first, the responsible Negro community. Second, they must be discredited to the white community, both the responsible community and to "liberals" who have vestiges of sympathy for militant black nationalist [sic] simply because they are Negroes. Third, these groups must be discredited in the eyes of Negro radicals, the followers of the movement. This last area requires entirely different tactics from the first two. Publicity about violent tendencies and radical statements merely enhances black nationalists to the last group; it adds "respectability" in a different way.

5. A final goal should be to prevent the long-range GROWTH of militant black organizations, especially among youth. Specific tactics to prevent these groups from converting young people must be developed. [...]

TARGETS

Primary targets of the Counterintelligence Program, Black Nationalist-Hate Groups, should be the most violent and radical groups and their leaders. We should emphasize those leaders and organizations that are nationwide in scope and are most capable of disrupting this country. These targets, members, and followers of the:

Student Nonviolent Coordinating Committee (SNCC)

Southern Christian Leadership Conference (SCLC)

Revolutionary Action Movement (RAM)

NATION OF ISLAM (NOI) [emphasis added]

Offices handling these cases and those of Stokely Carmichael of SNCC, H. Rap Brown of SNCC, Martin Luther King of SCLC, Maxwell Stanford of RAM, and Elijah Muhammed of NOI, should be alert for counterintelligence suggestions. [...]

A Post-Racial Society?

Excerpt from Clarence Thomas Confirmation Hearings

HEARING OF THE SENATE JUDICIARY COMMITTEE ON THE NOMINATION OF CLARENCE THOMAS TO THE SUPREME COURT

FRIDAY, OCTOBER 11, 1991 (9:03 P.M. EDT)

SEN. BIDEN: (Sounds gavel.) The committee will please come to order.

Judge, it's a tough day and a tough night for you, I know. Let me ask, do you have anything you'd like to say before we begin? And I understand that your preference is—which is totally and completely understandable—that we go one hour tonight, 30 minutes on each side. Am I correct in that?

JUDGE THOMAS: That's right.

SEN. BIDEN: Do you have anything you'd like to say?

JUDGE THOMAS: Senator, I would like to start by saying unequivocally, uncategorically, that I deny each and every single allegation against me today that suggested in any way that I had conversations of a sexual nature or about pornographic material with Anita Hill, that I ever attempted to date her, that I ever had any personal sexual interest in her, or that I in any way ever harassed her.

A second, and I think more important point, I think that this today is a travesty. I think that it is disgusting. I think that this hearing should never occur in America. This is a case in which this sleaze, this dirt, was searched for by staffers of members of this committee, was then leaked to the media, and this committee and this body validated it and displayed it at prime time over our entire nation. How would any member on this committee, any person in this room, or any person in this country, would like sleaze said about him or her in this fashion? Or this dirt dredged up and this gossip and these lies displayed in this manner? How would any person like it?

The Supreme Court is not worth it. No job is worth it. I'm not here for that. I'm here for my name, my family, my life and my integrity. I think something is dreadfully wrong with this country when any person, any person in this free country would be subjected to this.

This is not a closed room. There was an FBI investigation. This is not an opportunity to talk about difficult matters privately or in a closed environment. This is a circus. It's a national disgrace. And from my standpoint as a black American, as far as I'm concerned, it is a high-tech lynching for uppity blacks who in any way deign to think for themselves, to do for themselves, to have different ideas, and it is a message that unless you kowtow to an old order, this is what will happen to you. You will be lynched, destroyed, caricatured by a committee of the US Senate rather than hung from a tree.

Barak Obama Speech on Race, March 18, 2008

We the people, in order to form a more perfect union."

Two hundred and twenty one years ago, in a hall that still stands across the street, a group of men gathered and, with these simple words, launched America's improbable experiment in democracy. Farmers and scholars; statesmen and patriots who had traveled across an ocean to escape tyranny and persecution finally made real their declaration of independence at a Philadelphia convention that lasted through the spring of 1787.

The document they produced was eventually signed but ultimately unfinished. It was stained by this nation's original sin of slavery, a question that divided the colonies and brought the convention to a stalemate until the founders chose to allow the slave trade to continue for at least twenty more years, and to leave any final resolution to future generations.

Of course, the answer to the slavery question was already embedded within our Constitution - a Constitution that had at is very core the ideal of equal citizenship under the law; a Constitution that promised its people liberty, and justice, and a union that could be and should be perfected over time.

And yet words on a parchment would not be enough to deliver slaves from bondage, or provide men and women of every color and creed their full rights and obligations as citizens of the United States. What would be needed were Americans in successive generations who were willing to do their part - through protests and struggle, on the streets and in the courts, through a civil war and civil disobedience and always at great risk - to narrow that gap between the promise of our ideals and the reality of their time.

This was one of the tasks we set forth at the beginning of this campaign - to continue the long march of those who came before us, a march for a more just, more equal, more free, more caring and more prosperous America. I chose to run for the presidency at this moment in history because I believe deeply that we cannot solve the challenges of our time unless we solve them together - unless we perfect our union by understanding that we may have different stories, but we hold common hopes; that we may not look the same and we may not have come from the same place, but we all want to move in the same direction - towards a better future for of children and our grandchildren.

This belief comes from my unyielding faith in the decency and generosity of the American people. But it also comes from my own American story.

I am the son of a black man from Kenya and a white woman from Kansas. I was raised with the help of a white grandfather who survived a Depression to serve in Patton's Army during World War II and a white grandmother who worked on a bomber assembly line at Fort Leavenworth while he was overseas. I've gone to some of the best schools in America and lived in one of the world's poorest nations. I am married to a black American who carries within her the blood of slaves and slave-owners - an inheritance we pass on to our two precious daughters. I have brothers, sisters, nieces, nephews, uncles and cousins, of every race and every hue, scattered across three continents, and for as long as I live, I will never forget that in no other country on Earth is my story even possible.

It's a story that hasn't made me the most conventional candidate. But it is a story that has seared into my genetic makeup the idea that this nation is more than the sum of its parts – that out of many, we are truly one.

Throughout the first year of this campaign, against all predictions to the contrary, we saw how hungry the American people were for this message of unity. Despite the temptation to view my candidacy through a purely racial lens, we won commanding victories in states with some of the whitest populations in the country. In South Carolina, where the Confederate Flag still flies, we built a powerful coalition of African Americans and white Americans.

This is not to say that race has not been an issue in the campaign. At various stages in the campaign, some commentators have deemed me either "too black" or "not black enough." We saw racial tensions bubble to the surface during the week before the South Carolina primary. The press has scoured every exit poll for the latest evidence of racial polarization, not just in terms of white and black, but black and brown as well.

And yet, it has only been in the last couple of weeks that the discussion of race in this campaign has taken a particularly divisive turn.

On one end of the spectrum, we've heard the implication that my candidacy is somehow an exercise in affirmative action; that it's based solely on the desire of wide-eyed liberals to purchase racial reconciliation on the cheap. On the other end, we've heard my former pastor, Reverend Jeremiah Wright, use incendiary language to express views that have the potential not only to widen the racial divide, but views that denigrate both the greatness and the goodness of our nation; that rightly offend white and black alike.

I have already condemned, in unequivocal terms, the statements of Reverend Wright that have caused such controversy. For some, nagging questions remain. Did I know him to be an occasionally fierce critic of American domestic and foreign policy? Of course. Did I ever hear him make remarks that could be considered controversial while I sat in church? Yes. Did I strongly disagree with many of his political views? Absolutely – just as I'm sure many of you have heard remarks from your pastors, priests, or rabbis with which you strongly disagreed.

But the remarks that have caused this recent firestorm weren't simply controversial. They weren't simply a religious leader's effort to speak out against perceived injustice. Instead, they expressed a profoundly distorted view of this country – a view that sees white racism as endemic, and that elevates what is wrong with America above all that we know is right with America; a view that sees the conflicts in the Middle East as rooted primarily in the actions of stalwart allies like Israel, instead of emanating from the perverse and hateful ideologies of radical Islam.

As such, Reverend Wright's comments were not only wrong but divisive, divisive at a time when we need unity; racially charged at a time when we need to come together to solve a set of monumental problems – two wars, a terrorist threat, a falling economy, a chronic health care crisis and potentially devastating climate change; problems that are neither black or white or Latino or Asian, but rather problems that confront us all.

Given my background, my politics, and my professed values and ideals, there will no doubt be those for whom my statements of condemnation are not enough. Why associate myself with Reverend Wright in the first place, they may ask? Why not join another church? And I confess that if all that I knew of Reverend Wright were the snippets of those sermons that have run in an endless loop on the television and You Tube, or if Trinity United Church of Christ conformed to the caricatures being peddled by some commentators, there is no doubt that I would react in much the same way

But the truth is, that isn't all that I know of the man. The man I met more than twenty years ago is a man who helped introduce me to my Christian faith, a man who spoke to me about our obligations to love one another; to care for the sick and lift up the poor. He is a man who served his country as a U.S. Marine; who has studied and lectured at some of the finest universities and seminaries in the country, and who for over thirty years led a church that serves the community by doing God's work here on

Earth - by housing the homeless, ministering to the needy, providing day care services and scholarships and prison ministries, and reaching out to those suffering from HIV/AIDS.

In my first book, Dreams From My Father, I described the experience of my first service at Trinity:

> "People began to shout, to rise from their seats and clap and cry out, a forceful wind carrying the reverend's voice up into the rafters....And in that single note - hope! - I heard something else; at the foot of that cross, inside the thousands of churches across the city, I imagined the stories of ordinary black people merging with the stories of David and Goliath, Moses and Pharaoh, the Christians in the lion's den, Ezekiel's field of dry bones. Those stories - of survival, and freedom, and hope - became our story, my story; the blood that had spilled was our blood, the tears our tears; until this black church, on this bright day, seemed once more a vessel carrying the story of a people into future generations and into a larger world. Our trials and triumphs became at once unique and universal, black and more than black; in chronicling our journey, the stories and songs gave us a means to reclaim memories that we didn't need to feel shame about...memories that all people might study and cherish - and with which we could start to rebuild."

That has been my experience at Trinity. Like other predominantly black churches across the country, Trinity embodies the black community in its entirety - the doctor and the welfare mom, the model student and the former gang-banger. Like other black churches, Trinity's services are full of raucous laughter and sometimes bawdy humor. They are full of dancing, clapping, screaming and shouting that may seem jarring to the untrained ear. The church contains in full the kindness and cruelty, the fierce intelligence and the shocking ignorance, the struggles and successes, the love and yes, the bitterness and bias that make up the black experience in America.

And this helps explain, perhaps, my relationship with Reverend Wright. As imperfect as he may be, he has been like family to me. He strengthened my faith, officiated my wedding, and baptized my children. Not once in my conversations with him have I heard him talk about any ethnic group in derogatory terms, or treat whites with whom he interacted with anything but courtesy and respect. He contains within him the contradictions - the good and the bad - of the community that he has served diligently for so many years.

I can no more disown him than I can disown the black community. I can no more disown him than I can my white grandmother - a woman who helped raise me, a woman who sacrificed again and again for me, a woman who loves me as much as she loves anything in this world, but a woman who once confessed her fear of black men who passed by her on the street, and who on more than one occasion has uttered racial or ethnic stereotypes that made me cringe.

These people are a part of me. And they are a part of America, this country that I love.

Some will see this as an attempt to justify or excuse comments that are simply inexcusable. I can assure you it is not. I suppose the politically safe thing would be to move on from this episode and just hope that it fades into the woodwork. We can dismiss Reverend Wright as a crank or a demagogue, just as some have dismissed Geraldine Ferraro, in the aftermath of her recent statements, as harboring some deep-seated racial bias.

But race is an issue that I believe this nation cannot afford to ignore right now. We would be making the same mistake that Reverend Wright made in his offending sermons about America - to simplify and stereotype and amplify the negative to the point that it distorts reality.

The fact is that the comments that have been made and the issues that have surfaced over the last few weeks reflect the complexities of race in this country that we've never really worked through - a part of our union that we have yet to perfect. And if we walk away now, if we simply retreat into our respective corners, we will never be able to come together and solve challenges like health care, or education, or the need to find good jobs for every American.

Understanding this reality requires a reminder of how we arrived at this point. As William Faulkner once wrote, "The past isn't dead and buried. In fact, it isn't even past." We do not need to recite here the history of racial injustice in this country. But we do need to remind ourselves that so many of the disparities that exist in the African-American community today can be directly traced to inequalities passed on from an earlier generation that suffered under the brutal legacy of slavery and Jim Crow.

Segregated schools were, and are, inferior schools; we still haven't fixed them, fifty years after Brown v. Board of Education, and the inferior education they provided, then and now, helps explain the pervasive achievement gap between today's black and white students.

Legalized discrimination - where blacks were prevented, often through violence, from owning property, or loans were not granted to African-American business owners, or black home-owners could not access FHA mortgages, or blacks were excluded from unions, or the police force, or fire departments - meant that black families could not amass any meaningful wealth to bequeath to future generations. That history helps explain the wealth and income gap between black and white, and the con-centrated pockets of poverty that persists in so many of today's urban and rural communities.

A lack of economic opportunity among black men, and the shame and frustration that came from not being able to provide for one's family, contributed to the erosion of black families - a problem that welfare policies for many years may have worsened. And the lack of basic services in so many urban black neighborhoods - parks for kids to play in, police walking the beat, regular garbage pick-up and building code enforcement - all helped create a cycle of violence, blight and neglect that continue to haunt us.

This is the reality in which Reverend Wright and other African-Americans of his generation grew up. They came of age in the late fifties and early sixties, a time when segregation was still the law of the land and opportunity was systematically constricted. What's remarkable is not how many failed in the face of discrim-ination, but rather how many men and women overcame the odds; how many were able to make a way out of no way for those like me who would come after them.

But for all those who scratched and clawed their way to get a piece of the American Dream, there were many who didn't make it - those who were ultimately defeated, in one way or another, by

discrimination. That legacy of defeat was passed on to future generations - those young men and increasingly young women who
we see standing on street corners or languishing in our prisons,
without hope or prospects for the future. Even for those blacks
who did make it, questions of race, and racism, continue to define
their worldview in fundamental ways. For the men and women of
Reverend Wright's generation, the memories of humiliation and
doubt and fear have not gone away; nor has the anger and the bitterness of those years. That anger may not get expressed in public,
in front of white co-workers or white friends. But it does find
voice in the barbershop or around the kitchen table. At times, that
anger is exploited by politicians, to gin up votes along racial lines,
or to make up for a politician's own failings.

And occasionally it finds voice in the church on Sunday morning, in the pulpit and in the pews. The fact that so many people
are surprised to hear that anger in some of Reverend Wright's
sermons simply reminds us of the old truism that the most segregated hour in American life occurs on Sunday morning. That
anger is not always productive; indeed, all too often it distracts
attention from solving real problems; it keeps us from squarely
facing our own complicity in our condition, and prevents the
African-American community from forging the alliances it needs
to bring about real change. But the anger is real; it is powerful;
and to simply wish it away, to condemn it without understanding
its roots, only serves to widen the chasm of misunderstanding
that exists between the races.

In fact, a similar anger exists within segments of the white community. Most working- and middle-class white Americans don't
feel that they have been particularly privileged by their race.
Their experience is the immigrant experience - as far as they're
concerned, no one's handed them anything, they've built it from
scratch. They've worked hard all their lives, many times only to
see their jobs shipped overseas or their pension dumped after a
lifetime of labor. They are anxious about their futures, and feel
their dreams slipping away; in an era of stagnant wages and global
competition, opportunity comes to be seen as a zero sum game,
in which your dreams come at my expense. So when they are
told to bus their children to a school across town; when they
hear that an African American is getting an advantage in landing

a good job or a spot in a good college because of an injustice that they themselves never committed; when they're told that their fears about crime in urban neighborhoods are somehow prejudiced, resentment builds over time.

Like the anger within the black community, these resentments aren't always expressed in polite company. But they have helped shape the political landscape for at least a generation. Anger over welfare and affirmative action helped forge the Reagan Coalition. Politicians routinely exploited fears of crime for their own electoral ends. Talk show hosts and conservative commentators built entire careers unmasking bogus claims of racism while dismissing legitimate discussions of racial injustice and inequality as mere political correctness or reverse racism.

Just as black anger often proved counterproductive, so have these white resentments distracted attention from the real culprits of the middle class squeeze - a corporate culture rife with inside dealing, questionable accounting practices, and short-term greed; a Washington dominated by lobbyists and special interests; economic policies that favor the few over the many. And yet, to wish away the resentments of white Americans, to label them as misguided or even racist, without recognizing they are grounded in legitimate concerns - this too widens the racial divide, and blocks the path to understanding.

This is where we are right now. It's a racial stalemate we've been stuck in for years. Contrary to the claims of some of my critics, black and white, I have never been so naïve as to believe that we can get beyond our racial divisions in a single election cycle, or with a single candidacy - particularly a candidacy as imperfect as my own.

But I have asserted a firm conviction - a conviction rooted in my faith in God and my faith in the American people - that working together we can move beyond some of our old racial wounds, and that in fact we have no choice is we are to continue on the path of a more perfect union.

For the African-American community, that path means embracing the burdens of our past without becoming victims of our past. It means continuing to insist on a full measure of justice in every aspect of American life. But it also means binding our particular grievances - for better health care, and better schools, and better jobs – to the larger aspirations of all Americans—the white woman struggling to break the glass ceiling, the white man whose been laid off, the immigrant trying to feed his family. And it means taking full responsibility for own lives – by demanding more from our fathers, and spending more time with our children, and reading to them, and teaching them that while they may face challenges and discrimination in their own lives, they must never succumb to despair or cynicism; they must always believe that they can write their own destiny.

Ironically, this quintessentially American – and yes, conservative – notion of self-help found frequent expression in Reverend Wright's sermons. But what my former pastor too often failed to understand is that embarking on a program of self-help also requires a belief that society can change.

The profound mistake of Reverend Wright's sermons is not that he spoke about racism in our society. It's that he spoke as if our society was static; as if no progress has been made; as if this country – a country that has made it possible for one of his own members to run for the highest office in the land and build a coalition of white and black; Latino and Asian, rich and poor, young and old—is still irrevocably bound to a tragic past. But what we know—what we have seen – is that America can change. That is true genius of this nation. What we have already achieved gives us hope – the audacity to hope – for what we can and must achieve tomorrow.

In the white community, the path to a more perfect union means acknowledging that what ails the African-American community does not just exist in the minds of black people; that the legacy of discrimination – and current incidents of discrimination, while less overt than in the past – are real and must be addressed. Not just with words, but with deeds – by investing in our schools and our communities; by enforcing our civil rights laws and ensuring fairness in our criminal justice system; by providing this generation with ladders of opportunity that were unavailable for previous generations. It requires all Americans to realize that your dreams do not have to come at the expense of my dreams; that investing in the health, welfare, and education of black and brown and white children will ultimately help all of America prosper.

In the end, then, what is called for is nothing more, and nothing less, than what all the world's great religions demand – that we do unto others as we would have them do unto us. Let us be our brother's keeper, Scripture tells us. Let us be our sister's keeper. Let us find that common stake we all have in one another, and let our politics reflect that spirit as well.

For we have a choice in this country. We can accept a politics that breeds division, and conflict, and cynicism. We can tackle race only as spectacle - as we did in the OJ trial - or in the wake of tragedy, as we did in the aftermath of Katrina - or as fodder for the nightly news. We can play Reverend Wright's sermons on every channel, every day and talk about them from now until the election, and make the only question in this campaign whether or not the American people think that I somehow believe or sympathize with his most offensive words. We can pounce on some gaffe by a Hillary supporter as evidence that she's playing the race card, or we can speculate on whether white men will all flock to John McCain in the general election regardless of his policies.

We can do that.

But if we do, I can tell you that in the next election, we'll be talking about some other distraction. And then another one. And then another one. And nothing will change.

That is one option. Or, at this moment, in this election, we can come together and say, "Not this time." This time we want to talk about the crumbling schools that are stealing the future of black children and white children and Asian children and Hispanic children and Native American children. This time we want to reject the cynicism that tells us that these kids can't learn; that those kids who don't look like us are somebody else's problem. The children of America are not those kids, they are our kids, and we will not let them fall behind in a 21st century economy. Not this time.

This time we want to talk about how the lines in the Emergency Room are filled with whites and blacks and Hispanics who do not have health care; who don't have the power on their own to overcome the special interests in Washington, but who can take them on if we do it together.

This time we want to talk about the shuttered mills that once provided a decent life for men and women of every race, and the homes for sale that once belonged to Americans from every religion, every region, every walk of life. This time we want to talk about the fact that the real problem is not that someone who doesn't look like you might take your job; it's that the corporation you work for will ship it overseas for nothing more than a profit.

This time we want to talk about the men and women of every color and creed who serve together, and fight together, and bleed together under the same proud flag. We want to talk about how to bring them home from a war that never should've been authorized and never should've been waged, and we want to talk about how we'll show our patriotism by caring for them, and their families, and giving them the benefits they have earned.

I would not be running for President if I didn't believe with all my heart that this is what the vast majority of Americans want for this country. This union may never be perfect, but generation after generation has shown that it can always be perfected. And today, whenever I find myself feeling doubtful or cynical about this possibility, what gives me the most hope is the next generation - the young people whose attitudes and beliefs and openness to change have already made history in this election.

There is one story in particularly that I'd like to leave you with today - a story I told when I had the great honor of speaking on Dr. King's birthday at his home church, Ebenezer Baptist, in Atlanta.

There is a young, twenty-three year old white woman named Ashley Baia who organized for our campaign in Florence, South Carolina. She had been working to organize a mostly African-American community since the beginning of this campaign, and one day she was at a roundtable discussion where everyone went around telling their story and why they were there.

And Ashley said that when she was nine years old, her mother got cancer. And because she had to miss days of work, she was let go and lost her health care. They had to file for bankruptcy, and that's when Ashley decided that she had to do something to help her mom.

She knew that food was one of their most expensive costs, and so Ashley convinced her mother that what she really liked and really wanted to eat more than anything else was mustard and relish sandwiches. Because that was the cheapest way to eat.

She did this for a year until her mom got better, and she told everyone at the roundtable that the reason she joined our campaign was so that she could help the millions of other children in the country who want and need to help their parents too.

Now Ashley might have made a different choice. Perhaps somebody told her along the way that the source of her mother's problems were blacks who were on welfare and too lazy to work, or Hispanics who were coming into the country illegally. But she didn't. She sought out allies in her fight against injustice.

Anyway, Ashley finishes her story and then goes around the room and asks everyone else why they're supporting the campaign. They all have different stories and reasons. Many bring up a specific issue. And finally they come to this elderly black man who's been sitting there quietly the entire time. And Ashley asks him why he's there. And he does not bring up a specific issue. He does not say health care or the economy. He does not say education or the war. He does not say that he was there because of Barack Obama. He simply says to everyone in the room, "I am here because of Ashley."

"I'm here because of Ashley." By itself, that single moment of recognition between that young white girl and that old black man is not enough. It is not enough to give health care to the sick, or jobs to the jobless, or education to our children.

But it is where we start. It is where our union grows stronger. And as so many generations have come to realize over the course of the two-hundred and twenty one years since a band of patriots signed that document in Philadelphia, that is where the perfection begins.

VIII

The U.S. and the Middle East

In the first decade of the 21st Century, the world has been torn by conflicts in the Middle East, and this chapter aims to put these current crises in historical perspective.

From the earlier part of the 20th Century, the great western powers hoped to gain influence and control over the Middle East because of its vast reserves of oil, a goal that was accelerated after World War II. At the same time, the creation of the state of Israel created new tensions in a region that was already tense over western actions. Then, the rise of Islamic political groups, first in Iran and then throughout the region, added to the boiling political mix. The outcome was a series of wars that damaged American credibility and made the world a more dangerous place. And, as with the cold war, the need to confront Islamic "terrorism," spilled onto the home front, as political repression and even torture became part of the American political system.

The Middle East Becomes Important

Balfour Declaration 1917

November 2nd, 1917

Dear Lord Rothschild,

I have much pleasure in conveying to you, on behalf of His Majesty's Government, the following declaration of sympathy with Jewish Zionist aspirations which has been submitted to, and approved by, the Cabinet.

"His Majesty's Government view with favour the establishment in Palestine of a national home for the Jewish people, and will use their best endeavours to facilitate the achievement of this object, it being clearly understood that nothing shall be done which may prejudice the civil and religious rights of existing non-Jewish communities in Palestine, or the rights and political status enjoyed by Jews in any other country."

I should be grateful if you would bring this declaration to the knowledge of the Zionist Federation.

Yours sincerely,

Arthur James Balfour

Anti-Americanism in Arab World, May 1, 1950

From the Secretary of State Dean Acheson to Embassies in the Middle East

Anti-Americanism is resurging in the Arab world. The bombings at our Legations in Beirut and Damascus; vitriolic public statements by Syria's Dawalibi, Iraq's Suwaidi and other high officials; diatribes and fantastic rumors in the vernacular press of Syria, Egypt and Iraq; all testify to the reenkindling of Arab animosity against the United States. Whether prompted by Communists or Moslem extremists, whether encouraged by irresponsible journalists or by weak government officials who seek to divert attention from their own inadequacies, or whether attributable to a sincere objection to America's part in Palestine developments, the current emotionalism bodes no good for the interests of the United States, nor for that matter for the best interests of the Arab states themselves.

Our best efforts must be directed toward stemming this tide of anti-Americanism. In this campaign our public affairs media can help. It is suggested that our information output be concentrated along the following lines: a) Corrective versions should be sent directly and immediately to the authors of fantastic stories such as the Syrian newspaper article about a $20,000,000 USIE program in Syria. These corrective stories should be intended and delivered so as to persuade the author of the error in his assertions and also to enlist his cooperation in correcting the misconceptions he has promulgated. b) Difficult as it may be, we must on every occasion reaffirm our current policy of impartiality in the Palestine dispute; above all we should keep reiterating, that the Palestine issue notwithstanding, the United States has a sincere interest in maintaining strong friendship with the Arab world and in cooperating with it in its hoped-for progress and development. c) Difficult as it may be, we must also seek to re-direct the attention of Arab peoples to their own internal problems and encourage them to devote their energies to the tremendous social and economic improvements so long overdue in their own countries. d) Finally, we must try to impress upon the Arab countries the fact that the dissipation of their energies in fanaticism against the United States or against Israel coupled with a lack of attention to their own pressing problems will lead to worse conditions which can only benefit their avowed enemies.

Positive, aggressive action along the lines suggested above should be taken not in a spirit of righteous indignation or anger, but in a sincere and friendly manner. The editor of a diatribe against the United States might, for example, be visited privately by one of our public affairs officers in the field to discuss the newspaper's attitude and to seek placement for a corrective article prepared carefully under the supervision of our chief of mission. Other better counter-actions may suggest themselves. In this connection, it may be pointed out the the Department itself is confronted with a critical public relations problem on the home front as a result of which the Secretary and other high Department officials have taken it upon themselves to carry the Department's story to the people through public speeches, articles for publication, and personal contacts. This program on the home front is already producing favorable results. It might also prove effective in the field.

ACESON

The Present Situation in Iran, November 20, 1952

1. It is of critical importance to the United States that Iran remain an independent and sovereign nation, not dominated by the USSR, Because of its key strategic position, its petroleum resources, its vulnerability to intervention or armed attack by. the USSR, and its vulnerability to political subversion, Iran must be regarded as a continuing objective of Soviet expansion. The loss of Iran by default or by Soviet intervention would:

    a. Be a major threat to the security of the entire Kiddle Hast, including Pakistan and India.

    b. Permit communist denial to the free world of access to Iranian oil and seriously threaten the loss of other Middle Eastern oil,

    c. Increase the Soviet Union's capability to threaten important United States-United Kingdom lines of communication,

    d. Damage United States, prestige in nearby countries and with the exception of Turkey and possibly Pakistan, seriously weaken, if not destroy, their will to resist communist pressures.

    e. Set pff a series of military, political and economic developments, the consequences of which would seriously endanger the security interests of the United States.

2. Present trends in Iran are unfavorable to the maintenance of control by a non-communist regime for an extended period of time. In wresting the political initiative from the Shah, the landlords, and other traditional holders of power, the National Front politicians now in power have at least temporarily eliminated every alternative to their own rule except the Communist Tudeh Party. However, the ability of the National Front to maintain control of the situation indefinitely is uncertain. The political upheaval which brought the nationalists to power has heightened popular desire for promised economic and social betterment and has increased; social unrest. At the same time, nationalist failure to restore the oil industry to operation has led to near-exhaustion of the government's financial reserves and to deficit financing to meet current expenses, and is likely to produce a progressive deterioration of the economy at large.

3. It is now estimated that communist forces will probably not gain oontrol of the Iranian government during 1953. Nevertheless, the Iranian situation contains very great elements: of instability. Any US policy regarding Iran must accordingly take into account the danger that the communists might be enabled to gain the ascendency as a result of such possible developments as a struggle for power within the National Front, more effective communist infiltration of the government than now appears probable, government failure to maintain the security forces and to take effective action against communist activity, or a major crop failure. It is clear that the United Kingdom no longer possesses the capability unilaterally to assure stability in the area. If present trends continue unchecked, Iran could be effectively lost to the free world in advance of an actual Communist takeover of the Iranian Government. Failure to arrest present trends in Iran involves a serious risk to the national security of the United States.

4. For the reasons outlined above, the major United States policy objective with respect to Iran is to prevent the country from coming under communist control. The United States should, therefore, be prepared to pursue the policies

which would be most effective in accomplishing this objective. In the light of the present situation the United States should adopt and pursue the following policies:

a. Continue to assist in every practicable way to effect an early and equitable liquidation of the oil controversy.

b. Be prepared to take the necessary measures to help Iran to start up her oil industry and to secure markets for her oil so that Iran may benefit from substantial oil revenues.

c. Be prepared to provide prompt tini ted States budgetary aid to Iran if, pending restoration of her oil industry and oil markets, such aid is necessary to halt a serious deterioration of the financial and political situation in Iran,

In carrying out a, b, and c above, the United States should:

(1) Maintain full consultation with the United Kingdom.

(2) Avoid unnecessarily sacrificing legitimate United Kingdom interests or unnecessarily impairing United States-United Kingdom relations.

(3) Not permit the United Kingdom to veto any United States actions which the United States considers essential to the achievement of the policy objective set forth above.

(4) Be prepared to avail itself of the authority of the President to approve voluntary agreements and programs under Section 708 (a) and (b) of the Defense Production Act of 1950, as amended,

d. Recognize the strength of Iranian nationalist feeling; try to direct it into constructive channels and be ready to exploit any opportunity to do so, bearing in mind the desirability of strengthening in Iran the ability and desire of the Iranian people to resist communist pressure.

e. Continue present programs of military, economic and technical assistance to the extent they will help to restore stability and increase internal security, and be prepared to increase such assistance to support Iranian resistance to communist pressure.

f. Encourage the adoption by the Iranian Government of necessary financial, ôtaâieial afid administrative and other reforms.

g. Continue special political measures designed to assist in achieving the above purposes.

h. Plan now for the eventual inclusion of Iran in any regional defense arrangement which may be developed in the Middle East if such inclusion should later prove feasible.

5. In the event of either an attempted or an actual communist seizure of power in one or more of the provinces of Iran or in Tehran, the United States should support a non-communist Iranian Government, including participation in the military support of such a government if necessary and useful. Preparations for such an eventuality should include:

a. Plans for the specific military, economic, diplomatic, and psychological measures which should be taken to support a non-oomraunist Iranian Government or to prevent all or part of Iran or adjacent areas from railing under communist domination,

b. Politico-military discussions with the British Government and such other governments as may be appropriate, with a view to determining (l) courses of action which might be Pursued and (2) the allocation of responsibility in carrying out such courses of action in the area.

c. Preparatory measures for the implementation of special political operations in Iran and adjacent Middle eastern areas, including the procurement of such equipment as may he required, Effective liaison with the United Kingdom should he maintained with respect to such operations.

    d. Perfection of plans concerning the handling of the matter by the United Nations if and when that becomes necessary.

6. In the event that a communist government achieves complete control of Iran so rapidly that no non-communist Iranian Government available to request assistance, the position of the United States would have to be determined in the light of the situation at the time, although politico-military-economic discussions leading to plans for meeting such a situation should be carried on with the British Government and with such other governements as may be appropriate. In this contingency, the United States should make every feasible effort, particularly through special political operations, to endeavor to develop or maintain localized centers of resistance and to harass, undermine, and if possible, to bring about the overthrow of the communist government.

7. In the event of a Soviet attack by organized USSR military forces against Iran, the United States in common prudence would have to proceed on the assumption that global war is probably imminent. Accordingly, the United States should then immediately:

    a. Decide in the light of the circumstances existing at the time whether to attempt to localize the action or to treat it as a *casus belli*. In either case necessary measures should include direct diplomatic action and resort to the United Nations with the objectives of:

        (1) Making clear to the world the aggressive character of the Soviet action,

        (2) Making clear to the world United States preference for a peaceful solution and the conditions upon which the United States would,'in concert with other members of the United Nations, accept such a settlement,

        (3) Obtaining the authorization of the United Nations for member nations to-take appropriate action in the name of the United Nations to assist Iran,

b. Consider a direct approach to the highest Soviet leaders.

c. Place itself in the best possible position to meet the increased threat of global war.

d. Consult with selected allies to perfect coordinated plans.

e. Take action against the aggressor to the extent and in the manner which would best contribute to the security of the United States,

f. Prepare to maintain, if necessary, an Iranian Government-in-exile,

United Nations Security Council Resolution 242

NOVEMBER 22, 1967

The Security Council,

Expressing its continuing concern with the grave situation in the Middle East,

Emphasizing the inadmissibility of the acquisition of territory by war and the need to work for a just and lasting peace in which every State in the area can live in security,

Emphasizing further that all Member States in their acceptance of the Charter of the United Nations have undertaken a commitment to act in accordance with Article 2 of the Charter,

Affirms that the fulfillment of Charter principles requires the establishment of a just and lasting peace in the Middle East which should include the application of both the following principles:

Withdrawal of Israeli armed forces from territories occupied in the recent conflict;

Termination of all claims or states of belligerency and respect for and acknowledgement of the sovereignty, territorial integrity and political independence of every State in the area and their right to live in peace within secure and recognized boundaries free from threats or acts of force;

Affirms further the necessity

For guaranteeing freedom of navigation through international waterways in the area;

For achieving a just settlement of the refugee problem;

For guaranteeing the territorial inviolability and political independence of every State in the area, through measures including the establishment of demilitarized zones;

Requests the Secretary General to designate a Special Representative to proceed to the Middle East to establish and maintain contacts with the States concerned in order to promote agreement and assist efforts to achieve a peaceful and accepted settlement in accordance with the provisions and principles in this resolution;

Requests the Secretary-General to report to the Security Council on the progress of the efforts of the Special Representative as soon as possible.

United Nations Security Council Resolution 338

The Security Council,

Calls upon all parties to present fighting to cease all firing and terminate all military activity immediately, no later than 12 hours after the moment of the adoption of this decision, in the positions after the moment of the adoption of this decision, in the positions they now occupy; Calls upon all parties concerned to start immediately after the cease-fire the implementation of Security Council Resolution 242 (1967) in all of its parts;

Decides that, immediately and concurrently with the cease-fire, negotiations start between the parties concerned under appropriate auspices aimed at establishing a just and durable peace in the Middle East.

The Americans Go to War(s)

Excerpts From Iraqi Document on Saddam Hussein Meeting with U.S. Envoy, July 25, 1990

SADDAM HUSSEIN: I have summoned you today to hold comprehensive political discussions with you. This is a message to President Bush. You know that we did not have relations with the U.S. until 1984 and you know the circumstances and reasons which caused them to be severed. The decision to establish relations with the U.S. were taken in 1980 during the two months prior to the war between us and Iran.

When the war started, and to avoid misinterpretation, we postponed the establishment of relations hoping that the war would end soon.

But because the war lasted for a long time, and to emphasize the fact that we are a non-aligned country, it was important to re-establish relations with the U.S. And we choose to do this in 1984.

It is natural to say that the U.S. is not like Britain, for example, with the latter's historic relations with Middle Eastern countries, including Iraq. In addition, there were no relations between Iraq and the U.S. between 1967 and 1984. One can conclude it would be difficult for the U.S. to have a full understanding of many matters in Iraq. When relations were re-established we hoped for a better understanding and for better cooperation because we too do not understand the background of many American decisions. We dealt with each other during the war and we had dealings on various levels. The most important of those levels were with the foreign ministers.

U.S.-Iraq Rifts

We had hoped for a better common understanding and a better chance of cooperation to benefit both our peoples and the rest of the Arab nations.

But these better relations have suffered from various rifts. The worst of these was in 1986, only two years after establishing relations, with what was known as Irangate, which happened during the year that Iran occupied the Fao peninsula.

It was natural then to say that old relations and complexity of interests could absorb many mistakes. But when interests are limited and relations are not that old, then there isn't a deep understanding and mistakes could have a negative effect. Sometimes the effect of an error can be larger than the error itself.

Despite all of that, we accepted the apology, via his envoy, of the American President regarding Irangate, and we wiped the slate clean. And we shouldn't unearth the past except when new events remind us that old mistakes were not just a matter of coincidence.

Our suspicions increased after we liberated the Fao peninsula. The media began to involve itself in our politics. And our suspicions began to surface anew, because we began to question whether the U.S. felt uneasy with the outcome of the war when we liberated our land.

It was clear to us that certain parties in the United States—and I don't say the President himself—but certain parties who had links with the intelligence community and with the State Department—and I don't say the Secretary of State himself—I say that these parties did not like the fact that we liberated our land. Some parties began to prepare studies entitles: "Who will succeed Saddam Hussein?" They began to contact gulf states to make them fear Iraq, to persuade them not to give Iraq economic aid. And we have evidence of these activities.

Iraqi Policy on Oil

Iraq came out of the war burdened with $40 billion debts, excluding the aid given by Arab states, some of whom consider that too to be a debt although they knew—and you knew too—that without Iraq they would not have had these sums and the future of the region would have been entirely different.

We began to face the policy of the drop in the price of oil. Then we saw the United States, which always talks of democracy but which has no time for the other point of view. Then the media campaign against Saddam Hussein was started by the official American media. The United States thought that the situation in Iraq was like Poland, Romania or Czechoslovakia. We were disturbed by this campaign but we were not disturbed too much because we had hoped that, in a few months, those who are decision makers in America would have a chance to find the facts and see whether this media campaign had had any effect on the lives of Iraqis. We had hoped that soon the American authorities would make the correct decision regarding their relations with Iraq. Those with good relations can sometimes afford to disagree.

But when planned and deliberate policy forces the price of oil down without good commercial reasons, then that means another war against Iraq. Because military war kills people by bleeding them, and economic war kills their humanity by depriving them of their chance to have a good standard of living. As you know, we gave rivers of blood in a war that lasted eight years, but we did not lose our humanity. Iraqis have a right to live proudly. We do not accept that anyone could injure Iraqi pride or the Iraqi right to have high standards of living.

Kuwait and the U.A.E. were at the front of this policy aimed at lowering Iraq's position and depriving its people of higher economic standards. And you know that our relations with the Emirates and Kuwait had been good. On top of all that, while we were busy at war, the state of Kuwait began to expand at the expense of our territory.

You may say this is propaganda, but I would direct you to one document, the Military Patrol Line, which is the borderline endorsed by the Arab League in 1961 for military patrols not to cross the Iraq-Kuwait border.

But go and look for yourselves. You will see the Kuwaiti border patrols, the Kuwaiti farms, the Kuwaiti oil installations—all built as closely as possible to this line to establish that land as Kuwaiti territory.

Conflicting Interests

Since then, the Kuwaiti Government has been stable while the Iraqi Government has undergone many changes. Even after 1968 and for 10 years afterwards, we were too busy with our own problems. First in the north then the 1973 war, and other problems. Then came the war with Iran which started 10 years ago.

We believe that the United States must understand that people who live in luxury and economic security can each an understanding with the United States on what are legitimate joint interests. But the starved and the economically deprived cannot reach the same understanding.

We do not accept threats from anyone because we do not threaten anyone. But we say clearly that we hope that the U.S. will not entertain too many illusions and will seek new friends rather than increase the number of its enemies.

I have read the American statements speaking of friends in the area. Of course, it is the right of everyone to choose their friends. We can have no objections. But you know you are not the ones who protected your friends during the war with Iran. I assure you, had the Iranians overrun the region, the American troops would not have stopped them, except by the use of nuclear weapons.

I do not belittle you. But I hold this view by looking at the geography and nature of American society into account. Yours is a society which cannot accept 10,000 dead in one battle.

You know that Iran agreed to the cease-fire not because the United States had bombed one of the oil platforms after the liberation of the Fao. Is this Iraq's reward for its role in securing the stability of the region and for protecting it from an unknown flood?

Protecting the Oil Flow

So what can it mean when America says it will now protect its friends? It can only mean prejudice against Iraq. This stance plus maneuvers and statements which have been made has encouraged the U.A.E. and Kuwait to disregard Iraqi rights.

I say to you clearly that Iraq's rights, which are mentioned in the memorandum, we will take one by one. That might not happen now or after a month or after one year, but we will take it all. We are not the kind of people who will relinquish their rights. There is no historic right, or legitimacy, or need, for the U.A.E. and Kuwait to deprive us of our rights. If they are needy, we too are needy.

The United States must have a better understanding of the situation and declare who it wants to have relations with and who its enemies are. But it should not make enemies simply because others have different points of view regarding the Arab-Israeli conflict.

We clearly understand America's statement that it wants an easy flow of oil. We understanding American staying that it seeks friendship with the states in the region, and to encourage their joint interests. But we cannot understand the attempt to encourage some parties to hard Iraq's interests.

The United States wants to secure the flow of oil. This understandable and known. But it must not deploy methods which the United States says it disapproves of—flexing muscles and pressure.

If you use pressure, we will deploy pressure and force. We know that you can harm us although we do not threaten you. But we too can harm you. Everyone can cause harm according to their ability and their size. We cannot come all the way to you in the United States, but individual Arabs may reach you.

War and Friendship

You can come to Iraq with aircraft and missiles but do not push us to the point where we cease to care. And when we feel that you want to injure our pride and take away the Iraqis' chance of a high standard of living, then we will cease to care and death will be the choice for us. Then we would not care if you fired 100missiles for each missile we fired. Because without pride life would have no value.

It is not reasonable to ask our people to bleed rivers of blood for eight years then to tell them, "Now you have to accept aggression from Kuwait, the U.A.E., or from the U.S. or from Israel."

We do not put all these countries in the same boat. First, we are hurt and upset that such disagreement is taking place between us and Kuwait and the U.A.E. The solution must be found within an Arab framework and through direct bilateral relations. We do not place America among the enemies. We pace it where we want our friends to be and we try to be friends. But repeated American statements last year make it apparent that America did not regard us as friends. Well the Americans are free.

When we seek friendship we want pride, liberty and our right to choose.

We want to deal according to our status as we deal with the others according to their statuses.

We consider the others' interests while we look after our own. And we expect the others to consider our interests while they are dealing with their own. What does it mean when the Zionist war minister is summoned to the United States now? What do they mean, these fiery statements coming out of Israel during the past few days and the talk of war being expected now more than at any other time?

★   ★   ★

I do not believe that anyone would lose by making friends with Iraq. In my opinion, the American President has not made mistakes regarding the Arabs, although his decision to freeze dialogue with the P.L.O. was wrong. But it appears that this decision was made to appease the Zionist lobby or as a piece of strategy to cool the Zionist anger, before trying again. I hope that our latter conclusion is the correct one. But we will carry on saying it was the wrong decision.

You are appeasing the usurper in so many ways—economically, politically and militarily as well as in the media. When will the time come when, for every three appeasements to the usurper, you praise the Arabs just once?

APRIL GLASPIE: I thank you, Mr. President, and it is a great pleasure for a diplomat to meet and talk directly with the President. I clearly understand your message. We studied history at school That taught us to say freedom or death. I think you know well that we as a people have our experience with the colonialists.

Mr. President, you mentioned many things during this meeting which I cannot comment on on behalf of my Government. But with your permission, I will comment on two points. You spoke of friendship and I believe it was clear from the letters sent by our President to you on the occasion of your National Day that he emphasizes —

HUSSEIN: He was kind and his expressions met with our regard and respect.

Directive on Relations

GLASPIE: As you know, he directed the United States Administration to reject the suggestion of implementing trade sanctions.

HUSSEIN: There is nothing left for us to buy from America. Only wheat. Because every time we want to buy something, they say it is forbidden. I am afraid that one day you will say, "You are going to make gunpowder out of wheat."

GLASPIE: I have a direct instruction from the President to seek better relations with Iraq.

HUSSEIN: But how? We too have this desire. But matters are running contrary to this desire.

GLASPIE: This is less likely to happen the more we talk. For example, you mentioned the issue of the article published by the American Information Agency and that was sad. And a formal apology was presented.

HUSSEIN: Your stance is generous. We are Arabs. It is enough for us that someone says, "I am sorry. I made a mistake." Then we carry on. But the media campaign continued. And it is full of stories. If the stories were true, no one would get upset. But we understand from its continuation that there is a determination.

GLASPIE: I saw the Diane Sawyer program on ABC. And what happened in that program was cheap and unjust. And this is a real picture of what happens in the American media—even to American politicians themselves. These are the methods the Western media employs. I am pleased that you add your voice to the diplomats who stand up to the media. Because your appearance in the media, even for five minutes, would help us to make the American people understand Iraq. This would increase mutual understanding. If they American President had control of the media, his job would be much easier.

Mr. President, not only do I want to say that President Bush wanted better and deeper relations with Iraq, but he also wants an Iraqi contribution to peace and prosperity in the Middle East. President Bush is an intelligent man. He is not going to declare an economic war against Iraq.

You are right. It is true what you say that we do not want higher prices for oil. But I would ask you to examine the possibility of not charging too high a price for oil.

HUSSEIN: We do not want too high prices for oil. And I remind you that in 1974 I gave Tariq Aziz the idea for an article he wrote which criticized the policy of keeping oil prices high. It was the first Arab article which expressed this view.

Shifting Price of Oil

TARIQ AZIZ: Our policy in OPEC opposes sudden jumps in oil prices.

HUSSEIN: Twenty-five dollars a barrel is not a high price.

GLASPIE: We have many Americans who would like to see the price go above $25 because they come from oil-producing states.

HUSSEIN: The price at one stage had dropped to $12 a barrel and a reduction in the modest Iraqi budget of $6 billion to $7 billion is a disaster.

GLASPIE: I think I understand this. I have lived here for years. I admire your extraordinary efforts to rebuild your country. I know you need funds. We understand that and our opinion is that you should have the opportunity to rebuild your country. But we have no opinion on the Arab-Arab conflicts, like your border disagreement with Kuwait.

I was in the American Embassy in Kuwait during the late 60's. The instruction we had during this period was that we should express no opinion on this issue and that the issue is not associated with America. James Baker has directed our official spokesmen to emphasize this instruction. We hope you can solve this problem using any suitable methods via Klibi or via President Mubarak. All that we hope is that these issues are solved quickly. With regard to all of this, can I ask you to see how the issue appears to us?

My assessment after 25 years' service in this area is that your objective must have strong backing from your Arab brothers. I now speak of oil But you, Mr. President, have fought through a horrific and painful war. Frankly, we can see only that you have deployed massive troops in the south. Normally that would not be any of our business. But when this happens in the context of what you said on your national day, then when we read the details in the two letters of the Foreign Minister, then when we see the Iraqi point of view that the measures taken by the U.A.E. and Kuwait is, in the final analysis, parallel to military aggression against Iraq, then it would be reasonable for me to be concerned. And for this reason, I received an instruction to ask you, in the spirit of friendship—not in the spirit of confrontation—regarding your intentions.

I simply describe the position of my Government. And I do not mean that the situation is a simple situation. But our concern is a simple one.

HUSSEIN: We do not ask people not to be concerned when peace is at issue. This is a noble human feeling which we all feel. It is natural for you as a superpower to be concerned. But what we ask is not to express your concern in a way that would make an aggressor believe that he is getting support for his aggression.

We want to find a just solution which will give us our rights but not deprive others of their rights. But at the same time, we want the others to know that our patience is running out regarding their action, which is harming even the milk our children drink, and the pensions of the widow who lost her husband during the war, and the pensions of the orphans who lost their parents.

As a country, we have the right to prosper. We lost so many opportunities, and the others should value the Iraqi role in their protection. Even this Iraqi [the President points to their interpreter] feels bitter like all other Iraqis. We are not aggressors but we do not accept aggression either. We sent them envoys and handwritten letters. We tried everything. We asked the Servant of the Two Shrines—King Fahd—to hold a four-member summit, but he suggested a meeting between the Oil Ministers. We agreed. And as you know, the meeting took place in Jidda. They reached an agreement which did not express what we wanted, but we agreed.

Only two days after the meeting, the Kuwaiti Oil Minister made a statement that contradicted the agreement. We also discussed the issue during the Baghdad summit. I told the Arab Kings and Presidents that some brothers are fighting an economic war against us. And that not all wars use weapons and we regard this kind of war as a military action against us. Because if the capability of our army is lowered then, if Iran renewed the war, it could achieve goals which it could not achieve before. And if we lowered the standard of our defenses, then this could encourage Israel to attack us. I said that before the Arab Kings and Presidents. Only I did not mention Kuwait and U.A.E. by name, because they were my guests.

Before this, I had sent them envoys reminding them that our war had included their defense. Therefore the aid they gave us should not be regarded as a debt. We did not more than the United States would have done against someone who attacked its interests.

I talked about the same thing with a number of other Arab states. I explained the situation t brother King Fahd a few times, by sending envoys and on the telephone. I talked with brother King Hussein and with Sheik Zaid after the conclusion of the summit. I walked with the Sheik to the plane when he was leaving Mosul. He told me, "Just wait until I get home." But after he had reached his destination, the statements that came from there were very bad—not from him, but from his Minister of Oil.

And after the Jidda agreement, we received some intelligence that they were talking of sticking to the agreement for two months only. Then they would change their policy. Now tell us, if the American President found himself in this situation, what would he do? I said it was very difficult for me to talk about these issues in public. But we must tell the Iraqi people who face economic difficulties who was responsible for that.

Talks with Mubarak

GLASPIE: I spent four beautiful years in Egypt.

HUSSEIN: The Egyptian people are kind and good and ancient. The oil people are supposed to help the Egyptian people, but they are mean beyond belief. It is painful to admit it, but some of them are disliked by Arabs because of their greed.

GLASPIE: Mr. President, it would be helpful if you could give us an assessment of the effort made by your Arab brothers and whether they have achieved anything.

HUSSEIN: On this subject, we agreed with President Mubarak that the Prime Minister of Kuwait would meet with the deputy chairman of the Revolution Command Council in Saudi Arabia, because the Saudis initiated contact with us, aided by President Mubarak's efforts. He just telephoned me a short while ago to say the Kuwaitis have agreed to that suggestion.

GLASPIE: Congratulations.

HUSSEIN: A protocol meeting will be held in Saudi Arabia. Then the meeting will be transferred to Baghdad for deeper discussion directly between Kuwait and Iraq. We hope we will reach some result. We hope that the long-term view and the real interests will overcome Kuwaiti greed.

GLASPIE: May I ask you when you expect Sheik Saad to come to Baghdad?

HUSSEIN: I suppose it would be on Saturday or Monday at the latest. I told brother Mubarak that the agreement should be in Baghdad Saturday or Sunday. You know that brother Mubarak's visits have always been a good omen.

GLASPIE: This is good news. Congratulations.

HUSSEIN: Brother President Mubarak told me they were scared. They said troops were only 20 kilometers north of the Arab League line. I said to him that regardless of what is there, whether they are police, border guards or army, and regardless of how many are there, and what they are doing, assure the Kuwaitis and give them our word that we are not going to do anything until we meet with them. When we meet and when we see that there is hope, then nothing will happen. But if we are unable to find a solution, then it will be natural that Iraq will not accept death, even though wisdom is above everything else. There you have good news.

AZIZ: This is a journalistic exclusive.

GLASPIE: I am planning to go to the United States next Monday. I hope I will meet with President Bush in Washington next week. I thought to postpone my trip because of the difficulties we are facing. But now I will fly on Monday.

Osama Bin Laden: A Case Study, Prepared by Sandia National Laboratories, 1999

PART I: SUMMARY AND ANALYSIS

Abstract

This document provides an open-source examination of the threat posed by Osama bin Laden, his al Qaeda organization, and allied terrorist organizations. It includes a summary of the relevant history, the lessons learned from the 1998 African embassy bombings and from the follow-on cruise-missile strikes, the threat of future attacks using weapons of mass destruction, and a set of observations, conclusions and recommendations.

Executive Summary

This study represents an attempt to assess the threat posed by Osama bin Laden, his al Qaeda organization, his associates, and affiliated organizations. The report consists of two parts. Part II, which was completed first, consists of a detailed compilation of open-source historical information related to the lives and activities of Osama bin Laden and of other relevant individuals and organizations. The data compiled in Part II are organized by timeframe, by topic, or by region and are presented in a viewgraph format. Part I consists of a high-level summary of Part II, an analysis of the overall level of the threat, lessons learned, and options for the future. Part I is presented in a report format.

The study and the findings of this study can only be understood properly when examined in context. To this end, several constraints and caveats are important:

- The study consists of an analysis of existing data that was gathered from existing reports: No new data was collected or generated as a part of this study.

- The study relies exclusively upon second-hand sources of information (e.g., news media).

- The study relied exclusively upon open-source information.

- The completeness of the study was resource-limited.

- When this study was first started, there was no intent to publish. For that reason, source citations and archives are incomplete.

- The historical summary contains some inconsistencies. Resource limitations precluded the effective resolution of all such inconsistencies.

- The findings and conclusions are subject to change as new data emerges over time.

Findings

- Osama bin Laden is not a new threat. He is a capable adversary with many strengths. Likewise, his al Qaeda organization poses a significant threat and possesses many strengths and assets. However, it also has a number of exploitable weaknesses.

- The 7 August 1998 African embassy bombings should not be taken to imply that our intelligence and physical protection programs are a failure. On the contrary, many positive findings emerge after examining the full story in detail. On the other hand, there are many lessons learned and recommendations for future improvement.

- The 20 August 1998 retaliatory cruise missile strikes did little to help solve the problem posed by bin Laden and may ultimately prove to have done more harm than good. However, the issue is complex, and there are a wide range of possible advantages to retaliation which motivate such strikes.

- The risk of future attacks by Osama bin Laden or his associates using weapons of mass destruction (WMDs) is not insignificant. We find that the risk is greatest for radiological dispersion incidents, followed by use of low-end chemical or biological agents. A detailed set of findings and a quantitative assessment of various options is included in the body of this report.

- Many options exist for our future response to the bin Laden threat (and to the terrorist threat in general). The body of this report contains a list of options for intelligence collection and law enforcement, vulnerability reductions, military options, diplomatic options, options for sponsor states, and more. It is our finding that the root cause of the Islamic militant threat is the widespread and deep-seated discontent among a large segment of the Islamic world, as opposed to the actions or agitation of any one individual or group of individuals. As such, the diplomatic options are likely to provide the broadest and most effective long-term reduction in the threat. However, the threat can never be, and never will be, eliminated completely.

General conclusions

- Terrorism is not dead (although it has shifted from Marxist-oriented to religious-oriented)

- State sponsorship of terrorism is not over (although it has shifted from Soviet-dominated to third-world-dominated)

- Terrorism can be unpredictable and future threats may evolve from very unexpected sources

- Terrorism is a global phenomenon

- Our problems with terrorism are exacerbated by our position and by our image in the world

- Religion is a powerful motivational factor in modern terrorism

- Religion is a protective shield which complicates counter-terrorism

- Killing is an explicit goal of many modern terrorists

- Modern terrorism is not easily countered

- Despite repeated attacks over a period of many years, the truck bomb remains a very potent weapon and remains difficult to defend against

- Despite repeated warnings over a period of many months, the Nairobi bombing was not prevented

- Although the African bombings represent a failure of sorts, we do NOT find negligence to have been a significant contributing factor

- Although we may have underestimated the local threat in East Africa,, we were more the victims of resource constraints than of poor intelligence or of a poor threat response

- Our overall counter-terrorist capabilities are strong

- We have a record of successes that we can be proud of

- However, the terrorist can always seek out the weakest targets

- The "war" against terrorism will never be "won": terrorism will always be a world problem

- We are seeing increasing attention domestically to terrorism as a threat to national security

- We are seeing increasing worldwide recognition of terrorism as a global phenomena

- We are seeing improvements in the global response to terrorism

WMD terrorism

- Current terrorist interest in WMD agents and weapons suggests a trend toward new terrorist capabilities in the future

- However, the timing of any evolution towards new methods and capabilities is highly uncertain

- Furthermore, the current effectiveness and availability of explosive devices make it likely that the vehicle bomb will remain a dominant tool for some time yet .

- In addition the apparent inability of al Qaeda to acquire and employ WMD agents or weapons (even after years of trying and with significant resources at their disposal), suggests that the threat of WMD terrorism may be smaller at the present time than we currently seem to imagine

- Nonetheless, the obstacles standing in the way of WMD acquisition and employment are not insurmountable and some forms of WMD employment must be considered quite plausible in the future

Introduction

This study began immediately following the tragic bombings of the U.S. embassies in Nairobi and Dar es Salaam in August of 1998. It follows in the footsteps of several earlier studies in which analysts at Sandia National Laboratories attempted to piece together a complete and coherent picture of various terrorist groups in order to understand how terrorist threats were evolving and what that meant for those of us tasked with the protection of nuclear explosive devices from seizure and use by such groups. In the course of these studies, we have found that the first and most difficult task is simply to gather together and organize the vast wealth of information which becomes available following any international terrorist incident.

Even though we all follow events in the media, it is difficult, if not impossible, to get a clear and coherent understanding of major terrorist events, and what they mean for the future, by following the news in the order in which it becomes available. Different bits of information which are closely related may emerge months apart. Some bits of information do not even seem to be related when they are digested months apart, but it becomes apparent that they are related, and that the relationship can lead to important lessons, when they are seen side-by-side. For that reason, we begin a painstaking process of gathering huge amounts of data as it becomes available and assembling it in an order that makes sense. Once this process is complete, it is as if a large puzzle has been assembled: a big picture often emerges which was not recognizable from the pieces alone. In fact, many different pictures, or lessons, emerge from various corners of the puzzle.

An example might help to illustrate the value of this process. Consider the Aum Shinrikyo cult and their involvement with various chemical and biological agents. Most observers, including the vast majority of site security personnel, security systems designers (scientists and technologists), and military officers know very little about the cult, their capabilities, and what they tried to do. Many in fact, remain unaware that the Tokyo sarin incident was not the only attempt to use chem/bio agents nor that the cult was involved with many agents other than sarin. A good compilation of the facts reveals many things, among them the fact that the cult was involved with many agents other than sarin alone, that they tried biological agents before turning to chemi-cal agents and that they were capable of more sophisticated attacks than that for which they are best-known, namely the punctured plastic bags on the Tokyo subway trains.

A similar story exists for Osama bin Laden. Most people had never heard of him prior to the August 1998 African embassy bombings and still know nothing of his involvement in a wide variety of other terrorist acts and of his affiliations with various guerilla groups. An examination of bin Laden's activities makes it clear that bin Laden has been involved in fighting for Islamic causes since long before the East African embassy bombings, that he has had significant state support (as opposed to being the free-lance agent sometimes portrayed in press articles), and that he is far more of a terrorist sponsor (and instigator) than an arms-car-rying terrorist himself.

Bin Ladin Determined to Strike in US, President's Daily Briefing, August 6, 2001

Clandestine, foreign government, and media reports indicate bin Laden since 1997 has wanted to conduct terrorist attacks in the US. Bin Laden implied in U.S. television interviews in 1997 and 1998 that his followers would follow the example of World Trade Center bomber Ramzi Yousef and "bring the fighting to America."

After U.S. missile strikes on his base in Afghanistan in 1998, bin Laden told followers he wanted to retaliate in Washington, according to a—— service.

An Egyptian Islamic Jihad (EIJ) operative told - - service at the same time that bin Laden was planning to exploit the operative's access to the U.S. to mount a terrorist strike.

The millennium plotting in Canada in 1999 may have been part of bin Laden's first serious attempt to implement a terrorist strike in the U.S.

Convicted plotter Ahmed Ressam has told the FBI that he conceived the idea to attack Los Angeles International Airport himself, but that in —-, Laden lieutenant Abu Zubaydah encouraged him and helped facilitate the operation. Ressam also said that in 1998 Abu Zubaydah was planning his own U.S. attack.

> Ressam says bin Laden was aware of the Los Angeles operation.

Although Bin Laden has not succeeded, his attacks against the U.S. Embassies in Kenya and Tanzania in 1998 demonstrate that he prepares operations years in advance and is not deterred by setbacks. Bin Laden associates surveyed our embassies in Nairobi and Dar es Salaam as early as 1993, and some members of the Nairobi cell planning the bombings were arrested and deported in 1997.

Al Qaeda members—including some who are U.S. citizens—have resided in or traveled to the U.S. for years, and the group apparently maintains a support structure that could aid attacks.

Two al-Qaeda members found guilty in the conspiracy to bomb our embassies in East Africa were U.S. citizens, and a senior EIJ member lived in California in the mid-1990s.

> A clandestine source said in 1998 that a bin Laden cell in New York was recruiting Muslim-American youth for attacks.

We have not been able to corroborate some of the more sensational threat reporting, such as that from a —— service in 1998 saying that Bin Laden wanted to hijack a U.S. aircraft to gain the release of "Blind Sheikh" Omar Abdel Rahman and other U.S.-held extremists.

Nevertheless, FBI information since that time indicates patterns of suspicious activity in this country consistent with preparations for hijackings or other types of attacks, including recent surveillance of federal buildings in New York.

The FBI is conducting approximately 70 full-field investigations throughout the U.S. that it considers bin Laden-related. CIA and the FBI are investigating a call to our embassy in the UAE in May saying that a group or bin Laden supporters was in the U.S. planning attacks with explosives.

G.W. Bush: "Axis of Evil" Speech, January 29, 2002

THE PRESIDENT: Thank you very much. Mr. Speaker, Vice President Cheney, members of Congress, distinguished guests, fellow citizens: As we gather tonight, our nation is at war, our economy is in recession, and the civilized world faces unprecedented dangers. Yet the state of our Union has never been stronger. (Applause.)

We last met in an hour of shock and suffering. In four short months, our nation has comforted the victims, begun to rebuild New York and the Pentagon, rallied a great coalition, captured, arrested, and rid the world of thousands of terrorists, destroyed Afghanistan's terrorist training camps, saved a people from starvation, and freed a country from brutal oppression. (Applause.)

The American flag flies again over our embassy in Kabul. Terrorists who once occupied Afghanistan now occupy cells at Guantanamo Bay. (Applause.) And terrorist leaders who urged followers to sacrifice their lives are running for their own. (Applause.)

America and Afghanistan are now allies against terror. We'll be partners in rebuilding that country. And this evening we welcome the distinguished interim leader of a liberated Afghanistan: Chairman Hamid Karzai. (Applause.)

The last time we met in this chamber, the mothers and daughters of Afghanistan were captives in their own homes, forbidden from working or going to school. Today women are free, and are part of Afghanistan's new government. And we welcome the new Minister of Women's Affairs, Doctor Sima Samar. (Applause.)

Our progress is a tribute to the spirit of the Afghan people, to the resolve of our coalition, and to the might of the United

States military. (Applause.) When I called our troops into action, I did so with complete confidence in their courage and skill. And tonight, thanks to them, we are winning the war on terror. (Applause.) The man and women of our Armed Forces have delivered a message now clear to every enemy of the United States: Even 7,000 miles away, across oceans and continents, on mountaintops and in caves—you will not escape the justice of this nation. (Applause.)

For many Americans, these four months have brought sorrow, and pain that will never completely go away. Every day a retired firefighter returns to Ground Zero, to feel closer to his two sons who died there. At a memorial in New York, a little boy left his football with a note for his lost father: Dear Daddy, please take this to heaven. I don't want to play football until I can play with you again some day.

Last month, at the grave of her husband, Michael, a CIA officer and Marine who died in Mazur-e-Sharif, Shannon Spann said these words of farewell: "Semper Fi, my love." Shannon is with us tonight. (Applause.)

Shannon, I assure you and all who have lost a loved one that our cause is just, and our country will never forget the debt we owe Michael and all who gave their lives for freedom.

Our cause is just, and it continues. Our discoveries in Afghanistan confirmed our worst fears, and showed us the true scope of the task ahead. We have seen the depth of our enemies' hatred in videos, where they laugh about the loss of innocent life. And the depth of their hatred is equaled by the madness of the destruction they design. We have found diagrams of American nuclear power plants and public water facilities, detailed instructions for making chemical weapons, surveillance maps of American cities, and thorough descriptions of landmarks in America and throughout the world.

What we have found in Afghanistan confirms that, far from ending there, our war against terror is only beginning. Most of the 19 men who hijacked planes on September the 11th were trained in Afghanistan's camps, and so were tens of thousands of others. Thousands of dangerous killers, schooled in the methods of murder, often supported by outlaw regimes, are now spread throughout the world like ticking time bombs, set to go off without warning.

Thanks to the work of our law enforcement officials and coalition partners, hundreds of terrorists have been arrested. Yet, tens of thousands of trained terrorists are still at large. These enemies view the entire world as a battlefield, and we must pursue them wherever they are. (Applause.) So long as training camps operate, so long as nations harbor terrorists, freedom is at risk. And America and our allies must not, and will not, allow it. (Applause.)

Our nation will continue to be steadfast and patient and persistent in the pursuit of two great objectives. First, we will shut down terrorist camps, disrupt terrorist plans, and bring terrorists to justice. And, second, we must prevent the terrorists and regimes who seek chemical, biological or nuclear weapons from threatening the United States and the world. (Applause.)

Our military has put the terror training camps of Afghanistan out of business, yet camps still exist in at least a dozen countries. A terrorist underworld—including groups like Hamas, Hezbollah, Islamic Jihad, Jaish-i-Mohammed—operates in remote jungles and deserts, and hides in the centers of large cities.

While the most visible military action is in Afghanistan, America is acting elsewhere. We now have troops in the Philippines, helping to train that country's armed forces to go after terrorist cells that have executed an American, and still hold hostages. Our soldiers, working with the Bosnian government, seized terrorists who were plotting to bomb our embassy. Our Navy is patrolling the coast of Africa to block the shipment of weapons and the establishment of terrorist camps in Somalia.

My hope is that all nations will heed our call, and eliminate the terrorist parasites who threaten their countries and our own. Many nations are acting forcefully. Pakistan is now cracking down on terror, and I admire the strong leadership of President Musharraf. (Applause.)

But some governments will be timid in the face of terror. And make no mistake about it: If they do not act, America will. (Applause.)

Our second goal is to prevent regimes that sponsor terror from threatening America or our friends and allies with weapons of mass destruction. Some of these regimes have been pretty quiet since September the 11th. But we know their true nature. North Korea is a regime arming with missiles and weapons of mass destruction, while starving its citizens.

Iran aggressively pursues these weapons and exports terror, while an unelected few repress the Iranian people's hope for freedom.

Iraq continues to flaunt its hostility toward America and to support terror. The Iraqi regime has plotted to develop anthrax, and nerve gas, and nuclear weapons for over a decade. This is a regime that has already used poison gas to murder thousands of its own citizens—leaving the bodies of mothers huddled over their dead children. This is a regime that agreed to international inspections—then kicked out the inspectors. This is a regime that has something to hide from the civilized world.

States like these, and their terrorist allies, constitute an axis of evil, arming to threaten the peace of the world. By seeking weapons of mass destruction, these regimes pose a grave and growing danger. They could provide these arms to terrorists, giving them the means to match their hatred. They could attack our allies or attempt to blackmail the United States. In any of these cases, the price of indifference would be catastrophic.

We will work closely with our coalition to deny terrorists and their state sponsors the materials, technology, and expertise to make and deliver weapons of mass destruction. We will develop and deploy effective missile defenses to protect America and our allies from sudden attack. (Applause.) And all nations should know: America will do what is necessary to ensure our nation's security.

We'll be deliberate, yet time is not on our side. I will not wait on events, while dangers gather. I will not stand by, as peril draws closer and closer. The United States of America will not permit the world's most dangerous regimes to threaten us with the world's most destructive weapons. (Applause.)

Our war on terror is well begun, but it is only begun. This campaign may not be finished on our watch—yet it must be and it will be waged on our watch.

We can't stop short. If we stop now—leaving terror camps intact and terror states unchecked—our sense of security would be false and temporary. History has called America and our allies to action, and it is both our responsibility and our privilege to fight freedom's fight. (Applause.)

Our first priority must always be the security of our nation, and that will be reflected in the budget I send to Congress. My budget supports three great goals for America: We will win this war; we'll protect our homeland; and we will revive our economy.

September the 11th brought out the best in America, and the best in this Congress. And I join the American people in applauding your unity and resolve. (Applause.) Now Americans deserve to have this same spirit directed toward addressing problems here at home. I'm a proud member of my party—yet as we act to win the war, protect our people, and create jobs in America, we must act, first and foremost, not as Republicans, not as Democrats, but as Americans. (Applause.)

It costs a lot to fight this war. We have spent more than a billion dollars a month—over $30 million a day—and we must be prepared for future operations. Afghanistan proved that expensive precision weapons defeat the enemy and spare innocent lives, and we need more of them. We need to replace aging aircraft and make our military more agile, to put our troops anywhere in the world quickly and safely. Our men and women in uniform deserve the best weapons, the best equipment, the best training—and they also deserve another pay raise. (Applause.)

My budget includes the largest increase in defense spending in two decades—because while the price of freedom and security is high, it is never too high. Whatever it costs to defend our country, we will pay. (Applause.)

The next priority of my budget is to do everything possible to protect our citizens and strengthen our nation against the ongoing threat of another attack. Time and distance from the events of September the 11th will not make us safer unless we act on its lessons. America is no longer protected by vast oceans. We are protected from attack only by vigorous action abroad, and increased vigilance at home.

My budget nearly doubles funding for a sustained strategy of homeland security, focused on four key areas: bioterrorism, emergency response, airport and border security, and improved intelligence. We will develop vaccines to fight anthrax and other deadly diseases. We'll increase funding to help states and communities train and equip our heroic police and firefighters. (Applause.) We will improve intelligence collection and sharing, expand patrols at our borders, strengthen the security of air travel, and use technology to track the arrivals and departures of visitors to the United States. (Applause.)

Homeland security will make America not only stronger, but, in many ways, better. Knowledge gained from bioterrorism research will improve public health. Stronger police and fire departments will mean safer neighborhoods. Stricter border enforcement will help combat illegal drugs. (Applause.) And as government works to better secure our homeland, America will continue to depend on the eyes and ears of alert citizens.

A few days before Christmas, an airline flight attendant spotted a passenger lighting a match. The crew and passengers quickly subdued the man, who had been trained by al Qaeda and was armed with explosives. The people on that plane were alert and, as a result, likely saved nearly 200 lives. And tonight we welcome and thank flight attendants Hermis Moutardier and Christina Jones. (Applause.)

Once we have funded our national security and our homeland security, the final great priority of my budget is economic security for the American people. (Applause.) To achieve these great national objectives—to win the war, protect the homeland, and revitalize our economy—our budget will run a deficit that will be small and short-term, so long as Congress restrains spending and acts in a fiscally responsible manner. (Applause.) We have clear priorities and we must act at home with the same purpose and resolve we have shown overseas: We'll prevail in the war, and we will defeat this recession. (Applause.)

Americans who have lost their jobs need our help and I support extending unemployment benefits and direct assistance for health care coverage. (Applause.) Yet, American workers want more than unemployment checks—they want a steady paycheck. (Applause.) When America works, America prospers, so my economic security plan can be summed up in one word: jobs. (Applause.)

Good jobs begin with good schools, and here we've made a fine start. (Applause.)   Republicans and Democrats worked together to achieve historic education reform so that no child is left behind. I was proud to work with members of both parties: Chairman John Boehner and Congressman George Miller. (Applause.)   Senator Judd Gregg. (Applause.)   And I was so proud of our work, I even had nice things to say about my friend, Ted Kennedy. (Laughter and applause.)   I know the folks at the Crawford coffee shop couldn't believe I'd say such a thing—(laughter)—but our work on this bill shows what is possible if we set aside posturing and focus on results. (Applause.)

There is more to do. We need to prepare our children to read and succeed in school with improved Head Start and early childhood development programs. (Applause.) We must upgrade our teacher colleges and teacher training and launch a major recruiting drive with a great goal for America: a quality teacher in every classroom. (Applause.)

Good jobs also depend on reliable and affordable energy. This Congress must act to encourage conservation, promote technology, build infrastructure, and it must act to increase energy production at home so America is less dependent on foreign oil. (Applause.)

Good jobs depend on expanded trade. Selling into new markets creates new jobs, so I ask Congress to finally approve trade promotion authority. (Applause.)   On these two key issues, trade and energy, the House of Representatives has acted to create jobs, and I urge the Senate to pass this legislation. (Applause.)

Good jobs depend on sound tax policy. (Applause.)   Last year, some in this hall thought my tax relief plan was too small; some thought it was too big. (Applause.)   But when the checks arrived in the mail, most Americans thought tax relief was just about right. (Applause.)   Congress listened to the people and responded by reducing tax rates, doubling the child credit, and ending the death tax. For the sake of long-term growth and to help Americans plan for the future, let's make these tax cuts permanent. (Applause.)

The way out of this recession, the way to create jobs, is to grow the economy by encouraging investment in factories and equipment, and by speeding up tax relief so people have more money to spend. For the sake of American workers, let's pass a stimulus package. (Applause.)

Good jobs must be the aim of welfare reform. As we reauthorize these important reforms, we must always remember the goal is to reduce dependency on government and offer every American the dignity of a job. (Applause.)

Americans know economic security can vanish in an instant without health security. I ask Congress to join me this year to enact a patients' bill of rights—(applause)—to give uninsured workers credits to help buy health coverage—(applause)—to approve an historic increase in the spending for veterans' health—(applause)—and to give seniors a sound and modern Medicare system that includes coverage for prescription drugs. (Applause.)

A good job should lead to security in retirement. I ask Congress to enact new safeguards for 401K and pension plans. (Applause.) Employees who have worked hard and saved all their lives should not have to risk losing everything if their company fails. (Applause.) Through stricter accounting standards and tougher disclosure requirements, corporate America must be made more accountable to employees and shareholders and held to the highest standards of conduct. (Applause.)

Retirement security also depends upon keeping the commitments of Social Security, and we will. We must make Social Security financially stable and allow personal retirement accounts for younger workers who choose them. (Applause.)

Members, you and I will work together in the months ahead on other issues: productive farm policy—(applause)—a cleaner environment—(applause)—broader home ownership, especially among minorities—(applause)—and ways to encourage the good work of charities and faith-based groups. (Applause.) I ask you to join me on these important domestic issues in the same spirit of cooperation we've applied to our war against terrorism. (Applause.)

During these last few months, I've been humbled and privileged to see the true character of this country in a time of testing. Our enemies believed America was weak and materialistic, that we would splinter in fear and selfishness. They were as wrong as they are evil. (Applause.)

The American people have responded magnificently, with courage and compassion, strength and resolve. As I have met the heroes, hugged the families, and looked into the tired faces of rescuers, I have stood in awe of the American people.

And I hope you will join me—I hope you will join me in expressing thanks to one American for the strength and calm and comfort she brings to our nation in crisis, our First Lady, Laura Bush. (Applause.)

None of us would ever wish the evil that was done on September the 11th. Yet after America was attacked, it was as if our entire country looked into a mirror and saw our better selves. We were reminded that we are citizens, with obligations to each other, to our country, and to history. We began to think less of the goods we can accumulate, and more about the good we can do.

For too long our culture has said, "If it feels good, do it." Now America is embracing a new ethic and a new creed: "Let's roll." (Applause.) In the sacrifice of soldiers, the fierce brotherhood of firefighters, and the bravery and generosity of ordinary citizens, we have glimpsed what a new culture of responsibility could look like. We want to be a nation that serves goals larger than self. We've been offered a unique opportunity, and we must not let this moment pass. (Applause.)

My call tonight is for every American to commit at least two years—4,000 hours over the rest of your lifetime—to the service of your neighbors and your nation. (Applause.) Many are already serving, and I thank you. If you aren't sure how to help, I've got a good place to start. To sustain and extend the best that has emerged in America, I invite you to join the new USA Freedom Corps. The Freedom Corps will focus on three areas of need: responding in case of crisis at home; rebuilding our communities; and extending American compassion throughout the world.

One purpose of the USA Freedom Corps will be homeland security. America needs retired doctors and nurses who can be mobilized in major emergencies; volunteers to help police and fire
departments; transportation and utility workers well-trained in
spotting danger.

Our country also needs citizens working to rebuild our communities. We need mentors to love children, especially children
whose parents are in prison. And we need more talented teachers in troubled schools. USA Freedom Corps will expand and
improve the good efforts of AmeriCorps and Senior Corps to
recruit more than 200,000 new volunteers.

And America needs citizens to extend the compassion of our
country to every part of the world. So we will renew the promise of the Peace Corps, double its volunteers over the next five
years—(applause)—and ask it to join a new effort to encourage
development and education and opportunity in the Islamic
world. (Applause.)

This time of adversity offers a unique moment of opportunity—a
moment we must seize to change our culture. Through the
gathering momentum of millions of acts of service and decency
and kindness, I know we can overcome evil with greater good.
(Applause.) And we have a great opportunity during this time
of war to lead the world toward the values that will bring lasting
peace.

All fathers and mothers, in all societies, want their children to be
educated, and live free from poverty and violence. No people
on Earth yearn to be oppressed, or aspire to servitude, or eagerly
await the midnight knock of the secret police.

If anyone doubts this, let them look to Afghanistan, where the
Islamic "street" greeted the fall of tyranny with song and celebration. Let the skeptics look to Islam's own rich history, with its
centuries of learning, and tolerance and progress. America will
lead by defending liberty and justice because they are right and
true and unchanging for all people everywhere. (Applause.)

No nation owns these aspirations, and no nation is exempt from
them. We have no intention of imposing our culture. But
America will always stand firm for the non-negotiable demands
of human dignity: the rule of law; limits on the power of the

state; respect for women; private property; free speech; equal justice; and religious tolerance. (Applause.)

America will take the side of brave men and women who advocate these values around the world, including the Islamic world, because we have a greater objective than eliminating threats and containing resentment. We seek a just and peaceful world beyond the war on terror.

In this moment of opportunity, a common danger is erasing old rivalries. America is working with Russia and China and India, in ways we have never before, to achieve peace and prosperity. In every region, free markets and free trade and free societies are proving their power to lift lives. Together with friends and allies from Europe to Asia, and Africa to Latin America, we will demonstrate that the forces of terror cannot stop the momentum of freedom. (Applause.)

The last time I spoke here, I expressed the hope that life would return to normal. In some ways, it has. In others, it never will. Those of us who have lived through these challenging times have been changed by them. We've come to know truths that we will never question: evil is real, and it must be opposed. (Applause.) Beyond all differences of race or creed, we are one country, mourning together and facing danger together. Deep in the American character, there is honor, and it is stronger than cynicism. And many have discovered again that even in tragedy—especially in tragedy—God is near. (Applause.)

In a single instant, we realized that this will be a decisive decade in the history of liberty, that we've been called to a unique role in human events. Rarely has the world faced a choice more clear or consequential.

Our enemies send other people's children on missions of suicide and murder. They embrace tyranny and death as a cause and a creed. We stand for a different choice, made long ago, on the day of our founding. We affirm it again today. We choose freedom and the dignity of every life. (Applause.)

Steadfast in our purpose, we now press on. We have known freedom's price. We have shown freedom's power. And in this great conflict, my fellow Americans, we will see freedom's victory.

Thank you all. May God bless. (Applause.)